SWORDS
OF THE
BRITISH ARMY

THE REGULATION PATTERNS 1788 TO 1914

THE REVISED EDITION

BY
BRIAN ROBSON

SWORDS
OF THE BRITISH ARMY

THE REGULATION PATTERNS 1788 TO 1914

THE REVISED EDITION

BY

BRIAN ROBSON

Copyright © National Army Museum, 2011

The right of Brian Robson to be identified as the author of this work has been asserted by him in accordance with the Copyright, Designs and Patents Act 1988

ISBN 9781845749170

Published jointly by

The Naval & Military Press Ltd
Unit 10 Ridgewood Industrial Park,
Uckfield, East Sussex,
TN22 5QE England

Tel: +44 (0) 1825 749494
Fax: +44 (0) 1825 765701

www.naval-military-press.com
www.military-genealogy.com
www.militarymaproom.com

and

The National Army Museum, London
www.nam.ac.uk

Printed and bound by MCRL Overseas Printing

Contents

	Foreword	iv
	Preface	vi
	Introduction to the Revised Edition	ix
	Abbreviations	xvi
1.	The Eighteenth Century Background	1
2.	Cavalry Troopers' Swords 1788-1878	4
3.	Cavalry Troopers' Swords 1878-1914	38
4.	Cavalry Officers' Swords	74
5.	Household Cavalry Troopers' Swords	106
6.	Household Cavalry Officers' Swords	124
	Colour section between pages 141-142	
7.	Infantry Officers' Swords	142
8.	Scottish Infantry Swords	172
9.	General and Staff Officers' Swords	202
10.	Sergeants' Swords (excluding Scottish Regiments)	211
11.	Corps and Departmental Swords	226
12.	Drummers', Band and Pioneer Swords	251
13.	Practice Swords	264
	Appendix 1. Sword Knots	271
	Appendix 2. Markings on Swords	276
	Appendix 3. *The Marking of Arms,* 1912	284
	Appendix 4. *The List of Changes*	290
	Select Bibliography	296
	Index	302

Foreword

It is a remarkable author who, once having written a standard work - *Swords of the British Army* published in 1975 - does not rest upon his laurels but has the necessary scholarly inquisitiveness, zeal and perseverance to re-evaluate, present anew and, by so doing, surpass his original achievements to the advantage of all students and collectors in his field. It is a great pleasure, therefore, to introduce the Revised Edition of this excellent and informative study by Brian Robson, CB - all the more so on account of the author's steadfast support for the National Army Museum (NAM) over so many years, both as Deputy Under-Secretary of State for the Army, and for Personnel and Logistics in the Ministry of Defence from 1982 to 1986, and as a Member of Council, the Museum's governing body, from 1982 to 1993.

A noted military historian, founding Member and Council Member of the Army Records Society and, at the time of writing, Chairman of the Council of the Society for Army Historical Research, no one is better qualified than Brian Robson to display an objective approach to military history and the effects - for good or ill - of advances in weapons technology. This is reflected not only in this present book but in his scholarly accounts of the Victorian Army's campaigns in Afghanistan, 1878-80 and in the Sudan, 1884-85. Brian Robson has also published an edition of the Indian papers of Field Marshal Lord Roberts for the Army Records Society; he is a contributor to the new edition of the *Dictionary of National Biography*, as well as writing chapters and essays which have appeared in a number of National Army Museum publications since the 1980s.

Not only has Brian Robson undertaken substantial rewriting for this second and fully revised edition of *Swords of the British Army*, but it is a matter of pride that the National Army Museum has acted as the publisher of this new volume, thus contributing in support of the author not only the NAM's fine collection of British Army swords, as well as the associated curatorial and conservation skills of the relevant members of the Museum's staff, but also the in-house experience of publishing high quality academic books. Editing is the key duty of all publishers and for this book that has been undertaken by Michael Baldwin, Alan Guy, and Keith Miller, who also carried out additional research for the project. Text production is by Patricia Fell, while Marion Harding has performed the duties of Assistant Editor. The book's design is by Derek Buick, and photography by Nigel Armstrong, Ian Jones and Karen Millar. The swords have been conserved for photography by Martin Hinchcliffe. Sarah Godwin, Ray Seabrook and Paul Tew joined the team to ensure that the swords were available for public display, with Roy Mandeville constructing the specialist fittings. Gratitude is owed also to Miss Anna

Frankum of Penningtons, Solicitors, who guided us through the complexities of copyright legislation and Wilkinson Sword Limited, the Company pre-eminent in the field of modern sword production, for its financial sponsorship.

The National Army Museum is honoured and delighted to be able to undertake the publication of this notable book written by Brian Robson, which will be of importance to all readers of the first edition as well as to the substantial number of new students and collectors world-wide who are interested in this fascinating and complex subject.

Ian G Robertson
Director

March 1996
National Army Museum

Preface

The publication of any book, and particularly of a revised edition, requires a justification.

When this book was first published twenty years ago, it broke new ground by setting out to trace the development of British military swords from 1788 onwards, and to identify and describe all the regulation patterns introduced after that date, using, wherever possible, original official documents, contemporary paintings and drawings, and extant sword specimens - in other words, to put the subject on to a firm, scholarly basis.

The book was well received by collectors and serious students, and it has substantially withstood the test of time. Its conclusions and identifications - with one exception - have not been seriously challenged and have attracted general agreement. It is clear from the many comments received that it has proved of value to all those interested in the subject and in uniform generally. What was in 1975 new and hitherto unestablished is now generally accepted wisdom.

The one identification on which doubt has been cast is that of the Pattern 1788 Heavy Cavalry sword, and although what has been questioned has been largely the strength of the evidential chain, there remains a legitimate doubt about the identity of this pattern. I have thought it right therefore to set out the present evidence more fully in justification of the original conclusion, including one major new piece of evidence which greatly strengthens the original thesis.

In fact, what has been surprising has been the relative absence of new work on the subject, despite the growth of interest. Apart from a handful of articles of varying value, virtually nothing fresh has appeared in twenty years, with the distinguished exception of A V B Norman's *The Rapier and the Small Sword 1460-1820*, which has thrown a great deal of valuable tangential light on certain patterns.

Given the pioneering nature of the original book, it was inevitable that it should contain some errors of fact and omission, and some areas where the material available did not enable precise conclusions to be drawn. As was to be expected, the very appearance of the book produced a mass of new information, which has grown over the succeeding twenty years. This additional material has enabled errors to be corrected and 'weak' areas to be filled in or strengthened. Almost every chapter now contains new material and photographs, and the opportunity has been taken to correct a number of textual errors and misprints.

From the mass of correspondence and new evidence, three points have emerged which were insufficiently emphasised in the first edition. It is now clear that manufacturing tolerances were much looser in the eighteenth and early nineteenth centuries than had perhaps been realised, and that manufacturers were looser in their interpretation of sealed patterns than had originally been assumed. Indeed, in the absence of detailed drawings and specifications to guide manufacture, and with manufacturers being obliged to copy a single, sealed model, this is perhaps what one should have expected. Sword manufacture was, in any case, based to a considerable extent upon individual craftsmen as, in some senses, it has remained until today.

The second and third points are linked to the first. It is now clear that, to a greater extent than had been realised, both regiments and individuals went in for purchasing and using swords of non-regulation pattern. A classic example is the four-bar-hilted swords which appear to have had something of a vogue in the Royal Artillery in the middle of the nineteenth century. Not only did individuals purchase fighting swords to a pattern which met their particular tastes but regiments adopted patterns which had no basis in the regulations. This is, perhaps, most clearly seen in the Scottish regiments but it is also apparent in regiments such as the 6th (Carabiniers) Dragoon Guards and the 4th Light Dragoons. At the very end of our period, the 10th Hussars adopted their own variation of the Pattern 1912 cavalry officers' sword. The existence of variations of this kind has tempted many collectors and students to assume that they have unearthed a new and hitherto unidentified regulation pattern whereas, in fact, they have found either a somewhat free copy of a sealed pattern or an individual variation of the kind just mentioned. That in no way diminishes the value of the discovery but it needs to be stressed that a regulation pattern was exactly what the term implies - a pattern laid down by the official authorities for common adoption by the arm or particular portion of the arm of service. It follows that for every regulation pattern there will exist documented evidence - whether in the form of a General Order or *Dress Regulations* or official correspondence. If no such evidence can be found, then the presumption must be that the sword in question is not a regulation pattern, even if it exists in some numbers.

The third point is the realisation that regiments were often slow to adopt a new regulation pattern, partly from conservatism, sometimes for reasons of economy (swords do not wear out all that quickly), partly from élitism.

In producing this second edition, I am grateful, in the first instance, to the Council of the National Army Museum for agreeing to undertake publication, and to the Director (Ian Robertson), the Assistant Director (Collections) (Dr Alan Guy), the Head of the Department of Weapons, Equipment and Vehicles (Michael Baldwin) and to their staffs, particularly Keith Miller, who have done so much of the laborious work behind publication. I hope that they will feel that the result is a worthy addition to the Museum's distinguished list of publications.

I am indebted equally to two friends and colleagues of long standing - Stephen Wood, Keeper of the Scottish United Services Museum, and A V B (Nick) Norman, late Master of the Royal Armouries. They have provided help, hospitality and knowledge in equally generous proportions. Without their assistance and stimulation, this present edition would probably not have seen the light of day. I fear that they will weep over its imperfection even so.

A major contribution has been made by Geoff R Worrall, who, in the best traditions of scholarship, has made available his unrivalled knowledge of British cavalry swords, amassed over some 25 years of collecting and study.

The Hon. David McAlpine has allowed me to inspect his remarkable collection of cavalry uniforms and equipment, and I have received unstinting support and help from William (Bill) Reid, a former distinguished Director of the NAM, Herbert Woodend and Howard Mitchell of the Pattern Room at the Royal Ordnance Factory, Nottingham, from Philip Lankester and Bridget Clifford of the Royal Armouries. Others to whom I am in debt include Major Paddy Kersting, Curator of the Household Cavalry Museum, Windsor; Captain David Horn, Curator of the Guards Museum, London; Lieutenant-Colonel R B Merton, Regimental Secretary of the King's Royal Hussars; Brigadier Ken Timbers and Mr P W G Annis of the Royal Artillery Institution, Woolwich, and Richard Brown. I owe particular debts to Dr J P Puype of the Legermuseum at Delft; Mr Paul Doyle of the National Museum of Ireland, Dublin; Glasgow Art Gallery and Museum and the Castle Museum, York; Mr B W Reeder, who has made many suggestive points, and to Mr Richard Dellar. Mr Pat Shipp read the draft with his unrivalled eye for errors. I have benefited over the years from innumerable correspondents all over the world - I thank them all. But while others are largely responsible for the merits of this book, I alone am responsible for its defects.

Since the first edition, there have been two organisational changes of consequence. The Pattern Room of the old Royal Small Arms Factory at Enfield now resides in the privatised Royal Ordnance Factory at Nottingham; The Armouries of the Tower of London, now called the Royal Armouries, are to be located at Leeds in 1996. Many will miss the charm and convenience of their original locations.

Finally, in approaching this task, I have been ever mindful of what Francis Bacon said 400 years ago:

'If a man will begin with certainties, he shall end in doubts: but if he will be content to begin with doubts, he shall end in certainties'.
Francis Bacon *The Advancement of Learning* [1605]

Brian Robson	January 1996
	Hove

Introduction to the Revised Edition

The primary purpose of this book is to identify and describe all the regulation patterns of sword which have been introduced into the British Army since 1788.

The first attempt to do this was made by Charles ffoulkes and Captain E C Hopkinson in their book *Sword, Lance and Bayonet*, published in 1938 and based upon a series of articles which had appeared earlier in the *Journal of the Society for Army Historical Research*. It was reprinted unamended in 1967. It was a pioneering effort and was largely based upon the material which ffoulkes had found at the Tower of London where he was in charge of the Armouries, although he did some research via the regiments. Not surprisingly, it contained many gaps and a number of serious errors. A second attempt was made by John Wilkinson Latham in his *British Military Swords*, published in 1966. Latham, from his long family and personal connection with the celebrated firm of Wilkinsons, had unique opportunities to consult the firm's records of swordmaking and his book was handsomely illustrated, but, unfortunately, it reproduced most of the errors of the previous work and introduced some of its own. There was, therefore, room for a serious attempt at putting the subject on a proper, academic basis. The result was the first edition of this book, published exactly twenty years ago by Arms and Armour Press.

In preparing this and the previous edition, I have sought to make it something more than an academic catalogue by tracing, wherever possible, the background and origins of each pattern, and giving some indication of its effectiveness as a weapon. In doing this, some digression into the origins and organisation of the various regiments and corps of the British Army has been unavoidable. I have chosen to conclude the book at 1914, partly because no distinct new patterns have been introduced since then, and partly to avoid the tedious complications of the various regimental amalgamations since then. In one or two instances, however, I have transgressed beyond this self-imposed limit in order to complete the story.

This book does not deal with the swords adopted by the various volunteer units which have sprung up at various times, such as the Yeomanry, the Fencibles and the Volunteers. There are two reasons for this limitation. In the first place, it would require a book on its own, and, even then, the story could not be complete because full records of all of these units do not exist. In the second place, although there are many important exceptions, the swords of these units tended to conform to the patterns of the Regular Army and, indeed, as the nineteenth century progressed, many units, particularly in the Yeomanry, were equipped with swords which were surplus to Regular requirements.

There is no absolute agreement among students of the subject on the terms to be used to describe swords. What for one is a 'chamfer' is a 'latchet' or 'false edge' for another. I have used those terms which appear to me to be broadly standard (Figures 1-5), and, in any case, I have endeavoured wherever possible to provide a photograph to supplement or replace a detailed written description. For American students, I would point out that what I call 'locket', 'band' and 'chape' are the equivalents of the American terms 'throat', 'middle band' and 'tip'. What I call a 'shoe' on a scabbard is sometimes called a 'drag', and some British authorities use the terms 'backstrap' or 'spine' where I have preferred to use the older term 'backpiece'.

A particular problem arises over the term 'pommel'. Originally, the pommel was a distinct feature which terminated the grip, as indeed it still is, for example, in the Scottish cross-hilt. But, increasingly, the pommel has become an extension of the backpiece, sometimes fairly distinct as in the common lion's head pattern, but sometimes, also, indistinguishable from the backpiece. Some authorities distinguish the latter case by referring to it as a 'pommel cap'; in *Rules and Regulations for the Sword Exercise of the Cavalry* (1796), it is called 'The Head of the Backpiece'. I have chosen to use the term 'pommel' for all these cases. In the same publication, what is now generally called a 'langet' was termed the 'ear'. I have used the term 'ear', in what I believe to be the normal, present-day use, to denote the small protrusions often found on the backpiece which were riveted together through the grip and tang to secure the grip to

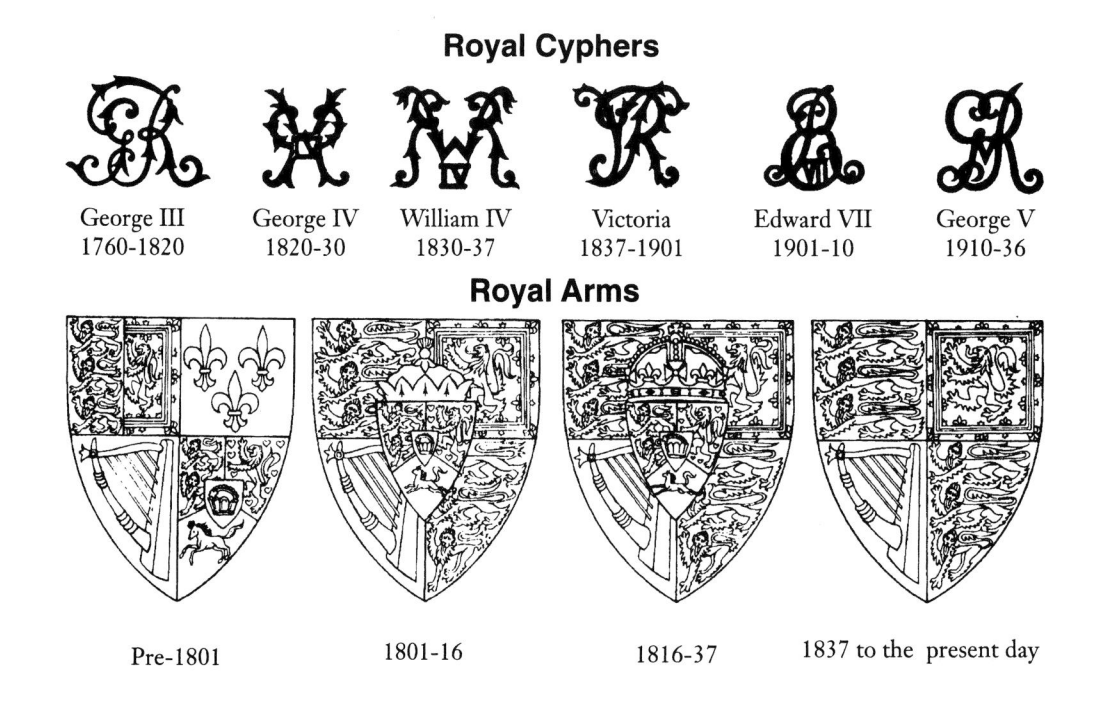

Royal Cyphers

George III	George IV	William IV	Victoria	Edward VII	George V
1760-1820	1820-30	1830-37	1837-1901	1901-10	1910-36

Royal Arms

| Pre-1801 | 1801-16 | 1816-37 | 1837 to the present day |

the blade. 'Shell' and 'boatshell' guards are sometimes called 'counter' guards by American writers.

A continuous source of confusion and misunderstanding lies in the use of the terms 'basket' and 'half-basket' in describing guards or hilts. The fact of the matter is that the terms have no precise meaning and in official documents are often used indiscriminately. A guard which effectively protects the whole hand, as in the traditional Scottish broadsword, can properly be described as a 'basket' guard but between that and a simple knuckebow or stirrup hilt there is an infinite variety of designs to which the term 'half-basket' can and has been applied. Certainly, to describe a hilt as 'basket' or 'half-basket' means very little in the absence of a drawing or photograph. Attempts have been made, and will, no doubt, continue to be made, to establish a precise sequence of forms of basket hilt but so far none has achieved any real degree of acceptance.

In the first edition, I chose to reverse the use of the terms 'scroll' and 'honeysuckle' in referring to the design of guards because it seemed to my eye to make more sense. In fact, it seems to have caused confusion in some quarters and certainly has not been generally followed. In the present edition, I have therefore reverted to the traditional usage, which has the incidental advantage of coming into line with the usage in *Dress Regulations*.

A word needs to be said about the design of sword blades. The ideal sword blade needs to be strong but light, and stiff but flexible. If a sword blade is too light, then it will be easily bent or broken; if it is too heavy, it becomes too difficult to wield effectively. It needs to be stiff so that it does not bend when a blow is made with it, but a blade which is too stiff is likely to shatter on contact with another hard object, just like a piece of glass. These mutually contradictory qualities are not easily reconciled in one piece of metal and therein lies the art of the blade maker. To achieve stiffness with the right degree of flexibility is primarily a question of the composition of the steel and its subsequent tempering to remove stresses and strains. To achieve strength with lightness is primarily a matter of design. In British military swords, there have been four basic designs of blade. The simplest design, and one much practised in the eighteenth century, was simply to produce a plain, heavy blade, often of lenticular, wedge or diamond section. The second design consists of a circular rib along the back of the blade - the so-called pipe-back or, as it was sometimes called because of its cross-section, the key-hole blade. The third and commonest design consists of a blade with one or more grooves (or fullers) running longitudinally along the blade. Such blades are, in effect, a form of I-girder, most easily seen in the Pattern 1892 infantry blade. The fourth method, adopted, for example, in the Pattern 1908 cavalry blade, consists of a narrow blade with a relatively very wide back, thus producing, in effect, a T-shaped girder. There are variations on each of these basic designs. A chamfered or latchet blade is one where the last few inches of the back are double edged and form a discontinuity with the rest of the blade (see, for example, Plate 69); in some relatively rare forms, the discontinuity is marked by a continuation of the pipe-back rib (see Plate 66).

It is generally accepted that for cutting or slashing, a curved blade is desirable since this produced a slicing form of cut. Conversely, a straight blade is the most desirable form for thrusting, making the blade an extension of the outstretched arm and giving additional penetrating force. Cutting or slashing requires above all a handy, manoeuvrable sword and has thus traditionally been the type of sword adopted by the physically smaller Oriental races and light cavalry. The thrusting sword, because it tends to be longer to provide maximum reach, tends also to be heavier, at least in military applications, and has thus been more often than not the weapon of the heavy cavalry since, in the thrust, impetus is of vital importance. Inevitably, constant attempts have been made to produce swords equally effective for cutting and thrusting; indeed, the history of the British cavalry troopers' sword in the nineteenth century is a history of such attempts. Almost equally inevitably, it is a history of relative failure, producing swords which were not ideal for either form of usage. It may be noted that penetrating wounds are basically more severe and disabling than slicing wounds.

The points of military swords come in basically three forms - spear, hatchet, and clipped (Figure 6). Spear points, in one form or another, are the commonest while clipped points, which seem to serve very little purpose, are the least common.

A distinct problem arises in classifying the various orders of dress with which particular patterns of sword were worn. The definitions laid down in the first *Dress Regulations* in 1822, and used in subsequent editions, were as follows:

Dress: Dress Reviews, Royal Birthdays and other particular occasions when troops were assembled.

Full Dress: Royal Drawing Rooms, Levées and similar occasions.

Undress: General use, on all occasions not otherwise specified.

As the nineteenth century progressed, Dress and Full Dress tended to merge, except perhaps in the cavalry, and various types of campaigning dress were introduced for active service. By the end of the century the basic distinction was between Full Dress and Service Dress.

No amount of description or illustration is a substitute for examining, and, if possible, handling, actual specimens of sword. The most comprehensive collection is probably still that of the Royal Armouries, formerly in the Tower of London and now to be re-located at Leeds (1996). It is closely followed by that at the National Army Museum (NAM). The Scottish United Services Museum (SUSM) has a particularly important collection of Scottish swords, and the Pattern Room at the Royal Ordnance Factory at Nottingham has a most important collection of sealed patterns from the

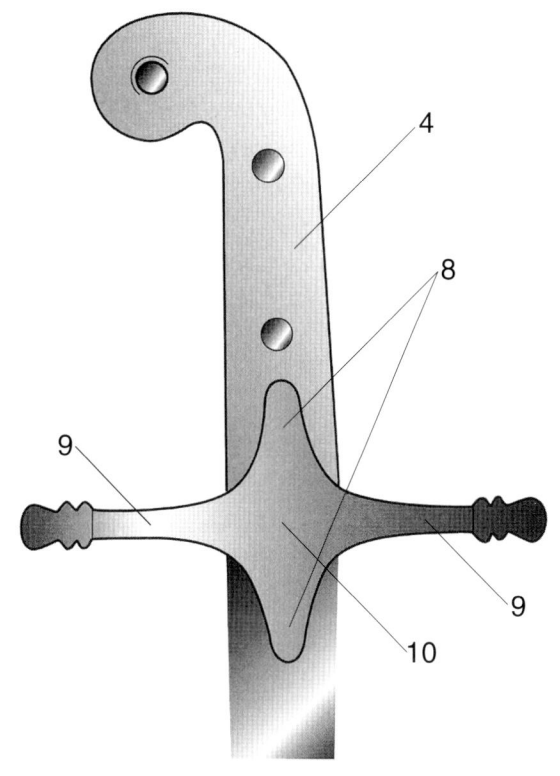

Fig. 1

Fig. 2

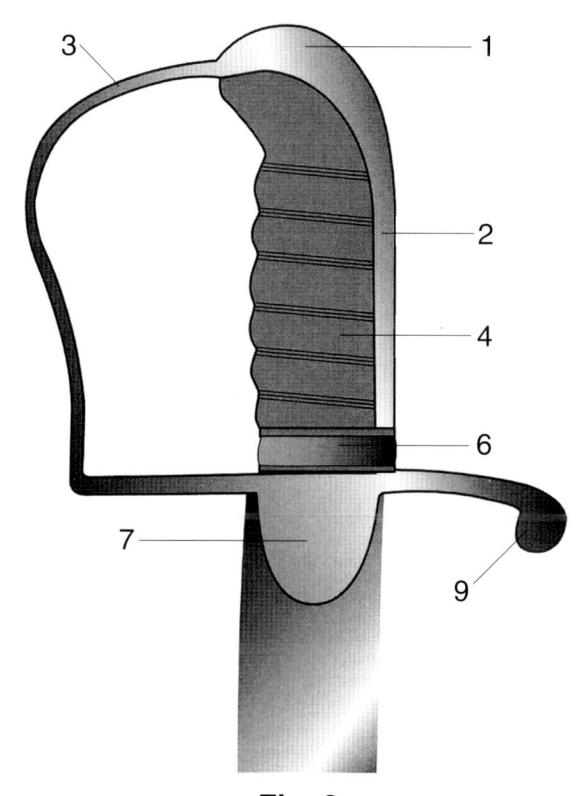

Fig. 3

Nomenclature of Sword Hilts, (Figs. 1-3):

1. Pommel
2. Backpiece
3. Guard
4. Grip
5. Ear
6. Ferrule
7. Langet
8. Double langets
9. Quillon
10. Écusson
11. Tang button

xiii

Fig. 4

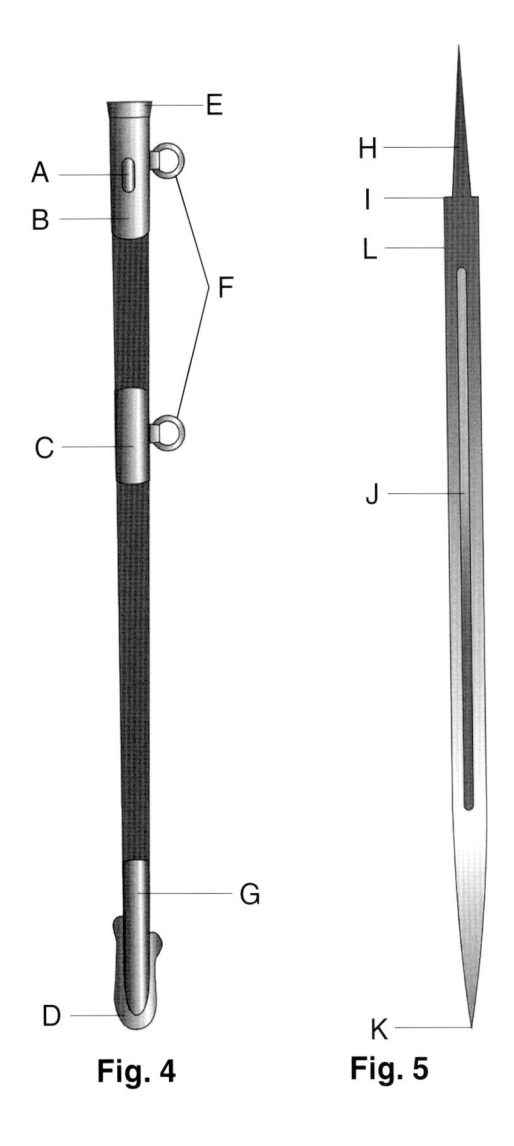

Fig. 5

Nomenclature of the scabbard and blade, (Figs. 4-5):

A. Frog button
B. Locket
C. Band
D. Shoe
E. Mouthpiece
F. Loose ring
G. Chape
H. Tang
I. Shoulder
J. Fuller
K. Spear point
L. Ricasso

Sword Points, (Fig. 6):

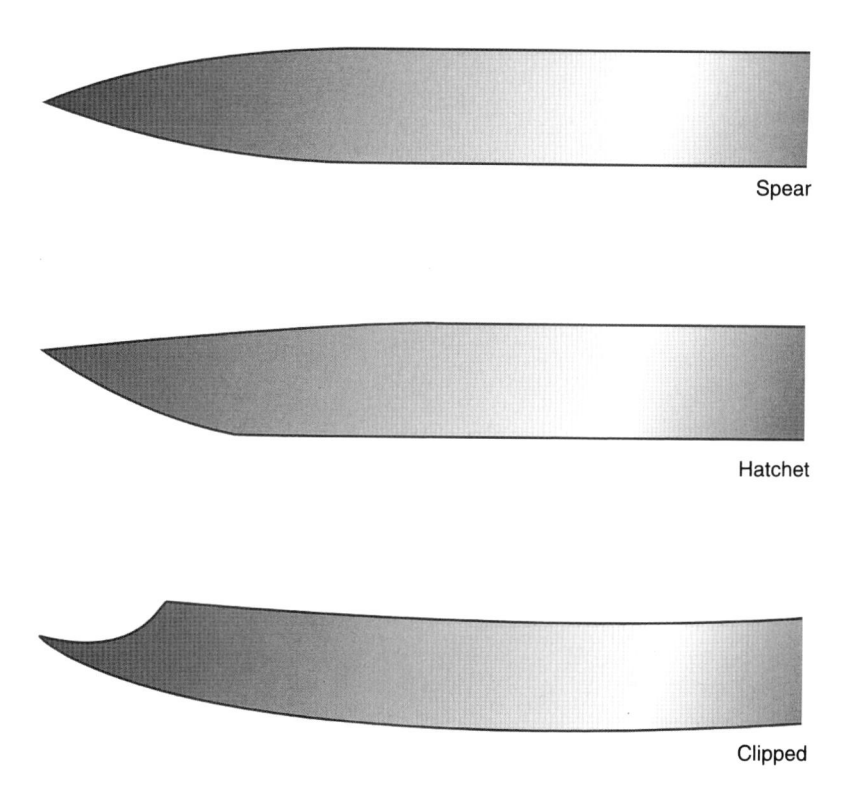

Spear

Hatchet

Clipped

middle of the nineteenth century onwards. The Royal Collection at Windsor has a large and valuable collection of swords, both British and foreign, associated with the Royal Family, which, in important cases, provide clues to the origins of the British regulation patterns. Finally, there are important swords to be found in the numerous regimental and corps museums. There are also some important private collections.

Measurements throughout are in inches because those are the units used in official papers. A precise measure of the curvature of a blade is difficult to devise. Some writers use the term 'rise' - the maximum distance between the back of the blade and a straight edge laid along it, but this by itself is not an accurate measure of curvature which depends also on the length of the blade. The most accurate measure of curvature would be the ratio of 'rise' to length but to most people that would be confusing rather than illuminating. I have fallen back upon descriptions such as 'slightly curved', relying wherever possible on the illustrations to clarify. Blades are described with point uppermost and the back towards the holder; hilts are described with pommel uppermost. These are the conventions used in official papers and the ways in which blade and hilt decoration was normally intended to be viewed. Scabbards are described with the mouth uppermost. Many hilts, blades and scabbard mounts were gilded, i.e., covered chemically with a thin layer of gold. The adjective commonly used in contemporary documents is 'gilt' and that is the sense in which it is used here.

Abbreviations

C-in-C	Commander-in-Chief
DGDQA	Director General of Defence Quality Assurance
FM	Field Marshal
5DG	5th Dragoon Guards
HCM	Household Cavalry Museum
HMSO	Her Majesty's Stationery Office
HRH	His Royal Highness
JAAS	*Journal of the Arms and Armour Society*
JRUSI	*Journal of the Royal United Services Institution*
JSAHR	*Journal of the Society for Army Historical Research*
LC	*List of Changes*
MoD	Ministry of Defence
NAM	National Army Museum
PRAI	*Proceedings of the Royal Artillery Institution*
PRO	Public Record Office
RA	Royal Artillery
RHA	Royal Horse Artillery
RHG	Royal Horse Guards
RSAF	Royal Small Arms Factory (Enfield)
RUSI	Royal United Services Institution
SUSM	Scottish United Services Museum

1. The Eighteenth Century Background

The British Army has never been a wholly unified, homogeneous organisation. Its constituent parts have, at times, appeared more notable for their diversity and rivalry than for their cohesion. Even today, after a long and bitter process of amalgamation and unification, the various regiments and corps preserve, and wield, a marked degree of independence and difference.

In the eighteenth century, these tendencies can be seen in their most extreme form. There was not one Army but two. The first, under the command and control of the Commander-in-Chief, with his office at the Horse Guards in London, comprised the cavalry and the infantry. He shared the duties of administering this Army with the Secretary at War, who had his office in the War Office and who, among a curious mélange of duties, was responsible to Parliament for the financial expenditure on the Army.[1] The Commander-in-Chief, however, was not subordinate to the Secretary at War; if he was subordinate to anyone, it was to the Sovereign.

The second Regular Army came under the control and direction of the Master-General of the Ordnance, who, in addition to acting as a Minister of Supply, was responsible for the Artillery and Engineers. The MGO was one of the great officers of state and normally a member of the Cabinet. When the Marquess of Granby was offered the choice of the post of Commander-in-Chief or Master-General of the Ordnance in 1763, he unhesitatingly chose the latter.

When a force was sent on active service, the Commander-in-Chief applied to the MGO for the necessary units of artillery and engineers. These then came under the operational control of the force commander but remained, for purposes of personnel administration, promotion, posting etc, under the direct, if distant, control of the MGO, whose headquarters remained physically and administratively quite distinct from either the War Office or the Horse Guards. It was a system not unlike that of the Admiralty and the Navy Board in this same period.

The existence of two Armies led inevitably to friction and confusion, and to the bizarre spectacle of parallel units being set up to perform essentially the same function. In 1800, for example, the Commander-in-Chief, exasperated by the system under which the Engineers came under the control of the MGO, created his own corps of engineers - the Royal Staff Corps - which existed in parallel with the Corps of Royal Engineers until 1838.[2]

The Eighteenth Century Background

It could be argued that there was a third Army, composed of the Militia and the various Volunteer units, which came in peacetime under the control of the Home Secretary and the Lords Lieutenant of the counties.

The fragmentation at the top was paralleled at regimental level where the colonel of the regiment was responsible for recruiting it, purchasing its clothing and equipment, and distributing its pay. In return, he received certain bulk allowances from the War Office. The system permitted and encouraged grave abuses, and led colonels to regard their regiment as a source of private profit. During much of the eighteenth century, the regiments were, in fact, called after their colonel at the time being.[3]

The system encouraged a lack of uniformity, not merely in terms of clothing and equipment but in matters of administration and even drill. There was no universally applied system of infantry drill in the British Army until 1792 when Dundas produced his famous drill book based on the Prussian system.[4] Even words of command differed between regiments so that a brigade commander sometimes found it awkward to drill his brigade on parade.

The difficulties that all this presented to a commander can be imagined but even more serious were the problems created on active service by a system under which each regiment purchased its own uniforms and equipment from its own private contractors. Since each regiment was free to choose its own suppliers, differences in patterns abounded and were fiercely defended as the symbols of independence and individuality. But these differences meant that the centralised supply of clothing and necessaries, with the exception of a few items such as muskets (but not swords), ammunition and shoes, was virtually impossible. If a regiment on active service abroad suffered serious losses of equipment or clothing, it might be months before they could be replaced. The system might be able to cope with a short campaign; it was bound to break down in face of a prolonged war. A similar system - the *silladar* system - operated in the Indian Army Cavalry regiments. Exactly as in the eighteenth century British Army, the predictable result was wide variations in patterns among the regiments and major problems of re-supply on prolonged active service.[5] The system broke down completely during the First World War and was abolished in 1922.

The decline and fall of the archaic British Army system is clearly illustrated in this book, particularly in relation to cavalry swords. Prior to 1788, the system allowed each regiment to select its own pattern of sword and to purchase them from their own choice of supplier, British or German. When, in 1788, the military authorities decided upon a modest degree of standardisation, it was necessary to ask each cavalry regiment to send in a specimen of its swords in order to decide on the most suitable. Even when two standard patterns had been chosen, it was still left to the regiments to arrange their own procurement and, since there were no detailed drawings or manufacturing specifications and the official descriptions were ambiguous, the result was a wide variation in the actual swords themselves.

It was the bitter experience of the opening years of the war against Revolutionary France, which broke out in 1793, which forced the Army authorities not merely to adopt absolutely standard patterns of sword and to lay down detailed standards of quality but to take over responsibility for procuring, storing and issuing cavalry swords. Even so, the old system lingered on in the Household Cavalry for nearly another 100 years.

The standardisation of patterns, the introduction of detailed specifications, the adoption of uniform standards of proof, the concentration of the sources of manufacture and the consequent elimination of problems of supply are the underlying themes of the chapters which follow.

Chapter 1: Notes

1. The precise position of the Secretary at War defies simple description; for a detailed analysis, see Olive Anderson, 'The Constitutional Position of the Secretary at War 1642-1859' *JSAHR*, Vol XXXVI, 1958, pp165-69. The post was absorbed into that of Secretary of State for War after the administrative disasters of the Crimean War. In 1870, the Commander-in-Chief became subject to the political control of the Secretary of State and in 1904 the post of C-in-C was abolished as part of the Esher Committee's reforms and replaced by that of Chief of the Imperial General Staff.

2. The memorial to the Royal Staff Corps lies in the Royal Military Canal, from Hythe in Kent to Rye in Sussex, which the Corps was responsible for constructing as an invasion defence against Napoleon, and which still remains basically intact. The post of Master-General of the Ordnance was abolished in 1855 as a direct result of the scandals of the Crimean War but revived again in 1904 as part of the new General Staff.

3. Regimental administration of the eighteenth century, including matters of procurement and quality control, is described by Alan J Guy, *Oeconomy and Discipline : Officership and Administration in the British Army, 1714-1763*, Manchester (1985).

4. *Rules and Regulations for the Movements of His Majesty's Infantry*, London (1792). A standard drill for cavalry also by Dundas, appeared in 1795.

5. In the Second Afghan War, a fire, which destroyed the equipment of three troops of the 13th Bengal Lancers in March 1880, crippled the regiment operationally for several months - see Brian Robson, *The Road to Kabul: the Second Afghan War 1878-1881*, London (1986) pp56-57.

2. Cavalry Troopers' Swords 1788-1878

The effective history of the cavalry troopers' sword in the British Army begins in 1788 - 'effective' because before that date the pattern of sword used in a cavalry regiment depended largely upon the whim or individual fancy of the colonel of that regiment. That situation arose from the fact that, in essence, he was the proprietor of that regiment - indeed, before 1788, the regiment was often called after its colonel, who was usually a general officer. In return for certain fixed allowances from the Government, he undertook to clothe and equip his regiment to the fairly broad standards laid down by the Army authorities. In consequence, no two regiments necessarily carried the same pattern of sword, and since each colonel was free to choose his own source of supply - British or foreign - there was no uniformity of quality. The problems of replenishment and augmentation that this was liable to create during a war can well be imagined.

1   Sword, 15th Light Dragoons, Officer, *c*1763
Blade length and width: 35in x 1¼in.
Blade type: straight, single edged, flat back, unfullered.
Guard: simple cross-hilt with recurved guard, in steel.
Hilt mounts: steel.
Grip: wood, covered with fishskin, bound with silver wire.
Scabbard: black leather, with steel chape and locket with frog hook.
Note: by Jefferys, Strand, London; royal cypher of George III and initials 'WB' (Captain William Brook, who served with the regiment 1759-65). Troopers carried a plain version with unchiselled hilt.

(NAM 7205-70)

Cavalry Troopers' Swords 1788-1878

Despite this apparently chaotic situation, a very broad convention had grown up in the period immediately before 1788, under which the heavy cavalry regiments generally carried long, heavy, straight swords, with some form of basket hilt, while the light cavalry tended to carry shorter, lighter, curved swords, usually with some form of knucklebow guard, although the 15th Light Dragoons carried a simple cross-hilt, (Plate 1). But any attempt at a detailed history of cavalry swords before 1788 would, in practice, be a catalogue of unconnected patterns of doubtful attribution.

It may have been the harsh lessons of the American War of Independence (1775-83) which forced a change in this system. On 30 November 1787, the Commander-in-Chief wrote to all colonels of heavy dragoon regiments:

> 'It being also His Majesty's intention to have an inspection made, of all the Regimental Swords now worn by the several Corps of Cavalry, in order to fix upon one for the general use of the whole, you will therefore be so good as to forward to my office in Crown Street Westminster, by the first convenient opportunity, one of the Uniform Swords at present worn by the private Men of the ...Regiment of Dragoons under your command.[1]

A similar request went to the colonels of light dragoon regiments.

A Board of General Officers, under the chairmanship of General Henry Seymour Conway,[2] was set up to consider swords, carbines and other items of equipment and clothing for the cavalry, and to make recommendations for standard patterns. For swords, the detailed terms of reference were:

> 'Regimental Swords
> for the Heavy Dragoons.
> The Form of the Hilts;- & the Length, Breadth & Shape of the Blades both for Officers & Men, to be fixed upon by the General Officers, commanding Reg^{ts} of Heavy Drag^s for H M's approbation;- & their opinion to be given, whether German Blades are preferable to those of British Manufacture.
>
> The same Points, for the Reg^{ts} of L^t D^{ns} to be determined upon by their respective Colonels;- & whether Sabres, or Swords, are most proper for their use.[3]

These terms of reference are of interest because they spotlight the high reputation of German (mainly Solingen) manufacturers and the lower reputation of British firms, a rivalry which was to linger on until almost the last decade of the nineteenth century. They are also of interest because they make a clear distinction between sabres (curved) and swords (straight) which has not subsequently been universally followed in the British Army.

The Board thus constituted met for the first time on 31 May 1788 and continued its deliberations until 16 June 1788. Having inspected the various patterns of sword already in service, it recommended that the pattern to be adopted for the heavy cavalry should be as follows:

> 'That the Hilts of the Swords for the Regiments of Dragoon Guards and Dragoons should be half Basket, the same form as those of the 6th or Inniskilling Regiment of Dragoons;- The Grip, from the Guard to the point of the Button, to be Seven Inches and five Eighths. - The Blades to be three Feet three Inches from the Guard to the Point;- The Breadth of the Blade at the Shoulder to be One Inch and five twelfths, - and the Back [of the blade] to be three Eighths of an Inch thick, and to finish about fourteen Inches from the Point.[4]

For the light cavalry, the pattern recommended was described thus:

> 'The Hilts to be of the same form as those now used by the Light Dragoons, - and to be Five Inches long in the Grip. - The Blades to be Thirty Six Inches long, - and the Curve in the Centre to be One Inch and three Quarters from the strait line:- The Breadth to be One Inch and One Half at the Shoulder, - The Blade to be three Eighths of an Inch thick, and to finish about Eleven Inches from the Point.[5]

It was recommended that the officers' swords should be uniform with those of the men.

At its second meeting, on 7 June 1788, the Board went into the thorny subject of German versus British manufacture, taking evidence from three well-known British manufacturers - Messrs Thomas Gill, Samuel Harvey and James Woolley - and, on the German side, the equally well-known importer of Solingen blades, John Justus Runkel.[6] It is clear from the evidence given that there were in existence no specific, uniform standards of proof for military swords, and that accordingly there were acute differences of opinion among makers over what constituted suitable proof. Gill believed that blades should be subjected to bending tests and struck on the edge on a bar of iron; he thought that striking on a flat surface was a fallacious test. Harvey agreed on bending but disagreed about striking on a flat surface. Woolley was in favour of bending only. No doubt their views reflected their existing practice. All agreed, however, that in the past many British swords had been bad and defective. In tests carried out there and then before the Board, swords provided by Runkel proved superior on the whole to those of the three manufacturers. Furthermore, Runkel claimed that, provided no import duty was levied, he could provide swords cheaper than the English manufacturers.

In face of this conflicting evidence, the Board recommended that the tests to be adopted in future for all cavalry swords should be striking on a piece of wood or iron, and bending, in a machine produced before the Board, at a rate of 2 inches per foot of the blade length. The bending test, in particular, was a very severe one, as we shall see later, and could be achieved in practice only with a blade in which flexibility took precedence over stiffness and strength. The Board recommended further that the Treasury should impose a levy on foreign swords to equalise competitive conditions and that then the colonels of regiments should be free to use whichever source they pleased.

These recommendations were duly accepted and circulated to the colonels of all cavalry regiments.

As was the custom, the recommendations were not accompanied by drawings or detailed manufacturing specifications and the precise identification of these 1788 patterns is a matter of considerable difficulty since the descriptions themselves are notable for their imprecision.

In the case of the proposed light cavalry pattern, the only detailed information given is the size and curvature of the blade and the length of the grip. No information is given as to the *form* of the blade, i.e., fullered or unfullered, and if fullered, the number and dimensions of the fullers. The reference to the hilts being of the same form as those then in use is in itself almost incomprehensible since there was no single pattern of hilt in use in the light cavalry, each regiment choosing its own.

In the face of these ambiguities, it is tempting to believe that the Board was not attempting to lay down a specification for a single, standard pattern of sword for the light cavalry but was taking a first tentative step towards standardisation by specifying a common size and shape of blade. That could be considered a sensible approach, given the existing diversity and quasi-proprietorial rights which the regimental colonels exercised over their regiments. By adopting this approach, the expense to the colonel of altering the swords of the regiment would have been substantially reduced, while a useful first step towards eventual full standardisation would have been achieved. It is also worth noting Major John Gaspard Le Marchant's comment in 1793 (see below) that scarcely two regiments had the same sword.

Nevertheless, a sufficient number of swords of similar form exist to suggest that there was a genuine Pattern 1788 Light Cavalry sword even if in slightly different forms. What might be considered to be the archetypal version is that shown, for example, in George Stubbs' painting of the 10th Light Dragoons in 1793, in the Royal Collection at Windsor,[7] and in the figures used to illustrate Le Marchant's *Rules and Regulations for the Sword Exercise of the Cavalry*, printed in

Cavalry Troopers' Swords 1788-1878

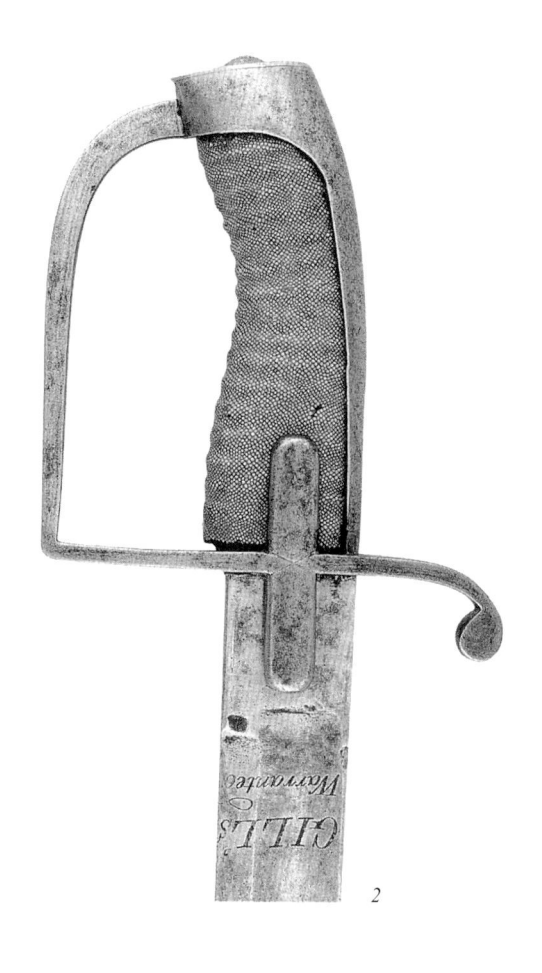

2   Sword, Light Cavalry, Pattern 1788

Blade length and width: 36in. x 1¼in.
Blade type: curved, flat back, single broad fuller each side almost to spear point, double edged last 6in.
Guard: straight knucklebow in steel, double langets.
Hilt mounts: steel.
Grip: wood, covered in fishskin.
Scabbard: wood, covered with tooled leather, and encased in iron or steel sheath, black japanned. Two loose rings on small v-shaped mounts.
Note: blade marked 'Gill's Warranted'; it is possible that this is an officer's sword to the 1788 pattern.

(NAM 8507-54)

3   Sword, Light Cavalry, Pattern 1788 - overall view of sword

(NAM 8507-54)

4   Sword, Light Cavalry, Pattern 1788 - overall view of scabbard

(NAM 8507-54)

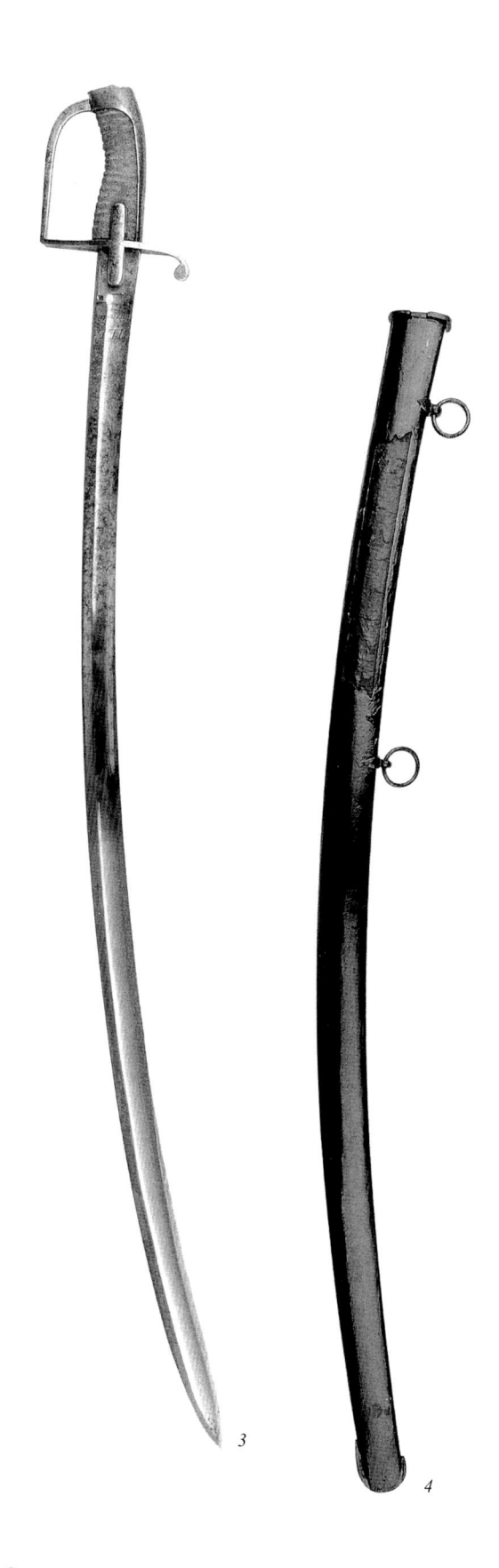

8

1796, just before the 1788 pattern was replaced. In this version, the hilt consists of a straight knucklebow, in steel, with straight, double langets, and a plain backpiece and pommel cap, (Plate 2). But there are innumerable variants from this period, differing in the form of the pommel, the shape of the langets, the use of single-or double-fullered blades, and in the form of the blade point. Many swords were made in Solingen and these tend to have the double-fullered blades known in the French Army as '*à la Montmorency*', viz. with a narrow fuller close to the back of the blade and a broader fuller in parallel on each side, both fullers running to the point. English versions tend, by contrast, to have blades with a single broad fuller running to the point each side, (Plate 3). A further distinguishing mark of English-made swords of this pattern is the disc-shaped quillon, often curved downwards. But these distinctions are not invariable.[8]

An interesting feature of these swords is the grip, which consists of a wooden former fitted over the spike tang and bound with cord or string and then covered with wet fishskin or leather; as it dried, it shrank and moulded itself to the turns of cord, thus producing a ridged grip. This contrasts with later methods in which the wooden former was often ridged itself and the fishskin covering bound externally with wire.

Scabbards were of iron or black leather, with iron mounts, or, in the case of many Solingen swords, of wood, with a long iron chape and locket joined by iron strips along the edges, giving the superficial appearance of an iron scabbard with wooden inserts; where the wood shows it is covered with leather, (Plate 4).

These variations can be ascribed to a number of causes, including the personal predilictions of regimental officers and manufacturers, and variations in manufacturing tolerances. But the principal cause was almost certainly the imprecision inherent in a system which provided no detailed, dimensioned drawings but required a manufacturer to copy from a single sealed model.

The identification of the 1788 Pattern Heavy Cavalry sword presents a highly intractable problem. While, on the face of it, the specification laid down by the Board was very precise, it contains, on closer examination, serious ambiguities and gaps. Dated heavy cavalry swords of this period are very uncommon and contemporary portraits and drawings either fail to show the swords at all or do so in a crude and imprecise way.

The starting point in the process must clearly be the identification of the hilt carried by the Inniskillings in 1788. As it happens, the Glasgow Art Gallery and Museum contains a sword of this regiment, the blade of which is marked on the back as having been made at the *Fabrique Royale* at Hertzberg in Hanover in 1779, (Plates 5, 6). This would seem in all probability to be a specimen of the sword referred to in the Inspection Return for the regiment in May 1777 which noted that a new set of swords was in the making. The date on the blade does not, of course, prove that the hilt itself is contemporaneous. There is however no indica-

Cavalry Troopers' Swords 1788-1878

5   Sword, Inniskilling Dragoons, 1779
Blade length and width: 33½in. x 1⅜in. x ⅜in.
Blade type: straight, double edged, one broad, one narrow fuller.
Guard: wrought iron basket.
Hilt mounts: wrought iron.
Grip: wood, covered in fishskin.
Note: the three short fullers in the blade at the shoulder are unusual in military swords. The blade was originally at least 2in. longer.
   (Glasgow Art Gallery and Museum, Reg No '84-13)

6   Sword, Inniskilling Dragoons, 1779
- back of the blade
   (Glasgow Art Gallery and Museum, Reg No '84-13)

Cavalry Troopers' Swords 1788-1878

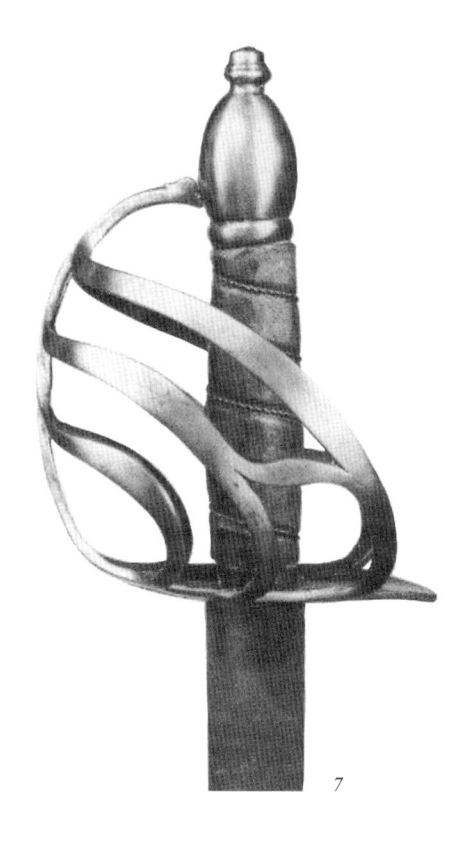

7   Sword, Heavy Cavalry, Pattern 1788
Note: marked 'Inniskilling' on the blade. Manufactured at Hertzberg.
(The Royal Collection © Her Majesty the Queen; Windsor - North Corridor 901)

8   Sword, Heavy Cavalry, Pattern 1788
Blade length and width: 38¼in. x 1¼in.
Blade type: straight, flat back, unfullered, spear point.
Guard: wrought iron or steel basket.
Hilt mounts: wrought iron or steel 7in. overall.
Grip: wood, covered with fishskin, bound with steel wire, 5in. long.
Scabbard: black leather, steel locket with frog hook and chape.
Note: made by James Woolley, Birmingham, 1793.
(SUSM 1992-82)

tion that the hilt is not contemporary with the blade. If one assumes, for argument's sake, that the hilt is a later addition, then that would move its date even closer to 1788 and thus strengthen the conclusion that this is indeed the hilt in use in 1788. If, *per contra*, the hilt has been re-bladed, of which there is no evidence, then one is forced to conclude that this was done because the regiment wished to retain this pattern of hilt post-1779; the alternative possibility, and one which seems highly improbable, is that the sword was first re-bladed and then re-hilted again after 1779 and before 1788. Faced with these complications, it seems logical to accept that the hilt of the Glasgow sword is indeed that carried by the Inniskillings in 1788 and the one that the Board had in mind in framing its recommendations. It should be noted that an almost identical sword, marked 'Inniskilling' on the blade, and also made at Hertzberg, is in the Royal Collection at Windsor, (Plate 7); unfortunately, it is not dated and no date of acquisition is recorded.

The Glasgow sword has been shortened in its career and originally must have measured at least 36 inches; the length of the hilt is approximately 7 inches, which compares with the $7^5/8$ths inches recommended in 1788. The Windsor sword has a blade length of 37 inches and a hilt length of $7^5/16$ths inches. It is fair to assume that the two swords are contemporaneous and the original catalogue entry suggests that the Windsor sword has its original hilt.

If one assumes for the moment that the Glasgow and Windsor hilts are the pattern prescribed by the Board of General Officers in 1788, then the question immediately arises as to whether there are any dated swords post-1788 with this hilt and which otherwise match the dimensions laid down in 1788. In fact, exactly such a sword has recently come into the collection of the Scottish United Services Museum (SUSM) in Edinburgh, (Plate 8), dated 1793; there is also one in NAM dated 1793 with hatchet point (6310-111).

At least three other swords exist which closely match the previous three. Two in the Royal Armouries (Nos IX-606 and 607, Plates 9, 10) match the dimensions of the 1788 pattern very closely, particularly IX-607:

	1788 Pattern	**IX-607**
Length of hilt	$7^5/8$in.	$7^1/4$in.
Length of blade	39in.	40in.
Width at shoulder	$1^5/12$in.	$1^7/16$in.
Thickness at shoulder	$3/8$in.	$3/8$in.

These two swords are both marked 'Inconquerable' on the blade, a motto which A N Ingram believed was awarded to the 2nd Irish Horse (subsequently the 5th Dragoon Guards) in 1788.[9] Unfortunately, this potentially important fact cannot be substantiated and thus used as an aid to dating.

Cavalry Troopers' Swords 1788-1878

9   Sword, Heavy Cavalry, Pattern 1788
Blade length and width: 36 1/2in. x 1 7/16in. x 3/8in.
Blade type: straight, flat back, broad fuller to within 1in. of spear point.
Guard: wrought iron basket.
Hilt mounts: wrought iron, 7 1/4in. overall.
Grip: wood, covered with fishskin and bound with steel wire; length 5 1/4in.
Scabbard: black leather, the wrought iron locket with long frog hook; here the chape is missing.
(Royal Armouries IX-606)

10   Sword, Heavy Cavalry, Pattern 1788
Blade length and width: 40in. x 1 7/16in. x 3/8in.
Blade type: straight, flat back, broad fuller to within 1in. of spear point.
Guard: wrought iron basket.
Hilt mounts: wrought iron.
Grip: wood, covered with fishskin, bound with steel wire.
Scabbard: black leather, the wrought iron locket with long belt hook and chape.
Note: the blade decoration is more elaborate than RA IX-606.
(Royal Armouries IX-607)

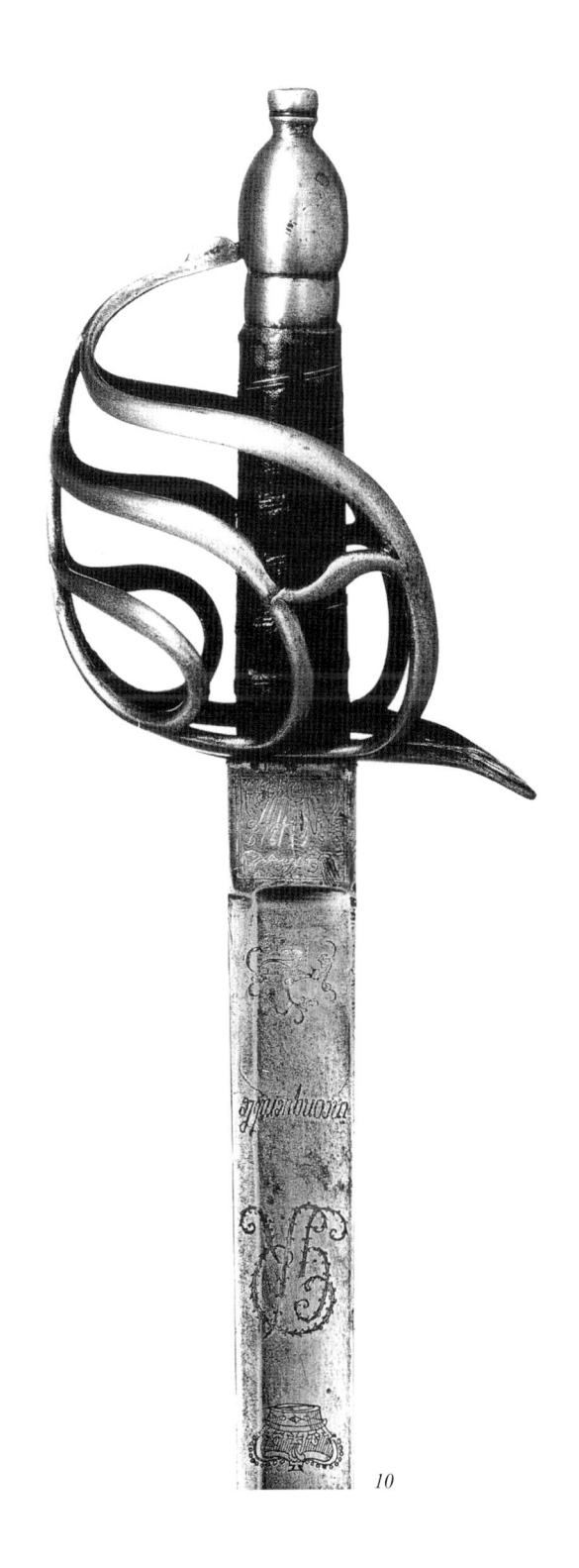

A third, almost identical sword is in the Legermuseum in Delft, Holland, its blade marked '3rd or Prince of Wales's Regiment of Dragoon Guards', a title awarded in 1765, (Plates 11, 12). The regiment was in England between 1765 and 1793, when it embarked for Flanders, and it may be a relic of the campaign in the Low Countries in 1793-95.

There is other, collateral evidence. Lieutenant-Colonel Charles Hamilton Smith's drawings of the death of Major-General Mansel at Beaumont in 1794 show very clearly a hilt of the Glasgow pattern on a sword carried by a heavy cavalry trooper.[10] A contemporary description of the 4th Dragoons in 1792 describes them as carrying a heavy, straight sword with a basket hilt,[11] while Le Marchant, on service with the heavy cavalry in Flanders in 1793 refers to their swords as having 'a wide, long and heavy blade, with a cumbrous fantastic handle'.[12]

It should be noted, however, that whereas the blades of the swords in the Royal Armouries and the Legermuseum have a single broad fuller each side, running to within an inch of the point, the Glasgow sword has one broad and one narrow fuller each side, starting at some distance from the shoulder, and three very short fullers in the ricasso. The Windsor sword has the same feature of three short fullers in the ricasso but has two narrow fullers starting $6^{1}/2$ inches from the shoulder, one of which runs virtually to the point. The SUSM sword has an unfullered blade. These differences may simply reflect the fact that the original specifications did not lay down the precise form of the blade but merely its dimensions.

In all cases, where they survive, the scabbards are of black leather with steel chape and locket, the latter with a frog hook, the swords at that time being carried in a frog on a shoulder belt.

Whilst this body of evidence constitutes a powerful case for concluding that the Pattern 1788 Heavy Cavalry sword is that shown in Plate 10, it is necessary to consider an alternative view for which there is evidence. The 1788 Board's recommendations referred to a 'half-basket', of the 'form' of the Inniskillings. This has suggested to some students that the hilt was intended to be literally *half* of the Glasgow hilt - that is to say, with bars only on one side. And indeed swords with hilts of this 'half-basket' form, and with blades of roughly the right dimensions, exist in considerable quantities in the Royal Armouries and elsewhere, (Plate 13). The disparity in numbers adds, if anything, to this thesis. On the other hand, the terms 'basket' and 'half-basket' had no precise meaning at this time or even later, and were used interchangeably. By itself, the term 'half-basket' cannot prove or disprove either thesis, and the absence of dates on these alternative swords is a weakness in the alternative theory.

The fact of the matter is that, in the absence of detailed manufacturing specifications and drawings, we do not know with certainty what the Pattern 1788 Heavy Cavalry sword was, although the author still inclines to the first hypothesis.

Cavalry Troopers' Swords 1788-1878

11

12

11   Sword, Heavy Cavalry, Pattern 1788
Blade length and width: 39⅞in. x 1⅜in.
Blade type: straight, flat back, broad fuller each side to within 1in. of spear point.
Guard: iron or steel basket.
Hilt mounts: iron or steel, 7½in. overall.
Grip: wood, bound with fishskin and brass wire.
(Legermuseum, Delft, Reg No 017045)

12   Sword, Heavy Cavalry, Pattern 1788
- detail of blade
Note: the title 'Prince of Wales" was granted in 1765 and the regiment was in England from 1765 until it embarked for Flanders in 1793.
(Legermuseum, Delft, Reg No 017045)

13   Sword, Heavy Cavalry, c1788
Blade length and width: 38¾in. x 1¼in.
Blade type: straight, flat back, one broad and one narrow fuller each side, spear point.
Guard: three-bar guard, with side ring.
Hilt mounts: iron or steel pommel and ferrule.
Grip: wood, covered with leather and bound with steel wire.
Note: typical of a large number of undated swords in the Royal Armouries which may possibly represent the Pattern 1788 Heavy Cavalry sword.
(Royal Armouries IX-1848)

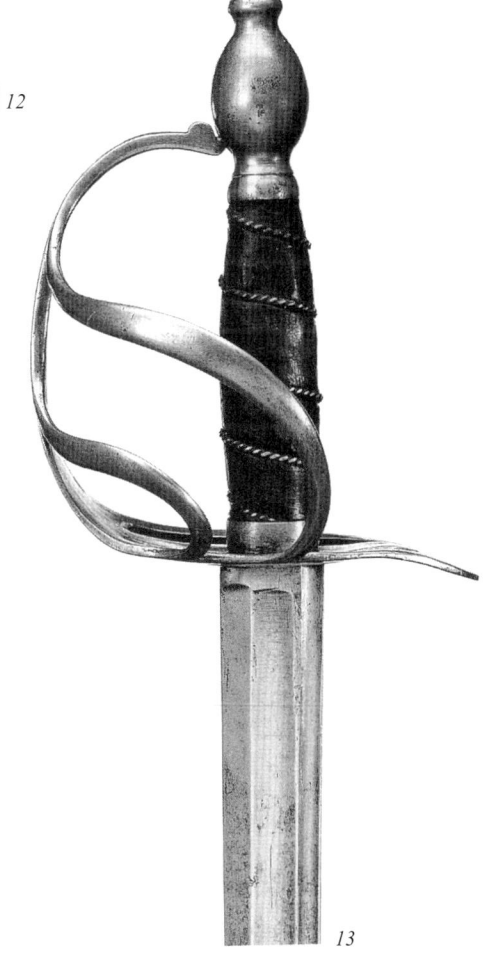

13

Although the Pattern 1788 Light Cavalry swords are marginally better swords for practical use than the Heavy Cavalry pattern, neither can be considered a masterpiece of design. The Light Cavalry swords are badly balanced, provide only minimal protection to the hand and are not sufficiently curved to be good slashing swords and not straight enough to be good thrusting swords. The Heavy Cavalry swords of this period are monstrosities - heavy, cumbersome, badly balanced and far too long. Moreover, although a measure of standardisation had been introduced into the designs, it is clear from subsequent experience that uniformity of quality lagged behind. What is also clear, both from the relative scarcity of existing specimens and from Le Marchant's comments on the patterns of sword in use in the Low Countries in 1793-94, (see below), is that re-equipment with the 1788 patterns was protracted, and had not been fully achieved by the time that new patterns were introduced in 1796.

The new patterns of sword received their first real test in the Flanders expedition of 1793. One of the officers accompanying that expedition was Major J G Le Marchant, in command of a squadron of the 2nd Dragoon Guards. He was probably unique in the British Army at that time in having devoted a great deal of rigorous thought to the question of the proper design of sword for cavalry. His views had been set out as early as 1789 in a paper entitled 'Remarks on the construction of swords adapted to the use of Cavalry',[13] written when he was still a cornet in the 6th Dragoons.

Le Marchant's thesis was that when cavalry charged it was the actual impetus of man and horse which did the damage, and that the sword played little part; for this purpose, therefore, the actual form of the sword was relatively unimportant. The sword came into its own only in subsequent individual encounters with other horsemen or infantry - what Le Marchant termed 'desultory encounters':

> 'I have only to repeat that in a Charge of Cavalry, the first advantage is to be derived exclusively from the Impulse - and not the Sword, in that case it can be of no importance what Construction the Sword is of, relative to the Use that may be made of it by Troops collectively formed. Therefore the Weapon should be adapted to the service of the Cavalry in desultory attacks against an enemy broken and in disorder.

In such encounters, Le Marchant was convinced that what was wanted was not a long, straight, heavy sword but a light, curved, slashing sword on the lines of the Oriental scimitar, and he adduced in support the success and effectiveness of the Persian, Tartar, Turkish, Arab and Hungarian light cavalry. He pointed out that a thrusting sword could never be made long enough in practice to equal the reach of an infantryman's musket and bayonet, whereas with a slashing sword a cavalryman could cut at his opponent's arm and disable him.

Clearly, neither of the 1788 patterns met Le Marchant's requirements and his experience in the field only served to confirm his views:

'I have been busily engaged in making drawings of all the articles in the military equipages of our Allies which differ from our own, such as saddles, accoutrements, arms etc. I have also paid particular observation to the mode of training the Austrian cavalry to the use of the sabre, in which their superiority over us is incredible.[14]

Participation in the cavalry action at Cassel in June 1793 alongside the Austrians confirmed him in his views, and he accordingly put himself under an Austrian sergeant for instruction.

Apart from the inferiority of British training, the swords themselves seemed to Le Marchant grossly inferior. They were so brittle that they often broke at the first blow, but the greatest defect was that they were so heavy and so badly balanced that they tended to twist in the man's hand, thus inflicting a bruise rather than a wound. The surgeons told him that many of the wounds to British cavalrymen and their horses were actually inflicted by their own swords. Le Marchant recorded that:

'The swords then in use by the British cavalry were of various descriptions, scarcely 2 regiments having the same pattern; but one of the most popular was a wide, long and heavy blade, mounted with a cumbrous, fantastic handle.[15]

(The latter description is a fair description of the Pattern 1788 Heavy Cavalry sword. It is only fair to record, in passing, that at Villers-en-Couches and at Beaumont in April 1794, the British cavalry achieved stunning successes against the French infantry).

Le Marchant returned home in 1794 and set to work to design a new sword, visiting Sheffield and Birmingham, and consulting the leading swordmakers, including Henry Osborne, who shared much of his thinking about swords. Together, it would appear, they evolved the design of a new slashing sword, with a 31 1/2 inch blade which Le Marchant submitted to the Commander-in-Chief (the Duke of York) early in 1796, with a memorial entitled 'A Plan for Constructing and Mounting in a Different Manner the Swords of the Cavalry'.[16] No copy of this memorial has yet been found but it is clear from the circumstantial evidence that the sword proposed was very similar to the later Pattern 1796 Light Cavalry sword except that it was slightly shorter in the blade. What is almost certainly a drawing of the hilt of Le Marchant's new pattern is included in *Rules and Regulations for the Sword Exercise of the Cavalry*; it differs only in the most minor detail from that subsequently adopted. The new method of 'constructing and mounting' cannot now be ascertained with certainty but it almost certainly referred to the method of riveting the backpiece and grip to the tang (see below).

Le Marchant's work was considered early in 1796 by a Board of Cavalry General Officers, appointed to consider the general equipment of the cavalry, and the results promulgated in June 1796. On swords, the recommendations were as follows:

> '[Heavy Cavalry] The swords having been found, from long, and repeated Experience, to be unmanageable, owing to the Length of the Blade, and the Weight of the Hilt, a Sword thirty five inches long in the Blade, is to be substituted in lieu of those, now in use; - and the Rivet which fixes the Back of the Hilt, to the middle of the Handle, must go through the Shank of the Blade; and the Back to be well riveted, near the Guard. The Shank of the Blade, to be large, and the Top of the Scabbard, made to take off, for the easier repairing of the same, as p.pattern sent herewith.
> [Light Cavalry] The Sabre is to be of the same pattern, as the one last approved of by His Majesty; - and the Length of the Blade to be from 32 Inches, and a half, to 33 Inches, measur'd in a straight Line from the Hilt, to the Point, but not to exceed the latter measure. The Scabbard to be the same, as that for the Heavy Cavalry.[17]

These descriptions are notable for their imprecision and they were not accompanied by drawings or manufacturing specifications; instead, manufacturers were expected to take their own measurements and specifications from the pattern swords available for inspection at the office of the Comptrollers of Army Accounts, in London. In these circumstances, it was inevitable that wide variations in manufacturing tolerances occurred and that actual specimens differ in details. Within a month of the Board's recommendations having been accepted and promulgated, Henry Osborne had tendered to supply 3,000 of each pattern within seven months, at a cost of seventeen shillings each. Orders also went at this time to Brunn, Prosser, Gill, Egg and Davies.[18] From the distribution of surviving specimens it seems that the majority of the two Pattern 1796 swords were made initially in Birmingham, as was to be expected.

It is clear that Le Marchant's ideas had not been fully accepted since a separate sword, with a straight blade, had been adopted for the heavy cavalry, although the light cavalry sword was clearly his design. But the heavy cavalry sword was, in fact, almost a direct copy of the Austrian heavy cavalry sword, the *Pallasche fur Kurassiere, Dragoner und Chevaux-Legers, Model 1775*,[19] and this may owe something to Le Marchant's earlier observations in Flanders; that sword is well shown in J B Seele's painting of Austrian dragoons, dated 1799, in the Royal Collection at Windsor.[20]

Cavalry Troopers' Swords 1788-1878

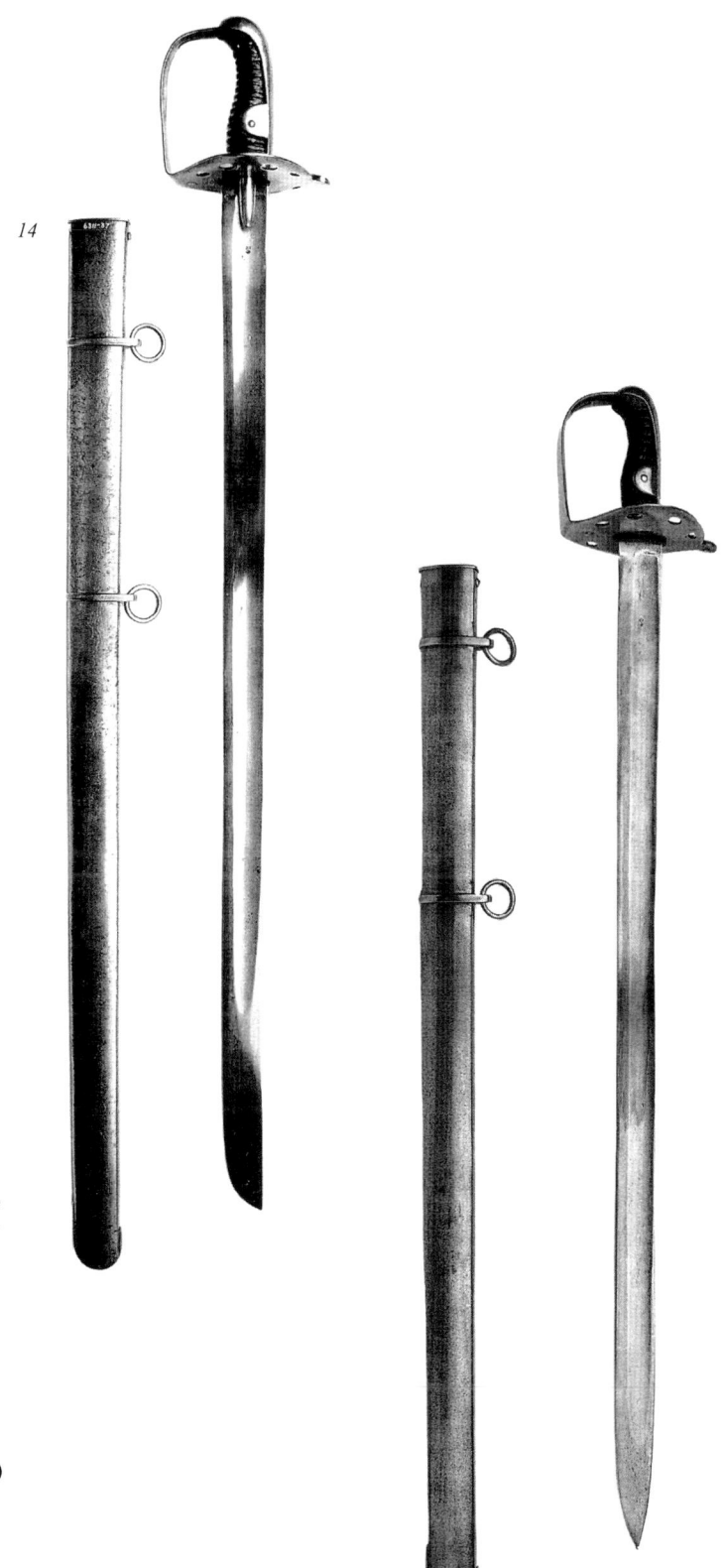

14 Sword, Heavy Cavalry, Pattern 1796

Blade length and width: 35in. x 1 1/2in.
Blade type: straight, flat back, single edged except for last 12 in. single broad fuller each side to within 8in. of hatchet point.
Guard: wrought iron or steel knucklebow broadening out at base into a pear-shaped disc pierced with holes round edge. The disc is reinforced on the inside with a thin plate and the sword knot slit is near the pommel.
Hilt mounts: wrought iron.
Grip: wood, bound with cord and covered with leather.
Scabbard: wrought iron, two thin bands and loose rings, narrow shoe. Lined with pine strips soaked in oil or paraffin wax.
Sword weight: 2lbs 6ozs.
Scabbard weight: 2lbs 3ozs.

(NAM 6311-37)

15 Sword, Heavy Cavalry, Pattern 1796 - with spear point and without langets.

(NAM 7510-91)

Cavalry Troopers' Swords 1788-1878

16 Sword, Heavy Cavalry, Pattern 1796
- with inner edge of disc and langets removed
(NAM 7510-91)

17 Sword, Heavy Cavalry, Pattern 1796
Blade length and width: 35in. x 1⁷/₁₆in.
Blade type: straight, flat back, hatchet point, single broad fuller each side to within 8in. of point.
Guard: steel 'disc' with raised rim.
Hilt mounts: steel.
Grip: wood, covered with leather and bound with steel wire.
Note: traces of red wax on grip suggest that this may have been some sort of sealed pattern although this version with raised rim was never standard. A similar sword (RA IX-968) is reputed to be that of Sergeant Shaw, 1st Life Guards; this has a standard steel scabbard, and a view mark of a crown over the figure '1'.
(Royal Armouries IX-1282)

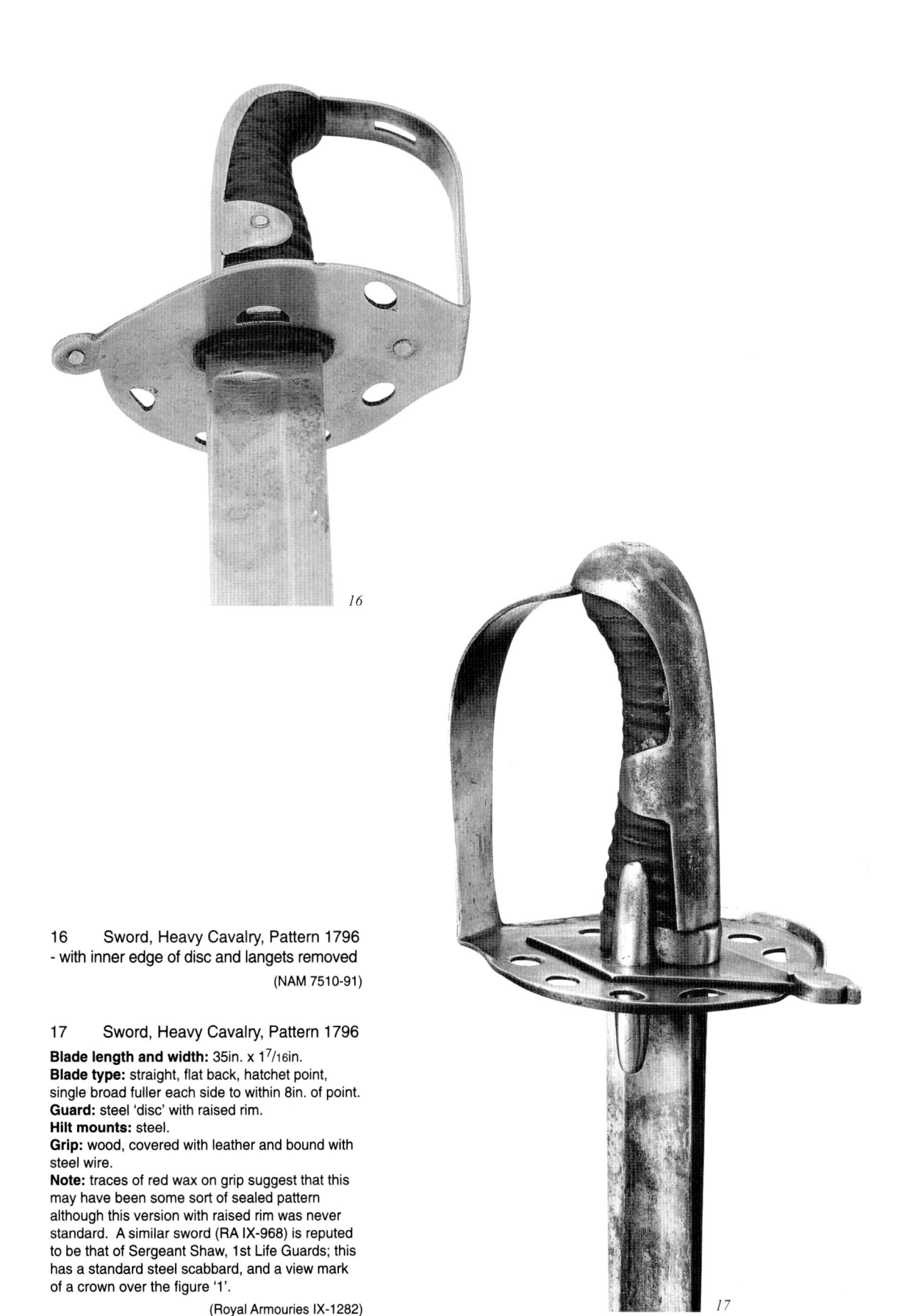

The Pattern 1796 Heavy Cavalry sword is the well-known disc-hilted sword, (Plates 14-17). With its straight, broad, hatchet-pointed blade, it offended against all Le Marchant's precepts. The hatchet point and broad blade made it useless for thrusting and its lack of curvature made it an inefficient slashing sword. Writing of the cavalry action at Bienvenida in the Peninsula in April 1812, Captain William Bragge of the 3rd Dragoons remarked:

'It is worthy of remark that scarcely one Frenchman died of his wounds although dreadfully chopped, whereas 12 English Dragoons were killed on the spot and others dangerously wounded by thrusts. If our men had used their swords so, three times the number of French would have been killed.[21]

In the hands of a very powerful man, the sword was still capable of great execution. Sergeant Ewart, of the 2nd (Royal Scots Greys) Dragoons, writing of his experiences at Waterloo, recalled that:

'One made a thrust at my groin. I parried it off and cut him down through the head. A lancer came at me - I threw the lance off and cut him through the chin and upwards through the teeth. Next, a foot-soldier fired at me and then charged me with his bayonet, which I also had the good luck to parry and then I cut him down through the head. This ended it.

The sword believed to be Ewart's is preserved in the SUSM and is a standard Pattern 1796 Heavy Cavalry sword, with a semi-spear point.[22] But Ewart was a giant of a man, 6 feet 4 inches tall, and probably any sword would have been devastating in his hands. On a lighter note, aficionados of Bernard Cornwell's series of Richard Sharpe novels, set in the Peninsular War, will remember that the hero habitually carried a Pattern 1796 disc-hilted sword for preference, even though a rifleman.

Nevertheless, the inability to thrust with this sword led to many swords being converted to a spear point by a simple grinding operation, (Plate 15). James Smithies, of the 1st (Royal) Dragoons, writing of the period immediately before Waterloo, recalled that: 'For the first time ever known in our army, the cavalry were ordered to grind the backs of their swords',[23] and he goes on to record the general view of the men that this was to enable them to deal more effectively with the heavily armoured French cuirassiers, who carried a splendid thrusting sword. Whether at a later stage some swords were made *ab initio* with spear points is at present uncertain but certainly numbers of spear-pointed swords with 33 inch blades and standard scabbards cut down to match exist.

Two other modifications are frequently encountered. The long, narrow langets which are a feature of the original pattern serve very little use in practice and were very often removed. Similarly, the sharp inner edge of the disc guard cut into the man's side and frayed his uniform jacket and many swords have this inner edge ground away - the alteration can usually be detected by the remains of the original holes in the disc, (Plate 16). What seems to be a later variant has a raised rim to the disc; the sword alleged to have been carried by the famous Sergeant Shaw, of the Life Guards, is of this pattern, and what may be the pattern sword is in the Royal Armouries, (Plate 17). The purpose of the rim, apart from smoothing the sharp edge of the guard, may have been to accommodate a leather hilt lining since there is evidence that such linings were in use in the Waterloo period in the Household Cavalry at least.[24]

The first issues of the disc-hilted sword appear to have been to the 1st (Royal) Dragoons early in 1797.[25] Despite its crude design and unhandiness, the Pattern 1796 Heavy Cavalry sword remained in service for more than 30 years and had its share of glory in the great heavy cavalry charges at Salamanca, Garcia Hernandez and Waterloo.

The Pattern 1796 Light Cavalry sword is the equally well-known stirrup-hilted sword, (Plate 18), basically Le Marchant's own design, although heavily influenced by contemporary European, and particularly Austrian, designs. With its curved blade, it was a good slashing sword and it feels heavier than it actually is - at approximately 2lbs 2ozs, it is lighter than any of its successors and very significantly lighter than the Pattern 1908 Cavalry Sword.

Cornet Francis Hall, of the 14th Light Dragoons, who was at the cavalry action at Fuentes d'Onoro in May 1811, wrote that:

> 'Their broadswords, ably wielded, flashed over the French-men's heads and obliged them to cower in their saddlebows. The alarm was, indeed, greater than the hurt, for their cloaks were so well rolled across their left shoulders that it was no easy matter to give a mortal blow with the broad edge of a sabre whereas their swords, which were straight and pointed, though their effect on the eyes was less formidable, were capable of inflicting a much severer wound.[26]

The principal defect of this sword is the guard, which gives only a minimal protection to the hand. The scabbard, like that of the heavy cavalry sword, is of iron and weighs more than the sword itself. It is wood lined but the lining was apt to disintegrate under active service conditions, leaving the sword to become blunt. Given the weight and size of the scabbard, suspended as it was by loose rings, it must have been virtually impossible to hide the approach of a body of light cavalry thus armed. Like the heavy cavalry sword, the Pattern 1796 Light Cavalry sword remained in service in the Regular Army for more than thirty years and lingered on in Yeomanry regiments until the 1860s. In India, discarded light cavalry blades were eagerly sought after by the native troopers of the Indian cavalry regiments to re-blade their own

Cavalry Troopers' Swords 1788-1878

18   Sword, Light Cavalry, Pattern 1796

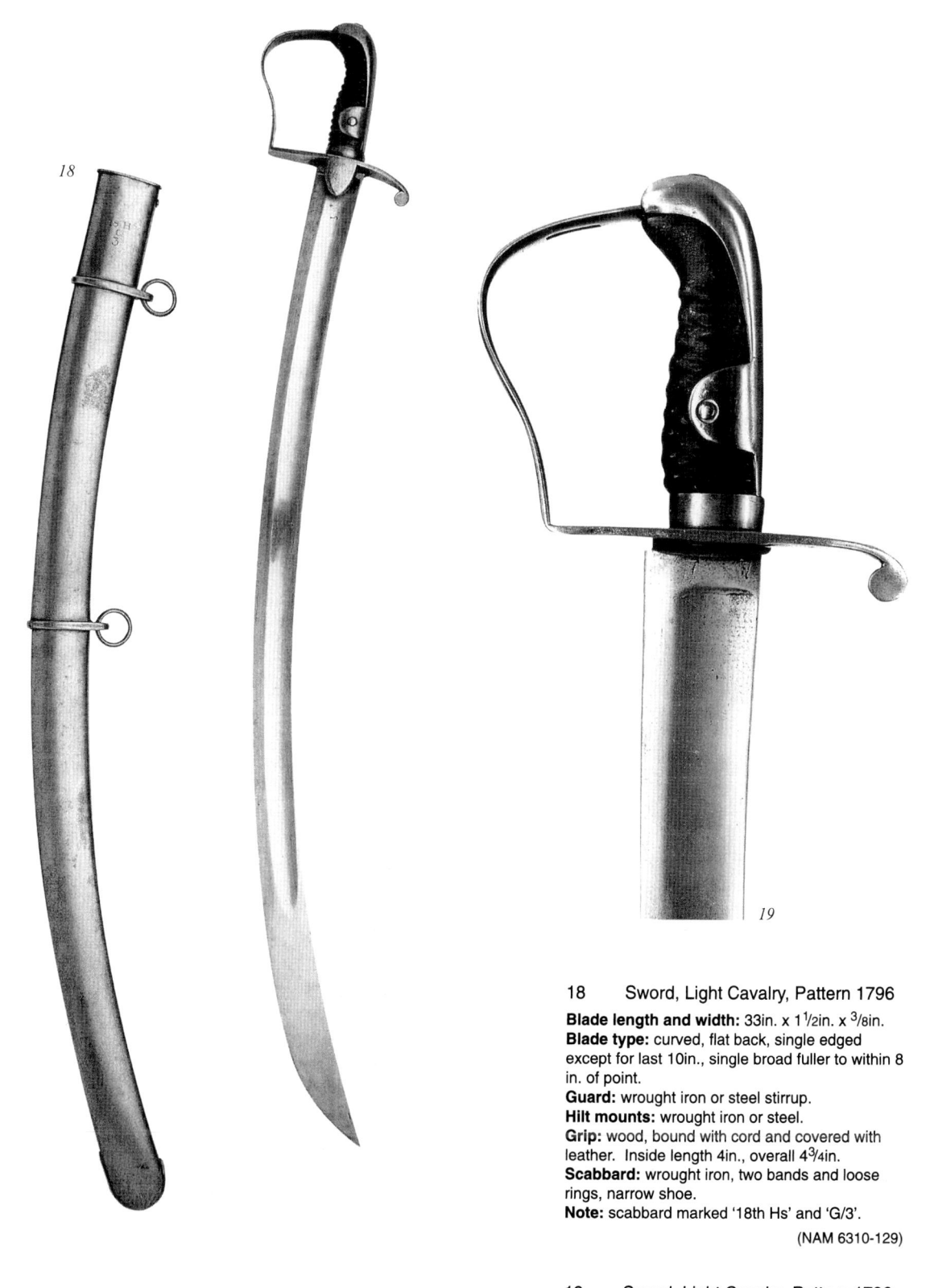

Blade length and width: 33in. x 1½in. x ⅜in.
Blade type: curved, flat back, single edged except for last 10in., single broad fuller to within 8 in. of point.
Guard: wrought iron or steel stirrup.
Hilt mounts: wrought iron or steel.
Grip: wood, bound with cord and covered with leather. Inside length 4in., overall 4¾in.
Scabbard: wrought iron, two bands and loose rings, narrow shoe.
Note: scabbard marked '18th Hs' and 'G/3'.

(NAM 6310-129)

19   Sword, Light Cavalry, Pattern 1796

Note: the normal shield-shaped langets are not present.

(Royal Armouries IX-249)

swords - a delicate compliment which Le Marchant would have appreciated, although the superior quality of the steel was perhaps the real attraction.[27] A further compliment was paid when the Prussian Army used this sword as the model for the Prussian cavalry sabre, Model 1811.[28]

In later specimens, the langets are sometimes removed, (Plate 19); otherwise, the only significant official modification was to the scabbard which, at the end of 1796, was increased in weight by 5-6 ozs.

The introduction of the 1796 Patterns was accompanied by two other changes of importance. Swords were in future to be worn suspended by slings from waistbelts (instead of shoulder belts); in consequence scabbards had loose rings for suspension in place of the older frog hook. Even more important, the delays experienced at the beginning of the war in 1793 in obtaining supplies of new swords from the private manufacturers and the wretched quality of many of those supplied led to the decision that in future the Board of Ordnance would maintain a reserve of properly tested swords at the Tower of London to meet any sudden expansion.[29]

John Gaspard Le Marchant was killed as a major-general, leading the heavy cavalry charge at the Battle of Salamanca in 1812, before he had had a chance to prove whether he was the cavalry leader of genius whom Wellington needed.

On 10 December 1821, the Adjutant-General's office wrote to the Board of Ordnance, requesting it to issue 296 swords 'of the new pattern for light cavalry' to the 4th Light Dragoons, who were under orders for India. The Board of Ordnance was forced to reply that it had no knowledge of any new pattern and in reply the Adjutant-General forwarded two new pattern swords, made by Prosser, which the King had recently approved for heavy and light cavalry respectively.[30] This was the first appearance of the Pattern 1821 cavalry swords. The surviving correspondence contains no clear description of these two new patterns but, from a memorandum prepared for the Master-General of the Ordnance at the time and from subsequent correspondence in the same files, their identity is quite clear.[31]

The Pattern 1821 Heavy Cavalry sword, (Plate 20), could hardly fail to be an improvement on its 1796 predecessor. It had a slightly curved, spear-pointed, fullered blade which improved both its thrusting and slashing capabilities, and a sheet-steel, bowl-shaped guard which gave good protection to the hand and proved to be the precursor of all subsequent British cavalry guards except for the Pattern 1853. Its construction followed Le Marchant's principle of having the hilt riveted to the blade, through the ears on the backpiece.

The Pattern 1821 Light Cavalry sword followed the same principle of construction and had an almost identical blade but mated with a new, three-bar guard, (Plate 21).[32] The origin of this pattern is not entirely clear but it closely resembles the French Light Cavalry sword Model 1816.[33] Given the post-1815 penchant for imitating French military fashion it may be that the origin of this sword need be sought no further. The guard gave better protection to the hand than its pred-

Cavalry Troopers' Swords 1788-1878

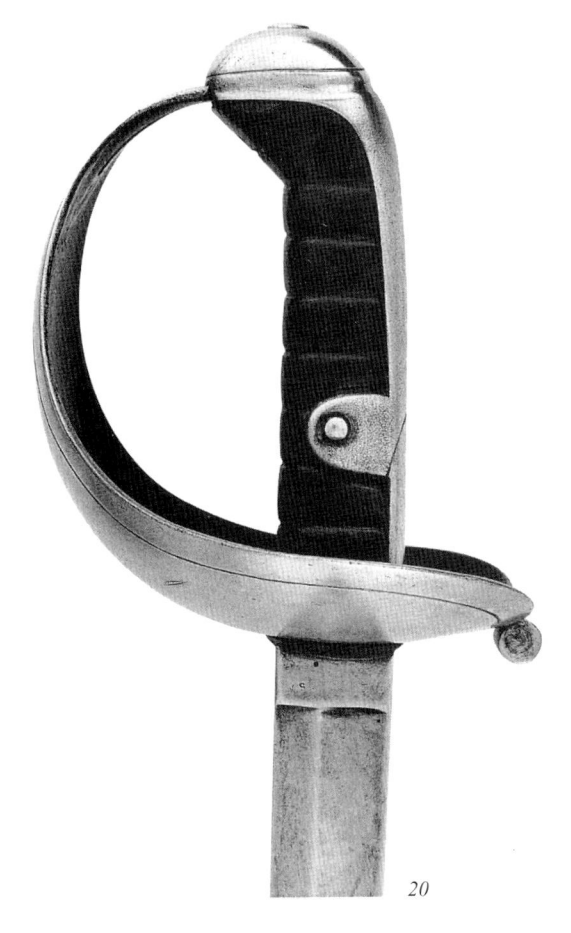

20

20 Sword, Heavy Cavalry, Pattern 1821

Blade length and width: 36½in. x 1¼in. x 7/16in.
Blade type: slightly curved, flat back, single wide fuller to within 9 in. of spear point; last 10½in. double edged.
Guard: steel bowl with sword knot slit near pommel.
Hilt mounts: steel.
Grip: wood, covered with leather.
Scabbard: steel; two loose rings on narrow bands 2½in. and 12½in. from mouth of scabbard; large shoe.
Note: the guard formed the basis of the hilt of the naval cutlass Pattern 1842.

(NAM 9508-2)

21 Sword, Light Cavalry, Pattern 1821

Blade length and width: 35½in. x 1¼in.
Blade type: slightly curved, flat back, single broad fuller to within 8in. of spear point; double edged for last 10in..
Guard: steel, three-bar.
Hilt mounts: steel, with stepped backpiece.
Grip: wood, covered with leather; length 4⅞in.
Scabbard: steel, with two loose rings and large shoe.

(NAM 5602-54)

21

ecessor, although by no means perfect - to modern hands, at least, it appears distinctly constricted. But as a sword, it was closely imitated in the United States Army's Dragoon sabre produced under the Ames contract of 1833, and in the US Topographical Engineers' sword of 1838, albeit with shorter blades.[34]

The Pattern 1821 swords marked the beginning of a long line of cut-and-thrust swords in the British cavalry which lasted throughout the nineteenth century.

With the rundown in the size of the Army after 1815, there were substantial quantities of both 1796 patterns in store. The light cavalry pattern could be used to arm the Yeomanry and so manufacture of the new Pattern 1821 Light Cavalry swords was started in March 1823, at a cost of eighteen shillings per sword, excluding the scabbard.[35] By March 1825, some 6,000 of the new light cavalry pattern had been produced and it was agreed that manufacture at Enfield at least should cease so that a start could be made on the new Pattern 1821 Heavy Cavalry sword, manufacture of which had been deferred originally because of the 34,000 swords of the 1796 heavy cavalry pattern still in stock, for which there was no alternative use.

The Chief Storekeeper at the Royal Small Arms Factory (RSAF) Enfield now took the opportunity to point out to the Board of Ordnance that the Pattern 1821 Heavy Cavalry blade as designed was proportionately thinner and weaker than the corresponding light cavalry design and he recommended that it should be made heavier and stiffer.[36] This was agreed and the Board ordered 2,000 of the stiffer version to be made at Enfield. This order was completed by November 1827 when manufacture ceased.

By this time, complaints had begun to accumulate about the Pattern 1821 Light Cavalry swords. Both the 8th Hussars and the 17th Lancers had reported that the sword and scabbard were too light and were constantly breaking or having to be repaired. The Storekeeper at the Tower, who was responsible for the issue of swords to units, was of the view that the new swords were not as good or fit for service as the old Pattern 1796 swords. In the face of this evidence, a committee was set up under Lieutenant-General Sir Herbert Taylor, Surveyor-General of the Ordnance, to investigate the whole question of the Pattern 1821 swords;[37] the other members were to be Major-General Sir Hussey Vivian (Inspector-General of Cavalry), Major-General William Millar (Royal Artillery), Lieutenant-Colonel Edward Keane (6th Dragoons) and Lieutenant-Colonel Joseph Thackwell (15th Hussars).[38]

The Committee reported in July 1828. It recommended that:

(a) the existing Pattern 1821 scabbards for both the heavy and light cavalry swords should be scrapped and replaced by new wrought steel scabbards weighing 2lbs 6ozs;

(b) three of the light cavalry swords and three modified by the Committee, together with three wrought iron and three steel scabbards, should be issued to each light cavalry regiment for trials;

(c) three of the heavy cavalry swords and three new pattern scabbards should be issued to each regiment of heavy cavalry for trials.

These recommendations were not fully implemented. No troop trials appear to have taken place but the modified light cavalry sword suggested by the Committee, together with a new steel scabbard, was sealed to act as a pattern for subsequent manufacture. What these modifications were is not entirely clear but they would seem to have been confined to increasing by a few ounces the weight of the blade and the scabbard. It does not appear that any significant action was taken in respect of the heavy cavalry sword.

There matters rested until 1833 when, in October of that year, the authorities at Enfield were asked to comment on a sword submitted by Lieutenant William Miller, of the 8th Hussars. After careful examination, Enfield did not think that Miller's sword was any improvement on the existing patterns but it took the opportunity to raise again the recommendations of the 1828 Committee on the light cavalry sword, and to press for them to be put into effect. This proposal was rejected on the grounds that there were by now large stocks of the Pattern 1821 sword in hand and that it was therefore undesirable to introduce modifications until further large-scale manufacture was required. In December 1835, a further order for 1,000 heavy cavalry swords was placed on Enfield, which again pressed for the 1828 Committee's recommendations to be implemented.[39] As a result, reports were called for from all regiments which had received either of the 1821 patterns.

The regiments themselves had little criticism of either sword, although there were some criticisms of the quality of manufacture, but there was almost unanimous criticism of the scabbards which were considered far too weak. Enfield itself thought that there were only three well-founded criticisms of the 1821 swords:

(a) the light cavalry guard was too constricted;

(b) the fuller in both swords was too deep (implying that the blades were too weak);

(c) both scabbards were too weak.

Swords and scabbards modified by Enfield to remedy these defects were then sent to the regiments for comment. The only apparent modification to the heavy cavalry pattern thus made was to reduce the depth of the fuller, making the blade heavier and stiffer. In the light cavalry sword, the pommel was made larger and the bars of the guard were extended to give more room for the hand. The modified scabbards were of steel and the metal heavier in gauge.

The modified heavy cavalry sword was unanimously approved and became the basis of all future manufacture. The modified hilt of the light cavalry sword was still not generally agreed and there was a strong body of opinion in favour of an iron scabbard because it was considered easier and cheaper to repair. Nevertheless, a modified light cavalry sword, with steel scabbard, was sent to the 12th Lancers for trial. No record of the results of this trial has been found[40] but in the event no significant modifications were made to the Pattern 1821 Light Cavalry sword before it was superseded by the Universal Pattern 1853 sword. But there was an administrative change of some importance in February 1844, when a War Office circular announced that as from 1 April 1844 all cavalry troopers' swords would be purchased direct by the Board of Ordnance and provided to the regiments as a public issue.[41] This reflected in some measure the fact that private manufacture of swords on a large scale had declined in Britain. By 1844, most of the great names - Gill, Osborne, Woolley, Harvey - had disappeared. Wilkinson & Son had not yet embarked upon the large-scale manufacture of troopers' swords and the firm of Mole & Son was virtually the only private manufacturer engaged upon large-scale manufacture. This firm continued to receive substantial orders from the Board of Ordnance and its successors but an increasing proportion of swords was henceforth made at the RSAF Enfield.

A major event in the history of British military swords occurred in 1853 with the introduction of the Sword, Cavalry, Pattern 1853, for all regiments of cavalry. Not only was it the first universal pattern of cavalry sword in the British Army but its basic characteristics as a compromise cut-and-thrust sword were reproduced in all subsequent cavalry swords down to 1908. It also embodied Charles Reeves' patent tang, first shown to the War Office in 1850 and subsequently patented in 1853, in which the tang was a continuation of the blade, instead of being welded on separately; this form of tang was embodied in all subsequent cavalry troopers' swords down to, and including, the Pattern 1899.

The origins of the Pattern 1853 sword, (Plates 22, 23) are obscure although it was, in all probability, a design produced at Enfield to remedy the perceived disadvantages of the 1821 patterns about which Enfield had not been consulted originally. The 1853 sword is, in fact, quite different from its immediate predecessors. The blade has a narrower, shallower fuller and this, taken in conjunction with an increase in weight, makes for a stiffer, sturdier blade. The extension of the blade to form the tang removes a major source of weakness in previous designs and there is a significant degree of cast-off, i.e. the hilt is set at an angle to the blade. The grip is simply a chequered leather strip riveted to each side of the tang. The scabbard is of wrought iron, as is the three-bar guard.

Cavalry Troopers' Swords 1788-1878

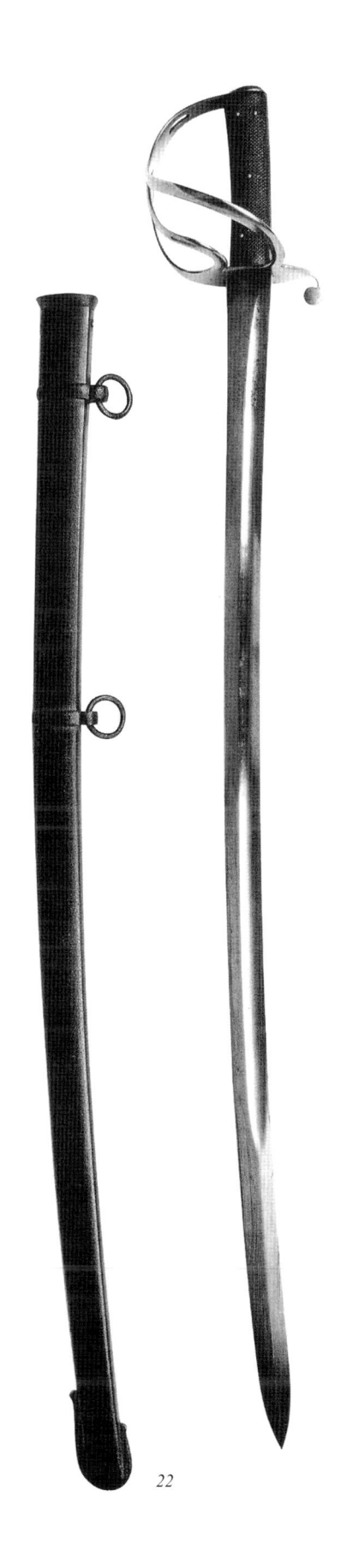

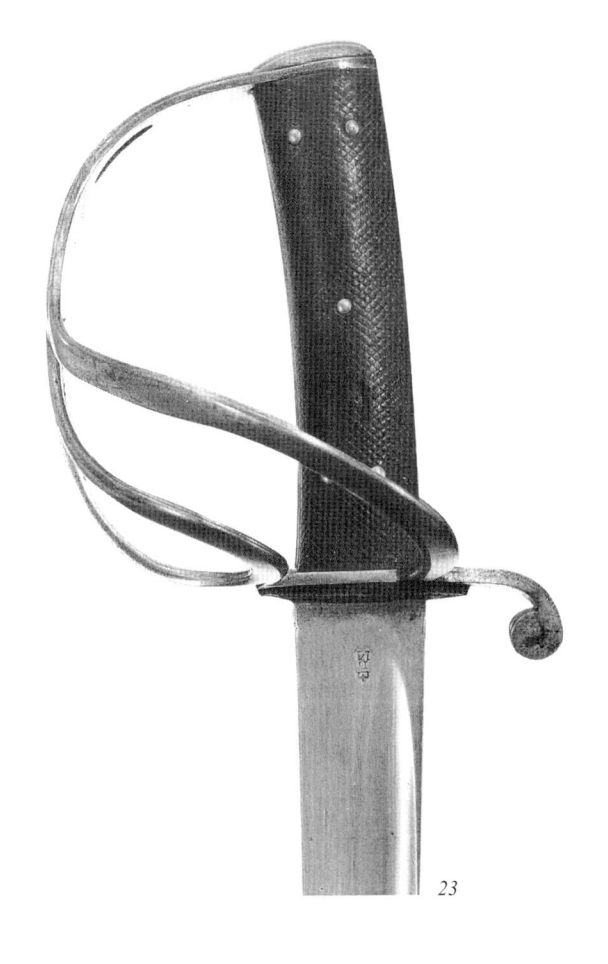

22   Sword, Cavalry, Pattern 1853

Blade length and width: 35½in. x 1¼in.
Blade type: curved, flat back, single fuller each side to within 9½in. of spear point, double edged for last 9in.
Guard: three-bar of malleable wrought iron, sword knot slit near pommel.
Grip: chequered leather strips riveted through tang.
Scabbard: malleable wrought iron, two bands with loose rings, 3¼in. and 12½in. from mouth.
Sword weight: 2lbs 7¾ozs.
Scabbard weight: 2lbs 1¼ozs.

(NAM 7205-7-38)

23   Sword, Cavalry, Pattern 1853
- close-up of hilt

(Royal Armouries 1X-341)

Apart from the lack of protection inherent in a three-bar guard and the compromise nature of the blade, the major defect is probably in the grip, which is almost round in section and therefore liable to twist in the hand. In the heat of battle, it must have been difficult to cut effectively with it. A circular memorandum from the Adjutant-General of 6 October 1854 stated that this sword was 'essentially a thrusting weapon', but elsewhere referred to it as 'an efficient cutting and thrusting weapon'. The truth was, as these extracts reveal, that, like its immediate successors, it was intended as both a cut and thrust sword and, like all such compromise patterns, not outstanding in either role.

No sooner was it issued than complaints about it began to surface. In March 1854, the commanding officer of the 11th Hussars, in Ireland, complained that some of the new swords were badly tempered and of a very inferior description; three swords issued in the past year had 'bent like hoops'.[42] Enfield, touched to its professional quick, examined the offending swords and then laid the blame on the unit for subjecting the swords to improper and unauthorised tests after issue. A few months later, Lieutenant-Colonel Henry Darby Griffith, commanding the 2nd (Royal Scots Greys) Dragoons, at Manchester, made similar complaints, and again Enfield concluded that the regiment was to blame for testing the swords itself too severely. This cannot have been of much comfort to Griffith, by that time in action in the Crimea where the swords were proving even more unsatisfactory. In a letter to the War Office in December 1854, he commented that:

> 'Our swords are very defective - as in our engagement [the charge of the Heavy Brigade at Balaclava] when our men made a thrust with the sword they all bent and would not go into a man's body and many of our poor fellows got sadly wounded and some lost their lives entirely from the unserviceable state of their arms. They were quite good enough for Home Service but quite unfit for active service.'[43]

Such damaging complaints could not go unheeded, particularly in the middle of a war which had already attracted unfortunate publicity on its administration. The Enfield authorities therefore requested a committee of officers to investigate the truth or otherwise of these complaints, and early in January 1855 Major William Neville Custance (6th Dragoon Guards)[44] and Cornet John Limbert (Adjutant, 1st Life Guards) were deputed to examine specimens of the swords being manufactured. In their presence, at the Tower of London, the approved manufacturing tests were applied to new swords just made at Enfield and by private firms at Birmingham. Of 76 swords made at Birmingham, one broke under test; of 240 made at Enfield, four broke. The Committee accordingly reported that in their view the swords were excellent weapons, made of the best materials, and concluded that swords about which regiments had complained must have been over-strained by unofficial tests in the regiments themselves.

There can be little doubt that Custance and Limbert were broadly correct in their views, although evidence later in the century suggested that the very best materials were not always used, partly out of ignorance. There is much evidence later that regiments were accustomed to carrying out their own unofficial tests on new swords, in ignorance of the fact that bending swords unnecessarily inevitably weakened blades through metal fatigue. It may well be that when regiments had to provide their own swords they were more careful with them.

It is not now possible to determine what proportion of the troops involved in the celebrated charges of the Heavy and Light Brigades at Balaclava on 25 October 1854 were armed with the Pattern 1853 sword. Certainly, the 11th Hussars and the 2nd Dragoons were at least partially, if not wholly, armed with the new

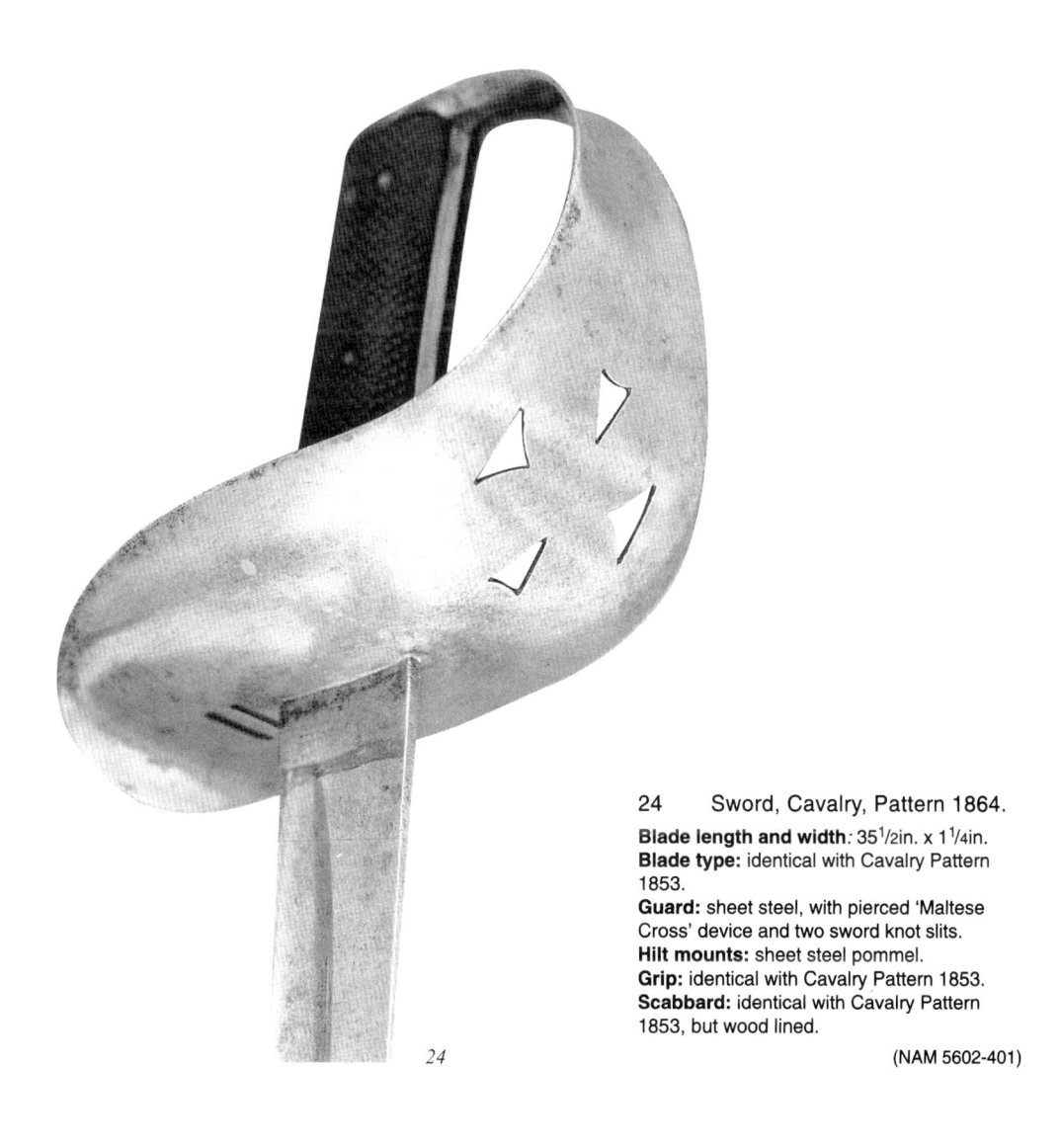

24   Sword, Cavalry, Pattern 1864.
Blade length and width: 35 1/2in. x 1 1/4in.
Blade type: identical with Cavalry Pattern 1853.
Guard: sheet steel, with pierced 'Maltese Cross' device and two sword knot slits.
Hilt mounts: sheet steel pommel.
Grip: identical with Cavalry Pattern 1853.
Scabbard: identical with Cavalry Pattern 1853, but wood lined.

(NAM 5602-401)

swords. Moreover, a process of 'cannibalisation' was going on at home whereby regiments going to the Crimea were being re-equipped with Pattern 1853 swords taken from regiments remaining in England.[45] It may therefore be that as much as half of the troops involved had the new swords while the remainder was equipped with the Pattern 1821 swords. In any event, the effect of these swords, properly used, was not necessarily as negligible as Griffith had claimed. Sir Evelyn Wood, who was present in the Crimea at the time, wrote afterwards:

> 'The Naval brigade sent doctors down to the wounded, [at Balaclava] and they described to us that evening the effect of some of the sword-cuts inflicted by our Heavy dragoons on the heads of the Russians as appalling; in some cases the head-dress and skull being divided down to the chin. The edge of the sword was used, for the greatcoats worn by the Russians were difficult to pierce with the point.[46]

The Pattern 1853 sword was to have a relatively short life. The wrought iron bars of the guard proved liable to breakage, presumably because of the brittle nature of the metal used, and in July 1861 a committee under Major-General John Lawrenson prepared a new pattern of cavalry sword, which would appear to have involved basically a new guard.[47] No action on it was taken at the time and the pattern sword has since disappeared. Two years later, in October 1863, the Superintendent of the RSAF submitted a new guard for the Pattern 1853 sword which he stated had been prepared by him in November 1861 at the request of the Commander-in-Chief;[48] the logical implication is that this was the pattern prepared for Lawrenson's committee. This new guard was approved by the Secretary of State for War, without trial, on 3 December 1863 and by the Commander-in-Chief in March 1864; initially, it would seem, for swords needing new hilts. No official approval for it to replace the Pattern 1853 in all subsequent manufacture can be traced but in practice that is what happened and the new guard, mated to the Pattern 1853 blade, became the Sword, Cavalry, Pattern 1864, formally adopted into service in March 1864, (Plate 24).[49]

Because the guard had not been subjected to trials before adoption, it was discovered only after introduction that the edges of the guard, which were not turned over or beaded, frayed the men's clothing. This objection was voiced strongly by Royal Artillery users and the Regiment was allowed in 1876 to revert to the Pattern 1853 sword.

The Pattern 1864 sword was to enjoy a relatively long life, possibly because its introduction coincided with a period in which the cavalry was not engaged in active service on any significant scale. With the outbreak of the Second Afghan War in November 1878, that period came to an end.

Chapter 2: Notes

1. Public Record Office (PRO). WO 3/27, p23.

2. Henry Seymour Conway (1721-95), served in Flanders 1742-45, at Culloden 1746, Flanders 1747, Rochefort Expedition 1757, Germany 1761-63. Lieutenant-General of Ordnance 1767-72. Commander-in-Chief 1782-84. Field Marshal 1790. He was a politician as well as a soldier.

3. PRO. WO 26/33, p302 - an undated draft but obviously prepared early in 1788.

4. PRO. WO 3/37, pp358-86.

5. *Ibid*.

6. Thomas Gill, in business as a swordmaker from *c*1783 until his death in 1801, was a fierce protagonist of English (and particularly his own) blades. Samuel Harvey was in business from 1778 until 1795, and James Woolley from 1785 until at least 1797. Runkel was the leading supplier of Solingen blades to the British market and blades marked with his name are perhaps the commonest named blades found on British swords. For details of the three English manufacturers, see W E May & P G W Annis, *Swords for Sea Service*, Vol II, London (1970) pp317, 322.

7. See reproduction in *JSAHR*, Vol XIII, 1933, p58.

8. See the drawing of a sword of the 7th Light Dragoons by Woolley, dated 1794, in G R B Barrett, *The 7th Queen's Own Hussars*, Vol II, London (1914) p253. For a useful discussion of the Pattern 1788 Light Cavalry sword, see an article by G R Worrall in *Classic Arms and Militaria*, Vol I, No 7, 1994, pp20-23.

9. See A N Ingram, 'Mid-eighteenth century cavalry swords' *JSAHR*, Vol XXIX, 1951, p30, footnote.

10. Royal Collection, Windsor, Catalogue No 1132.

11. 'Philo Scotus' (Philip Ainslie), *Reminiscences of a Scottish Gentleman commencing in 1787*, London (1861)

12. D Le Marchant, *Memoirs of the late Major-Genl Le Marchant*, London (1841) p49.

13. Royal Military Academy Sandhurst Library 'Le Marchant Papers' Packet 14 Fl.

14. Le Marchant, *Memoirs*, p32

15. *Ibid.*, p49

16. The *Memoirs* give the date of this memorial as 1797 but that is clearly a mistake since the new patterns of sword, one of which is based on Le Marchant's design, were approved in 1796. There is no copy of the memorial in the British Library, the Royal Archives or the Ministry of Defence Library.

17. PRO. WO 3/29, pp43-44

18. PRO. WO 47/2561, Minutes of the Board of Ordnance, p736

19. See Eduard Wagner, *Hieb-und Stichwaffen*, Prague (1966) pp333, 375

20. See A E Haswell Miller and N P Dawnay, *Military Drawings and Paintings in the Royal Collection*, London (1966) Vol I, plate 161

21. S A C Cassels(ed.), *Peninsular Portrait 1811-1814: The letters of Captain William Bragge, Third (King's Own) Dragoons*, London (1963) p49

22. SUSM. L1956-9.

23. See *JSAHR*, Vol XXXIV, 1956, p20

24. The process of cutting off the langets and the inner edge of the disc seems to have begun almost as soon as the swords were issued - see a bill dated 31 December 1797 for 'cutting the hilts' of 364 swords of the 2nd Dragoon Guards in *JSAHR*, Vol XVII, 1938, p97. This may reflect the fact that the sword had been introduced without any trials. A hilt lining is shown in sketches of British and Russian equipment in the Royal Collection at Windsor, (Catalogue No 704).

25. PRO. WO 3/31, p52

26. *RUSI Journal*, Vol LVI, 1912, p1541

27. See *The Cavalry Journal*, Vol XIV, 1924, p108

28. Wagner, *op. cit.*, p218

29. An entry in the Secretary's Book at the War Office, which was a handy working record of precedents and data, for 1 April 1804, records that: 'it has been usual of late to supply regiments of cavalry with sabres and to call upon the Colonel for the value who receives an allowance from the War Office' - PRO. WO 55/1843.

30. These 1821 patterns illustrate a phenomenon which is exemplified in the swords in the Royal Collection at Windsor, viz. George IV's predilection for dabbling in the design of swords for the British Army, without any necessary liaison with the proper Army authorities in London.

31. Unless otherwise noted, this and the following twelve paragraphs are based upon the correspondence in PRO. WO 44/539.

32. There is some evidence that it was referred to at the time as the 'Pattern 1822' sword - for example, the commanding officer of the 11th Light Dragoons, writing to the Adjutant-General on 27 June 1836 noted that: 'the swords received from the Board of Ordnance of pattern of 1822 are considered perfectly efficient', PRO. WO 3/444. Until the start of the issue of the *List of Changes* in 1860, there was, in fact, no formalised system of nomenclature for swords. ffoulkes and Hopkinson, (p48), mistakenly referred to this sword as the 'Pattern 1830', confusing the date of issue with the date of adoption.

33. See Christian Ariés, *Armes Blanches Militaires Francaises*, Fascicule 2, Paris, (1967).

34. See Harold L Peterson, *The American Sword 1775-1945*, revised edition, Philadelphia (1965) pp31, 147

35. First issues were to the 8th Hussars and 17th Lancers in 1824 on their return from India. At least half of the 6,000 had been made by private manufacturers. The papers in PRO. WO 44/539 give an updated list of manufacturers who had received contracts; they included Prosser, Gill, Osborne, Woolley and Deakin. The average order was for 200.

36. Letter from Chief Storekeeper at Enfield to Board of Ordnance, 25 March 1825.

37. Herbert Taylor (1775-1839). Commissioned 1794. Service in the Low Countries 1793-95, North Holland 1799. Private Secretary to King George III, 1805-11, Military Secretary 1820-27, Surveyor-General of the Ordnance 1828 and then Adjutant-General.

38. Richard Hussey Vivian, 1st Baron Vivian (1775-1842). Commissioned 1793. Service in the Low Countries 1794-95, North Holland 1799, Peninsula 1813-14, Waterloo 1815. Inspector-General of Cavalry 1825-30, Master-General of the Ordnance 1835. Joseph Thackwell (1781-1859). Commissioned 1800. Service in Peninsula 1807-14, Waterloo 1815, First Afghan War 1838-39, Maratha War 1843-44, First Sikh War 1846, Second Sikh War 1848-49.

39. By this time at least 1,500 of the original batch of 2,138 Heavy Cavalry swords had been issued; the first issue of 231 going to the 5th Dragoon Guards in June 1832 - PRO. WO 3/444.

40. A sword in the Worrall Collection, by Osborne & Gunby, marked '12L' might conceivably be one of these trial swords, but the guard does not match that described in the papers.

41. War Office Circular 923, 28 February 1844, para 18: 'It has also been deemed expedient to direct that the supply of swords to the Cavalry shall in future be made by the Ordnance Department, in the same manner as all other arms'.

42. PRO. WO 44/701.

43. *Ibid*. The engagement referred to was the charge of the Heavy Brigade at Balaclava on 25 October 1854.

44. William Neville Custance. Commanded 6th Dragoon Guards in the Indian Mutiny, 1857-59.

45. It would appear that all the cavalry in the Crimea had the Pattern 1853 by the end of the war in 1856. A War Office letter of 23 May 1855 stated that: 'Both heavy and light cavalry are to be armed with one description of sword viz. the pattern of 1853. The Cavalry serving in the Crimea have all of them this weapon and those serving at home were deprived of theirs and given the old pattern of sword in exchange to enable the Ordnance to meet the demand in the case of the regiments on active service' PRO. WO 3/142.

46. Sir Evelyn Wood, *The Crimea in 1854 and 1894*, London (1895), p113

47. John Lawrenson. Commanded Heavy Cavalry Brigade in the Crimea 1855 and all cavalry in that theatre, 1855-56. Commanding Aldershot Cavalry Brigade in 1861. Almost unique in reaching rank of general and colonel of 13th Hussars without any honours of any kind.

48. See the *Memorandum submitted to 1885 Committee on Swords*, War Office (1885).

49. See *List of Changes (LC)* 887, 1 April 1864 and the sealed pattern at the Pattern Room, Nottingham (No 190), which is marked as having been approved on 8 March 1864.

3. Cavalry Troopers' Swords 1878-1914

The history of the British cavalry troopers' sword in the nineteenth century is largely one of complaint. How far the complaints arose genuinely from the defects of the swords themselves, and how far they were due to deficiencies in the training of the men, is hard to determine. Certainly, none of the regulation patterns issued during the period were ideal in design, construction or quality, primarily because of the continued attempt to produce a sword which was equally good for both cutting and thrusting. In the nature of things, this was an impossibility and those who tried encountered problems of weight, temper and balance which were never satisfactorily solved. But when expert opinion was divided on the merits of the cut versus the thrust,[1] the efforts of those who tried to produce a sword to do both are at least understandable.

There is, nevertheless, evidence to suggest that the faults were not confined to the swords themselves. The troopers were not always well-trained in the difficult art of mounted swordsmanship,[2] and insufficient attention was paid to the care and sharpening of swords.[3] Cavalry officers seem rarely to have given much thought to the theory and principles behind the design of swords and frequently expected it to do things for which it was not designed. Paradoxically, it was not until the South African War of 1899-1902 had demonstrated the uselessness of horsed cavalry as a shock weapon in the face of the magazine rifle and machine gun that serious attention was paid to the design of the cavalry sword. As has happened in many spheres of human activity, the peak of development coincided with the onset of obsolescence, on the eve of the war which demonstrated beyond argument that the day of the *arme blanche* was over.

The Pattern 1864 sword did not prove universally popular when it was introduced into service. It is rather a heavy and cumbersome weapon and it was criticised because the sharp inner edge of the guard damaged the clothing, while the guard was felt to constrict the hand. Many preferred the older, three-barred hilt and as mentioned in the previous chapter the Royal Artillery was allowed in 1876 to revert to the Pattern 1853 sword, although this was largely because of its uniformity with the officers' swords.[4]

The 1864 Pattern sword received its first real test in the Second Afghan War which broke out in November 1878. By then some 12,000 of the Pattern 1864 swords were in stock. Complaints, as well as swords, had accumulated and early in 1878 the Assistant-Adjutant-General (Colonel T D Baker)[5] approached the main Government sword contractor, Robert Mole & Son, of Birmingham, to see if a lighter sword and scabbard could be produced. In November 1878, Mole & Son submitted three swords and scabbards of a lighter pattern, with 35 1/2 inch blades, one of which was sent to the Superintendent of the Royal Small Arms Factory at Enfield for comment. His reactions were presumably not unfavourable because the firm was asked to produce a further six swords to this new pattern, as well as six more converted from existing Pattern 1864 swords in stock.[6] These twelve swords were then sent to the 5th Dragoon Guards and the 11th Hussars in June 1879 for trial.

These swords (known subsequently as the Sword, Cavalry, Experimental, Pattern 1880, Converted) followed the same general form as the Pattern 1864 but the blade was narrower, thinner and lighter, and the hilt was also smaller and lighter, although retaining the same bowl form with pierced 'Maltese Cross'. The bowl, however, had two sword knot slits, one near the pommel, as in the Pattern 1853 sword, and another at the bottom, near the blade. One assumes that it was not intended that the final design would retain both slits but rather that a decision on which one was handiest would emerge from trials. The whole sword weighed 2lb 2ozs, some 6ozs less than the 1864 sword. The steel scabbard had fixed loops on the back edge instead of loose rings, in order to reduce noise, and weighed 1lb 15 3/4ozs, fractionally lighter than the existing pattern.[7] As initial reports on the new design proved favourable, a further 800 swords, converted from Pattern 1864 swords, were ordered in March 1880 from Mole & Son, and these were issued to the 4th Hussars, 4th Dragoon Guards, and B, K, M Batteries of the Royal Artillery for more extended trials.[8]

Although lighter than the Pattern 1864, this Experimental Pattern 1880 sword was still heavier than the Pattern 1882 sword subsequently adopted, and Mole & Son were of the opinion later that it would have made a satisfactory and acceptable regulation pattern.[9] One may, perhaps, with hindsight, doubt this because, at 2lb 2ozs, it was much lighter than experience was to prove desirable.

But it was, in any case, rapidly superseded by another new design which had its origin in complaints being received from cavalry regiments taking part in the Second Afghan War about the weight and clumsiness of the Pattern 1864 sword. Consequently, in December 1879, while Mole & Son were awaiting War Office reactions to the Experimental Pattern 1880 swords, they received a further letter from the Assistant-Adjutant-General (Colonel A L Annesley),[10] asking if they could design an even lighter, smaller and shorter sword than the 1880 Experimental Pattern which was already considered too heavy and cumbersome, particularly for the light cavalry, (hussars and lancers). Annesley's letter may well have been the direct result of complaints from units in Afghanistan. Giving evidence before the Eden Commission in the summer of 1879 a succession of British cavalry officers who had served in Afghanistan criticised both the Pattern 1864 sword and, especially, the scabbard.

Cavalry Troopers' Swords 1878-1914

There was virtually unanimous agreement that the sword was too heavy and that a leather or leather-covered scabbard was required on active service.[11]

The manufacturers immediately pointed out that, while such a sword could obviously be made, they feared that it would lack durability. As things turned out, the War Office would have been well advised to ponder this warning but there is no evidence that it did so.[12] Later that month, in answer to the War Office's request, Mole & Son submitted a new and smaller sword. Known subsequently as the Sword, Cavalry, Experimental, Pattern 1880, New (to distinguish it from the Experimental, Pattern 1880, Converted), it was again very similar in form to the Pattern 1864 sword but the blade length was only 33 inches and the guard was smaller, lighter, and turned over at the edges to avoid fraying the clothing, (Plate 25). The accompanying scabbard had fixed loops, like the Converted Pattern, with a wooden lining, and weighed only 1lb 10ozs; the sword itself weighed a mere 1lb 15ozs, half a pound lighter than the Pattern 1864. It is not clear what, if any, tests were carried out, or

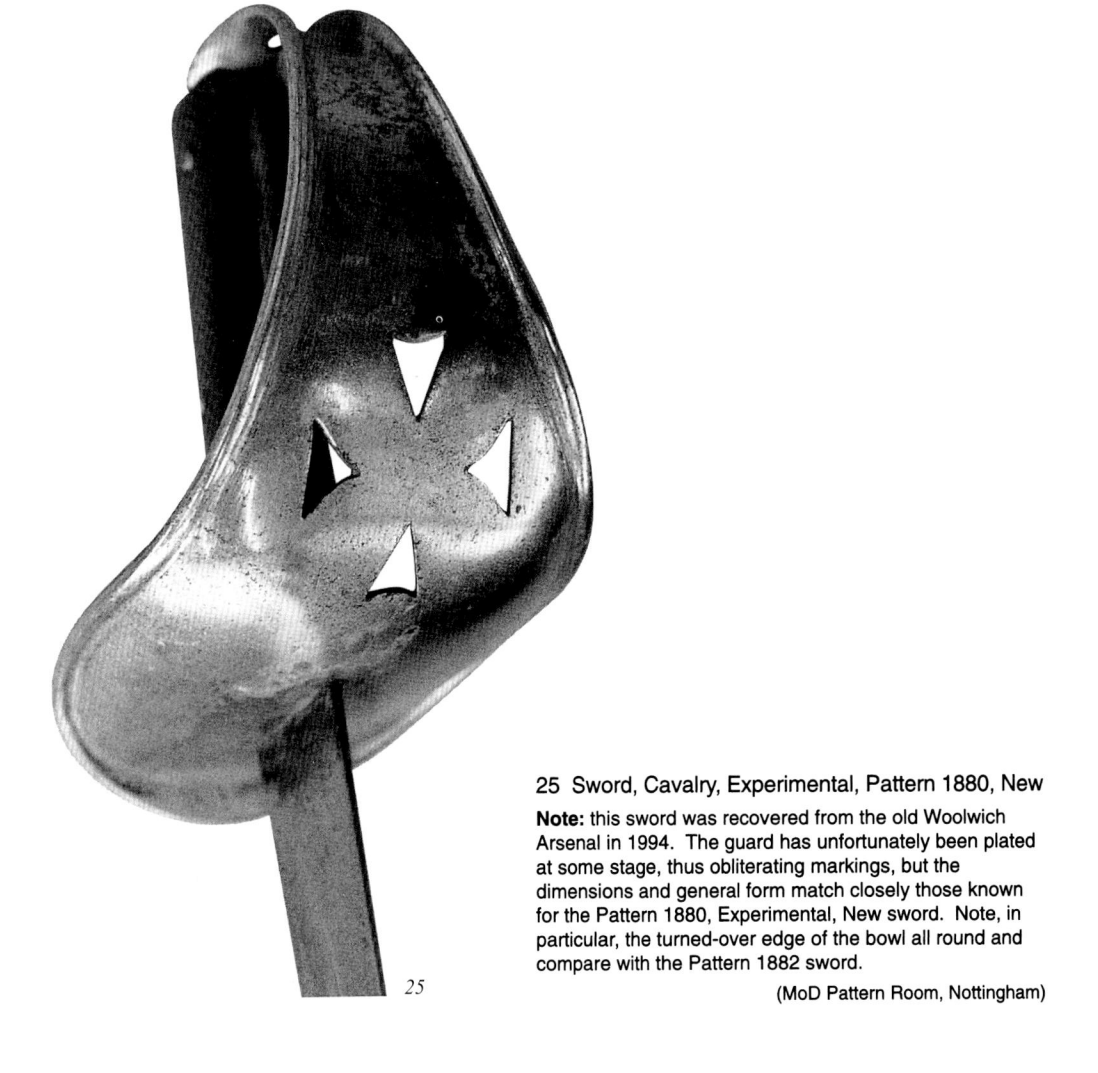

25 Sword, Cavalry, Experimental, Pattern 1880, New

Note: this sword was recovered from the old Woolwich Arsenal in 1994. The guard has unfortunately been plated at some stage, thus obliterating markings, but the dimensions and general form match closely those known for the Pattern 1880, Experimental, New sword. Note, in particular, the turned-over edge of the bowl all round and compare with the Pattern 1882 sword.

(MoD Pattern Room, Nottingham)

advice sought, before the War Office ordered 100 swords of this second experimental pattern in July 1880. These were issued to the 6th Dragoons, the 11th and 20th Hussars and G Battery, Royal Artillery. Two new models of sword were thus undergoing troop trials at the same time, by different units, and with no apparent attempt at cross-exchanging results.

The trials of the 800 Experimental, Pattern 1880, Converted swords elicited strong differences of opinion from the units. The cavalry regiments involved reported favourably, regarding the swords as a great improvement on the existing issue weapon. The Royal Artillery batteries complained that the hilt hurt the hand and damaged the clothing; they also objected to the fixed rings on the scabbard on the slightly irrelevant ground that they might hurt the wearer in the event of a fall, and they considered the sword knot slits too small. Inasmuch as these criticisms had any substance, they were much the same as those that the Regiment had directed against the Pattern 1864, and might therefore have been anticipated.

The trials of the 100 swords of the Experimental, Pattern 1880, New design produced greater consensus. The 11th Hussars and the 6th Dragoons thought the blade too short but regarded this defect as more than compensated by the greater lightness and handiness of the sword as a whole. The 6th Dragoons and G Battery R A thought that the guard was too small but the two hussar regiments had no complaints on this score. The 20th Hussars went so far as to regard the sword as eminently suitable for all medium and light cavalry regiments, and gave particular praise to the solid wood lining of the scabbard, a feature which was, henceforth, incorporated in all new cavalry patterns.

These generally favourable reactions, and the urgent need to order some swords straightaway, led the War Office to order 1,000 of the Experimental, Pattern 1880, New swords from Mole & Son in December 1880. Some of these swords went to re-equip the 4th Dragoon Guards who took them to Egypt in 1882. There they proved very satisfactory, although it is not clear whether they were used to any extent in action.

Concurrently, the Inspectors-General of Cavalry for Great Britain and Ireland and the Deputy-Adjutant-General of the Royal Artillery were asked for their comments on the new sword. This was a fatal, if perhaps inevitable, step since it opened the way to a wave of further criticism and suggestions. The Inspector-General of Cavalry for Ireland and the DAG, Royal Artillery thought the blade too short but agreed that this was more than made up for by the increased handiness of the sword. The Inspector-General for Great Britain refused to commit himself, saying that he had received differing opinions and suggesting that more extensive service trials were needed before a final decision was taken; he agreed, nevertheless, that the Pattern 1864 sword was quite unsuitable for medium and light cavalry.

In view of the generally favourable comments so far, the Superintendent at Enfield was instructed to make up a sword to the Experimental, Pattern 1880, New design but with a slightly modified guard to meet the criticisms made of it. The intention was that this modified model would form the sealed pattern for subsequent manufacture on a large scale. The Superintendent, however, now suggested that it might be better to defer adopting the new model until a completely satisfactory hilt had been designed. He thought that this needed to be bigger and more rounded to avoid damage to the soldiers' clothing.

The unfortunate consequences of the decision to seek further comments now began to manifest themselves. The Superintendent was ordered to submit a new hilt along the lines he had suggested, which he did in November 1881, and 24 swords of the Experimental New Pattern, but with the new Enfield hilt were then produced and issued in April 1882 to the 2nd Dragoon Guards, the 4th and 21st Hussars and to H and I Batteries, Royal Artillery. This new pattern was called the Sword, Experimental, Pattern 1881. By now, just over four years had elapsed since the Assistant-Adjutant-General's original initiative.

Even before the Experimental Pattern 1881 sword had been ordered, however, and shortly after submitting his modified Experimental, Pattern 1880, New sword, the Superintendent at Enfield had submitted stop-gap proposals to convert existing stocks of Pattern 1864 blades to produce a long and a short sword corresponding closely to the original Experimental, Pattern 1880, Converted and the Experimental, Pattern 1881 swords respectively. The 'Long' pattern was to be made by grinding down the thickness of the blade to produce a weight saving of some 2ozs while retaining the original length of $35^{1}/_{2}$ inches; the 'Short' pattern was to be made by grinding down the Pattern 1864 blades to a length of 33 inches and a total sword weight of 2lb $1^{1}/_{2}$ozs. There was to be a new scabbard for both swords, embodying fixed loops and a new, detachable mouthpiece secured by countersunk metal screws. The majority of conversions were to be to the 'Short' pattern but it was intended to issue the 'Long' pattern to the 4th and 5th Dragoon Guards and the 1st (Royal) and 2nd (Royal Scots Greys) Dragoons, which enlisted bigger men than the other cavalry regiments. Orders for the necessary conversions were issued to the RSAF Enfield in January 1882.

Meanwhile, the 24 swords of the Experimental, Pattern 1881 had received favourable reports from the units that had had them on trial, and in December 1882 the Surveyor-General of the Ordnance approved the sealing of 'Long' and 'Short' patterns based upon the 1881 sword. These new patterns were known subsequently as the Sword, Cavalry, Pattern 1882, Long and Short, and the first order, for 1,000 of the 'Short' version, was placed with Mole & Son in March 1883, together with a parallel order for 1,000 of the Pattern 1882, (Converted) Short swords.

Thus five years after the start of the process, no fewer than four new patterns of sword - the Patterns 1882, Converted, Long and Short and the Patterns 1882, Long and Short, New - had been adopted, the only obvious difference being the fact that, on average, the 'Converted' swords were some 2ozs heavier than the 'New' swords.

The relationship of these swords to the Experimental, Patterns 1880, Converted and New designs is clearly shown in the Table at the end of this chapter.

The Patterns 1882 Long and Short swords differed only in the weight and length of the blade and scabbard. The sheet-steel guard was very similar to that of the Pattern 1864 sword, retaining the 'Maltese Cross' piercing, but it was smaller and lighter, (Plates 26, 27). The Short, New blade was 33 inches long and the sword weighed approximately 2lbs, plus or minus 1oz. The Long, New blade was $35^{3}/_{8}$ inches long and the sword weighed 2lb $2^{1}/_{2}$ ozs, plus or minus 1 oz. The scabbard for both types was of sheet-steel, with a rounded shoe and two fixed loops on the back at $2^{1}/_{2}$ and $9^{1}/_{2}$ inches from the mouth. It had a solid wood lining and a detachable mouthpiece fastened by a screw each side, (Plate 28). The Short scabbard weighed 1lb 10ozs and the Long approximately 2 ozs more.

Although the Pattern 1882 swords were in some ways an improvement on their predecessor, being lighter and handier, and with a better designed guard and scabbard, they were still open to criticism on account of the grip, which was almost cylindrical and tended therefore to slip in tired hands. Above all, the blade was another compromise cut-and-thrust specimen, and not particularly good at either.

Experience was to show that the desire for lightness (and in the case of the Converted pattern, economy) had been taken too far, the blades being fatally weak.

It is not clear what further specific tests the War Office applied to the patterns before they were sent for manufacture, but they had undergone extensive trials in the hands of the troops, which might have been expected to show up any significant weaknesses. In his subsequent evidence to the 1887 Royal Commission on Warlike Stores, which investigated, *inter alia*, the failure of the Pattern 1882 swords, the Superintendent at Enfield (Colonel H T Arbuthnot) claimed that he had, from the first, made it clear to the Ordnance Department that, in his view, the new pattern blades were too light and that 2 ozs more metal in them would have produced a much more satisfactory blade.[13] Similarly, Mole & Son had, at the outset, expressed doubts about the strength of the original Experimental, Pattern 1880, New sword which had in due course become the Pattern 1882 Short (New) sword.

Opinions differed subsequently about the Pattern 1882 (Converted) blades. Colonel Arbuthnot, in his 1887 evidence, thought that they were very much better than the New pattern blades because they were thicker and stiffer.[14] Mole & Son, on the other hand, thought that the conversion had been false economy because the blades could not be expected to stand the same strains after grinding down as they had stood originally.[15] The Director of Contracts at the War Office came to the same conclusion.[16] They were, in all probability, right since other cases of grinding down fared disastrously, but it was unfortunate that no one saw fit to make these points when conversion was decided upon.

The War Office proceeded to issue the new swords as fast as they could be produced. The first production order was placed with Mole & Son in March 1883,[17]

Cavalry Troopers' Swords 1878-1914

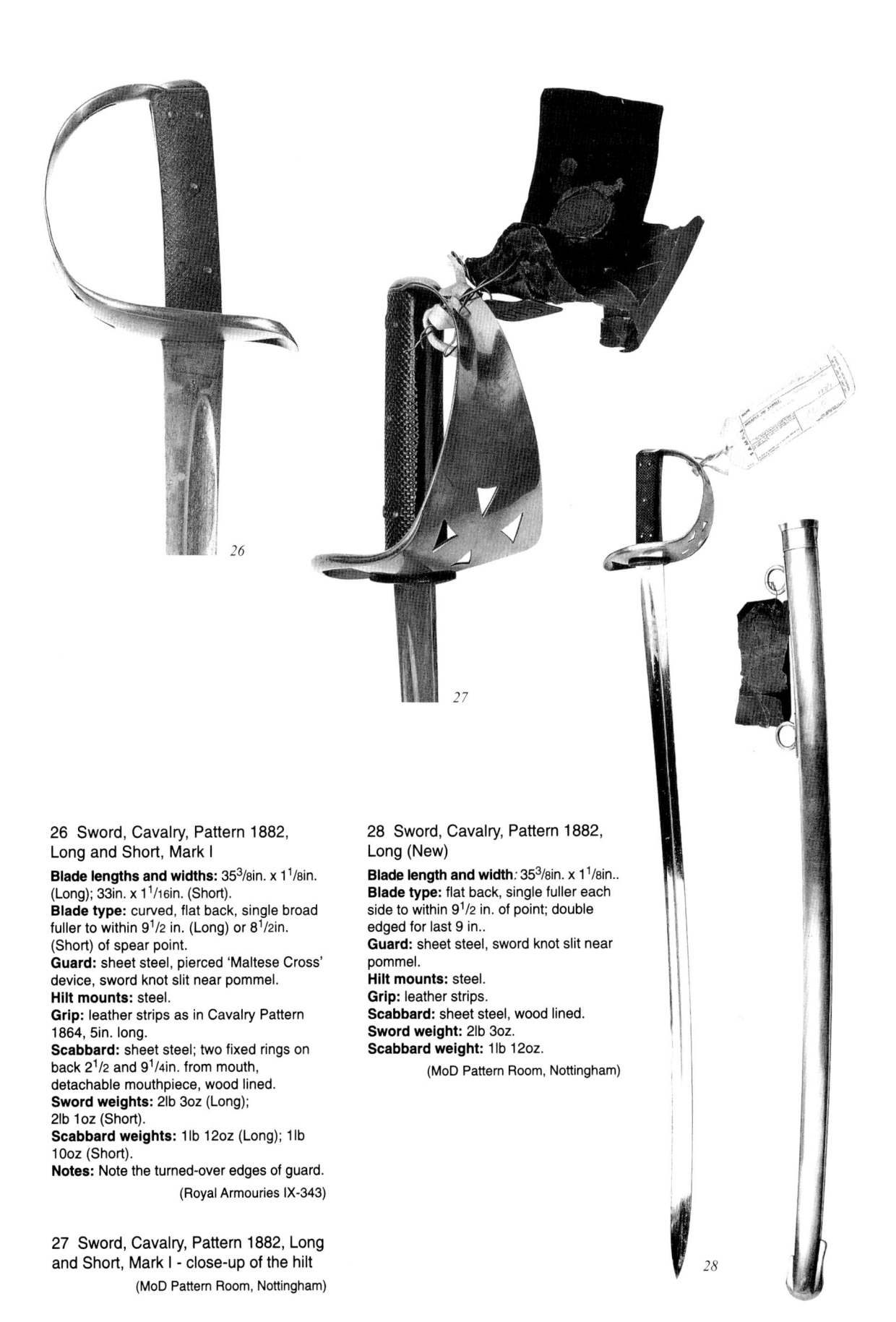

26 Sword, Cavalry, Pattern 1882, Long and Short, Mark I

Blade lengths and widths: 35^3/$_8$in. x 1^1/$_8$in. (Long); 33in. x 1^1/$_{16}$in. (Short).
Blade type: curved, flat back, single broad fuller to within 9^1/$_2$ in. (Long) or 8^1/$_2$in. (Short) of spear point.
Guard: sheet steel, pierced 'Maltese Cross' device, sword knot slit near pommel.
Hilt mounts: steel.
Grip: leather strips as in Cavalry Pattern 1864, 5in. long.
Scabbard: sheet steel; two fixed rings on back 2^1/$_2$ and 9^1/$_4$in. from mouth, detachable mouthpiece, wood lined.
Sword weights: 2lb 3oz (Long); 2lb 1oz (Short).
Scabbard weights: 1lb 12oz (Long); 1lb 10oz (Short).
Notes: Note the turned-over edges of guard.

(Royal Armouries IX-343)

27 Sword, Cavalry, Pattern 1882, Long and Short, Mark I - close-up of the hilt

(MoD Pattern Room, Nottingham)

28 Sword, Cavalry, Pattern 1882, Long (New)

Blade length and width: 35^3/$_8$in. x 1^1/$_8$in..
Blade type: flat back, single fuller each side to within 9^1/$_2$ in. of point; double edged for last 9 in..
Guard: sheet steel, sword knot slit near pommel.
Hilt mounts: steel.
Grip: leather strips.
Scabbard: sheet steel, wood lined.
Sword weight: 2lb 3oz.
Scabbard weight: 1lb 12oz.

(MoD Pattern Room, Nottingham)

although conversion of existing stocks of Pattern 1864 blades had been going on at Enfield for some time previously. The first actual issues appear to have been made in the latter half of 1883 and within a matter of months, complaints began to pour in.[18] By a not unfamiliar process, the swords which had received general approval in troop trials became the object of universal criticism when they became a general issue. In May 1884, shortly after receiving the new swords, the 7th and 15th Hussars (neither of which had participated in the service trials) complained that the blades were soft and easily bent. A month later, the 16th Lancers reported that 26 out of 78 new swords received had been damaged because of the softness of their blades. The unfortunate Colonel Arbuthnot was accordingly asked to examine the allegedly defective swords and to report. He reported that the swords in question had been overstrained as a result of unauthorised tests by the regiments. Nevertheless, he conceded that the blades, as designed, were too light at the point and that, although they made for a good cutting sword, they were generally too light for thrusting. He recommended obtaining reports from all the regiments which had received the new pattern swords.

Accordingly, in July 1884 a questionnaire was sent to all regiments, asking for comments on the new pattern swords and asking for views generally upon the desirable length, temper and design of a cavalry sword. At the same time, The General Officer Commanding at Aldershot (Lieutenant-General Sir Archibald Alison), under whom the 7th and 15th Hussars were serving, commented that if the swords which had been damaged had passed the official tests, then the tests must be inadequate, and he recommended the setting up of a committee to go into the whole matter. By this time, complaints had come in also from the 1st (Royal) Dragoons, and in October 1884 the War Office bowed to the inevitable and appointed a special committee to go into the whole question of cavalry swords.

The Chairman of the Committee was Major-General Sir Drury Curzon Drury Lowe, a noted cavalryman who had commanded the cavalry in Egypt in 1882 and led the pursuit after Tel-el-Kebir;[19] the other members were Sir Frederick Abel (Chemist to the War Office), Colonel Arbuthnot, Colonel E A Wood (10th Hussars), Major C F Call (Assistant- Superintendent, India Stores Department), Mr J F Latham (Messrs Wilkinson & Son), Mr F J Mappin MP (Turton & Son), and Mr G R Hunter (Director of Artillery and Stores, War Office), who acted as Secretary. The Committee was required to consider and advise on the patterns and quality of the swords and scabbards then in use in the cavalry. In practice, it limited itself to the 1882 patterns and did not deal with the earlier patterns, of which some were still in service, or with the patterns of sword peculiar to the Household Cavalry.

The Committee held some ten meetings, taking evidence from a wide range of users and manufacturers, and conducting extensive tests and trials. By the time it started work, the results of the questionnaire distributed in July 1884 were available. With one exception, all the regiments wanted a blade longer than the 33 inches of the 1882 Short patterns, and almost all regiments complained about the hilt damaging the clothing, even though the edges of the guard had been turned over precisely to meet this problem. Beyond this, there was no unanimity. The blade length recommended varied between the 34 inches recommended by some hussar regiments to the 39 inches preferred by the 1st Life Guards. Opinions as to where the sword should balance, how much it should weigh and what sort of strain it should stand varied equally widely. The 15th and 18th Hussars actually wanted a return to the Pattern 1853 sword which the Royal Artillery still carried. The request for suggestions to improve the present patterns brought few replies of any originality; the Royal Horse Guards suggested a leather scabbard to reduce noise and reflection from the metal, the 4th and 14th Hussars suggested a straight blade and the 10th Hussars wanted the same sword for both officers and men, a return to 1796. The general impression was that few officers had ever given much thought to the subject, probably because they had never been asked before.

As a first step, the Committee withdrew 60 of the Short pattern from the 2nd Dragoon Guards and the 7th, 10th, 15th and 20th Hussars for examination and testing. These swords fell into three groups:

(a) Pattern 1864 blades converted by Mole & Son;

(b) Pattern 1864 blades converted by Enfield;

(c) new blades made by Mole.

The tests, devised by Colonel Arbuthnot, consisted of striking the back and edge of the blade on a block of hard wood, and bending in a machine to a predetermined length. Of the swords in group (a), only four out of twelve passed, the remainder bending permanently or breaking. Of the swords in group (b), ten out of fourteen passed. In group (c), none passed. The difference in results between (a) and (b), when taken in conjunction with the differing views, previously recorded, between Colonel Arbuthnot and Mole & Son about the value of conversion suggests that the method of conversion may have been rather different. But the failure of all of the new blades is particularly striking.

In a second series of tests, at Knightsbridge Barracks in January 1885, five troopers from the 1st Life Guards and the 15th Hussars made a series of cuts against the carcasses of a horse and some sheep, both skinned and unskinned. Of the six Long pattern swords used, all broke or bent after no more than four cuts. Five out of six Short pattern swords fared the same. But of seven experimental swords made up to the Committee's own design, two came through undamaged. These experimental swords were made up with 33 and $34^{1}/_{2}$ inch blades, and a variety of scabbards.

What all of these tests seemed to show was that the Pattern 1882 swords were unsatisfactory, either in design or manufacture, and that, if anything, the commercially manufactured blades were worse than those made at Enfield. The Committee therefore went carefully into the question of manufacture, examining the representatives of two Sheffield steel-producing firms, (Sanderson & Co and Frith & Sons), as well as a representative of Mole & Son. It transpired that the best steel had not always been used and that there were acute differences of opinion among manufacturers as to the relative merits of oil and water hardening.

In its first report, presented in March 1885, the Committee came to the conclusion that the swords of the 1882 patterns were not satisfactory, and recommended that they should all be withdrawn for re-testing and that only those that passed these tests should be re-issued for service. (The tests were again devised by Colonel Arbuthnot, and were even more severe than those originally used for testing new Pattern 1882 blades. They involved striking on a hardwood block, bending in a machine to reduce the length by 5 inches (4³/4 inches for the Short patterns), and bending round a curved pattern). The swords to be re-issued should weigh between 2lbs 3ozs and 2lbs 5ozs in the case of the Long patterns, and between 2lbs 1¹/2 ozs and 2lbs 3ozs for the Short patterns. In effect, this meant that, in the case of the Short patterns, only the Converted pattern could be re-issued. Although the Committee was not to know it and acted in what it thought was a prudent fashion, there can be little doubt, in the light of later investigations, that the re-testing itself weakened the swords.

In its second report, issued in April 1885, the Committee dealt with the question of future design and manufacture. It noted that almost all of the regiments had expressed a preference for a longer blade than the 33 inches of the Short patterns, and that experience in the first campaign round Suakin, in the Sudan, in 1884, had shown that the 10th Hussars' troopers had been unable to reach their opponents lying prostrate. It recommended, therefore, a slightly longer blade and one which could withstand a severer test than the present 1882 patterns. The sword that the Committee recommended was to have a 34¹/2 inch blade, balancing approximately 5 inches from the shoulder and generally similar in form to the Pattern 1882 weapon. The recommended hilt was again very similar in form to its predecessor except that the grip was ¹/2 inch longer. The whole sword was to weigh between 2lbs 4¹/2 and 2lbs 6ozs. The Committee made no specific recommendation about the scabbard except to say that it could, with advantage, be made lighter. As regards manufacture, only the very best steel should be used in future, but whether oil or water hardening was to be employed was to be left to the individual manufacturer. Finally, the Committee recommended that a proportion of swords should be made each year at Enfield to act as a check upon commercial quality and costs (significantly, Mr Mappin alone dissented from this recommendation).

In a separate report, the military members of the Committee recommended that a specimen of the proposed sword should be sealed as the regulation pattern for all mounted services except the Household Cavalry. They suggested one change to the scabbard, preferring a fixed loop on either side, near the mouth, to the two fixed loops along the back of the 1882 pattern scabbards. The weight of the scabbard recommended was 1lb 6½ozs, rather lighter than either of the two 1882 patterns.

The successive recommendations of the Committee were accepted by the Commander-in-Chief and the War Office and the result was the Sword, Cavalry, Pattern 1885, officially adopted in November 1885, (Plate 29).[20] It can most readily be distinguished from earlier and later patterns by the length of the blade (34½ inches), and by the weight (2lbs 6 ozs ±1oz). The blade is very similar to earlier patterns, being slightly curved, spear-pointed, with a flat back and a single wide fuller each side, terminating 8½ inches from the point. The guard differed slightly from the 1882 patterns inasmuch as the top of it was flush with the top of the grip and into the angle between the top of the grip and the guard was fitted a triangular hand-stop. The guard is very slightly wider and the angle of the grip relative to the blade is slightly increased compared with earlier patterns. The grip is 5¼ inches long but otherwise unchanged from previous models. The scabbard, (Scabbard, Sword, Cavalry, Pattern 1885, Mark I), was lighter than the previous 1882 patterns at 1lb 8ozs and had a smaller shoe; the main change was the adoption of fixed loops on either side, some 2¼ inches from the mouth, (Plate 30). This device overcame the problem of a broken upper sling which had meant, in earlier patterns, that the scabbard tilted forwards and the sword was then liable to fall out; the new pattern meant that the sword and scabbard remained vertical even if one sling broke or was cut. This feature was adopted later in all subsequent cavalry patterns.

The failure of the Pattern 1882 swords and the decision to replace them entirely with the Pattern 1885 brought into acute focus the dearth of sword manufacturing capacity in Britain. The total War Office requirement for the new sword (including reserves and some for the Indian Army) was put at 30,000.[21] Only one commercial firm (Mole & Son) was engaged in large-scale manufacture and, even with the assistance of the RSAF Enfield, it could not produce this number of swords quickly. Moreover, it had expressed doubts as to the practicability of making blades to stand the new and more rigorous tests recommended by the Committee.[22] In order to keep Moles' capacity in being, the company was given an order for 9,500 swords, spread over three years. In accordance with one of the Committee's recommendations, Enfield was given an order for 2,000. For the remainder of the requirement, some 18,500 swords, the War Office turned to Solingen, as it had done many times before. The old-established and reputable firm of Weyersberg, Kirschbaum & Co. was asked to make a sample batch of 287 blades, of which 200 subsequently passed all the new tests. As a result, the firm then received the order for the remaining 18,000 or so blades required, at a price some four shillings below the English prices.

Cavalry Troopers' Swords 1878-1914

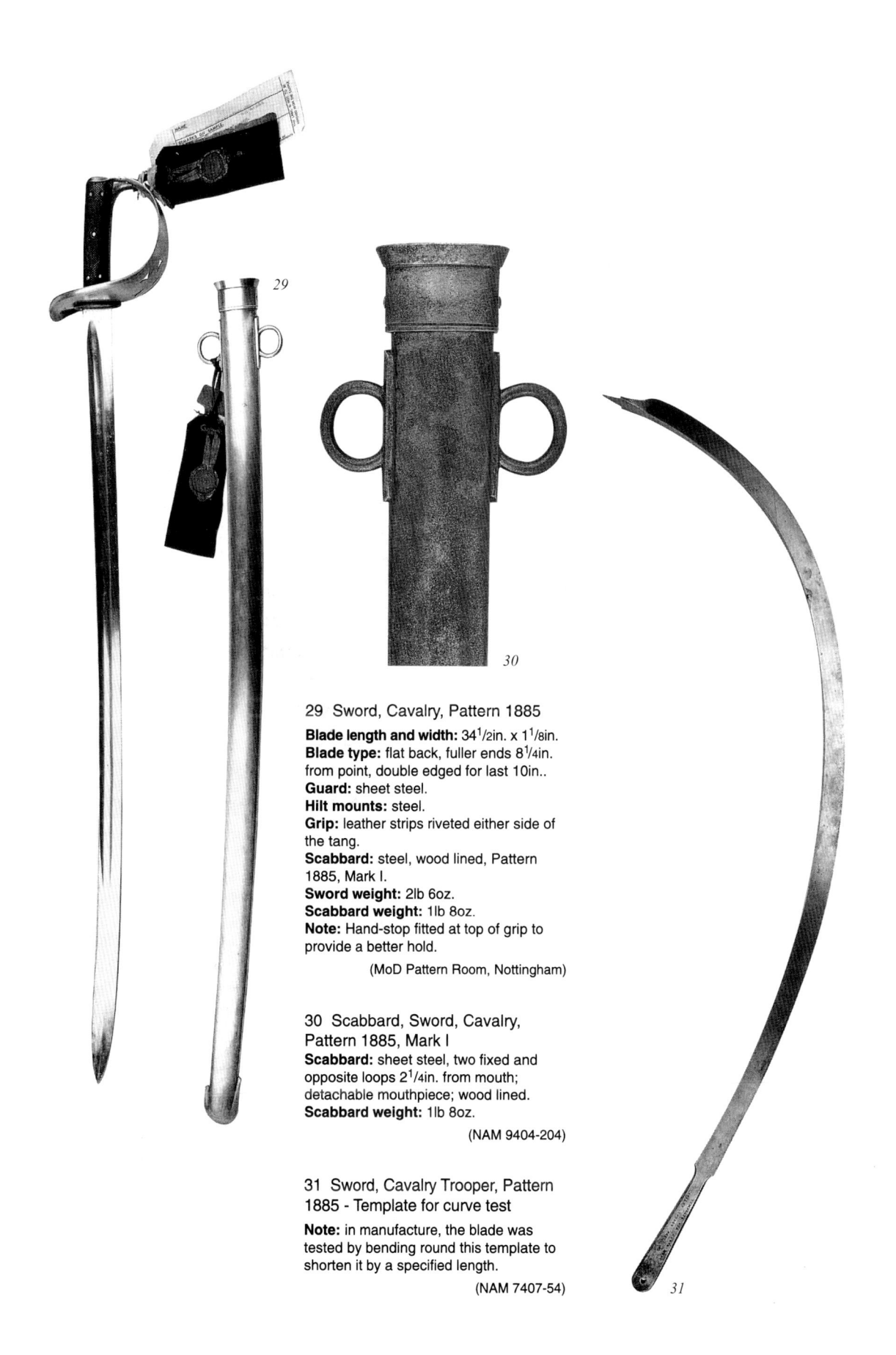

29

30

29 Sword, Cavalry, Pattern 1885
Blade length and width: 34$\frac{1}{2}$in. x 1$\frac{1}{8}$in.
Blade type: flat back, fuller ends 8$\frac{1}{4}$in. from point, double edged for last 10in..
Guard: sheet steel.
Hilt mounts: steel.
Grip: leather strips riveted either side of the tang.
Scabbard: steel, wood lined, Pattern 1885, Mark I.
Sword weight: 2lb 6oz.
Scabbard weight: 1lb 8oz.
Note: Hand-stop fitted at top of grip to provide a better hold.

(MoD Pattern Room, Nottingham)

30 Scabbard, Sword, Cavalry, Pattern 1885, Mark I
Scabbard: sheet steel, two fixed and opposite loops 2$\frac{1}{4}$in. from mouth; detachable mouthpiece; wood lined.
Scabbard weight: 1lb 8oz.

(NAM 9404-204)

31 Sword, Cavalry Trooper, Pattern 1885 - Template for curve test
Note: in manufacture, the blade was tested by bending round this template to shorten it by a specified length.

(NAM 7407-54)

31

49

This order was placed at the end of 1885 and completed in April 1887.[23] The decision to go to Solingen was subsequently severely criticised in the report of the 1887 Commission on War-like Stores, on the grounds that Enfield could easily have done the job. With the completion of the Solingen contract, no further sword contracts were placed abroad and Enfield and Mole became the primary peacetime producers.

In its desire to produce a sword which would be satisfactory, the 1884 Committee had deliberately increased the stringency of the tests to be applied to the new sword. The blade was to be struck on its edge and back by means of a machine, the force to be equal to the hardest blow that a man could strike against the trunk of an oak tree 2 feet in diameter. It was then to be bent round a rigid metal pattern, (Plate 31) so that the length from guard to point was shortened by 5 inches, and finally it was to be bent by pressure downwards on the hilt until the blade length had been reduced by 6 inches, the blade being bent both ways in this last test. These tests were very severe, especially the last one, and the Superintendent at Enfield thought it was too severe; in his view, shortening to $5^{1}/_{2}$ inches was enough. Nevertheless, these tests were approved for all new swords.[24]

The 1884 Committee had investigated the subject of cavalry swords with an unprecedented degree of thoroughness and the authorities at the War Office might reasonably have thought that the resulting Pattern 1885 sword would have a long and satisfactory life in service. That was not to be the case.

The first swords appear to have been issued in the middle of 1886, among the first regiments to receive them being the 2nd (Royal Scots Greys) Dragoons. As with any new weapon introduced into service, there was inevitably interest in its performance as compared with earlier weapons, and almost certainly a certain amount of unofficial testing went on in the regiments receiving the new swords. There is evidence that in some cases, swords were bent across a man's thigh, a test which, Sir Garnet Wolseley observed later, was likely to damage or break any sword. By the summer of 1888, sufficient doubts had begun to surface about the strength of the Pattern 1885 blade for the authorities in London to put in hand the manufacture of 200 experimental blades in October 1888. These blades retained the existing length of $34^{1}/_{2}$ inches but one group was $1^{1}/_{2}$ ozs heavier than the Pattern 1885, (1lb $8^{1}/_{2}$ozs against 1lb 7ozs), while the second group weighed 1lb 9ozs. Fifty of each group were ordered from Wilkinsons and from Enfield.[25]

Matters were accelerated by complaints arising from the experience of the 20th Hussars against the Mahdists round Suakin in December 1888.[26] Amid some exaggerated press reports of the failure of swords and revolvers, it emerged from a Board of Enquiry held at Suakin in December 1888 that four swords had been bent or broken. Two swords had been damaged as a result of horses trampling on them, a normal exigency of service. Two, however, had broken in hand-to-hand combat:

'Encountering one of the enemy's footmen, I made a downward cut at his head, and my sword broke about 3 inches from the hilt...

'I first engaged one of the enemy footmen on my off side, and cut his head open. I then became engaged with one of their cavalrymen on the same side. He was about to make a thrust at me with a spear, when I gave him a cut between the elbow and the hand, and he galloped off. I now found a mounted horseman on my near side, I delivered cut 3 at his neck, which he parried, and my sword flew into three pieces....As far as I am able to judge, my sword met that of my opponent about half way down the blade. My opponent's sword was a much heavier one than mine...

Neither of these incidents in themselves would seem particularly noteworthy. Some swords are bound to break in the circumstances of hand-to-hand fighting, and certainly any one cutting at a heavy Sudanese sword might expect an accident of this kind. Subsequent examination back in England of the remains of these two swords showed that they were of good quality. But these incidents coincided with serious complaints from the 5th Dragoon Guards in Ireland. A Board of Enquiry there held in December 1888, concluded that all the swords in the regiment's charge were inferior in quality and quite unfit for service; it recommended that the swords should be subjected to a scientific test by a competent War Office official. As an immediate step, all the swords of the cavalry regiments in Ireland (5th Dragoon Guards, 2nd Dragoons (Royal Scots Greys), 12th Lancers and 14th and 19th Hussars) were examined and re-tested on the spot by the Chief Inspector of Small Arms (Colonel W H King-Harman). It was considered undesirable to subject them to the same severe tests that they had received before acceptance into service and the re-testing in Ireland consisted of striking on an oak block and bending against a standard spring pressure.

Of the total of 2,876 swords examined, 2,138 had been made at Solingen, 490 by Mole & Son and 229 by the RSAF Enfield; the origins of the remaining nineteen are not stated. Of the Solingen swords, 76 (3.55%) had been bent or damaged in the regiments and further 117 (5.5%) bent or broke during re-testing. For the Mole swords, the figures were sixteen (3.27%) and 62 (12.7%) respectively, and for the Enfield swords the figures were five (2.2%) and twelve (5.2%). The results for Solingen and Enfield were very similar but the incidence of failure on re-testing among the Mole swords is significant.

In his report, Colonel King-Harman called attention to the fact that some of the regiments had been applying their own unofficial tests. Nevertheless, he concluded that the Pattern 1885 blade was too thin between the fullers and, in a large number of cases, too brittle. He also condemned the practice of issuing service swords to new recruits; he thought that each station should maintain a sufficient number of cast-off practice swords for use by recruits in training.

Wolseley, the Adjutant-General, in a covering minute to the report which was submitted to Parliament in February 1889, concluded that the blades were too thin between the fullers and that the tests laid down by the 1884 Committee were too severe. He was confident that with another 2$^{1}/_{2}$ ozs of metal added to the blade a good sword could be produced.

Two other investigations were under way. For purposes of comparison, a total of 22 foreign patterns of cavalry sword were obtained and examined.[27] They came from Germany, Russia, France, Spain, Italy and Egypt, and covered a very wide spectrum of blade designs and weights. The weights ranged from 1lb 15$^{1}/_{4}$ ozs for the Russian Cossack sword Pattern 1881 to 3lbs 9ozs for the German cuirassiers' sword, and the blade length varied from the 33 inches of the Austrian Universal Pattern to 38$^{1}/_{4}$ for the German cuirassiers' pattern. Some, such as the French heavy cavalry and German and Prussian cuirassiers' swords, had straight blades intended purely for thrusting; the majority followed the British example of being intended for both cutting and thrusting, although not necessarily equally effective. A wide variety of constructions was also present - diamond section, single fuller each side, double fullers each side, single fuller on one side only and piped back.

From this examination, Colonel King-Harman concluded that the main points to be borne in mind in designing a strong sword were to keep the blade as short and heavy as was practicable, the balance as far as possible towards the point, and the flexibility as high as possible. To achieve these desirable aims, the back of the blade should be as narrow as was consistent with stiffness, and the fullers as narrow and shallow as was consistent with lightness.

In parallel, two distinguished engineers, Sir Frederick Bramwell and Mr Benjamin Baker,[28] were asked in April 1889 to investigate the whole matter of testing, choice of materials and the form of the blade. It was the first time that sword blades had been subjected to detailed mathematical and chemical analysis. Their report, in August 1889, took the form of answers to a number of detailed questions posed by the Director of Artillery, who was responsible at the War Office for the procurement of weapons.[29] They dealt first with the question of testing. They saw no objection to the striking test but regarded the existing bending tests as far too severe. As they pointed out, it was well known in engineering circles that bending a piece of metal alternately one way and then the other, thus reversing the stresses, gravely weakened it and caused early failure. It was not surprising therefore that the initial severe tests, followed by casual bending in the hands of the regiments, followed finally by subsequent re-testing, had produced a high incidence of failure. They recommended that future bending tests of a sword should consist of reducing the length by 5 inches under a pressure of 39lbs, to each side; this test to be applied only once in the life of the blade, subsequent bending tests to be only to one side and the blade marked accordingly. They saw no reason to alter the existing fullered type of blade but they recommended the adoption of a uniform specification of steel as follows:

	per cent		per cent
Carbon	0.9 to 1.15	Phosphorus	not to exceed 0.02
Silicon	not to exceed 0.2	Sulphur	0.02
Manganese	0.15 to 0.35	Copper	trace only.

The annealed strength was to be at least 50 tons per square inch. No particular advantage was seen in adopting chrome steel at this stage.

Bramwell and Baker noted three manufacturing points:

(a) blades should be made by machine rolling rather than hand-hammering which depended too much on the skill of the individual workman;

(b) oil hardening should be used in preference to water hardening which occasionally produced cracking and warping;

(c) to maintain the necessary consistency of temperature, lead baths or gas-heated mufflers and pyrometers should be used.

These recommendations were to guide British sword manufacture until 1914.

The experimental blades were ready early in 1889, the Enfield blades being marked 'E' and the Wilkinson blades 'W'.[30] Chests containing a mixture of Enfield and Wilkinson blades were then sent to the 4th Dragoon Guards and the 4th Hussars in Ireland, and to the 11th and 19th Hussars at Aldershot, for the usual trials against dead sheep and horses. The results of these trials were by no means clear-cut. Not everyone thought that the new blades were a significant improvement on the Pattern 1885 swords and there was some division among users as to the relative merits of the Enfield and Wilkinson products. But there was now some urgency in settling on a design for early manufacture, since it was unthinkable that the Pattern 1885 sword should be put back into manufacture. Accordingly, the Pattern 1889 Experimental blade, mated with the Pattern 1885 hilt, was formally adopted into service in May 1890 as the Sword, Cavalry, Pattern 1890, (Plate 32).[31] It was, at 2lbs 9 ozs, some 3 ozs heavier than its 1885 predecessor, and the flat surface between the edge of the fuller and the back of the blade is very slightly wider (0.0625 of an inch). The swords are stamped '1890' or, more often, '/90'. Otherwise, they are almost identical with the Pattern 1885.

The scabbard was the Scabbard, Cavalry, Pattern 1885, Mark II, introduced in May 1889 to meet complaints that the 1885 Mark I scabbard was too light and easily damaged.[32] The Mark II was 6 ozs heavier, at 1lb 14½ ozs.

With the introduction of the Pattern 1890, the wheel had come full circle because it was actually heavier than the Pattern 1864, the weight of which had set the War Office off in 1878 on the quest for a lighter sword. But the long search for a satisfactory cavalry sword had even yet not reached its conclusion. The failures of the Patterns 1882 and 1885 swords in quick succession and the very thorough investigations which had taken place into the whole business of design had sparked off a wide interest in the subject at all levels. The Pattern 1890 sword may have been a slight improvement on its predecessor but it was in form not very different from the patterns of the last 30 years, and the examination of foreign patterns had showed that there was more than one way of tackling the problem. The Annual Accounts of the RSAF Enfield reveal that in the financial year 1896-97 two cavalry swords were made with experimental hilts enabling the thumb to be extended when grasping the sword. This suggests an emphasis on thrusting. Four more experimental swords were made in the following year although it is not clear whether these were of the same or different patterns. Four more experimental swords were made in 1898-99 and a batch of 100 in 1899-1900. From subsequent papers, we know that existing stocks of cavalry swords had been deliberately run down by 1899 in anticipation of the introduction of a new pattern.[33]

Unfortunately, the relevant War Office papers have been destroyed and it is not possible to reconstruct the processes which led to the introduction of the Sword, Cavalry, Pattern 1899, (Plate 33).[34] This was, once again, a variation upon a familiar theme. The 33½ inch blade was slightly curved, with a flat back and a single broad fuller each side, starting about 1¼ inches from the shoulder and finishing 7 inches from the point. The blade, although an inch shorter than its immediate predecessors (and only half an inch longer than the Pattern 1882 Short sword), was proportionately heavier and stronger. The main design change from the 1890 pattern was the bowl-shaped guard, which was solid and significantly larger, measuring some 5½ inches at its widest point; there was a pear-shaped reinforcing plate brazed on to the outside surrounding the exit point of the blade. The scabbard was virtually identical with its predecessor, the Pattern 1885 Mark II, but 1 inch shorter and proportionately slightly stronger. A number of Pattern 1899 swords were produced by converting Pattern 1890 blades and in these swords the fuller finishes some 8 inches from the point.[35]

The war which broke out in South Africa in 1899 was the first major conflict in which the British Army had been engaged for nearly half a century and, inevitably, it provided a searching test of organisation, tactics and equipment. The melancholy results of that examination can be read in the volumes of evidence produced before

Cavalry Troopers' Swords 1878-1914

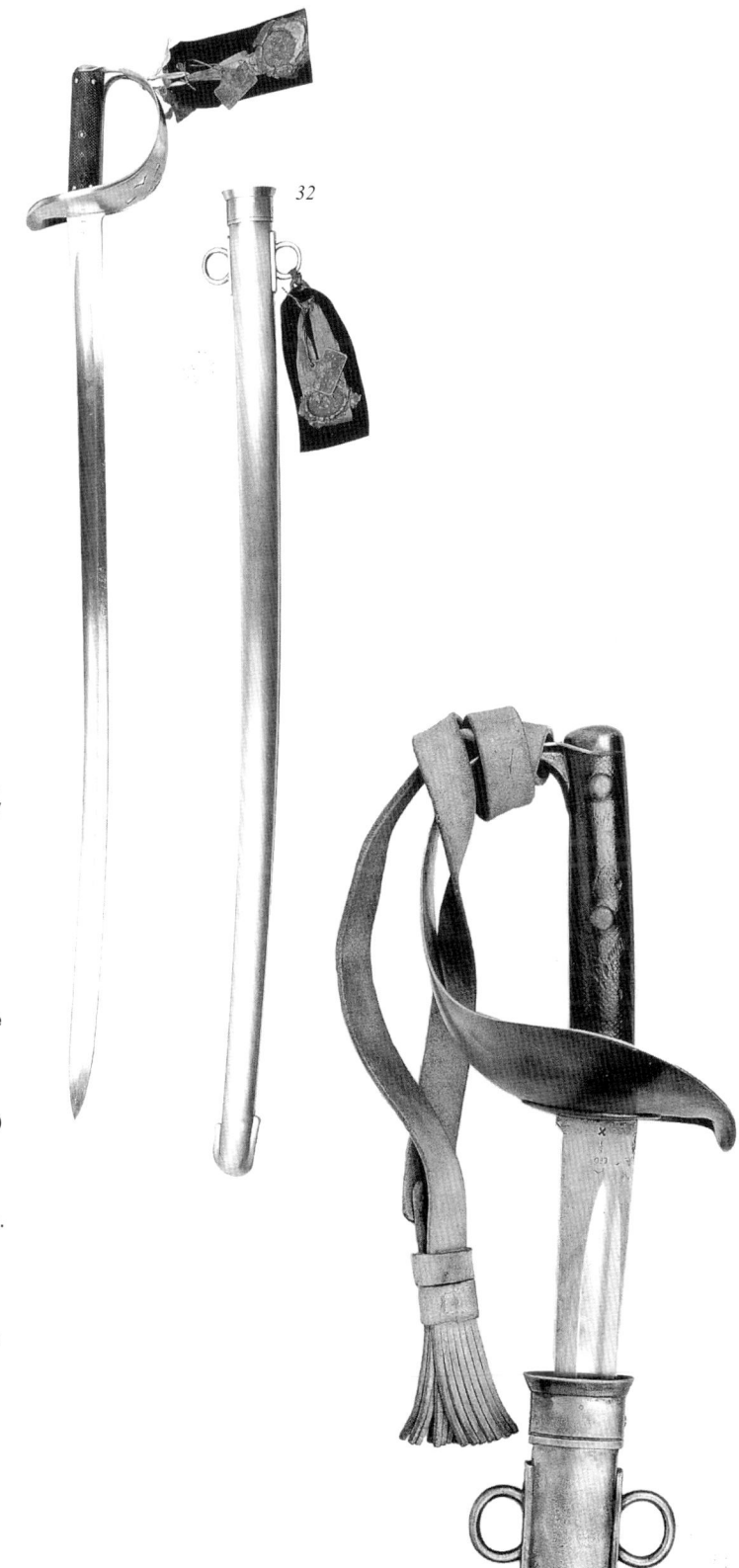

32 Sword, Cavalry, Pattern 1890

Blade length and width: 34 1/2in. x 1 1/8in.
Blade type: flat back, otherwise virtually identical with Cavalry Pattern 1885.
Guard: sheet steel.
Hilt mounts: steel.
Grip: leather strips fixed either side of the tang as in previous pattern.
Scabbard: Cavalry, Pattern 1885, Mark II.
Scabbard weight: 1lb 14 1/2oz.
Note: The flat surface between the edge of the fuller and the back of the blade (0.0625 in.) is slightly wider than in the Sword, Cavalry, Pattern 1885 blade.

(MoD Pattern Room, Nottingham)

33 Sword, Cavalry, Pattern 1899

Blade length and width: 33 1/2in. x 1 1/8in.
Blade type: slightly curved, flat back, single fuller each side to within 7 in. of spear point, double edged for last 8 in..
Guard: sheet steel bowl, with sword knot slit near pommel and pear-shaped reinforcing piece on outside surrounding blade. Inner edge turned over.
Hilt mounts: steel.
Grip: 6in. long, composed of leather strips secured through tang with three rivets.
Note: the guard does not have the pierced 'Maltese Cross' of preceding patterns and the grip is longer.

(NAM 7411-14)

the Royal Commission which was appointed subsequently to enquire into the conduct of the war.[36]

The regular cavalry regiments which went to South Africa were equipped initially with the Pattern 1890 sword and then, in the later stages, with the Pattern 1899, the Household Cavalry continuing to use throughout their own Pattern 1892 sword, (see Chapter 5).

Opportunities for mounted sword action were few and far between and by the end of the war many regiments had traded in their swords for rifles and bayonets, becoming, in effect, mounted infantrymen. None of the patterns of sword had proved satisfactory. Giving evidence to the Royal Commission, the cavalry commander, Major-General Sir John French stated: 'I think the present cavalry sword is the very worst that could possibly be used by mounted troops. I am trying hard to get it altered'.[37]

Colonel Robert Baden-Powell, another prominent cavalryman, declared: 'The present sword is a perfectly useless weapon to my mind, whether as a sword or anything else'.[38]

His views were echoed by another prominent cavalry officer, Major-General Douglas Haig. The Marquis of Tullibardine, who had commanded the Royal Horse Guards in South Africa, went even further: 'The present sword, and particularly the one we have got in the Household Cavalry [Household Cavalry, Pattern 1892, Mark I] no one could possibly use without falling off if he really cut with it'.[39]

The matter was caustically summed up thus by the commanding officer of the 18th Hussars, in September 1900:

> 'The present sword is in my opinion far too heavy and of very little use. The scabbard should be of leather. The present steel pattern is constantly being damaged, owing to horses rolling or falling, whereas the leather scabbard as used by officers, is much more serviceable, as well as lighter. The sword should be lighter and made with a view to using the point and not the cut. At the battle of Talana Hill, I had an excellent opportunity of watching the effect of the sword during the charge. A party of about 20 Boers were charged by half a squadron, 18th Hussars, the two parties met at full gallop and the Hussars did their best to cut down the enemy, till the latter threw their rifles away. The result was (as far as I could see) one man killed (by a point) and about 8 wounded but none appeared to be much cut about and I believe more damage would have been done had the men been armed with heavy sticks.

There was, however, no unanimity among these critics as to what should replace the existing patterns. French and Haig, for example, favoured a straight, thrusting sword whereas Baden-Powell wanted a light, slashing sword; other witnesses wanted the men equipped with rifles and bayonets. Even so, one can begin to detect for the first time a movement in favour of a thrusting sword.

The relative impotence of horsed cavalry in the face of barbed wire, magazine rifles and machine guns using smokeless propellant was not lost upon some authorities at the time. As early as September 1902, the Canadian Militia authorities had decided that the future of cavalry lay in 'the efficient use of the rifle'.[40] Even earlier, the General Officer Commanding in the Transvaal and Orange River colony had pointedly asked the War Office how it was intended to arm the cavalry in the future since many regiments had returned their swords and lances to store and re-equipped with rifles and bayonets.[41] Within a year of the end of the war, the War Office had reached the same conclusions as the Canadian authorities; a memorandum from the Commander-in-Chief (Lord Roberts) issued in 1903, stated that henceforth the primary arm of the cavalry was to be the rifle, although the sword was to be retained for shock action in those fleeting opportunities when it could be used to advantage.[42] The lance was to be abolished, however. (In practice, it crept in again in 1909 after Roberts' retirement and was not finally abolished until 1927).[43]

Experiments to improve the cavalry sword and scabbard began before the South African War ended.[44] The Annual Accounts of the RSAF Enfield for 1900-01 reveal that two experimental wooden scabbards had been produced, one with gun-metal and one with steel mounts. Next year, Enfield produced a leather scabbard and in 1902-3 a batch of 1,000 wooden scabbards with steel mounts were made, presumably for troop trials, (Plate 34). In the same year, Enfield also undertook experiments with a sword which could also be used as a bayonet, predictably without success. Clearly, the time had come to take the matter forward in a more formal way and in March 1903 a committee was set up under Sir John French to advise on the 'future pattern, weight and length of the cavalry sword'. The other members were the Inspector-General of Cavalry (Sir Douglas Haig), Brigadier-General M F Rimington, a cavalry commander in the recent war, and Major-General Henry Scobell, another cavalry veteran and now commanding the 1st Cavalry Brigade at Aldershot.[45]

The Committee was given very wide terms of reference and, although it has been overshadowed subsequently by the later 1906 Committee, it can be argued that the French Committee was the more seminal event. Given the chairman's expressed views, it is not surprising that the Committee quickly reached the basic conclusion that the future sword should be essentially a thrusting weapon. It dismissed the existing Pattern 1899 sword as clumsy, and settled instead upon a straight sword, with a narrow, chisel-edged blade, which it recommended in its final report of January 1904.

Two hundred swords were made up to this basic specification, of which 75 were made by Enfield and the remainder, it is assumed, by Wilkinsons. This Sword, Cavalry, Experimental, Pattern 1904, (Plate 35) had many of the characteristics of the

Cavalry Troopers' Swords 1878-1914

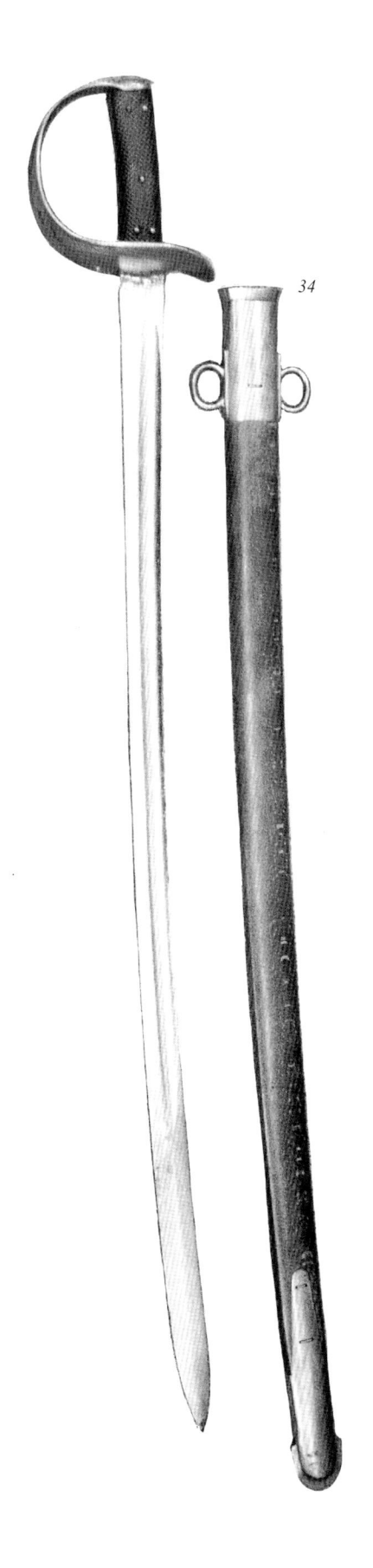

34 Scabbard, Cavalry, Experimental, Pattern 1900 with Pattern 1890 sword

Note: the scabbard is made of two pieces of wood, glued together and varnished. The mounts are of steel, stapled to the body. Weight 1lb 3oz.

(MoD Pattern Room, Nottingham)

35 Sword, Cavalry, Experimental, Pattern 1904

Blade length and width: 35$\frac{1}{4}$in. x 1in.
Blade type: straight, flat back, single narrow fuller each side, spear point.
Guard: sheet steel bowl, beaded edge, reinforcing piece outside surrounding blade shoulder; sword knot slit near pommel.
Hilt mounts: steel.
Grip: chequered plastic strips fastened through tang by three bolts.
Scabbard: leather, steel chape with fixed and opposite loops 2in. from mouth, steel locket.
Sword weight: 2lb 1$\frac{1}{2}$oz.
Scabbard weight: 12oz.
Note: The protuberance on the grip was designed to fit between the first and second fingers to provide a firmer grasp.

(MoD Pattern Room, Nottingham)

later Pattern 1908 sword, starting with the blade, which was straight, narrow, spear-pointed, 35$^{1}/_{2}$ inches long, but with a very wide back which made the cross-section almost T-shaped. The guard was a simple, sheet-steel bowl, with a reinforcing piece (or mullet) on the outside, as in the Pattern 1899 sword. The grip was of chequered vulcanite (an early form of thermoplastic), with a prominent knob about two thirds of the way down to give the fingers a better grip for thrusting; it was fastened to the tang by three large screw-bolts passing through the tang. The scabbard was of leather (with wooden liner) with steel chape and locket, the latter having two fixed and opposite loops, as in the Pattern 1885 scabbard. The sword weighed 2lbs 1$^{1}/_{2}$ozs and the scabbard 12ozs.

36 Sword, Cavalry, Officer, Experimental, Pattern 1904
Blade length and width: 35in. x 1in.
Blade type: straight, of almost triangular section with very wide back; unfullered, spear point.
Guard: nickel-plated steel bowl with engraved scroll pattern on outside; sword knot slit near pommel.
Hilt mounts: plated steel backpiece and chequered pommel.
Grip: wood, covered with fishskin and bound with silver wire.
Note: The guard is basically a solid version of the Cavalry, Officer, Pattern 1896 hilt.

(Wilkinson-Latham Collection)

An officers' version was produced, (Plate 36), in which the bowl was basically a solid version of the Pattern 1896 officers' sword, the blade was etched and decorated, and the grip was of wood, covered with fishskin and bound with silver wire. The backpiece and pommel were chequered.

In the design of its blade and grip, in the use of plastic for the grip and in its rigorous adoption of the thrusting principle, the Pattern 1904 Experimental sword marked a decisive break with the past, and was almost as different from the designs which had preceded it as the musket was from the breech-loading rifle. Although it was destined not to go into production, it heavily influenced succeeding designs which can be regarded as elaborations of it.

Cavalry Troopers' Swords 1878-1914

The troop trials of the 200 swords elicited general, if surprising, approval in principle although there were numerous criticisms of detail. Not all were in favour - Colonel T S Napier, the Inspector of Gymnasia, and Captain Alfred Hutton, a noted sword expert, were opposed in principle to a thrusting-only sword. Although the 1904 sword was not adopted, the need for a better sword than the present regulation pattern remained and in August 1905, four new designs were issued for trials. These were:

Pattern A - a straight, fullered blade, with plain bowl guard pierced at the bottom with a hole to take the thumb. The left edge of the bowl was turned over and there was a large cast-steel pommel secured by a recessed bun-nut;

Pattern B - the same hilt, mated to a Pattern 1889 blade, (Plate 37);

Pattern C - as A but with a Pattern 1899 pommel;

Pattern D - as B, but with a Pattern 1899 pommel.

(The decision to make up designs incorporating the 1899 blade showed that the old obsession with cut-and-thrust blades died hard).

Two swords of each design were issued to the 1st, 2nd, 3rd and 4th Cavalry Brigades, and to Hutton and Colonel M Fox (Chief Inspector of Physical Education at the Board of Education). None of these compromise designs proved acceptable and it was a pity that the authorities did not have the vision or the courage to continue

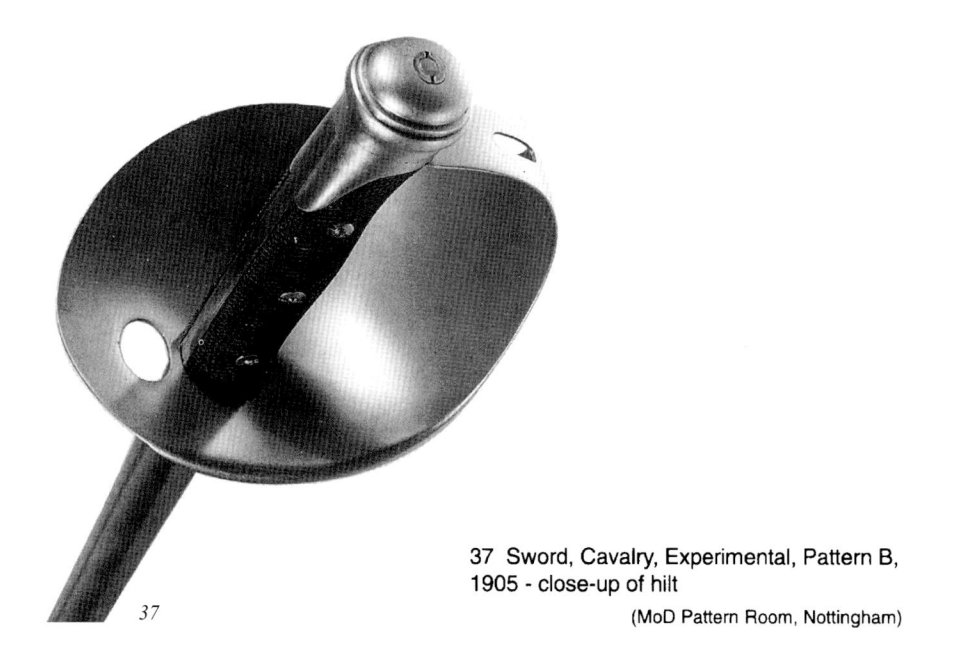

37 Sword, Cavalry, Experimental, Pattern B, 1905 - close-up of hilt
(MoD Pattern Room, Nottingham)

along the 1904 line of development. In desperation, one imagines, the Master-General of the Ordnance (Sir James Wolfe-Murray) proposed another committee.

The new Committee met in April 1906 under the chairmanship of Major-General Scobell,[46] the other members being Colonel Fox, Captain Hutton, Major A L Powell, Major R M Poore (7th Hussars), Major J A Bell-Smythe (1st (King's) Dragoon Guards), Major J B Jardine (5th Lancers), and Major B R Kirwan (Royal Artillery) (Secretary). When Jardine went to India in 1907, he was replaced by Major E S Tickell (14th Hussars) although Jardine signed the final report. Unlike previous committees, this was largely composed of regimental officers conversant at first hand with the needs and problems of mounted swordsmanship.

The terms of reference of the 1906 Committee were to recommend a sword for the cavalry and mounted services which should be primarily for thrusting but capable of being used as a cutting weapon, and to make recommendations for the future sword exercises. Given such terms of reference, the Committee might have been excused for designing yet another compromise sword, of the same general type which had afflicted the cavalry since 1821. Instead, with admirable courage, it went on to produce the most revolutionary design of sword ever introduced into the British or any other modern army.

At its first meeting, the Committee examined sixteen patterns of sword or hilt, viz:

(1) the Pattern 1899 sword

(2) the 1904 Experimental sword

(3) a Pattern 1899 sword modified by Wilkinsons

(4) a Dutch cavalry sword

(5) the French Model 1896 Light Cavalry sword

(6) the Egyptian Army cavalry sword, made by Wilkinsons

(7, (8), (9), (10) the 1905 Experimental patterns

(11) a design submitted by Scobell, the chairman

(12) a design submitted by Hutton

(13) a design submitted by the 21st Lancers

(14), (15), (16) three designs submitted by Fox.

(Although the papers are not specific, they imply that Nos 11-16 were designs of hilt rather than complete swords).

From these sixteen, the Committee retained Nos 11-16 for further study, suggesting that it had already made up its mind about the basic principle and form of the blade. Indeed, three days after this first meeting, the Committee met representatives of Wilkinson and Mole, by then the only large-scale commercial sword manufacturers in Britain, and asked them to submit specimen swords to the following specification:

Weight - 2lbs 6ozs
Blade length - 35 inches
Balance - $2^{1}/_{2}$-$2^{3}/_{4}$ inches from hilt
Hilt - to be on the lines of one of Fox's designs, the grip shaped to the hand in the thrusting position.
The blade was to be straight, narrow and with a chisel edge.

The specimen submitted by Wilkinsons in May 1906 was virtually identical to the 1904 Experimental sword and was rejected because the blade's T-shaped cross-section made it unsuitable for cutting.

(In reply to War Office criticisms about the cutting ability of this sword, Scobell claimed ingenuously that the last 10 inches of the blade could be sharpened and used for cutting).

Mole & Son submitted three models (A, B and C) in June 1906 (Plates 38, 39). After testing by soldiers, model A was selected for further trials, subject to some modifications of detail, viz.:

(a) a longer grip and heavier pommel, to bring the balance to within 3 inches of the hilt;

(b) the thumb depression in the grip to be deeper and the exit ramp smoother to reduce the shock when thrusting;

(c) the bowl to be wider and more open and to have a beaded edge;

(d) the front of the bowl to be bent over to facilitate carrying the sword at the 'Slope';

(e) the reinforcing mullet on the outside of the bowl to be extended by half an inch.

At the same time, the Committee recorded its view that the best material for the grip was aluminium.

A sword embodying these modifications and marked 'AA' was submitted by Mole & Son to the Committee and examined at its sixth meeting on 21 August 1906. This 'AA' sword weighed 2lbs $9^{1}/_{4}$ozs, some 3ozs more than the target weight but still some 2ozs less than the Pattern 1899 sword; it appears to have had an aluminium grip. As a result of its examination, the Committee asked for further minor modifications:

Cavalry Troopers' Swords 1878-1914

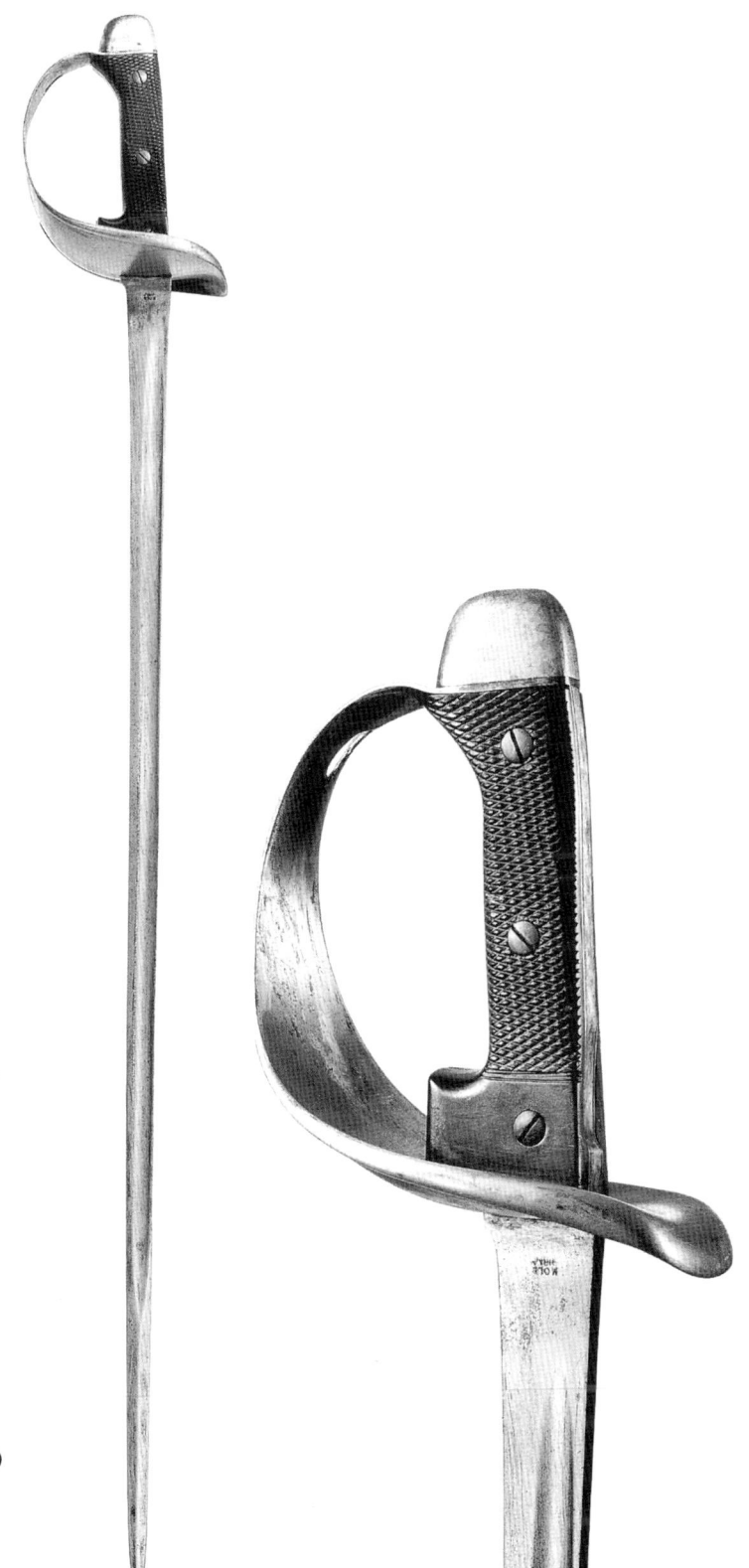

38 Sword, Cavalry, Experimental Pattern *c*1903-6

Blade length and width: 34½in. x 1in.
Blade type: straight, flat back, single fuller each side to within 7in. of spear point; double edged for last 9½in.
Guard: sheet steel bowl, with turned-over edges; sword knot slit near pommel.
Hilt mounts: steel.
Grip: black plastic strips fastened through tang by three bolts.
Sword weight: 2lb 14oz.
Scabbard weight: 12oz.
Note: Made by Mole & Son. It may be either design B or C submitted by the firm in 1906, but this identification is tentative.

(Royal Armouries IX - 1305)

39 Sword, Cavalry, Experimental Pattern *c*1903-6 - close-up of hilt

(Royal Armouries IX - 1305)

38

39

63

(a) the grip to be lengthened by a further half inch;

(b) the pommel to be made even heavier;

(c) the mullet to be oval instead of pear-shaped, and to extend a further three-eighths of an inch.

This modified AA model, with a wooden scabbard, was sent to Enfield in November 1906 so that a second specimen, with a vulcanite grip, could be made up. Enfield called attention to the weakness of the spike tang and proposed a Reeves-type tang, with the halves of the grip riveted either side. Enfield disliked the wooden scabbard, somewhat surprisingly, and recommended a leather-covered steel scabbard. Both of these recommendations were accepted by the Committee. The total cost of supplying models A, B, C, AA and modified AA was £29 14s 0d.

The sword was now close to the form finally adopted and 500 'modified AA' swords, as further modified by Enfield, and now known as the Sword, Cavalry, Pattern 1906, Mark 1 were made up, (Plates 40, 41, 42) and issued for troop trials at home and in India early in 1907. They were of two designs, by Mole and Wilkinson respectively, and it would appear from the reports that the only significant difference was in the angle of cast-off (the angle between the longitudinal axis of the grip and that of the blade), that of the Mole version being slightly greater. Some of the grips at least appear to have been made of wood. The only dissentient voice on the Committee appears to have been that of Hutton, who objected to the principle of a thrusting sword only, on the somewhat curious ground that it was more suited to a duellist than a soldier. By now, the sword had reached a weight of 2lbs 7ozs and that of the scabbard 1lb 4 ozs.

The troop trials went off satisfactorily, the only significant criticisms being of the grip, which was considered too rough, and the scabbard, which was thought too flimsy. The wooden grips had tended to split and all regiments were in favour of some form of composite material.

The report, together with a separate report from the Chief Inspector of Small Arms, were considered by the Committee at its eighth meeting in December 1907, when further minor changes were decided upon, viz.; the grip was to be of dermatine or gryphonite (early forms of plastic) and should have a metal ferrule at the base; the chequering was to be finer; the guard to be left unpolished and of thicker gauge steel; the mullet was to be extended into a V-shape, and the thickness of the blade between the fullers was to be increased from 0.6 to 0.7 inches. The Mole angle of cast-off was adopted and the scabbard was to be of steel only, with a shoe and a more curved mouthpiece.

Cavalry Troopers' Swords 1878-1914

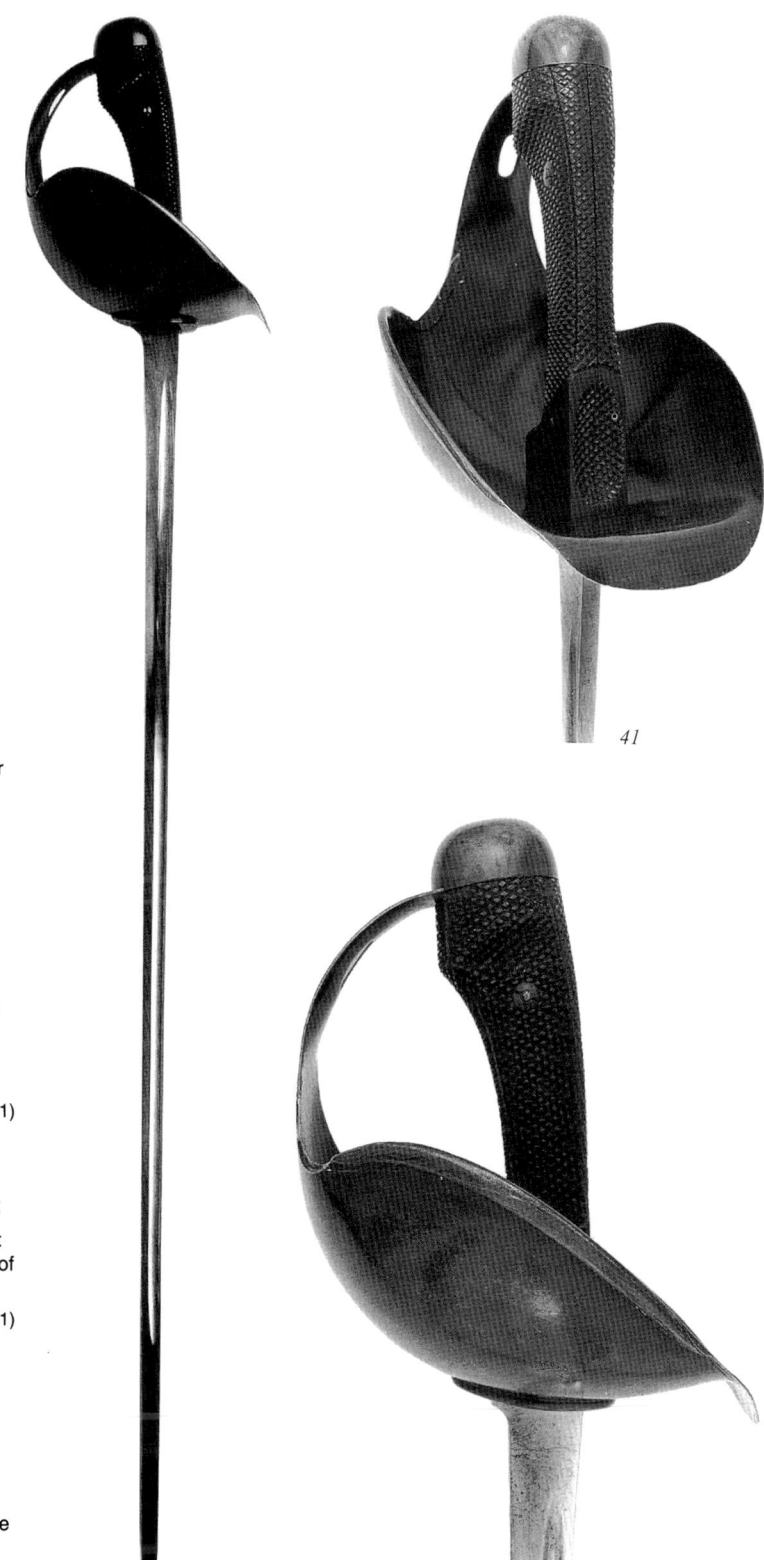

40 Sword, Cavalry, Pattern 1906, Mark I (Experimental)

Blade length and width: 35in. x 1in.
Blade type: straight, flat back, single fuller each side to within 6½in. of spear point; double edged for last 7½in..
Guard: sheet steel bowl with beaded edge on right side; oval strengthening piece outside surrounding blade shoulder; sword knot slit near pommel.
Hilt mounts: steel pommel.
Grip: black plastic, prominent thumb depression.
Scabbard: sheet steel covered with leather leaving steel tip exposed; wood lined.
Sword weight: 2lb 10oz.
Scabbard weight: 1lb 4oz.

(NAM 7205-7-1)

41 Sword, Cavalry, Pattern 1906, Mark I (Experimental) - inside of hilt

Note: The absence of a metal ferrule at base of grip, and beading on right side of guard only, should be noted.

(NAM 7205-7-1)

42 Sword, Cavalry, Pattern 1906, Mark I (Experimental) - outside of guard

Note: The oval reinforcing piece, the beading on the right side of the guard only and the shape of the blade near the shoulder should be noted. Compare blade shoulder with Plate 43.

(NAM 7205-7-1)

40

41

42

65

Further meetings in January and March 1908 produced more significant changes, somewhat surprisingly:

(a) the blade was now given a prominent shoulder, (compare Plates 42 and 43);

(b) the cast-off was increased;

(c) the scabbard was lightened, adapted more closely to the shape of the blade and given a simple square end;

(d) the mouth of the scabbard was extended by $1/8$ of an inch;

(e) the seating of the fixed loops on the scabbard was made narrower and lighter.

The Committee presented its final report on 28 April 1908, recommending the new sword for all cavalry units and the retention of the Pattern 1899 sword for other mounted services. The report was approved by the Army Council on 13 May 1908 and the new sword submitted to King Edward VII for his formal approval in June 1908. He was appalled by the design, which he called 'hideous', and wanted to know why a new sword was necessary at all, and why it should be for thrusting only. A high-level deputation, led by French and Haig, was hastily despatched to explain, and royal approval was given on 7 July 1908, the King stipulating only that the Household Cavalry were to retain their existing sword (Household Cavalry Pattern 1892, Mark II) for ceremonial purposes, carrying the new sword only on active service.

The estimated cost of manufacture of the Pattern 1908 sword was put at £1 2s $8^{1}/2$d and the scabbard at 8s 11d compared with £1 1s 6d and 8s 6d for the Pattern 1899 sword. In fact, the actual cost of the first batch made at Enfield as a check on commercial manufacturers' costs was £1 8s 8d and 12s $1^{1}/2$d. Some difficulty was encountered initially by the RSAF in manufacturing the bowl guard and in obtaining satisfactory gryphonite grips from contractors, and this probably accounts for the extra cost.

The Pattern 1908 sword was the last entirely new design to be adopted by the British Army and it has been regarded since its appearance as a masterpiece of design. It was without doubt the best sword ever produced for the British cavalry and probably for any cavalry but it is not difficult to understand the shock it created in conservative military circles, with its wicked, rapier-type blade and its pistol-shaped, plastic grip.

The pattern, sealed in July 1908, is known as the Sword, Cavalry, Pattern 1908, Mark 1, (Plates 43, 44). Although the blade could be, and was, sharpened along the last 18 inches, the cutting power was negligible and to that extent the Scobell Committee could be said to have evaded part of its remit. Blades are marked 'P'08' and in the original pattern the buff-piece (the leather washer round the shoulder of the blade,

Cavalry Troopers' Swords 1878-1914

43 Sword, Cavalry, Pattern 1908, Mark I
Blade length and width: 35¼in. x 1in. x 5¹/₁₆in.
Blade type: straight, flat back, single fuller each side to within 8in. of spear point; double edged for last 6 in..
Guard: sheet steel bowl with beaded edge; sword knot slit near pommel; very large pear-shaped reinforcing piece on outside near blade shoulder.
Hilt mounts: steel pommel.
Grip: plastic with steel ferrule at base and large depression for thumb.
Scabbard: sheet steel, square end, no shoe, detachable mouthpiece, two fixed and opposite loops 2¼in. from mouth; wood lined.
Sword weight: 2lb 15¾oz.
Scabbard weight: 1lb 6½oz.

(Royal Armouries IX - 700)

44 Scabbard, Cavalry, Pattern 1908, Mark I
(with Sword, Cavalry, Pattern 1908, Mark I)
Scabbard: sheet steel, wood lined.
Scabbard weight: 1lb 6½oz.
(Sealed Pattern No 1211).

(MoD Pattern Room, Nottingham)

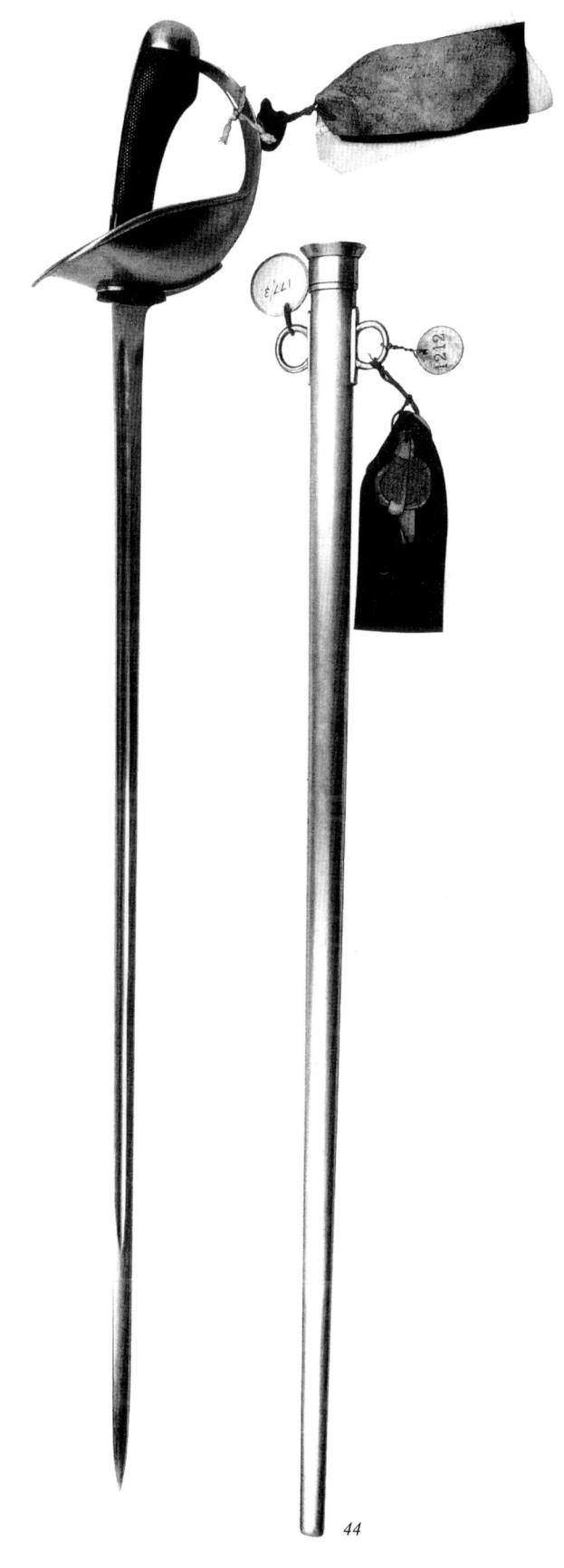

preventing moisture entering the scabbard) was simply slipped on over the blade. The grip, which is perhaps the most striking feature of the design, was modelled originally in gutta-percha (a material which becomes soft and malleable when warmed) by Colonel Fox, in order to achieve the right shape. It is designed so as to bring the sword automatically into the thrusting position when properly gripped; production grips were of red dermatine. The overall length of the sword (some 43 inches) meant that with the arm fully extended for thrusting and the rider leaning forward in the saddle the reach was approximately the same as that of the standard lance; in 1914, the British swordsmen had no difficulty in dealing effectively with the opposing German *Uhlans*.

Although the sword is actually heavier than its immediate predecessors, it feels lighter because of its perfect balance.

Service experience produced a number of minor modifications. In 1910, the sword knot slit was increased to 0.8 by 0.25 inches, the tang strengthened at the shoulder and the reinforcing mullet on the bowl extended by 1/4 inch in each direction so as to more adequately cover the mouth of the scabbard, which was at the same time made more concave in order to accommodate it.[47] In 1911, a serration was introduced at the shoulder of the blade to retain the buff-piece more securely[48] but this did not solve the problem and in 1912 the serration was abandoned and the buff-piece secured by a pin passing through the blade; the sword was then designated the Pattern 1908, Mark 1*, a new scabbard under the same designation having been introduced in 1911, made of slightly thicker steel so that it weighed 1lb 10 ozs.[49] In 1926 the sword became the Sword, No 1, Mark 1. In 1914, arrangements were made for the pommel and ferrule to be oil-blackened and for the bowl and scabbard to be painted khaki.

A modified version of the Pattern 1908 was adopted in 1918 for the Indian cavalry.[50] The blade is identical except that it is marked 'I[ndia] P[attern]'08'. The hilt, (Plate 45) is significantly smaller to suit the smaller hand of the Indian soldier and the guard lacks the reinforcing mullet. The most obvious difference is in the grip, which is, in effect, the lower part only of the British Army version, and only 5 1/2 inches long. It was originally specified to be of walnut, which is expensive and relatively scarce; later specimens often have dermatine grips, presumably as an economy. Although lighter (2lbs 2 ozs) than the British sword, it does not feel quite as well balanced because of the smaller hilt. The scabbard is identical to the Pattern 1908, Mark 1*.

Imitation being the sincerest form of flattery, it is gratifying to note that the United States Army's cavalry sword, Model 1913, perfected by George S Patton as a junior officer, is very similar to the Pattern 1908 and very obviously derived from it; in fact, a specimen of the Pattern 1908 was extensively trialled by the US Army before the Model 1913 was adopted.[51] The American sword also has a straight, narrow, thrusting blade, 35 inches long, but double edged. The guard is likewise a simple bowl in sheet steel but the grip does not compare with Fox's masterpiece. The scabbard was originally of stiffened webbing, an interesting innovation, but was later made of steel.

Cavalry Troopers' Swords 1878-1914

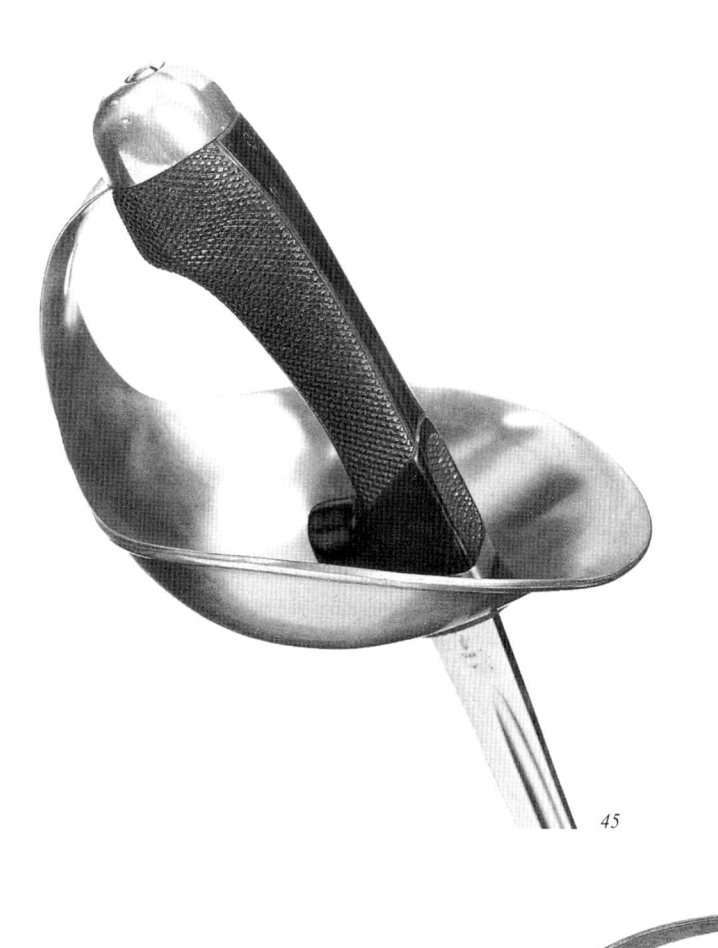

45 Sword, Cavalry, Pattern 1908, Mark I (top) and India Pattern 1908, Mark I - comparison of hilts

Guards: sheet steel in both cases.
Hilt mounts: pommel and ferrule at bottom of grip are of malleable cast iron in both cases.
Grips: dermatine or similar plastic (Pattern 1908, Mark I); walnut (India Pattern 1908, Mark I); grip lengths 6¾ and 5⅞in. respectively.
Note: The bowl of the India Pattern 1908, Mark I is smaller (4¾in. wide at its widest, against 5½in. for the Pattern 1908, Mark I) and there is no reinforcing piece on the outside.

(MoD Pattern Room, Nottingham)

(NAM 7812-12)

The dimensional relationship of cavalry sword patterns 1864-1899

Pattern	Length of blade (inches)	Length of grip (inches)	Weight of sword lb oz	Weight of scabbard lb oz	Length of scabbard (inches)	Notes
1864	35$^{1}/_{2}$	5	2 7$^{3}/_{4}$	2 1$^{1}/_{4}$	36$^{1}/_{4}$	
Experimental 1880 Converted	35$^{1}/_{2}$	5	2 2	1 15$^{3}/_{4}$	36$^{1}/_{4}$	
Experimental 1880 New	33	5	1 15	1 10	34	
Experimental 1881	33	5	2 1$^{1}/_{2}$	1 10	34	
1882 'Long', Converted	35$^{1}/_{2}$	5	2 4	1 12	36$^{1}/_{4}$	
1882 'Short', Converted	33	5	2 1$^{1}/_{2}$	1 10	34	
1882 'Long', New	35$^{3}/_{8}$	5	2 2$^{1}/_{2}$	1 11$^{1}/_{2}$	36$^{1}/_{4}$	
1882 'Short', New	33	5	2 0$^{1}/_{4}$	1 9$^{3}/_{4}$	34	
1884 Committee	34$^{1}/_{2}$	5$^{1}/_{4}$	2 5	1 6$^{1}/_{2}$	—	
1885	34$^{1}/_{2}$	5$^{3}/_{8}$	2 6	1 8	35$^{1}/_{2}$	Scabbard: Pattern 1885 Mark I
1890	34$^{1}/_{2}$	5$^{3}/_{8}$	2 9	1 14$^{1}/_{2}$	35$^{1}/_{2}$	Scabbard: Pattern 1885 Mark II
1899 New	33$^{1}/_{2}$	6	2 11	1 14$^{1}/_{4}$	34$^{1}/_{2}$	
1899 Converted	33$^{1}/_{2}$	6	2 11	1 14$^{1}/_{4}$	34$^{1}/_{2}$	Scabbard converted from Scabbard Pattern 1885 Mark I

Note: Weights are average: individual swords or scabbards might vary by up to 1 oz either way.

Chapter 3: Notes

1. The controversy lasted down to 1914 - see, for example, *The Cavalry Journal*, Vol II, 1907, pp76-79, and Vol III, 1908, pp194-98

2. *Ibid.*, Vol II, 1907, pp470-74.

3. *Ibid.*, Vol II, pp76-79 and Vol XIV, 1924, p108; and Baden-Powell's evidence to the Royal Commission investigating the South African War - answer to Question 19956 (Cd.1789) - London HMSO, (1903).

4. *LC* 2870, 1 January 1876.

5. Colonel Thomas Durand Baker (1837-93). Served in the Crimea, the Indian Mutiny, New Zealand, Second Afghan War. Quarter-Master General, War Office 1890-93.

6. The information in this paragraph is derived from a Memorandum prepared by Mole & Son in *Papers prepared for 1887 Royal Commission on War-like Stores - Section 17*, Ministry of Defence (MoD) Central Library.

7. See *Special Committee on Cavalry Swords and Scabbards - Reports and Proceedings, October 1884 to May 1885* - War Office, 1885

8. *Ibid.*, p30.

9. Mole Memorandum.

10. Arthur Lyttelton Annesley. Commissioned 11th Light Dragoons 1854. Service in Crimean War. Colonel 1877 and Assistant-Adjutant-General 1877-80. Adjutant-General, Bombay Army 1881-84.

11. See the *Report of Special Commission appointed by His Excellency the Governor-General in Council to enquire into the Organisation and Expenditure of the Army in India*, Simla, (1879). Note especially the evidence of Lieutenant-Colonel Lord Kerr and Major E A Wood (10th Hussars) in Vol II - Appendices, pp 242-332. For an account of this Commission (known as the Eden Commission after its chairman, Sir Ashley Eden), see Brian Robson 'The Eden Commission and the reform of the Indian Army 1879-1895', *JSAHR*, Vol LX, 1982, pp4-13.

12. Information in this and the next eight paragraphs is drawn from the 1884 Committee report.

13. *Report of the Royal Commission appointed to enquire into the system under which patterns of war-like stores are adopted and the stores obtained and passed for Her Majesty's service* (Cd 5062) London, HMSO, (1887) - answer to Question 5504.
    Henry Thomas Arbuthnot (1834-1919). Commissioned Royal Artillery 1853. Service in the Crimea and the Indian Mutiny. Colonel 1879 and Superintendent, Royal Small Arms Factory, Enfield 1880-87. Retired as honorary Major-General 1887.

14. *Ibid.*, Question 5542.

15. Mole Memorandum.

16. 1887 *Royal Commission*, Question 1204.

17. Mole Memorandum.

18. Information in this and succeeding paragraphs from report of 1884 Committee.

19. Sir Drury Curzon Drury Lowe (1830-1908). Commissioned 17th Lancers 1854. Service in the Crimea, Indian Mutiny, Zulu War, First Anglo-Boer War and Egypt 1882. Inspector-General of Cavalry 1885-90.

20. *LC* 4854, 1 January 1886.

21. 1887 *Royal Commission*, Question 724.

22. *Ibid.*, Question 1204.

23. *Ibid.*

24. See report of 1884 Committee.

25. See *Reports on alleged failures of cavalry swords and Pistols at Suakin* (Cd 5633) HMSO, (1889).

26. *Ibid.*, for information in this and the succeeding five paragraphs.

27. Colonel W H King-Harman, *Report on English and Foreign Swords (Cavalry)* War Office reference 77/26/1786 (September 1889).

28. Sir Frederick Bramwell (1818-1903). A distinguished civil and mechanical engineer, a Fellow of the Royal Society and former President of both the Institute of Civil Engineers and the Institute of Mechanical Engineers. A member of the Ordnance Committee from 1881. Benjamin Baker, (later Sir), a distinguished civil engineer.

29. *Cavalry Swords: Report by Sir F Bramwell and B Baker Esq, on best form and material to be employed in manufacture and tests to be applied,* 1st August 1889. War Office, (1889).

30. Information in this and succeeding paragraph from *Cavalry Swords*, a précis prepared in the War Office c1890. Some information can be gleaned also from RSAF's Annual Accounts for the period, printed in the annual volumes of *Parliamentary Papers*.

31. *LC* 6477, 1 September 1891.

32. *LC* 5731, 1 May 1889.

33. See the evidence of Sir Henry Brackenbury (Question 1600) before the *Royal Commission appointed to enquire into the military preparations and other matters concerned with the war in South Africa* (Cd 1789) London HMSO, (1903). Brackenbury stated that reserves had been run down to 80 in preparation for the introduction of a new sword.

34. *LC* 9880, 1 December 1899.

35. See pattern sword (No 1005) at The Pattern Room, Nottingham.

36. See note 33 above.

37. *Ibid.*, answer to Question 17230.

38. *Ibid.*, answer to Question 19945. Baden-Powell also remarked on the failure to keep the swords sharp, as compared with the Indian Army.

39. *Ibid.*, answer to Question 19962.

40. See Enclosure 1 on War Office file 54/Cavalry/430.

41. *Ibid.*, letter dated 4 July 1902.

42. Reference War Office file 54/Cavalry/430, dated 10 March 1903.

43. Abolished by Army Order 39 of March 1903, and reintroduced by Army Order 158 of June 1909.

44. The information in this and the succeeding six paragraphs is taken from a précis prepared for the Army Council in 1906 - see War Office file 54/Cavalry/861.

45. Sir John French, later 1st Earl of Ypres (1852-1925). Commissioned Militia 1870, into 8th Hussars 1875. Service in Sudan 1884-85 and South Africa 1899-1902, where he commanded the cavalry. Later Chief of the Imperial General Staff and Commander-in-Chief British Expeditionary Force 1914. Douglas Haig, 1st Earl (1861-1928). Commissioned 7th Hussars 1885. Service in Sudan 1897-98, South Africa 1899-1902. C-in-C France 1915-18. Sir Michael Rimington (1858-1928). Commissioned 6th Dragoons 1881. Service in Bechuanaland 1884-85, Zululand 1888, South Africa 1899-1900. Inspector of Cavalry in India. Sir Henry Scobell (1859-1912). Commissioned 2nd Dragoons (Royal Scots Greys) 1879. Service in South Africa 1899-1902. Commanding 1st Cavalry Brigade at Aldershot.

46. Information in this and succeeding fourteen paragraphs from War Office file 54/Cavalry/757, which contains, *inter alia*, the minutes of the Committee's meetings.

47. *LC* 15151, 1 August 1910 and *LC* 15212, 1 October 1910; see also pattern sword (1249) at the Pattern Room, Nottingham.

48. *LC* 15388, 1 March 1911.

49. *LC* 16089, 1 September 1912; see also the pattern sword (No 1295) at the Pattern Room, Nottingham, dated 28 March 1912.

50. The pattern sword, at the Pattern Room, Nottingham, is marked as approved 22 February 1918.

51. Peterson, *op. cit.*, p37.

4. Cavalry Officers' Swords

Before 1914, officers' swords were not an official issue and officers purchased them privately from retailers or manufacturers such as Gill, Tatham and Prosser in the earlier period, and Henry Wilkinson & Co pre-eminently in the second half of the nineteenth century.

This situation had two important consequences: in the first place, individual swords often varied in small (and, occasionally, not so small) ways from the prescribed pattern, and, in the second place, the Army authorities tended to be relatively relaxed in their imposition of uniformity so that many regiments devised their own patterns, the precise authority for which is generally obscure but tended to be hallowed by custom. A further consequence of the system of private purchase was that officers' swords were subject to no official standards of proof and suitability, although probably in practice most officers' swords were at least equal in quality to those of the other ranks; Wilkinsons in the later period based their reputation on the quality of their blades and set the standard for other makers to equal. Nevertheless, one must doubt whether patterns such as the 1821 infantry sword would have been adopted if the Royal Small Arms Factory Enfield had been involved.

Given that officers frequently had their swords tailored to fit the individual, wide variations exist among surviving specimens of the prescribed patterns.

The introduction of standard patterns of sword for the other ranks of the cavalry in 1788 was accompanied by an instruction that the officers' swords were to be uniform with those of the men.[1] By and large, that instruction seems to have been followed in the light cavalry as far as the service sword was concerned; between 1788 and 1796 they carried rather more ornate versions of the knucklebow-hilted swords prescribed for the troopers, (Plate 46).[2] Officers' swords can usually be distinguished by the presence of decoration on the blade, by the presence of a ferrule at the base of the grip and by the generally higher quality.[3]

In Full Dress and when dismounted or out of barracks, officers of some regiments carried more elaborate patterns of regimental design. The 10th Light Dragoons, always an elite regiment, carried a version with a particularly ornate hilt after 1788, (Plates 47, 48). This has a French flavour about it although it may be of Austrian origin since a similar pattern was carried earlier in at least one Austrian hussar regiment.[4] George, Prince of Wales was Colonel of the 10th and a notorious dabbler in matters of uniform and he may well have had a hand in the adoption of this pattern. Two specimens at Windsor - CH50, by Bland & Foster (1787-91) and CH

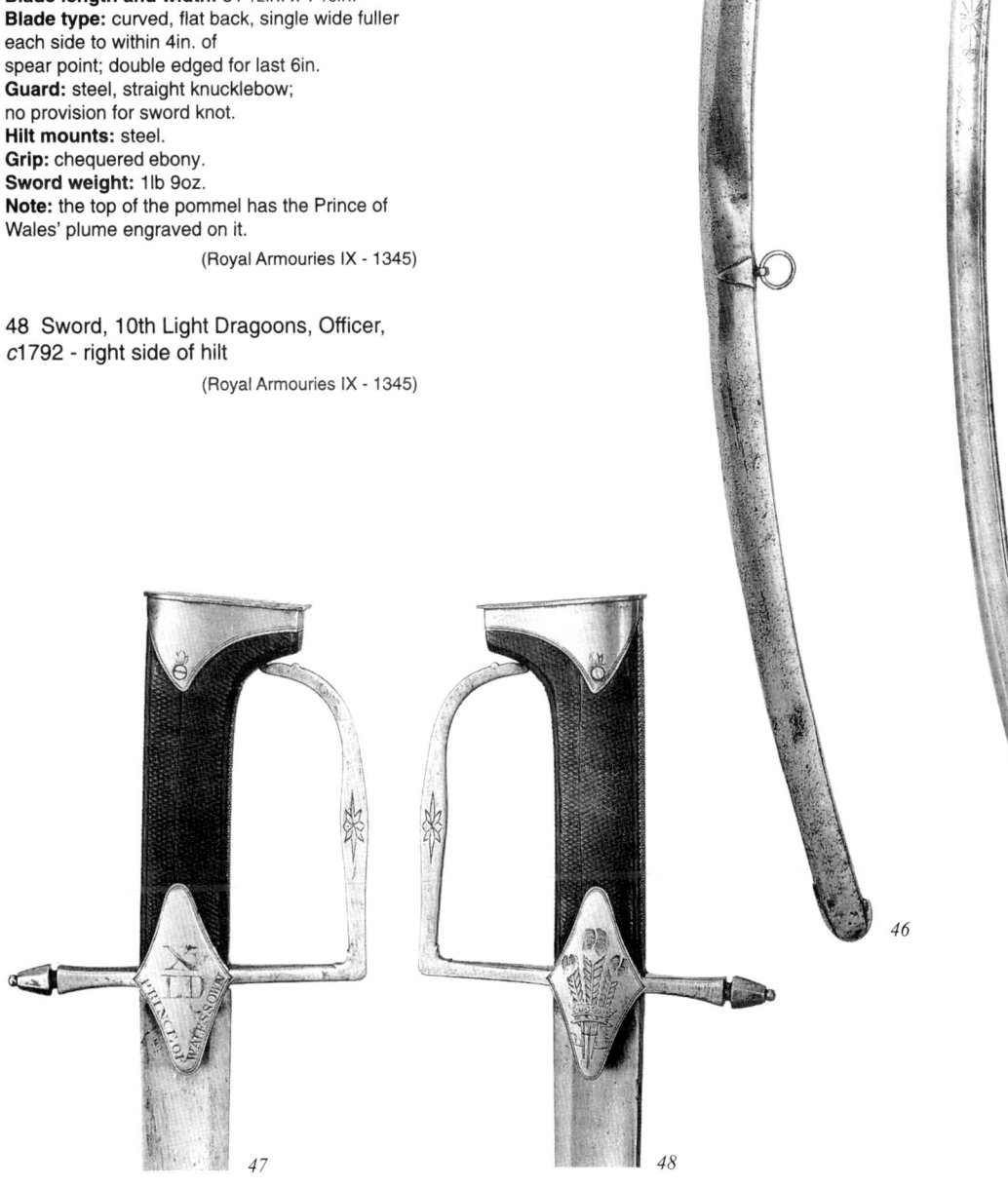

Cavalry Officers' Swords

46 Sword, 16th Light Dragoons, Officer, *c*1788

Blade length and width: 33in. x 1⁷/₁₆in.
Blade type: moderately curved, one narrow fuller near back and one broader fuller, of the French style known as '*à la Montmorency*'.
Guard: straight knucklebow in steel.
Hilt mounts: steel.
Grip: wood, covered in leather.
Scabbard: steel or wrought iron.
Note: blade marked 'The 16th Light Dragoons' and 'J.J.Runkel Sohlingen'. Scabbard by Woolley & Co (1790-97).

(NAM 6005-22)

47 Sword, 10th Light Dragoons, Officer, *c*1792

Blade length and width: 31½in. x 1³/₈in.
Blade type: curved, flat back, single wide fuller each side to within 4in. of
spear point; double edged for last 6in.
Guard: steel, straight knucklebow;
no provision for sword knot.
Hilt mounts: steel.
Grip: chequered ebony.
Sword weight: 1lb 9oz.
Note: the top of the pommel has the Prince of Wales' plume engraved on it.

(Royal Armouries IX - 1345)

48 Sword, 10th Light Dragoons, Officer, *c*1792 - right side of hilt

(Royal Armouries IX - 1345)

46

47

48

75

Cavalry Officers' Swords

49 Sword, 30th Light Dragoons, Officer, 1794-6

Blade type: curved, flat back, single fuller each side to within 1/4in. of spear point; double edged for last 7in.
Guard: steel, straight knucklebow; no provision for sword knot.
Hilt mounts: steel.
Grip: ebony.
Scabbard: wood, covered with leather, with steel locket, band and chape, and steel edges. Two loose rings, on locket and band.
Note: virtually identical with 10th Light Dragoons sword of same period. Blade by Thomas Gill.

(NAM 6310-119)

50 Sword, 30th Light Dragoons, Officer, 1794-6 - left side of hilt

(NAM 6310-119)

51 Sword, 30th Light Dragoons, Officer, 1794-6 - right side of hilt

(NAM 6310-119)

52 Sword, 7th Light Dragoons, Officer, c1794

Blade length and width: 31in. x 1 7/16in.
Blade type: curved, flat back, spear point, single broad fuller each side.
Guard: straight knucklebow in gilt brass, with double langets each side.
Hilt mounts: gilt brass.
Grip: wood, apparently bound in leather, and encased in gilt brass in fretwork design.
Scabbard: black leather, with elaborate gilt brass chape, locket and band, loose rings on locket and band. Left side of locket engraved 'VIILD'.
Note: almost identical swords with steel hilts were in use at same period in the 10th Light Dragoons.

(NAM 9406-218)

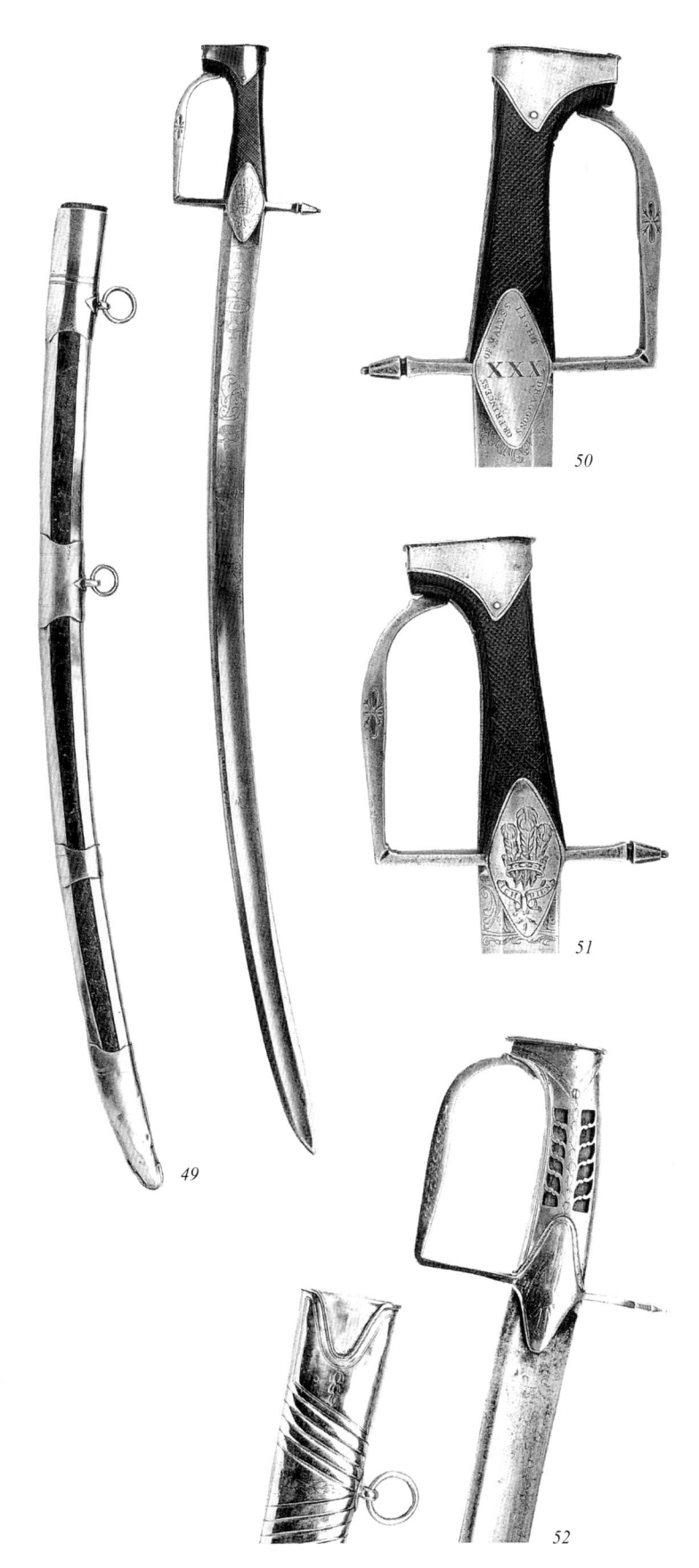

56, by Foster (1792-97) - show that these swords were in use in the period 1790-92, and may have been in use as early as 1788. A virtually identical sword was in use in the 30th (Princess of Wales') Light Dragoons during the short life of that regiment from 1794 to 1796, (Plates 49, 50, 51). Swords of the same pattern were also carried by the 7th Light Dragoons[5] and by at least two Yeomanry regiments.

A more elaborate version of this particular pattern, in which the grip is encased in a pierced or fretwork metal covering, in gilt brass or steel, also appears to date from the early 1790s. In the case of the 10th, the swords of this pattern (in steel) were purchased for the officers by the Prince of Wales himself in 1792,[6] and presumably replaced the previous pattern, although they may simply have been carried off duty, at evening functions. Those of the 7th Light Dragoons had a gilt brass hilt, (Plate 52).

Prior to 1788, the 15th Light Dragoons had carried as their service sword a pattern incorporating a folding three-bar hilt, (Plates 53, 54); a similar sword was carried at this time by some French light cavalry regiments from which it may have been adopted.[7] It almost certainly remained in use in the 15th after 1788.

The lack of absolute certainty as to the form of the Pattern 1788 Heavy Cavalry troopers' sword produces a similar lack of certainty as to the officers' sword since officially the two were to be the same. A sword in the NAM, (9502-70) made by Thomas Gill, dated 1794 on the blade and bearing the initials of George Mellifont, who served in the 4th (Royal Irish) Dragoon Guards from 1790-1800, is virtually identical to the Pattern 1788 troopers' swords identified in Chapter 2, although the outer bar on each side has been removed at some stage and the blade shortened to $36^{1}/_{2}$ inches, (Plate 55). Two other swords, with steel-barred hilts of not dissimilar form, are also in the NAM. The first, (Plates 56, 57) may have belonged to Lieutenant-Colonel John Callow, of the 3rd (King's Own) Dragoons, who served in the regiment from 1768 to 1799, when he was appointed Lieutenant-Governor of Quebec. The second sword, (Plate 58) is dated 1782 on the blade. Yet another sword of broadly similar type, marked 'KOD' [King's Own Dragoons] is in the Perth City Museum, (Inventory number 3C/1956).

What may be Pattern 1788 officers' swords at Windsor, (Laking 751 and Windsor 759, (originally Laking 749)) have bright steel barred hilts of Inniskilling form, with straight, decorated blades and white shagreen grip coverings. It seems probable, however, that these are Household Cavalry swords and they are therefore dealt with in Chapter 6.

Thus, while it cannot be claimed that a Pattern 1788 heavy cavalry officers' sword has been identified with certainty, possible examples all display the characteristics of a broad, straight blade and barred hilt of 'Inniskilling' form.

For dismounted wear, heavy cavalry officers were accustomed to carrying a lighter, smaller sword of regimental pattern. The *Standing Orders* of the 2nd Dragoons in 1795 refer to officers' 'broadswords' and to 'regimental small swords', and even the

Cavalry Officers' Swords

53

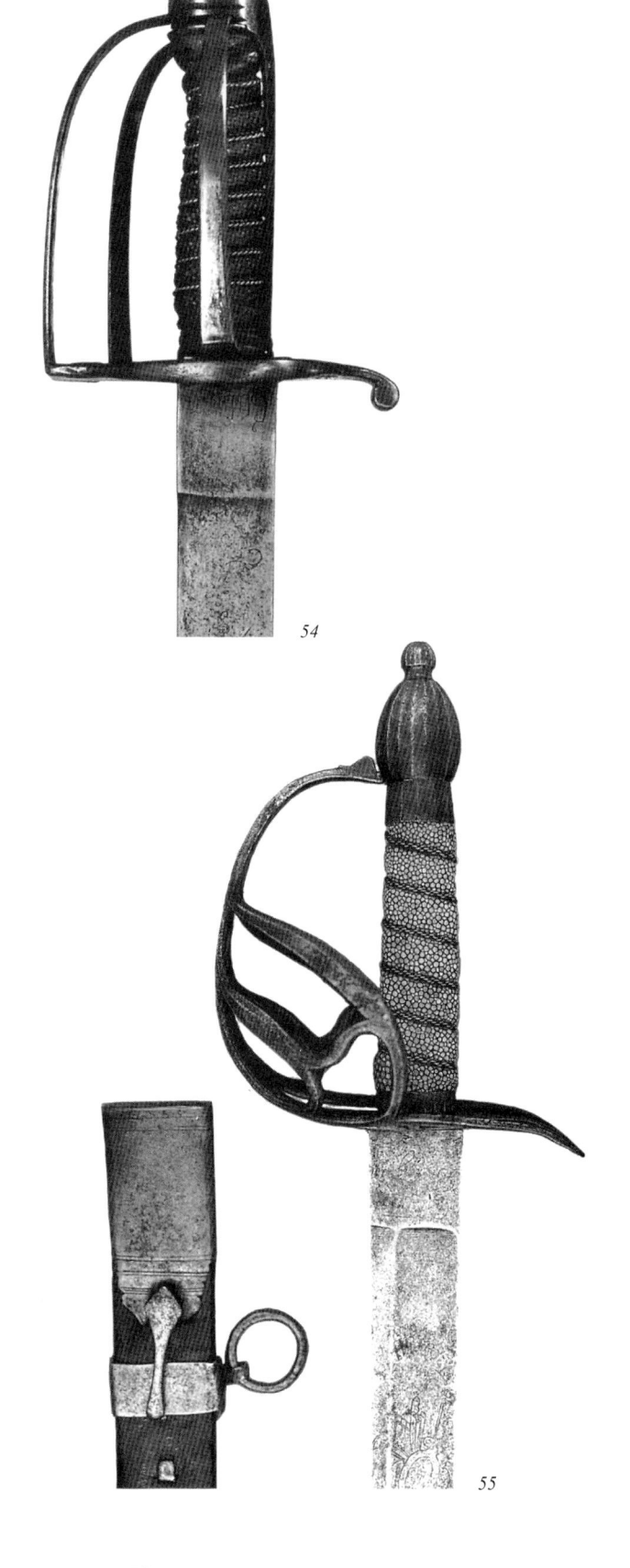

54

53 Sword, 15th Light Dragoons, Officer, *c*1790

Blade length and width: 36in. x 1¼in.
Blade type: very slightly curved, flat back, no fuller, single edged, clipped point.
Guard: steel, straight knucklebow.
Hilt mounts: steel.
Grip: wood, covered with fishskin and bound with steel wire; inside length 4¼in.
Sword weight: 2lb 3oz.
Note: Blade made by Cullum and marked 'King's Light Dragoons'.

(Royal Armouries IX - 331)

54 Sword, 15th Light Dragoons, Officer, *c*1790 - guard expanded

(Royal Armouries IX - 331)

55 Sword, Heavy Cavalry, Officer, Pattern 1788

Blade length and width: 36½in. x 1½in.
Blade type: straight, flat back.
Guard: wrought iron basket.
Hilt mounts: wrought iron.
Grip: wood, covered with fishskin and bound with copper wire.
Scabbard: black leather with wrought iron chape with long frog hook and later addition of two suspension rings.

(NAM 9502-70)

55

Cavalry Officers' Swords

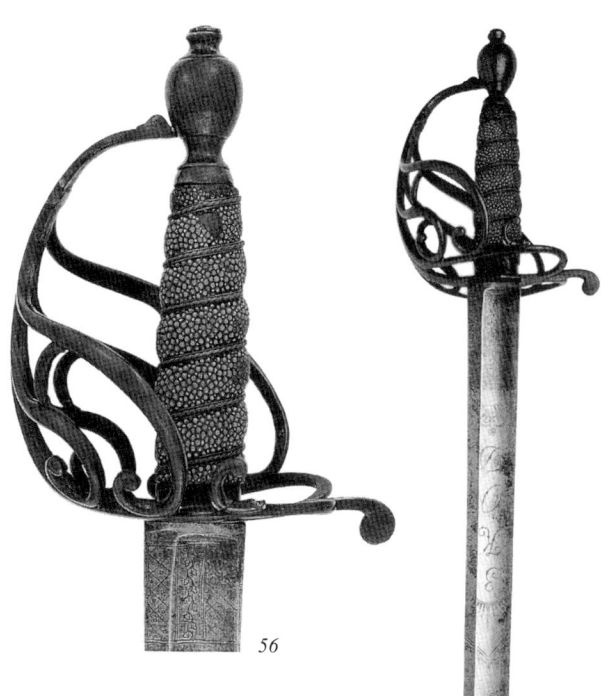

56, 57 Sword, Heavy Cavalry, Officer, Pattern 1788

Blade length and width: 37 1/4in. x 1 7/16in.
Blade type: straight, flat back.
Guard: wrought iron basket.
Hilt mounts: wrought iron.
Grip: wood, covered with sharkskin and bound with silver wire.
Sword weight: 2lb 5 3/4oz.
Note: the third or outside bar on the right side of the guard is missing.

(NAM 6005-71)

58 Sword, Heavy Cavalry, Officer, c1788

Blade length and width: 35 1/4in. x 1 3/8in.
Blade type: straight, flat back, single edged, spear point, single wide fuller.
Guard: steel basket hilt.
Hilt mounts: steel, with ovoid faceted pommel.
Grip: wood, covered with white sharkskin, bound with German silver wire. Inside length 6 in.
Note: blade by Runkel may be as early as 1782; marked with cypher of George III. Similar to the sword ascribed to Lieutenant-Colonel Callow. (NAM 6005-71).

(NAM 7708-3)

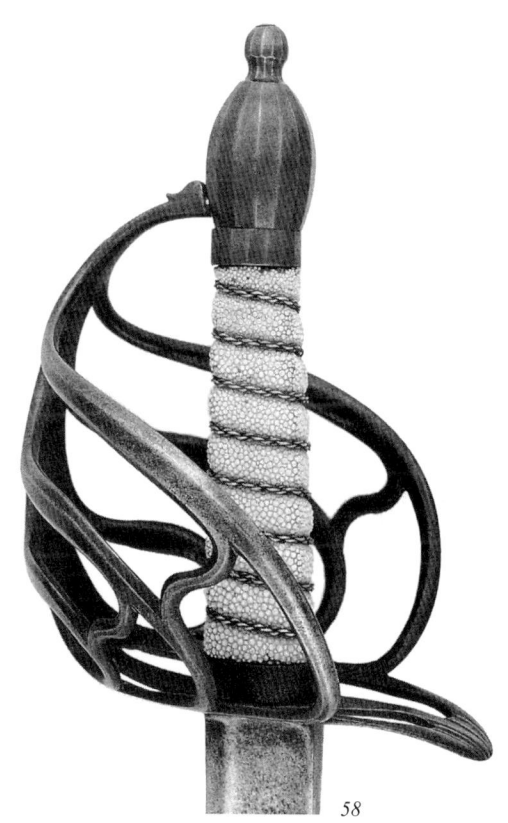

56
57
58

79

sergeants seem to have had a lighter sword for dismounted wear.[8] This was a logical development, given the length and clumsiness of the Pattern 1788 service sword and it is probable that some of these 'smallswords' were similar in pattern to the boatshell-hilted swords formally introduced in 1796, (see below).

The use of light pattern swords when dismounted appears to have been prevalent in light cavalry regiments also. A light pattern sword of the 16th Light Dragoons, however, followed the pattern of the 1786 infantry officers' sword, (Plate 129).

When the Pattern 1796 stirrup-hilted sword was introduced for light cavalry troopers, the principle of uniformity between officers' and troopers' swords was followed relatively closely, the officers' swords following the same general pattern but usually with decorated blades - sometimes blued and gilt, (Plate 59), sometimes simply etched or engraved,[9] and frequently with slightly more ornate hilts. The officers' hilts frequently show variations in their precise detail, as one would expect - these variations including the shape of the langet and of the ear on the backpiece, the absence of langets, the form of the right angle at the bottom of the stirrup and the faceting of the backpiece and stirrup.

Almost inevitably, the 10th Light Dragoons had their own different and more ornate versions. The first of these versions has a straight, squared, gilt knucklebow, with flat-topped pommel and decorated backpiece and diamond-shaped langets bearing the regiment's title and number and the royal cypher of George III or the regimental badge.[10] The stylistic affinity of these hilts with those of the earlier officers' swords of this regiment, (Plate 47) suggests that these particular 1796 pattern variations date from the years immediately after 1796 and presumably followed on from the 1788 patterns.

A second version of the Pattern 1796 officers' sword for the 10th follows much more closely the basic pattern but with the regimental badge of the Prince of Wales' feathers in silver fixed to langets of somewhat elaborate shield shape, (Plate 60). This sword is shown in Sir William Beechey's portrait of Sir Bellingham Graham, exhibited at the Royal Academy in 1814. For this and stylistic reasons, it seems likely that this version appeared later than the version with diamond-shaped langets and probably some time after 1800.

The stirrup-hilted swords of the 1796 pattern, with their heavy scabbards, were also an encumbrance when dismounted and from shortly after 1801 light cavalry officers in Full or Evening Dress began to carry mameluke-hilted sabres of regimental pattern and differing degrees of ostentation. The same development among Royal Artillery officers was ascribed in later years by General Cavalié Mercer to the influence of Abercromby's Egyptian campaign of 1801-02, and this explanation is almost certainly correct since the same development took place in the French army at the same time. But a second influence was the experience of light cavalry officers in India where the mameluke hilt, with an Oriental blade, was frequently carried by

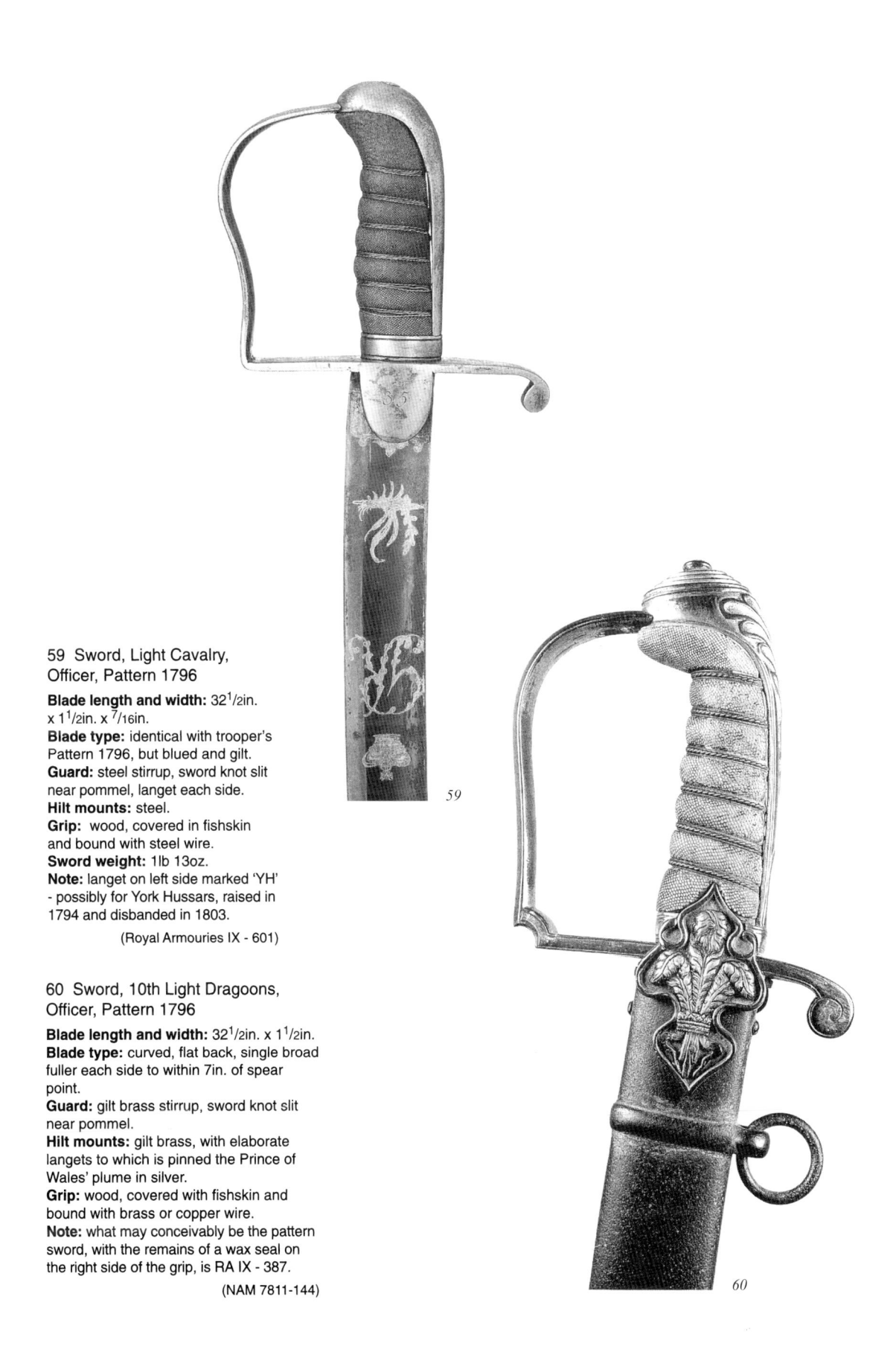

Cavalry Officers' Swords

59 Sword, Light Cavalry, Officer, Pattern 1796

Blade length and width: 32 1/2in. x 1 1/2in. x 7/16in.
Blade type: identical with trooper's Pattern 1796, but blued and gilt.
Guard: steel stirrup, sword knot slit near pommel, langet each side.
Hilt mounts: steel.
Grip: wood, covered in fishskin and bound with steel wire.
Sword weight: 1lb 13oz.
Note: langet on left side marked 'YH' - possibly for York Hussars, raised in 1794 and disbanded in 1803.

(Royal Armouries IX - 601)

60 Sword, 10th Light Dragoons, Officer, Pattern 1796

Blade length and width: 32 1/2in. x 1 1/2in.
Blade type: curved, flat back, single broad fuller each side to within 7in. of spear point.
Guard: gilt brass stirrup, sword knot slit near pommel.
Hilt mounts: gilt brass, with elaborate langets to which is pinned the Prince of Wales' plume in silver.
Grip: wood, covered with fishskin and bound with brass or copper wire.
Note: what may conceivably be the pattern sword, with the remains of a wax seal on the right side of the grip, is RA IX - 387.

(NAM 7811-144)

59

60

81

Army officers, including Wellington himself. This type of sword was basically Persian in origin but from Persia it spread outwards to Egypt, Turkey and India.

Sabres of this type are shown as early as 1807 in Denis Dighton's portraits of officers of the 7th and 15th Light Dragoons (Hussars) and they were almost certainly being carried before 1807. In due course, all those regiments which were designated hussars in the early part of the nineteenth century produced their own patterns, differing in the details of the decoration on the hilt, in the form of the curved blade and perhaps most notably in the ornateness of the scabbard, which seem originally to have been predominantly of leather-covered wood; steel scabbards became universal later in the century.[11] Charles Farmer, in his *Universal Dictionary*, published in 1810, stated that: 'The officers of Light Dragoons wear a steel sabre with a steel scabbard and stirrup hilt; and for a frock sword one of the same construction with the sabre, only, much lighter, with a leather scabbard'.[12]

The practice in the heavy cavalry of carrying a lighter sword when dismounted was officially recognised in 1796 with the introduction of a light, straight-bladed sword, with a gilt-brass boatshell guard and mounts, and a silver wire-bound grip, (Plate 61).[13] The top of the knucklebow was usually screwed to the pommel although sometimes pegged into it. The scabbard was of black leather, with gilt-brass locket, band and chape (embodying a shoe), and with two loose rings, (Plate 62). The design of this sword goes back well before 1796 - a specimen in the Royal Collection at Windsor, for example, (Windsor Catalogue 860) can be dated from the maker's name to pre-1792, and a closely similar hilt was in use in the Swedish cavalry even earlier.[14] It was almost certainly not a case of introducing a new pattern so much as standardising on an existing pattern. The original blades appear to have been lenticular in cross-section, with a narrow central fuller.[15]

The introduction of this light pattern sword accompanied the introduction of a new, heavy cavalry officers' service sword.[16] The blade is virtually identical with that of the Pattern 1796 heavy cavalry troopers' sword - that is to say, a straight, broad blade with a single wide fuller each side and a hatchet point, (see Chapter 2). But in the case of officers' swords it was frequently decorated in blued and gilt designs, (Plate 63), and more rarely in incised or etched decoration. The guard was of a new design of so-called 'ladder' pattern in steel (this is known by some collectors as the 'first honeysuckle pattern'), (Plate 64); the backpiece and pommel follow the same form as those of the troopers' sword, and the scabbard was virtually identical.

What appears to be the pattern sword is at Windsor (Laking 858) where it is catalogued as having been purchased as a pattern sword for officers of heavy dragoons; the blade is by Runkel but the hilt was made by Prosser. One suspects that it is based on a German or Austrian design. Farmer described it and the dismounted sword thus:

Cavalry Officers' Swords

61, 62 Sword, Heavy Cavalry, Officer, Dress, Pattern 1796

Blade length and width: 32³/₈in. x 1in.
Blade type: straight, flat back, single fuller each side to within 1in. of spear point.
Guard: gilt brass knucklebow and boatshell.
Hilt mounts: gilt brass.
Grip: wood, bound with silver wire.
Scabbard: black leather with gilt brass locket, frog hook, two loose rings, band and chape.
Note: middle band of scabbard and ring missing.

(NAM 7310-62)

63 Sword, Heavy Cavalry, Officer, Undress, Pattern 1796 - decorated blade

Note: the blued and gilt blade is typical of decorated blades of this period.

(NAM 6702-9)

64 Sword, Heavy Cavalry, Officer, Undress, Pattern 1796 - close-up of hilt

(NAM 6702-9)

61

62

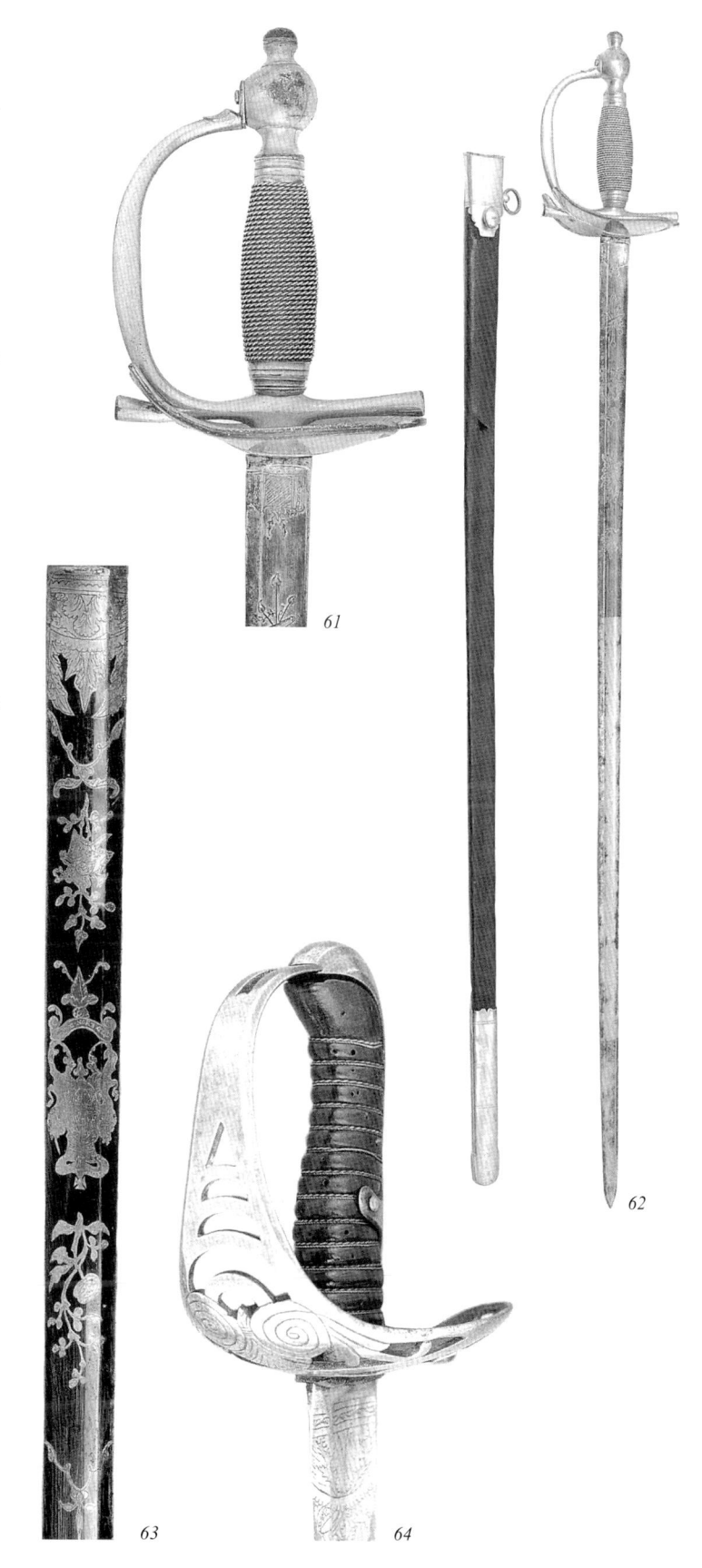

63 *64*

> 'Heavy dragoon officers wear a broad, straight, cut and thrust blade with a hanger point, mounted with a hilt with a shell as a guard. This is called their field sword or sword for service. They have also a second sword, called a frock sword, which has a two-edged blade, of lighter construction than their field sword. It is mounted with a gilt hilt, called a boat shell hilt. This is to replace their heavy field sword, and is worn chiefly when the officer is dismounted.

This new pattern is shown very clearly in drawings of officers of the 2nd Dragoons of the King's German Legion, c1810,[17] and in a fine portrait of Major Edward Wildman, of the 6th Dragoon Guards, c1818, now in the collection of the Hon. David McAlpine.[18] A fairly early sword of this pattern in the NAM, (Plate 65) appears to have belonged to Lieutenant H W Hutton, who joined the 4th Dragoon Guards in 1805 and seems to have left the regiment in 1810.

As discussed in Chapter 2, the Pattern 1796 heavy cavalry blade was an unsatisfactory fighting sword, heavy and clumsy, and almost equally unsatisfactory for cutting or thrusting. Troopers could do little about it, apart from minor modifications to the hilt and point, but officers could, and did, please themselves about the swords they actually carried for fighting, and in the second decade of the nineteenth century, possibly in the closing years of the Napoleonic War, a new type of blade began to appear on some officers' swords. This was a so-called 'pipe-backed' blade, in which a prominent round rib or pipe ran along the back of the blade. (It is sometimes known as a 'ramrod-back'). In what would seem to be the earliest form, the pipe runs almost to the point although since the blade narrows in thickness the last few inches tend to become in effect double edged. The purpose of the pipe was to enable the blade to be made narrower and better adapted for thrusting while retaining the same stiffness and strength. Later forms of the blade have a very prominent false edge added for the last 9 or 10 inches, (Plate 66). The purpose of this false edge is not entirely clear but may have been to add weight to the end of the blade to provide a better balance or more stiffness for cutting.

The precise origins of this blade on British swords is not known. Pipe-backed blades were in use in the French light cavalry from as early as 1805 and it may ultimately be derived from Oriental models - another relic perhaps of the French and British Egyptian campaigning of 1798-1802. At least two British specimens bear the rubric 'Prossers's Invention 1818'.[19] Given the evidence from the Windsor archives that Prosser was frequently employed to make up new patterns of swords and scabbards for George, Prince Regent,[20] it may well be that he was responsible, if not for the pipe-backed blade, for the addition of the prominent false edge. It may be significant that when the new Pattern 1821 swords appeared for troopers, the pattern swords themselves were made by Prosser, (see below).

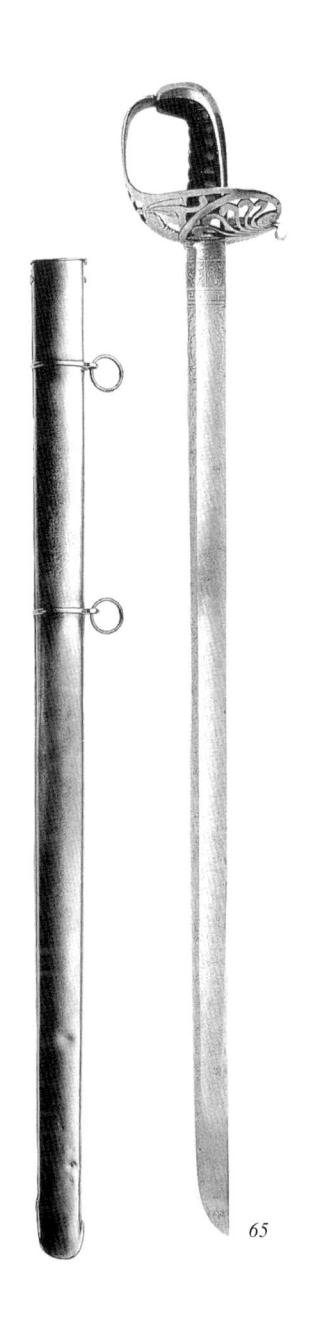

Cavalry Officers' Swords

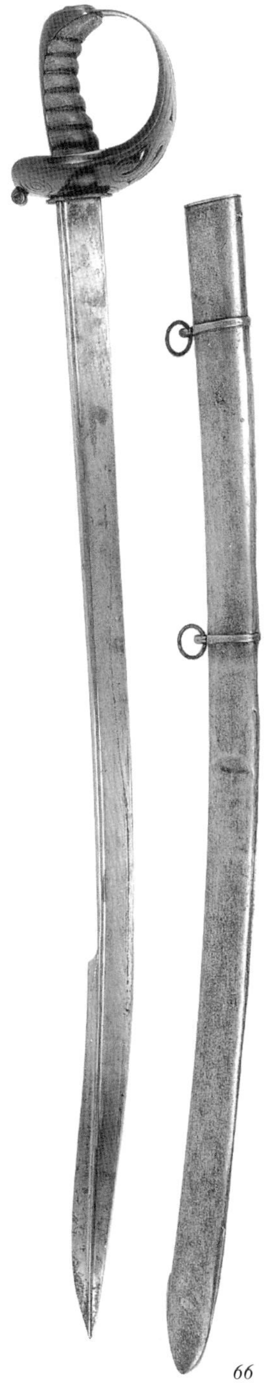

66 Sword, Cavalry, Officer, *c*1820

Blade length and width: 34 1/4in. x 1 3/8in.
Blade type: curved, pipe-backed to spear point, very prominent false edge for last 11 in.
Guard: steel bowl, pierced and engraved, sword knot slit near pommel.
Hilt mounts: steel backpiece and stepped pommel, with tang button.
Grip: fishskin on wood, bound originally with steel wire.
Scabbard: steel, with two narrow bands and loose rings, narrow shoe.
Note: the blade is engraved with battle honours of 4th Light Dragoons. Grip has been damaged and bent back.

(SUSM 1987-78)

67 Sword, Cavalry, Officer, *c*1820

Note: the curious, almost Celtic, decoration quite unlike any other contemporary British regulation pattern.

(SUSM 1987-78)

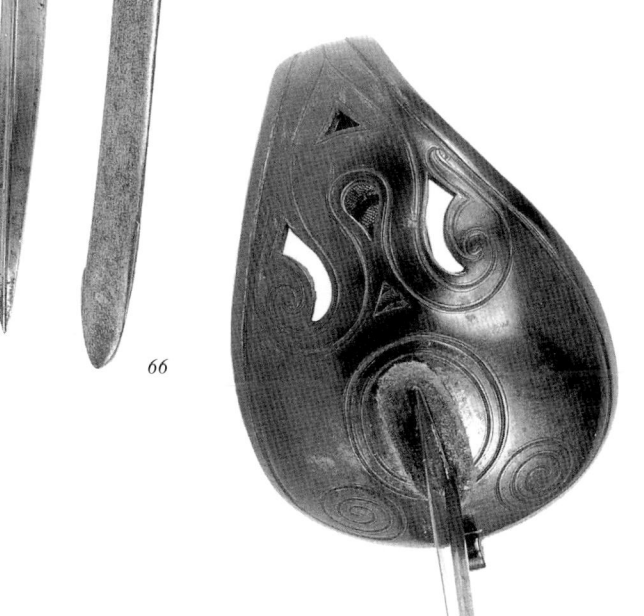

65

66

67

65 Sword, Heavy Cavalry, Officer, Undress, Pattern 1796

Blade length and width: 35in. x 1 1/2in.
Blade type: identical with Heavy Cavalry Troopers', Pattern 1796.
Guard: steel basket of 'ladder' (or 'first honeysuckle') pattern, with sword knot slit near pommel.
Hilt mounts: steel.
Grip: wood, covered with leather.
Scabbard: steel, with markedly concave mouth and two split rings for suspensions.
Note: recorded as belonging to H W Hutton, who joined the 4th Dragoon Guards in 1805 and retired in 1810. The blade is inscribed with the name of the regiment.

(NAM 6706-40-17)

These pipe-backed blades appear most numerously on swords fitted with versions of the Pattern 1796 stirrup hilt. But specimens also exist with Pattern 1796 heavy cavalry officers' 'ladder' hilts, (see, for example, SUSM 1994-53), and at least two specimens are known to the author with Pattern 1803 infantry officers' hilts. The example in the NAM, (8104-47), is marked to an officer of the 32nd Foot and bears the battle honours 'Peninsula' and 'Waterloo', awarded to the regiment in 1825 and 1827 respectively; it is clearly a re-bladed sword. A blade of this kind, mated to an unusual, bolt-on, three-bar, folding hilt, in the NAM, (8704-34) was made for an officer of the 3rd Bombay Light Cavalry, raised in 1820.

It has been suggested that this blade represents a new 'Waterloo Pattern', introduced between the Patterns 1796 and 1821.[21] It has to be said, however, that, as far as the present author is aware, with one possible exception, none of these blades can be dated positively to before June 1815, and there is no hard evidence that any of them were actually carried at Waterloo, although the possibility cannot be excluded. Such scanty documentary evidence as exists suggests strongly that no new regulation pattern was introduced between 1796-1821. (In passing, it may be noted that the pipe-backed blade with prominent false edge appeared also in the Pattern 1827 Naval Officers' sword).[22]

Note has, however, to be taken of a particular group of swords in which the pipe-back with prominent false edge is mated to an entirely new form of bowl hilt, (Plate 67).[23] This bowl guard is made of sheet steel, with a curious engraved or chased and pierced design which is almost Celtic in flavour. The piercings vary slightly between specimens and cannot be regarded as of significance, probably reflecting only the different makers. Specimens can be related to at least three regiments (2nd Dragoons, 3rd Dragoon Guards and 4th Dragoons); they would therefore seem to have been designed for heavy cavalry regiments in the first instance.

The earliest date that can be ascribed to the specimens known to the author is 1815 when the apparent owner, James Hadden, joined the 3rd Dragoon Guards.[24] The specimen in the SUSM would appear to be not earlier than 1819, based on the dates of award of the battle honours on the blade. The only reliable pictorial evidence is in a watercolour by Denis Dighton of a group of officers of the 2nd Dragoons, dated 1818, in which two officers are shown with what appears to be this hilt.[25] Another painting by Dighton shows the Union Brigade charging at Waterloo, with a 2nd Dragoons sergeant brandishing what might just possibly be this sword, although this is by no means clear.[26] A specimen in NAM by Odell of London can be dated between 1811-17, (NAM 9503-19).

Taking all the evidence into account, the likeliest date of introduction of this particular pattern is 1816-17. As with the pipe-backed blade considered earlier, there is no documentary evidence to suggest that this was in any way a regulation pattern or that it was carried by all the officers in any one regiment.

The real significance of these pipe-backed blades emerges in 1822 when the first edition of *Dress Regulations* prescribed new patterns of sword for both heavy and light cavalry officers which were to have pipe-backed blades, along with the infantry officers' sword. (Given the date of publication of these *Regulations*, it is clear that the new patterns had been adopted in 1821, at the same time as the parallel patterns for troopers (see Chapter 2); the new officers' patterns are therefore referred to here as the Patterns 1821).

For heavy cavalry officers, the *Regulations* prescribed two swords. The Dress sword was simply the Pattern 1796 boatshell-hilted sword, (Plate 61). The Undress (or service) sword was described thus: 'Steel basket hilt, pommel and shell; black fishskin grip with silver twisted wire; plain steel blade, to cut and thrust, thirty six inches long, one and a quarter inches wide at the shoulder'. The scabbard was to be of plain steel.

This description, confusing and ambiguous as it is, makes it quite clear that this was not simply the old 'ladder' hilted sword of 1796 whose dimensions were quite different. The reference to the new blade being made to cut and thrust makes it clear that the blade was intended to be curved, and the description of the grip is different, the majority of surviving Pattern 1796 swords having leather-covered grips.

The term 'plain blade' means in this context an unfullered, rather than an undecorated blade and the contemporary evidence shows that the new sword had a moderately curved, unfullered, pipe-backed blade, with a pierced basket guard of honeysuckle pattern (known to some collectors as the 'second honeysuckle pattern') which was to remain virtually unchanged for heavy cavalry officers down to 1912. A portrait of an officer of the 1st (Royal) Dragoons, *c*1832, shows this hilt exceptionally clearly,[27] and it is shown with almost photographic clarity in a painting of Captain John Carnegie of Tarrie in the uniform of the 2nd Dragoons in which he served from 1823 to 1830, (Plate 68). Below the picture, in the possession of the Earl of Southesk, hangs the actual sword, with its honeysuckle hilt, (Plate 69).

Other early swords of this pattern include one by Thomas Gill (1818-37), in the NAM where it is ascribed to Colonel Philip Dorville, (Plate 70), who was in the 1st Dragoons from 1795 to 1827, and two swords in the Royal Armouries (IX-836 and 1062), bearing the cypher of King George IV (1820-30).

Although the honeysuckle hilt remained virtually unchanged down to 1912, there were changes in the blade. As has been noted, the term 'plain' when applied to blades in *Dress Regulations* normally means an unfullered blade and although the sword of Lieutenant W E Marsland, 1st (King's) Dragoon Guards 1857-63, formerly in the Royal United Services Institution, has an absolutely flat, unfullered blade, the Carnegie, Dorville and Royal Armouries swords all have pipe-backed blades and it is clear that this was the standard blade. Inasmuch as plain meant unfullered this description could be used of a pipe-backed blade also.

From 1864 onwards, *Dress Regulations* describe the blade as 'grooved' - that is to say, fullered. This type of blade, however, appears on cavalry swords a good deal

Cavalry Officers' Swords

68

68 Portrait of Captain J S Carnegie of Tarrie in the uniform of the 2nd (North British) Dragoons, *c*1830

Note: the sword shown in the picture is that illustrated in Plate 69.

(Collection of the Earl of Southesk, Kinnaird Castle, Brechin)

69 Captain Carnegie's sword - Heavy Cavalry Officer, Undress, Pattern 1821

Note: the blade is pipe-backed, with prominent false edge and the guard is of pierced honeysuckle pattern.

(Collection of the Earl of Southesk, Kinnaird Castle, Brechin)

69

earlier than 1864, albeit perhaps unofficially. Wilkinsons were making blades of this type in the period 1850-54, before they started numbering their blades, and they made a sword of this type for a Colonel Steele in 1860.[28] On the other hand, *Dress Regulations* for 1900, in the case of the Army Service Corps, who carried the cavalry sword, gives the date of sealing of the pattern as 1863.

The blade length given in the 1822 *Dress Regulations* was 36 inches. In the 1857 *Regulations* the length is given as 35$^{1}/_{2}$ inches, only to revert to 36 inches in 1872 and to 35 inches in 1900. These changes are of little significance; Wilkinsons' sword registers show that there were variations in the length of heavy cavalry swords sold on the same day. In practice, the average length seems to have been 35 inches. It should be noted that this honeysuckle guard is not symmetrical, being wider on the outside than on the inside, (Plate 71).

Cavalry Officers' Swords

70 Sword, Heavy Cavalry, Officer, Undress, Pattern 1821

Blade length and width: 36 1/8in. x 1 1/4in.
Blade type: slightly curved, pipe-back, spear point, double edged for last 9 in.
Guard: steel basket in honeysuckle pattern, sword knot slit near pommel.
Hilt mounts: steel.
Grip: wood, covered with fishskin and bound with steel wire.
Note: the blade is marked 'T.Gill's Warranted' and with the cypher of George IV (1820-30). It is recorded as having belonged to Lieutenant-Colonel Philip Dorville, who joined the 1st (Royal) Dragoons in 1811 and went on half-pay as Lieutenant-Colonel in 1827; the sword therefore appears to date from 1821-27.

(NAM 5903-163)

71 Sword, Heavy Cavalry, Officer, Undress, 1887

Blade length and width: 35 1/4in. x 1 1/8in.
Blade type: flat back, single fuller each side to within 13in. of point; double edged for last 9 1/2in.
Guard: steel, sword knot slit near pommel.
Hilt mounts: steel.
Grip: wood, covered with fishskin and bound with steel wire.
Scabbard: nickel-plated steel; two bands with loose rings 2 1/2in. and 10 3/4 in. from mouth, wood lining.
Sword weight: 2lb 2oz.
Scabbard weight: 1lb 4oz.
Note: individual specimens vary slightly in length and weight according to maker and height of owner.

(NAM 5809-49-8)

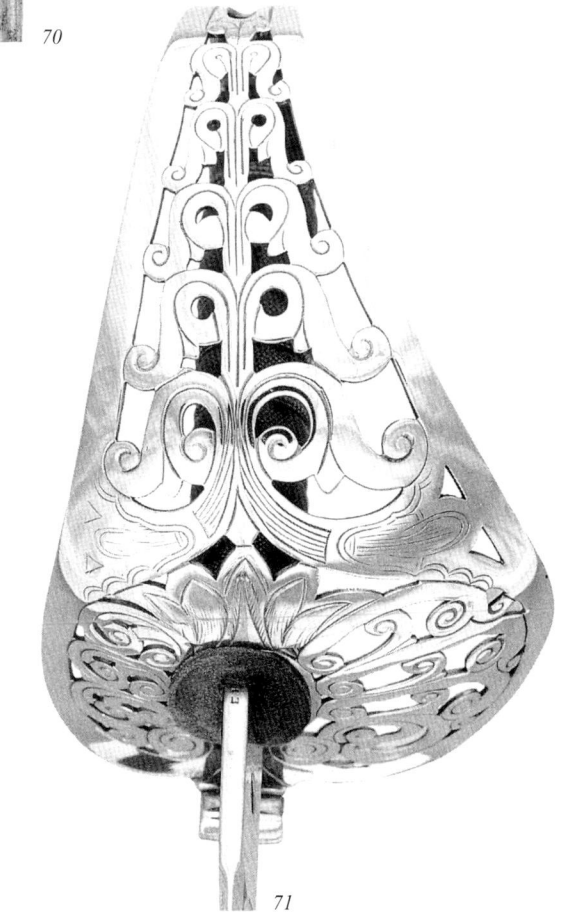

Cavalry Officers' Swords

A small number of heavy cavalry regiments carried mameluke-hilted sabres for a period in the nineteenth century, of the same general form as those of the light cavalry, (see below). Known specimens exist for the 1st (King's) Dragoon Guards, (Plate 72),[29] the 5th Dragoon Guards and the 6th Dragoon Guards, (Plate 73). These heavy cavalry sabres are rare and were clearly never a general fashion as they were in the light cavalry. The specimens seen by the author suggest that the fashion among the heavy cavalry dates to the first half of the century.

ffoulkes and Hopkinson in their *Sword, Lance and Bayonet* stated without evidence that the 'ladder' hilted sword for heavy cavalry officers was introduced in 1834 and replaced by a new 'scroll' pattern hilt in 1857, which in turn was replaced by a universal, 'honeysuckle' pattern in 1896.[30] Subsequent writers, such as J W Latham, tended to follow ffoulkes and Hopkinson in accepting what can now be seen to be a wholly incorrect sequence.

As we have seen, the ladder-hilted sword was introduced in 1796 and remained the regulation for heavy cavalry officers until 1821. Even if there had not been ample direct evidence for this, the form of the blade (identical with that of the Pattern 1796 heavy cavalry troopers' sword) and the shape and construction of the grip make it impossible on stylistic grounds for this sword to have been introduced as late as 1834. The length and width of the blade as given in the 1822 *Dress Regulations*, the fact that the blade was to be 'plain' (i.e. unfullered), the description of the blade as 'for cut and thrust' (which in the British Army normally indicates a moderately curved blade) and the use of fishskin and silver wire for covering the grip, all indicate that a new sword was being described which was not the ladder-hilted sword.

At the other end of the scale, as we shall see, there was no general introduction of a honeysuckle hilt in 1896 but the adoption by the light cavalry of the honeysuckle hilt carried by the heavy cavalry since 1821-22.

There remains therefore the mystery of ffoulkes and Hopkinson's 'scroll' hilt for heavy cavalry. A hilt of this pattern was introduced in 1857 for Royal Engineers officers, (see Chapter 11 and Plate 211 below), and in 1863, in a lecture to the Royal United Services Institution, John Latham of Wilkinsons referred to it thus: 'The Royal Engineers' is a very good guard, as is also that of the heavy cavalry, but both have the defect of being overbalanced, i.e. heavier on one side than on the other'.[31]

A careless reading might suggest that he was referring to identical hilts and it may well be that this was the source of ffoulkes and Hopkinson's statement; in retrospect, it can be seen that Latham was referring to two different hilts. They may also have been confused by the fact that *Dress Regulations* of 1857 describe the heavy cavalry officers' hilt as of 'scroll' pattern.

But while it is clear that guards of 'scroll' form were never a general regulation pattern for cavalry officers, it is true that a number of regimental patterns of 'scroll' form were adopted in the second half of the nineteenth century. The best known is probably that of the 6th Dragoon Guards, (Plate 74), which bears the initials of

Cavalry Officers' Swords

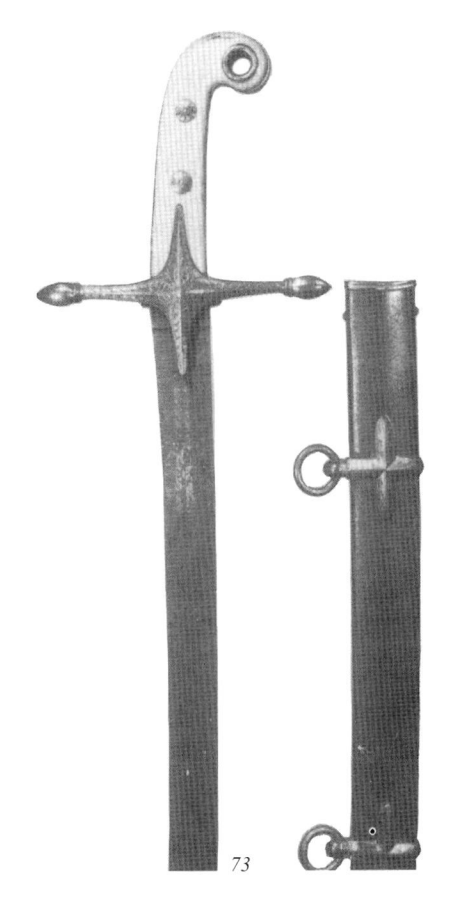

72 *73*

72 Sword, Levée, 1st (King's) Dragoon Guards
Hilt: gilt brass.
Grip: ivory.

(NAM 8407-94)

73 Sword, Levée,
6th Dragoon Guards
Hilt: gilt brass.
Grip: ivory, with two gilt brass floral-headed rivets.
Scabbard: steel, with mouthpiece, bands and loose rings and chape in brass.

(Collection G R Worrall)

Lieutenant L J Wheeler, who was commissioned into the regiment as quartermaster in 1899. A second specimen is illustrated in J W Latham's *British Military Swords*, and a specimen of the guard only is in the Royal Armouries. This pattern appears to have been adopted in 1877,[32] and to have remained in use until the introduction of the Pattern 1912 sword, (see below).

A design for a hilt for the 9th Lancers very similar to that just described is reproduced in J W Latham's book,[33] and there exists at least one specimen, that made for Lieutenant E B McInnis, who joined the regiment in 1875.[34]

A third pattern appears to have been carried at some time by officers of the 4th Light Dragoons in the period 1850-60, (Plate 75).[35] The 4th became hussars in 1861 and no specimen of this hilt marked to the regiment as hussars has been seen by the author. A very similar hilt, but without a regimental device on the guard, was sold by

Cavalry Officers' Swords

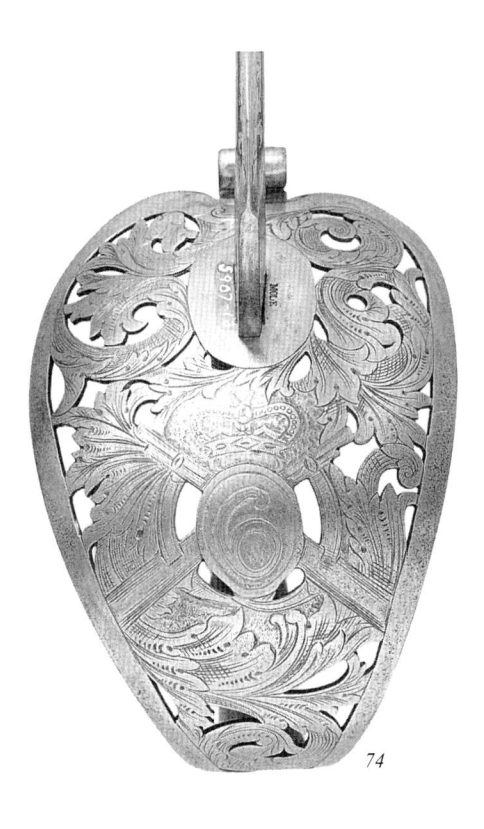

74 *75*

74 Sword, 6th Dragoon Guards (Carabiniers), Officer, Undress, 1877-1912

Note: this sword belonged to Lieutenant and Quartermaster L J Wheeler, who was commissioned in 1899. The Tudor Crown replaced the St Edward's Crown in 1901 on the accession of Edward VII.

(NAM 5907-13)

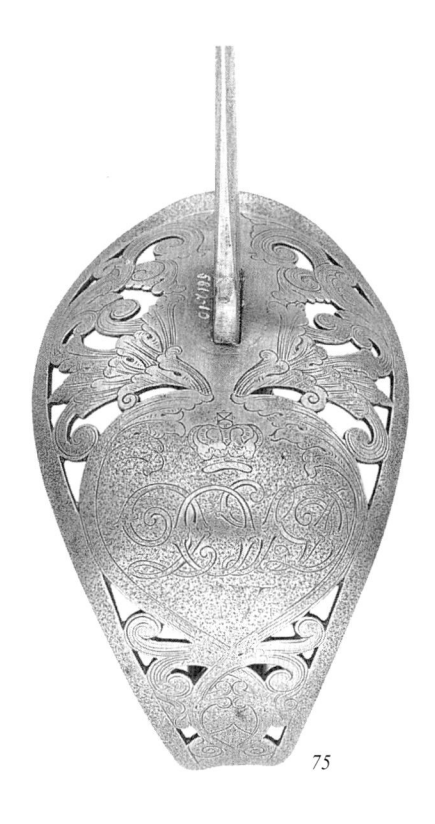

75 Sword, 4th Light Dragoons, Officer, Undress, c1860

Note: the blade bears battle honours up to 1856 and the sword was made by Charles Reeves, Toledo Works, Birmingham (1850-60). The 4th became Hussars in 1861 which dates the sword to c1860 but it is not known when this pattern was introduced into the regiment.

(NAM 5812-10)

Wilkinsons to Lieutenant C H Kempson, of the 1st (Royal) Dragoons, in March 1863, (Plate 76). In view of the paucity of specimens, it cannot be established with precision whether either of these patterns were adopted by all officers of these two regiments.

Yet another regimental pattern of hilt is that of the 4th Dragoon Guards, (Plate 77). This has a three-quarter basket hilt, pierced with a honeysuckle pattern. Like the Kempson sword, there is no backpiece and the pommel cap has a 'tail' somewhat like that of the 1832 Dress sword of the 2nd Life Guards, (Plate 117) but in this case, and that of the Kempson sword, absolutely plain. A number of specimens of this 4th Dragoon Guards guard exist and it seems probable that it was in general use in the regiment in the late 1840s and 1850s although no documents on its introduction and cessation have been located.

Cavalry Officers' Swords

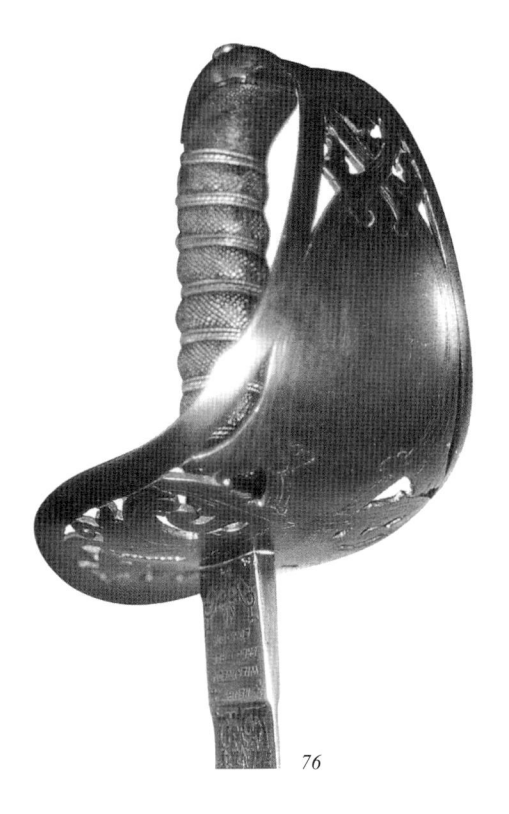

76 Sword, 1st (Royal) Dragoons, Officer, Undress, 1863

Note: sold to Lieutenant C H Kempson by Wilkinsons in March 1863.

(Private Collection)

77 Sword, 4th Dragoon Guards, Officer, Undress, c1850

Blade length and width: 35 1/2 in. x 1 1/4 in.
Blade type: slightly curved, flat back, single fuller each side to within 9 in. of spear point.
Guard: steel basket, honeysuckle pattern, inner edge turned up, stool turned down, sword knot slit near pommel.
Hilt mounts: steel.
Grip: wood, covered with fishskin and bound with steel wire.
Scabbard: steel, two bands and loose rings, large shoe.
Note: the sword of Edward Cooper Hodge, who joined the regiment in 1825 and commanded it in the Crimea. Note the form of the pommel, reminiscent of the 2nd Life Guards officers' Dress sword of 1832.

(NAM 8802-12)

The sword prescribed for light cavalry officers in the *Dress Regulations* of 1822 was also an entirely new pattern, (Plate 78), with a steel, three-bar hilt, a slightly curved, pipe-backed blade, 35 1/2 inches long, with spear point and double edged for the last 10 inches or so. The bars of the polished steel guard are fluted whereas those of the equivalent troopers' sword are plain, and the steel backpiece ends in a stepped pommel; some specimens have a 'step' in the backpiece which was presumably intended as a rudimentary thumb stop. The grip was of wood, covered with fishskin and bound with silver wire but unlike the troopers' sword, the backpiece does not

Cavalry Officers' Swords

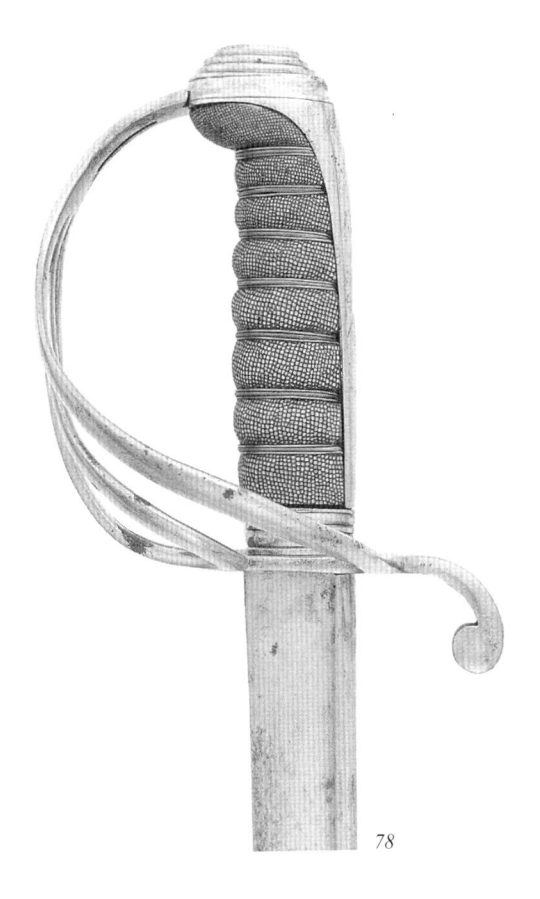

78 Sword, Light Cavalry, Officer, Undress, Pattern 1821

Blade length and width: 35½in. x 1¼in.
Blade type: spear point, double edged for last 10in.
Guard: steel, sword knot slit near pommel.
Hilt mounts: steel.
Grip: wood, covered with fishskin and bound with steel or German silver wire.
Scabbard: steel; two loose rings on bands 2½in. x 11¼in. from mouth; large shoe.

(NAM 6706-40-3)

79 Sword, Lancers, Officer, Full Dress, Pattern 1822

Blade length and width: 30½in. x 1¼in.
Blade type: curved, pipe-back, spear point, chamfer or double edge for last 10in.
Guard: gilt brass cross-guard.
Hilt mounts: gilt brass.
Grip: ivory; hole for sword knot at the top.
Scabbard: blue velvet, gilt brass locket, two bands with loose rings and chape, all elaborately moulded and chased.
Note: this sword is of the 17th Lancers.

(NAM 5911-2)

(See also Colour Plate I)

have ears riveted through the grip and tang. The scabbard was of steel, with two bands and loose rings, with a detachable mouthpiece and a prominent shoe. Generally, the officers' sword is a better quality version of the troopers' sword Pattern 1821.

For the new lancer regiments which had been introduced in 1816, there was, in addition, a mameluke-hilted Dress and Full Dress sword, with a velvet-covered scabbard. It was described in the *Dress Regulations* thus: 'White mameluke hilt, gilt cross, ornaments and mountings embossed, blade thirty inches long, ornamented on each side with lances, next number, above this two lances transverse, surmounted by a crown in bright work'.

For Full Dress, the scabbard was to be of crimson velvet, with richly gilt and chased mounts and two loose rings; for Dress it was to be of polished steel.

This description is reasonably precise except that it hides the fact that the blade was curved and spear-pointed. It also omits the fact that for the 17th Lancers, which converted to the role only in 1823, the scabbard was actually of blue velvet to match the colour of the tunic, (Plate 79).[36] At least one scabbard for this regiment exists covered in green velvet although this may be idiosyncratic.

The three lancer regiments existing in 1822 (9th, 12th and 16th Lancers) had apparently carried mameluke-hilted sabres from the beginning. For example, a Denis Dighton portrait of officers of the 9th Lancers in 1817, in the Royal Collection at Windsor, shows such sabres in both steel and what appears to be leather but is probably intended to be velvet-covered scabbards.[37] The only unsheathed sword has an unfullered blade decorated with crossed lances. It is clear therefore that not only did the lancer regiments follow the general light cavalry tradition of carrying mameluke-hilted sabres but that the *Dress Regulations* of 1822 were merely recording this custom. Nevertheless, the use of velvet-covered scabbards was unique in the British Army, as was the very precise instruction as to the decoration of the blades. In practice as was to be expected, there was a certain amount of variation between the swords of the different regiments, notably in relation to the shape of the quillon terminals, the design on the écusson and the ornamentation of the scabbard mounts. What is clear is that no expense was spared in making these regiments truly élite and again one senses the hand of George IV and the post-Waterloo fashion for copying French military style; indeed, of course, the introduction of lancer regiments into the British Army was directly due to encountering similar French regiments in the Peninsula and at Waterloo.

Although the 1822 *Dress Regulations*, as originally issued, made no provision for the carriage of mameluke-hilted sabres by the other regiments of light cavalry, these regiments, as we have seen, had been carrying such sabres since at least 1805 and it was inconceivable that they should not be allowed to carry on doing so when the new lancer regiments had been given this privilege. The *Dress Regulations* were therefore amended accordingly after 1822.[38] Mameluke-hilted sabres thus exist for most,

Cavalry Officers' Swords

80

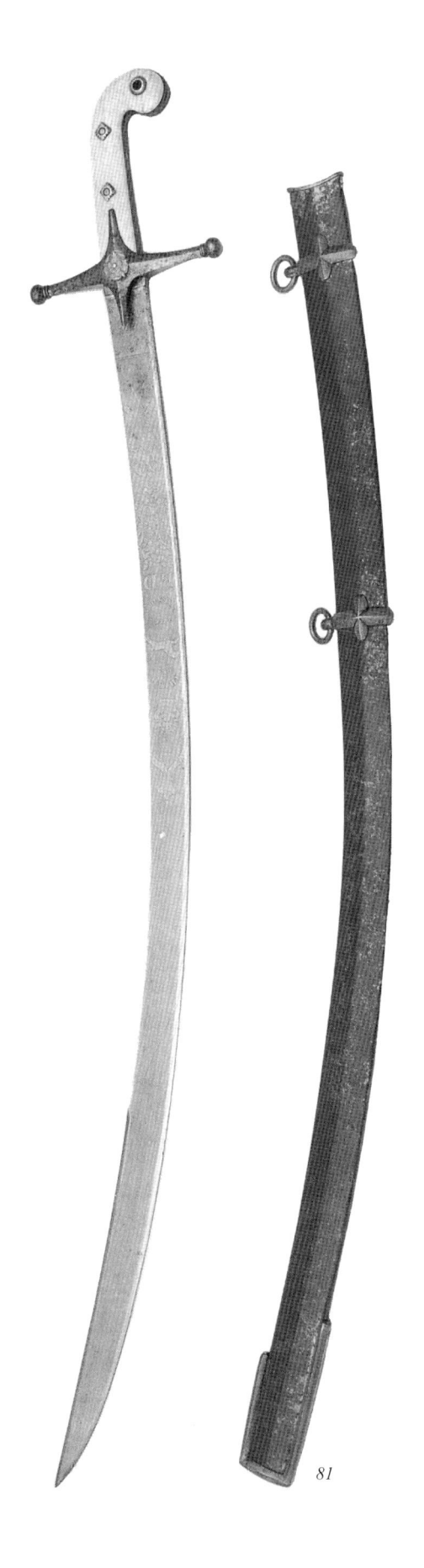

80 Sword, Levée, 16th Lancers, Officer, post-1832

Blade length and width: 30½in. x 1¼in.
Blade type: curved, unfullered, spear point.
Hilt mounts: gilt brass.
Grip: ivory.
Scabbard: steel; gilt mounts, two loose rings.
Note: unusually elaborate.

(NAM 7905-1)

81 Sword, Levée, 3rd (King's Own) Light Dragoons, Officer, c1830

Note: the cross-guard is in steel, with gilt brass rose on the écusson, and gilt brass floral-headed rivets in the ivory grip. The scabbard is steel with brass bands and loose rings. The sword is marked 'Prosser' and has the cypher of William IV (1830-37).

(NAM 7305-47)

81

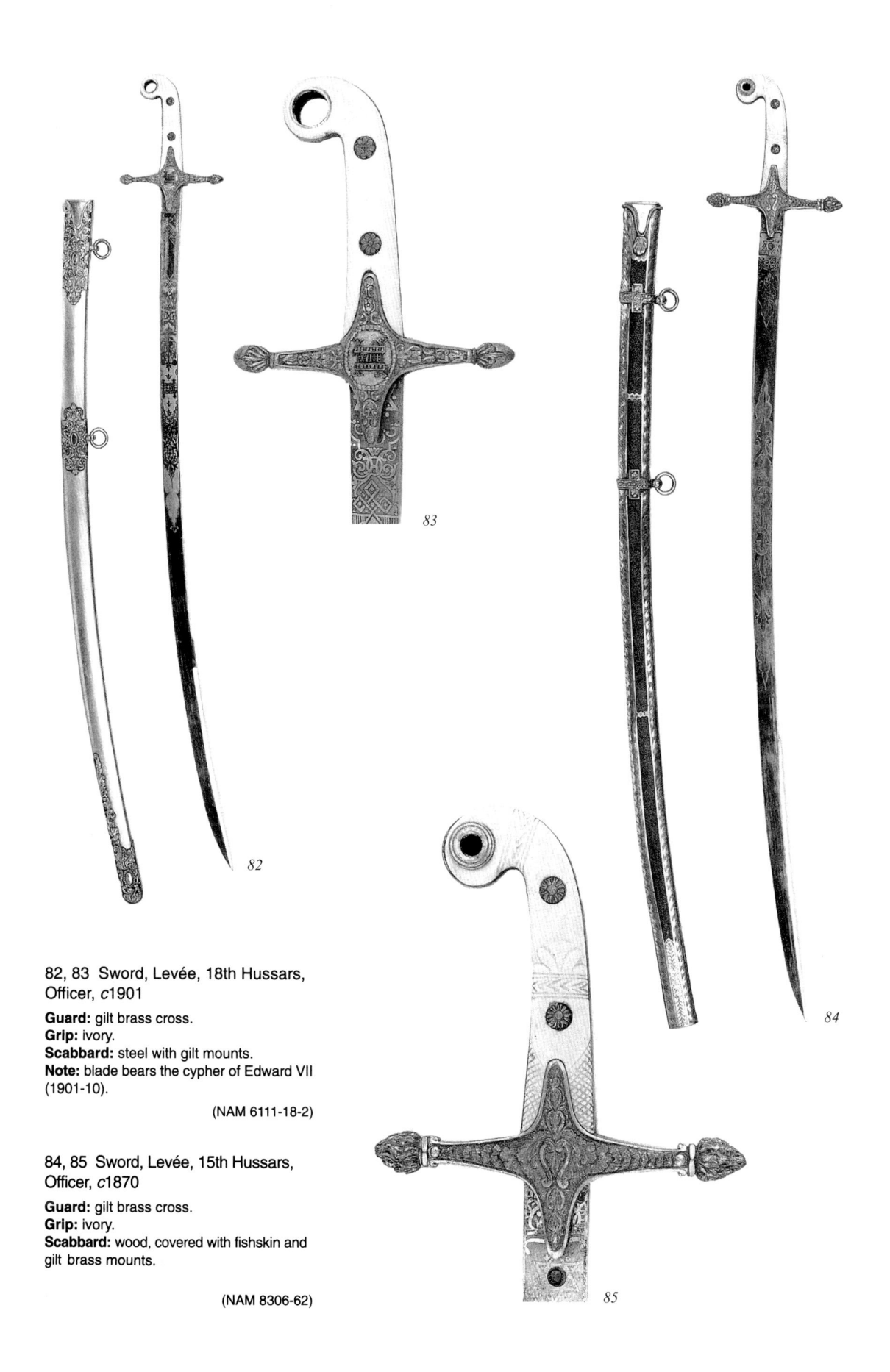

Cavalry Officers' Swords

82, 83 Sword, Levée, 18th Hussars, Officer, c1901

Guard: gilt brass cross.
Grip: ivory.
Scabbard: steel with gilt mounts.
Note: blade bears the cypher of Edward VII (1901-10).

(NAM 6111-18-2)

84, 85 Sword, Levée, 15th Hussars, Officer, c1870

Guard: gilt brass cross.
Grip: ivory.
Scabbard: wood, covered with fishskin and gilt brass mounts.

(NAM 8306-62)

but not all, of the light cavalry regiments, both in their pre- and post-1861 forms, when the remaining light dragoon regiments were re-designated hussars.

These sabres, (Plates 80-86), while all conforming to a single basic design, differ widely in detail, most notably in regard to:

(a) the form of the blade, which is sometimes pipe-backed but more normally with an unfullered blade ending in a false edge or latchet;

(b) the design of the quillon ends;

(c) the device on the écusson, which is sometimes in the form of the regimental badge or other device, as in the case of the 3rd, 11th and 18th, and sometimes, as in the 15th, a simple arabesque design;

(d) the construction of the scabbard - sometimes steel and in other cases, leather covered wood - and in the ornateness of the scabbard mounts.

There were relatively few major changes in cavalry officers' swords until 1896. The boatshell-hilted Dress sword of the heavy cavalry was discontinued in 1831 although a modified version continued in use in the Household Cavalry until 1857, (see Chapter 5). The mameluke-hilted sabres of the light cavalry were also officially discontinued in 1831 but in practice remained in use in some regiments at least, such as the 11th and 18th Hussars, until 1914.[39] The introduction of the fullered blade in the 1850s produced a change in the pommel and backpiece of the heavy cavalry officers' hilt, the stepped pommel being replaced by a hemispherical chequered pommel, and the lower part of the backpiece becoming chequered also to give a better grip for the thumb, (Plate 87).

In 1896, the differences which had existed since before 1788 in the patterns of service sword carried by light and heavy cavalry officers disappeared as a result of an Army Order of 1 June 1896 which ordered light cavalry officers to adopt the heavy cavalry officers' honeysuckle-hilted sword. It was a change long overdue since the troopers' swords had been unified since the pattern of 1853 and the heavy cavalry officers' guard was clearly superior to the light cavalry three-bar hilt. Moreover, the distinction between heavy and light cavalry in terms of their roles had largely disappeared. At this same time, a minor change in respect of the cavalry officers' hilt was introduced with the adoption of a universal pattern grip for all officers' swords, except for the General Officers'. This universal grip was familiar enough, being of ridged wood, covered with fishskin and bound with turns of silver wire but it was, if anything, slightly straighter than previous patterns, and its distinctive feature was that the length was variable between 5 and $5^{3}/4$ inches, according to the wearer's

Cavalry Officers' Swords

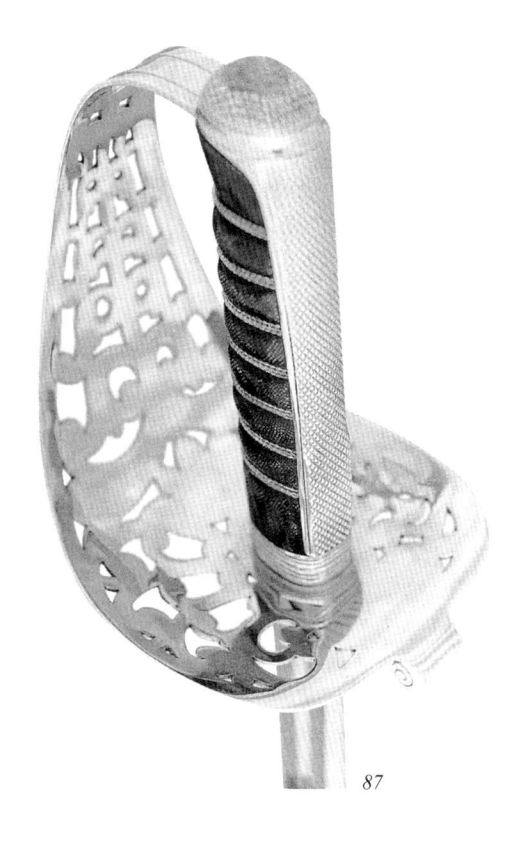

86 Sword, Levée, 19th Hussars, Officer, c1865
Guard: gilt brass cross, with crescent on right écusson and elephant and howdah on left.
Grip: ivory.
Scabbard: steel.
Note: blade bears battle honour 'Seringapatam'.

(NAM 8009-107)

87 Sword, Heavy Cavalry, Officer, Undress, late 19th century - inside of hilt

(NAM 5809-49-8)

hand. In this form, the sword weighed approximately 2lbs 1oz, with an authorised blade length of 36¹/16 inches.

As had been frequently pointed out over the years, a bright steel scabbard with loose rings was not the most practical pattern for active service and regiments had adopted various *ad hoc* expedients in the past to reduce reflections and quieten the noise. In 1879, during the Second Afghan War, the 6th Dragoon Guards had covered their scabbards with leather.[40] (Indian cavalry regiments had almost always used leather or leather-covered wooden scabbards). In the Egyptian expedition of 1882, the cavalry had browned their hilts and scabbards, sometimes by the simple process of allowing them to rust.[41] The deciding factor of change was the introduction of the Sam Browne belt for universal wear. By using a frog for suspending the sword, it avoided the awkward problem of fixing suspension rings to a leather scabbard. The widespread use of the Sam Browne started, as was to be expected, in India and in November 1898 its gradual introduction for use at home was authorised, to be shortly followed in September 1899 by Army Order 151 which prescribed its immediate adoption by officers of all branches for use when on active service. It was to be accompanied by a new wooden scabbard covered with brown leather, and with a steel chape and locket.[42] Two years later, in 1901, the steel mounts were abolished and the scabbard assumed its modern form with plated steel mouth and leather shoe.

Following the introduction of the revolutionary Pattern 1908 sword for cavalry troopers, a companion version for officers was introduced in 1912. In general terms, the Pattern 1912 sword is a more elaborate version of the troopers' sword, (Plates 88-90), the main differences being:

(a) the guard, which is of nickel-plated steel, has the previous honeysuckle pattern etched on to the outside, and there is no reinforcing piece on the outside;

(b) the grip is of wood, covered with black fishskin and bound with seventeen bands of twisted silver wire;

(c) the pommel is stepped, with a chequered top;

(d) there are two scabbards, a brown leather-covered wooden scabbard for use with the Sam Browne, and a plated steel scabbard, with two loose rings, for wear in Full Dress;

(e) some, but by no means all blades are etched and decorated.

The weight of the sword is approximately 2lbs 6ozs and the plated steel scabbard weighs 1lb 5¹/4ozs.

Cavalry Officers' Swords

88 Sword, Cavalry, Officer, Pattern 1912

Blade length and width: 35in. x 1in.
Blade type: virtually identical with that of the Sword, Cavalry, Pattern 1908, Mark 1 except for decoration and shape of the shoulder.
Guard: nickel-plated steel bowl, decorated on outside with 'scroll' design; sword knot slit near pommel.
Hilt mounts: nickel-plated steel.
Grip: wood, covered with fishskin and bound with silver-plated copper wire.
Scabbard: Dress scabbard is of plated steel with two loose rings on narrow bands; service scabbard is of wood covered with pigskin, and with a strap for attaching to frog.
Sword weight: 2lb 9oz.
Scabbard weight: 12oz (Service).
Note: the elaborate pommel is noteworthy. Individual swords and scabbards vary in weight because there was no rigidly enforced specification.

(Formerly Author's Collection)

89 Sword, Cavalry, Officer, Pattern 1912 - outside of guard

Note: as compared with the Troopers' Pattern 1908, there is no reinforcing piece on the outside of the guard and the edges of the guard are not beaded.

(NAM 8207-12)

90 Sword, Cavalry, Officer, Pattern 1912 - inside of guard

(NAM 8207-12)

Cavalry Officers' Swords

This sword has remained the regulation pattern. At least one regiment - almost predictably, the 6th Dragoon Guards - incorporated the regimental badge into the decoration of the guard.[43] The 10th Hussars, almost equally predictably, went further and adopted an extraordinary hilt, in which the bowl guard was replaced by an elongated three-bar hilt, (Plate 91). Since the guard gives inferior protection to the normal bowl guard, it is an inferior weapon as well as compellingly ugly; in some specimens the pommel is not stepped but domed and chequered.

Some swords exist in which the Pattern 1912 hilt has been attached to an ordinary Pattern 1908 troopers' blade.[44] These were presumably produced against the heavy demands of the First World War although it has been suggested that this was not an uncommon practice among Sheffield makers even in peacetime. These Pattern 1912/1908 swords are virtually identical with the normal Pattern 1912 swords except that they tend to be slightly heavier.

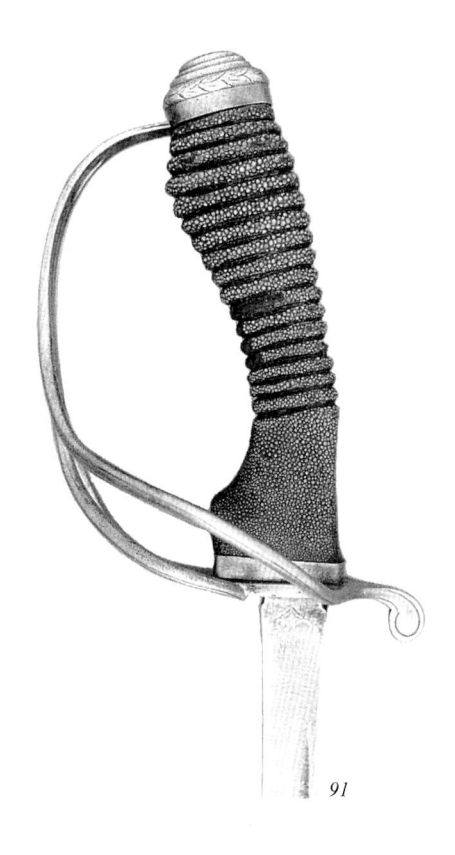

91   Sword, 10th Hussars, Officer, Pattern 1912

Blade type: identical with ordinary cavalry officers' Pattern 1912 (Plate 88).
Guard: plated steel, three-bar.
Hilt mounts: plated steel.
Grip: as for ordinary Pattern 1912.
Scabbard: as for ordinary Pattern 1912.
Note: the awkward junction of blade and hilt should be noted.

(NAM 7410-9)

Chapter 4: Notes

1. PRO. WO 3/37, pp34-41; also WO 71/11, p359.

2. An Inspection Return for the 12th Light Dragoons in June 1790 records that the officers' swords were 'pretty near shape and length lately ordered' - *JSAHR*, Vol III, 1924, p254.

3. Some swords of this type have sword knot slits which go transversely through the langets - see, for example, a portrait in the NAM of an officer of the 7th Light Dragoons *c*1793, (NAM 5807-20).

4. This pattern of sword, with a slightly different pommel, is shown in a print of George, Prince of Wales, by J R Smith, published in May 1792. A painting of a private of the Austrian Kalnoky Regiment of Hussars, *c*1748, in the Royal Collection at Windsor (Catalogue 177 - reproduced as a Plate 125 in Miller and Dawnay, *op. cit.*), shows a very similar hilt.

5. See, for example, a specimen formerly belonging to the late J R F Winsbury and now in the G R Worrall Collection.

6. I am indebted to Mr A V B Norman for this information. A sword of this pattern, which belonged to Francis Gregory, who served in the regiment between 1781 and 1794, is in the King's Royal Hussars Museum at Winchester.

7. See Claude Blair, *European and American Arms*, London (1962) p101, Figure (n).

8. See *JSAHR*, Vol XIII, 1934, p98.

9. A specimen with an etched blade by Thomas Gill is RA IX-835.

10. For illustrations of these and other officers' swords of the 1796 pattern, see a most useful article by G R Worrall, 'The 1796 Light Cavalry Sword - Part 1' in *Classic Arms and Militaria*, Vol I, No 9, 1994, pp44-48. This sword, with brass scabbard and slightly different-shaped langets, is shown in a portrait of Lieutenant Andrew Finucane, 10th Light Dragoons, *c*1810 (NAM 6405-28).

11. See the numerous pictures of light cavalry officers by Robert Dighton Junior in the Royal Collection at Windsor e.g. Nos. 747, 768, 771, 772 and 792. The Mamelukes were descended from Turkish slave soldiers and had become the effective rulers of Egypt by the time Napoleon invaded in 1798.

12. Charles Farmer, *A Universal Military Dictionary in English and French*, unpaginated edition, London (1810).

13. PRO. WO 3/29, p184.

14. See T Wise, *European Edged Weapons*, London (1980) p59.

15. An almost identical sword, copied from the British pattern, was adopted by the United States Army in 1832 for General and Staff Officers - see Peterson, *op. cit.*, p126.

16. General Order of 7 November 1796.

17. See *JSAHR*, Vol XXXIX, 1961, p191.

18. Reproduced in *JSAHR*, Vol XVII, 1938, p187.

19. NAM 8704-34; G R Worrall Collection.

20. See A V B Norman, 'The dating and identification of some swords in the Royal Collection at Windsor Castle' *JAAS*, Vol 9, 1979, p231.

21. See note 10 above.

22. May and Annis, *op. cit.*, Vol I, pp227-28; Vol II, Plate 39A.

23. See Richard Dellar, 'An enigmatic British cavalry sword', *Classic Arms and Militaria*, Vol I, No 6, 1994, pp19-22.

24. G R Worrall Collection.

25. Royal Collection 413, reproduced as Plate 308 in Miller and Dawnay, *op. cit.*

26. Royal Collection No 763 - reproduced in Oliver Millar, *Later Georgian pictures in the collection of Her Majesty the Queen*, London (1969) Plate 234.

27. Reproduced in C T Atkinson, *The History of the Royal Dragoons*, Privately printed, (1934).

28. See J W Latham, *British Military Swords from 1800 to the Present Day*, London (1966) Plate 49.

29. A specimen of this sword is in the Glasgow Museum and Art Gallery, (Accession No AA/NN/27) and Mr A V B Norman has informed me that yet another is at Dyrham Park, in Gloucestershire. A tailor's pattern, by Gieves, is in the Royal Armouries archives, Reference No I-235/33.

30. ffoulkes and Hopkinson, *op.cit.*, p52.

31. John Latham, 'The shape of sword blades', *RUSI Journal*, Vol IV, 1863, p410.

32. A drawing of this design, dated 7 December 1877, and signed on behalf of the lieutenant-colonel commanding the Carabiniers, is in the Wilkinson archives - see RA Wilkinson Archives, microfiche Reg 15.

33. J W Latham, *op. cit.*, p31.

34. I am indebted to Mr J D Morgan for details of this sword and its owner. See also his article 'A Special Regimental Pattern Sword of the Ninth Lancers' in *Classic Arms and Militaria*, Vol 1, No 12, 1994.

35. This sword is marked 'Reeves, Toledo Works, Birmingham': the Birmingham City Librarian informs me that Reeves operated at this address from 1850 to 1860. A sword of this pattern, supplied by Wilkinsons to Colonel Lear of the regiment, was in Wallis & Wallis' Sale 130, May 1966, Lot 668A.

36. *JSAHR*, Vol XLI, 1963, p30.

37. Royal Collection No 417 - reproduced in Miller and Dawnay, *op. cit.*, Plate 304.

38. See copy in MoD Central Library with manuscript amendments to 1826 - reference no C.8c.

39. A letter, dated 29 December 1892, reference 61002/4485, from the Duke of Cambridge to the Colonel of the 18th Hussars, records that: 'H.R.H. the C-in-C desires that the pattern of dress-sword now in use by the officers of the Regiment be discontinued, as H.R.H. sees no reason why the Regiment more than any other cavalry regiment should wear a dress sword'. But Wilkinsons made a sword of this pattern for an officer of this regiment as late as 1904, and similar swords for other regiments until 1914.

40. Uniforms Register of 5DG, formerly in the RUSI and now in the NAM, (6807-495)

41. Joseph Lehmann, *All Sir Garnet; A Life of Field-Marshal Lord Wolseley*, London (1964) p309.

42. Patterns 389 and 399, sealed on 4 January 1900.

43. J W Latham, *op. cit.*, p31 states that the 9th Lancers also had their badge on the outside of the bowl but the author has not seen specimens of this type.

44. See G R Worrall, 'The 1912 Cavalry Officers' sword and its variations', *Guns, Weapons and Militaria*, June 1982, p18.

5. Household Cavalry Troopers' Swords

The history of the troopers' swords of the Household Cavalry is poorly documented; actual dated specimens from the period before 1850 are relatively rare and the pictorial evidence is often confusing and contradictory. The lack of documentary evidence stems in large part from the peculiar position of the three regiments as the personal bodyguard of the Sovereign, with direct access to the royal person. In consequence, the regiments were, in matters of equipment and uniform, largely outside the control of the ordinary Army authorities; it would be a rash Adjutant-General who took it upon himself to dictate on matters of uniform and equipment to regiments so closely linked to the Sovereign and in which he was apt to take a close personal interest as his own Household troops. One illustration of this is the fact that until 1882, long after the rest of the Army, the Household Cavalry regiments chose their own patterns of sword and procured them direct from their own sources of manufacture, so that the Superintendent of the RSAF Enfield was forced to confess that he had no direct knowledge of the swords in use or the tests to which they had to conform. It was a system which could hardly have survived so long were it not for the fact that the regiments, as such, rarely went on active service.

The relative absence of documentary evidence and of datable specimens encourages a reliance on pictorial evidence, which can be dangerous. Few artists, especially in the earlier period, can be relied upon for precise detail in military pictures and to attempt to erect theories upon a glimpse of a scabbard or the apparent colour of a hilt, as some authorities have been tempted to do, is dangerous and unscholarly. It is equally dangerous to theorise on the basis of the existence of one or two specimens. These factors render the history of the Household Cavalry troopers' swords before 1820 still a matter of uncertainty.

The two regiments of Life Guards were formed in 1788 from the existing troops of Horse or Life Guards and Horse Grenadier Guards. The Royal Horse Guards (Blues) had existed as a regiment since 1661 but were not technically a part of the Household Cavalry until 1820; for ease of treatment, however, they will be included with the Life Guards in this chapter.

Between 1788 and 1796, evidence about the swords carried by these regiments is extremely sparse. Indeed, the author is not aware of any dated sword from this period which can be firmly assigned to any of them. There is no evidence that they were required to adopt the Pattern 1788 Heavy Cavalry sword, (see Chapter 2) and it seems highly probable that, for a time at least after 1788, they continued to carry their existing swords. A sword of the 2nd Troop of Horse Grenadier Guards is illustrated in Plate 92 and can reasonably be dated to the period 1763-1788, and may indeed be the pattern referred to in the accounts of Cox & Co, the regimental agents, in 1780, where the sum of £37 5s 2d is recorded as having been spent on new sword hilts for the 2nd Troop. A similar sword, made by Thomas Gill, dated 1788, and bearing a Garter star on the blade, may be a sword of a private of the Blues.[1] It is very similar to the Pattern 1788 Heavy Cavalry sword but with a faceted brass pommel. What appears to be the same pattern of sword is shown in a watercolour of a private of the Blues, painted by C J Smith in 1796.[2] We know that Gill made a complete set of swords for the 1st Life Guards in 1789[3] and one may make a tentative guess that between 1788 and 1796 all three regiments were carrying swords of the same generic pattern as the heavy cavalry, with long, straight blades and basket guards of curved brass or iron bars.

While there is firmer ground in respect of the swords carried after 1796, the picture is by no means wholly clear. The introduction of new patterns of sword for the ordinary light and heavy cavalry regiments in that year, (see Chapter 2), following war-time experience in Flanders and Holland, was bound to impact upon the Household Cavalry. On 14 November 1796, the Adjutant-General wrote to Colonel Stanley:

> 'I have it in Command from F.M. the D. of York, to acqt. you, for the information of H. G. the D. of Richmond, that H.M. has seen & approv'd of a Sword, for the use of the R. R. of Horse Guards, a Pattern of which is deposited by order of H.R.H. the D. of York, in the Office of the Comptroller's of Army Accounts, these to be had recourse to, as occasion may require.
> N.B. The Regts. of Life Guards, are to have the same Sword, as above.[4]

A fortnight later, the Adjutant-General's office sent a pattern sword, as approved by the King, to the Secretary of the Clothing Board for the purpose of regulating future supplies.[5] A first batch of 50 of these new swords reached the Royal Horse Guards on 9 July 1797, and thereafter further supplies trickled in until a final batch, making 482 in all, reached the regiment in December 1798.[6] One assumes that supplies reached the other two regiments of the Household Cavalry in much the same way, but somewhat later.

What precisely was the pattern of these new swords? A bill for £117 submitted to the Duke of Richmond in November 1798, by James Woolley & Co of Birmingham (and which clearly refers to the batch of 100 received in October 1798) refers specifically to '100 New Regulation Broadswords with best proof blades'.[7] This description, together with the fact that Woolley had been one of the earliest contractors for the Pattern 1796 Heavy Cavalry troopers' sword, (see page 18), would suggest that the new pattern referred to in the Adjutant-General's letter of November 1796 was simply the ordinary Pattern 1796 heavy cavalry sword. And there is a good deal of pictorial evidence that the 1796 disc-hilted sword was being carried by the Household Cavalry in the latter part of the Napoleonic Wars - for example, Charles Hamilton Smith's drawing of 25 November 1814 of men of the Royal Horse Guards; the same artist's drawing of 1 May 1815 of men of the 1st Life Guards[8], and Alexander Sauerweid's painting of a corporal of 'the Life Guards', c1816.[9]

If this was, indeed, the situation in the Household Cavalry in the period 1796-1816, what is one to make of the well-known brass-hilted swords, of which there are 58 in the Royal Armouries, (RA IX-256 to 314), which have been labelled as 'Household Cavalry 1805' for more than 70 years, as well as other specimens elsewhere? These swords have 'ladder' hilts, very similar in form to the those of the Pattern 1796 Heavy Cavalry officers' sword but the base of the guard is in the form of a star, (Plate 93); the blades are identical with that of the Pattern 1796 disc-hilted sword. The scabbards are of brass, with large frog hooks, (Plate 94). What appears to be the same, or a very similar, hilt is shown in a drawing by Robert Dighton Junior of an officer of the 2nd Life Guards c1802,[10] although the Royal Armouries' swords are clearly not officers' swords.

Stylistically, these swords are directly linked to the pattern of sword for heavy cavalry introduced in 1796. The general crudeness of manufacture, the absence of any decoration, the relatively large number of manufacturers and the quantity of surviving specimens makes it clear that these are not officers' swords. It is tempting to believe therefore that these represent the new Household Cavalry pattern introduced in 1796; in this case, Woolley's bill of 1798 might be read plausibly as referring to 'New Regulation Dragoon *blades*', rather than to complete *swords*.

A major difficulty with this theory is that, of the eight known makers represented in the Royal Armouries' swords, only three, (Dawes, Hadley and John Gill), are known to have been in business before 1808 and one, (Thomas Craven) was only in business after 1818. A further difficulty arises over the belt hook on the scabbards which shows that the swords were intended to be carried from a shoulder belt although this was not, in 1796, a part of the normal uniform. Nevertheless, the number of manufacturers suggests that enough of these swords were made to equip at least two, if not three, of the regiments of the Household Cavalry, although, as we shall see, it is more probable that only the two regiments of Life Guards were so equipped.

Taking all the evidence, it seems probable that these were indeed the swords carried by the Life Guards on home service between 1797 and 1820, and that the swords in the Royal Armouries and elsewhere represent the last replacements before new patterns were introduced in 1820. An extension of this hypothesis would be that the swords were for Full Dress only and that the service sword was the ordinary disc-hilt. A steel version of these brass hilts is known[11] and it has been suggested, on tenuous grounds, that it was carried by quartermasters.[12]

Household Cavalry Troopers' Swords

92

92 Sword, Horse Grenadier Guards (2nd Troop), *c*1780

Blade length and width: 38in. x 1 1/4in.
Blade type: straight, flat back, single fuller each side, single edge, spear point.
Guard: steel or wrought iron.
Hilt mounts: steel or wrought iron.
Grip: wood, covered with fishskin and bound with copper wire.
Note: the outside of the base of the guard is engraved '66 2ᵈTrp GG^DS'

(NAM 7108-21)

93 Sword, Heavy Cavalry (possibly Household Cavalry), *c*1808-1818

Blade length and width: 35in. x 1 3/8in. x 9/16in.
Blade type: identical with Heavy Cavalry, Pattern 1796.
Guard: brass, sword knot slit near pommel.
Hilt mounts: brass; the ears of the backpiece riveted through the tang.
Grip: wood, bound with cord and covered with leather; inside length 4 1/2in.
Scabbard: brass with long frog hook and large shoe.
Sword weight: 2lb 12oz.
Scabbard weight: 1lb 8oz.
Note: the weights of these swords vary between 2lb 11oz and 2lb 14oz. The scabbard weights vary from 1lb 7oz to 2lb 5oz.

(Royal Armouries IX-8135)

94 Sword, Household Cavalry, Trooper (?), *c*1808-18 - scabbard, with frog hook

(Royal Armouries IX-8135)

93

94

Household Cavalry Troopers' Swords

A composite regiment of the Household Cavalry served in the Peninsula and France between 1812 and 1814 and all three regiments served at Waterloo: the pictorial evidence makes it clear that the sword then used was basically the Pattern 1796 disc-hilted weapon, although it has been suggested that in this case the grip was slightly taller and narrower than the standard, and that the scabbard differed in having horizontally reeded bands. The sword reputed to have been used at Waterloo by the famous Sergeant Shaw, of the Life Guards, is in the Royal Armouries, (IX-968) and is a disc-hilted, Pattern 1796 heavy cavalry sword but with raised rim, (Plate 17).

A completely new pattern of sword was introduced for the 1st Life Guards in 1820. An extract from Regimental Orders of 20 May 1820 announced that:

> 'Orders are given for new swords of a pattern approved by His Majesty. As soon as it may be notified that they are to be delivered by Ordnance, they will be taken into wear, and officers will provide themselves afterwards with swords of a pattern which has also been approved by His Majesty.[13]

The new sword, (Plates 95, 96) is clearly illustrated in Hull's lithographs of a corporal of the regiment in King's Guard Order, published in May 1828, and of a standard bearer and farrier, published in February 1829. It is also very clearly shown in Dubois Drahonet's painting of Private George Roberts of the regiment, painted in 1832 and in his portrait of Regimental Corporal-Major Winterbottom, also painted in 1832.[14]

The guard of the new sword was a steel bowl, with twelve brass studs round the edge, and bearing the incised regimental cypher under a crown, the upper quarters of which were pierced. The slightly curved blade varies in actual specimens between $37^{1}/_{4}$ and $38^{3}/_{4}$ inches but it seems probable that the specified length was meant to be 38 inches. The bowl form of the guard echoes the guard of the Pattern 1821 Heavy Cavalry troopers' sword, (Plate 20).

This Pattern 1820 sword continued in use in the 1st Life Guards until replaced by the Pattern 1882 sword and thus had probably the longest service life of any regulation pattern before 1914. Earlier specimens appear to have had leather-covered grips but later versions have grips covered in fishskin and bound with wire.[15]

Problems begin to arise in identifying the patterns of sword carried in the 2nd Life Guards and Royal Horse Guards after 1820. A sword in the NAM, (7805-57), has a plain steel bowl guard similar to that of the Pattern 1821 Heavy Cavalry troopers' sword but with the addition of a brass grenade on the outside and twelve brass studs round the rim of the bowl, (Plate 97). What appears to be the same sword is shown in a crude painting of a private of the 2nd Life Guards, formerly in the possession of the late James Rowntree, to whom I am indebted for a photograph. This

Household Cavalry Troopers' Swords

95   Sword, 1st Life Guards, Trooper, Pattern 1820

Blade length and width: $38^{3}/_{4}$in. x $1^{1}/_{4}$in.
Blade type: slightly curved, flat back, fuller each side to within 10in. of spear point; double edged for last 10 in.
Guard: steel with brass studs.
Hilt mounts: steel, sword knot slit near pommel.
Grip: wood, covered in fishskin and bound with steel wire; inside length 5in.
Scabbard: steel or wrought iron, with two loose rings on bands and large shoe.
Sword weight: 2lb 13oz.

(NAM 7704-66)

96   Sword, 1st Life Guards, Trooper, Pattern 1820 - outside of guard

(NAM 7704-66)

97   Sword, 2nd Life Guards, Trooper, *c*1820

Note: the blade and hilt are virtually identical with those of the 1st Life Guards, Pattern 1820, except for the substitution of the grenade on the outside of the hilt. The blade is marked 'Enfield' and 'GR', which would suggest a date not later than 1820.

(NAM 7805-57)

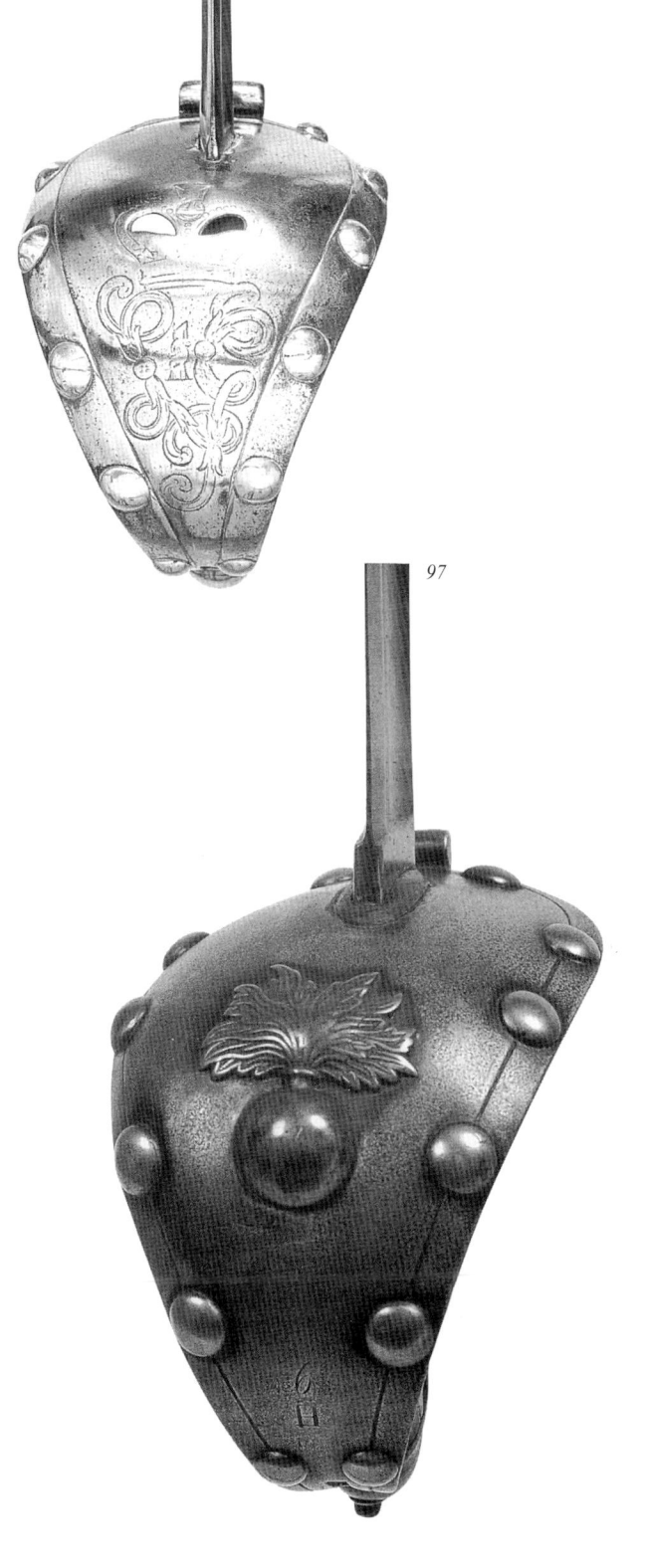

111

sword clearly echoes the 1st Life Guards Pattern 1820 and may therefore have been contemporaneous, if only for a relatively short period.

The series of oil paintings executed by the French artist Alexandre-Jean Dubois Drahonet for King William IV in 1832-34 includes, however, a portrait of Corporal Thomas Robinson of the 2nd Life Guards, painted in 1832,[16] showing him carrying a sword with a guard composed of curved brass or gilt bars, not dissimilar to the officers' Dress sword of this period (see Chapter 6). Drahonet was a very accurate artist and is not likely to have made a mistake; moreover, other prints showing the same pattern exist. The only sword known to the author which appears to match this painting is in the National Museum of Ireland, Dublin, (Plates 98, 99). It has a $38^{1}/_{2}$ inch blade and the scabbard shoe is similar to that on Household Cavalry officers' swords (see, for example, Plate 127). The maker, Andrews of Pall Mall, was a favourite supplier to the Household Division and the cypher of William IV (1830-37) strengthens the view that this may indeed be the sword depicted by Drahonet. It is not known when this four-bar-hilted sword was introduced; nor whether the steel bowl hilt referred to above preceded it or was intended as the service sword alongside the four-bar brass-hilted swords. (For four-bar-hilted swords of the 2nd Life Guards in steel, which appear however to be officers' swords, see Chapter 6 and Plate 124).

In 1833, the regiment received an issue of the ordinary Pattern 1821 Heavy Cavalry troopers' sword, (Plate 20). A letter from the office of the Ordnance Board to the office of the Commander-in-Chief on 22 April 1833 records that:

> 'Having submitted to the Board of Ordnance your letter dated the 17th instant and having communicated with the Board of Ordnance on the subject of the issue to the Second Regiment of Lifeguards of 354 swords of the approved pattern for Heavy cavalry, I now have the honour to acquaint you for the information of the Commander-in-Chief that the Board have ordered the same to be supplied.'[17]

Issues appear to have started shortly after this and to have been substantially completed by 1836, when the regiment was among those from whom comments were requested on the suitability of the Pattern 1821 swords, (see Chapter 2). At this point, the regiment seems to have been generally satisfied with the swords although it shared in the general criticism of the weakness of the scabbards. This sword is shown in a watercolour by Hull of men of the 2nd Life Guards c1833, now at Windsor, (Catalogue No 2194). What is not clear is whether these Pattern 1821 swords were issued in place of the four-bar brass-hilted swords or in addition, as the regiment's service sword, since the evidence shows the four-bar swords being carried by privates as late as the 1840s.

Difficulties also arise over the swords carried by the Royal Horse Guards after 1796. The memorial erected in 1817 to Major Robert Packe of this regiment, killed at

Household Cavalry Troopers' Swords

98 Sword, 2nd Life Guards (?), 1820-32

Blade length and width: 38 1/2in. x 1 1/4in.
Blade type: slightly curved, pipe-back, false edge for last 11in.
Guard: brass, four-bar, with sword knot slit near pommel.
Hilt mounts: plain brass pommel cap and pommel.
Grip: wood, covered in fishskin and bound with brass wire.
Scabbard: steel, two loose rings on bands, brass shoe.
Note: the blade is marked with cypher of William IV and the retailer's name 'Andrews, Pall Mall, Warranted'.

(National Museum of Ireland, No SE 112)

99 Sword, 2nd Life Guards (?), 1820-32 - view of hilt.

(National Museum of Ireland, No SE 112)

100 Sword, Royal Horse Guards, Trooper, c1796

Blade length and width: 34 1/2in. x 1/2in.
Blade type: straight, flat backed, single broad fuller each side, spear point.
Guard: steel or iron 'star' type with side bars.
Hilt mounts: steel or iron.
Grip: wood, covered with leather and bound with steel wire.

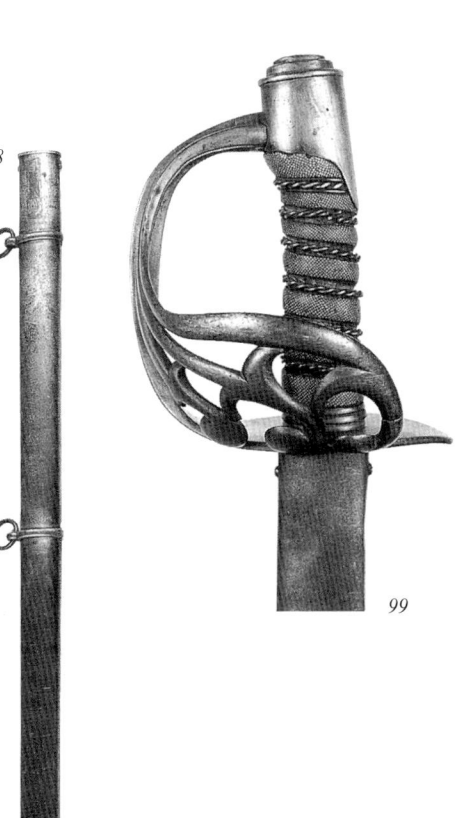

(NAM 8209-19)

Waterloo, shows the private soldiers carrying a sword with a guard which is in essence a Pattern 1796 Heavy Cavalry officers' hilt but with the addition of two curved bars on each side, (Plate 100). The blade is the same as that of the Pattern 1796 disc-hilted sword. A number of specimens exist in public and private collections[18] and it is well depicted, carried by a private of the Royal Horse Guards, in Sir David Wilkie's famous canvas 'Reading the Waterloo Despatches', painted in 1822 and now in the Wellington Museum at Apsley House: the uniform is correct for the period 1817-21.

The form of the hilt and of the blade relate it very directly to the heavy cavalry officers' and troopers' swords of 1796 and, in the absence of other evidence, it is reasonable to suppose that this was the new sword introduced for the Royal Horse Guards in that year, (see above). Indeed, a sword of this pattern in the Castle Museum at York is labelled as having belonged to the Royal Horse Guards. But, as with the brass-hilted swords attributed to the Life Guards, this requires the Woolley bill of November 1798 to be read as referring to blades rather than swords.

This sword can only have been carried until c1830 because in 1832 Dubois Drahonet painted two portraits of men of the Royal Horse Guards, Troop Corporal-Major Robert Goldie and Private Samuel Bowden, which shows them carrying long straight swords with guards composed of four, curved, brass or gilt bars, with brass pommels.[19] The portraits are absolutely clear in this respect and, given Dubois Drahonet's generally high standard of accuracy, there is no real room for doubt that these were the swords he actually saw being worn. (Kettle-Drummer George Rungeling, in the same series, is shown carrying a brass or gilt-hilted sword with what appears to be a boatshell guard).[20] Further pictures showing this sword worn by men of this regiment include two lithographs by R Walker c1842-48, and a painting by the same artist, showing the grip to have been fishskin-covered.[21]

Given this pictorial evidence, there would seem to be little doubt that this sword was actually carried in the 1830s and '40s, but to date the only specimen which matches these portraits is the sword in the National Museum of Ireland, (see above).

In any event, in 1848, the Royal Horse Guards received a new set of swords, made by Reeves, Greaves and Reeves, of Birmingham.[22] These swords, (Plates 101, 102), had long, slightly curved blades, with a new steel hilt of 'honeysuckle' design, with a brass pommel. Photographs taken in the 1870s and 1880s show this sword still in use.[23]

Photographs of the same era and from the same source,[24] however, show men of the 1st and 2nd Life Guards carrying a sword with a bowl hilt decorated with brass studs and the regimental cyphers applied in brass. While the photographs are clear and compelling, the author has not encountered any actual specimens, and it is not clear whether this represents a completely new design or work by the regimental armourer, using a Pattern 1820 bowl or even a Heavy Cavalry Pattern 1821 guard.

In 1882 a composite regiment of the Household Cavalry went to Egypt with Sir Garnet Wolseley and took part in the campaign to overthrow Arabi Pasha. Writing to

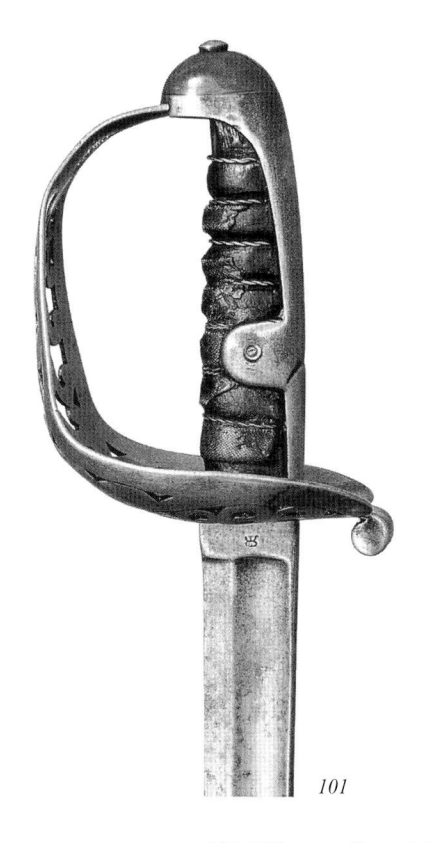

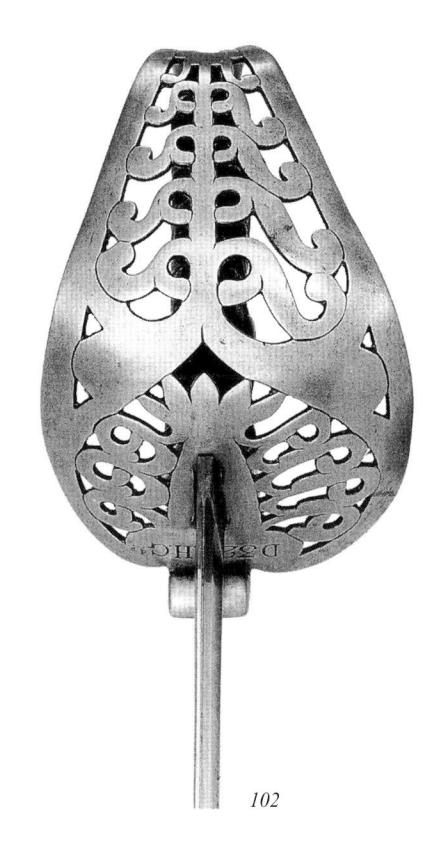

101, 102   Sword, Royal Horse Guards, Trooper, Pattern 1848

Blade length and width: 38in. x 1¼in.
Blade type: slightly curved, rounded back, single fuller each side to within 12½in. of spear point, double edged for last 12in.
Guard: steel basket of 'honeysuckle' form, with sword knot slit near pommel.
Hilt mounts: steel but with smooth brass hemispherical pommel; ears on backpiece riveted through tang.
Grip: wood, covered in fishskin and bound with brass wire.
Scabbard: steel, two bands with large domed bosses and loose rings.
Note: this specimen marked 'D32RH^{GD}', i.e. sword 32, D Troop, Royal Horse Guards.

(Royal Armouries IX-703)

the Duke of Cambridge about the action at Magfar on 24 August 1882, Wolseley reported that the Household Cavalry: 'with their heavy swords, cut men from the head to the waist-belt'.[25]

This may have been a slight exaggeration but it suggests that the swords then in use, in the right hands, were not ineffective. This is significant in view of later criticism.

Nevertheless, by 1882 the swords of all three regiments were in need of replacement in view of the length of time that they had been in service, and the decision had been taken that the replacements should be made at Enfield, rather than by a private manufacturer. What happened then sheds an interesting light upon the way in which swords had been procured by the regiments before. Having been entrusted with the job of providing new swords, the Superintendent at the RSAF Enfield (Colonel

Arbuthnot) not unreasonably asked to be provided with a detailed specification. No such specification was available, since it transpired that the swords had always been manufactured as a result of discussions between the regiments and the private firms.

In due course, Arbuthnot was provided with one of the Pattern 1820 swords of the 1st Life Guards and instructed to use that as a general pattern.[26] By his later testimony, Arbuthnot was not much impressed by this sword. The blade, in his opinion, was much too weak and in his own words: '...they were not swords at all to my mind, they were rapiers; they were perfectly straight blades and very long blades'.[27] He therefore obtained permission to lighten the hilt and put more strength into the blades. The original Pattern 1820 sword, which had been made by Wilkinsons, together with Arbuthnot's modified version were then submitted to the commanding officers of the three regiments for their views. Those of Lieutenant-Colonel Fred Burnaby, the famous traveller, commanding the Royal Horse Guards, are of particular interest:

> 'In reply to your letter of 22nd instant and accompanying correspondence, with reference to the relative merits of the Royal Small Arms Factory sword and the Wilkinson sword, I have the honour to acquaint you that I prefer the Wilkinson sword in preference to the other.
> I prefer, however, the hilt of the Small Arms Factory sword as it is larger and affords more protection to the hand. The ornamental work on the hilt should be closer to prevent a sword or bayonet thrust going through. As to the studs on the hilt, I think a plain hilt would be preferable. I entirely approve of the manner in which the Wilkinson sword is slung.[28]

As we have seen, the Wilkinson sword was almost certainly a relatively recent specimen of the Pattern 1820 sword; what may be the Royal Small Arms Factory sword is preserved in the Pattern Room at Nottingham, where it is labelled as having been received from the Tower of London in 1881. This latter sword, (Plate 103) has a blade of the same length as the Pattern 1820 sword but weighs some 5 ozs less, which indicates that considerable weight had been saved by the new hilt.

The result of Arbuthnot's work and the views of the commanding officers appeared in 1882 in the form of two new patterns - the Sword, Household Cavalry, Long, Pattern 1882, Mark I and the Sword, Household Cavalry, Short, Pattern 1882, Mark I.[29] The 'Long' sword had a blade length of 38 7/8 inches and weighed 2lbs 5 ozs (Plate 104). The scabbard had a lower loose ring 11 inches from the mouth, a fixed upper ring 3 1/2 inches from the mouth and a fixed loop on the inside (right side) opposite the upper fixed ring. The 'Short' sword, which was intended for bandsmen and trumpeters, had a 34 3/4 inch blade, the sword weighing 2lbs 2ozs. The scabbard had two loose rings and was minus the fixed loop on the inside. The guard for both swords was a 'scroll' design, in strapwork, embodying the initials 'HC' under a crown. Compared with the RSAF Enfield trial pattern, the guard lacks the former's brass studs round the edge of

Household Cavalry Troopers' Swords

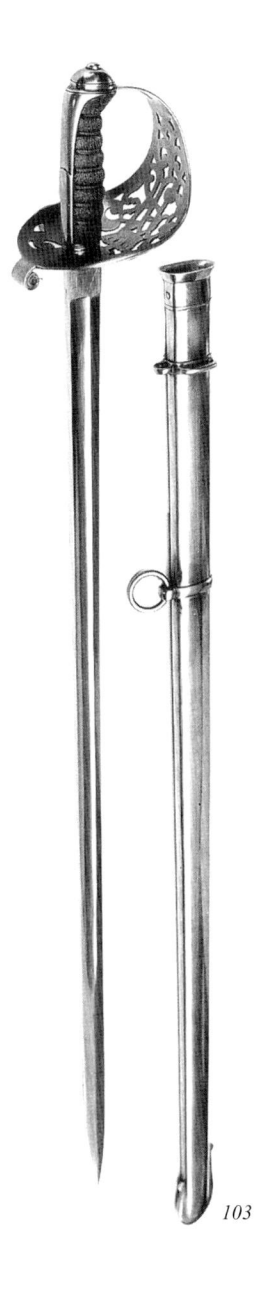

103   Sword, Household Cavalry, Experimental, Pattern 1881

Blade length and width: $38^7/_8$in. x $1^1/_8$in.
Blade type: flat back, fuller each side to within 13in. of point; double edged for last 15in.
Guard: steel, with brass studs.
Hilt mounts: steel.
Grip: wood, covered with fishskin and bound with brass wire.
Scabbard: steel, wood lined.
Sword weight: 2lb 8oz.
Scabbard weight: 2lb 1oz.

(MoD Pattern Room, Nottingham)

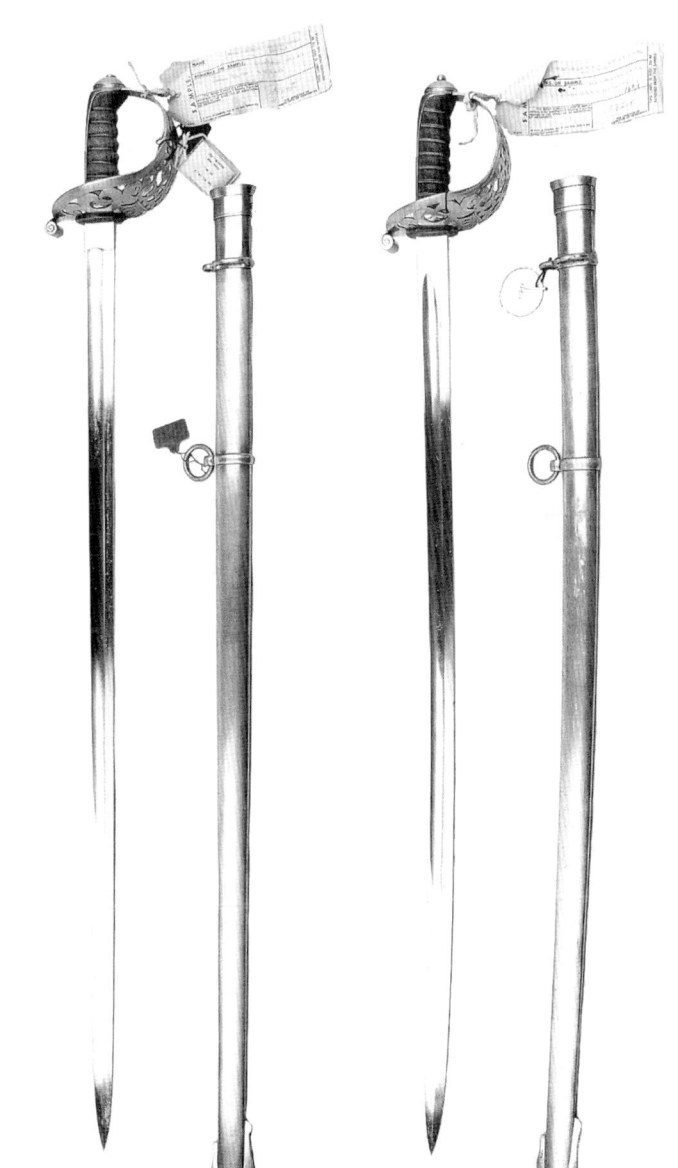

103

104   Sword, Household Cavalry, Long, Patterns 1882 (left) and 1888 - comparison of blades

Blade lengths and widths: $38^7/_8$in. x $1^3/_{16}$in. (Pattern 1882); $37^1/_8$in. x $1^1/_4$in. (Pattern 1888).
Guards: steel.
Hilt mounts: steel.
Grips: wood, covered with fishskin and bound with brass wire (Pattern 1882) or German silver wire (Pattern 1888).
Scabbards: steel.
Sword weights: 2lb 5oz (Pattern 1882); 2lb 9oz (Pattern 1888).
Scabbard weights: 1lb 14oz (Pattern 1882); 1lb 13oz (Pattern 1888).

(MoD Pattern Room, Nottingham)

104

the guard, and the backpiece does not have ears riveted through and ends in a true pommel.

Despite Arbuthnot's original strictures about strength, the 'Long' pattern sword weighed 3 ozs less than the Pattern 1864 Cavalry sword, which had a blade 3 inches shorter and it was only 2 ozs heavier than the Pattern 1882 Cavalry (Long) sword which also had a blade 3 inches shorter and was to be severely criticised for lack of strength. By implication, therefore, the Household Cavalry 'Long' pattern was too light in proportion to its length.

Early in 1886, a further supply of these swords was required. It would appear that already there were doubts about the merits of the Pattern 1882 swords, although they had never been tested on active service, since the Director of Artillery suggested to the Adjutant-General (Wolseley) that a committee should be set up, consisting of the Inspector-General of Cavalry and representatives of the three Household Cavalry regiments, to consider whether the 1882 patterns needed modification. Wolseley, instead, asked the three commanding officers for their views. The COs of the 2nd Life Guards and the Royal Horse Guards had no fault to find with the swords. The CO of the 1st Life Guards thought that, while the patterns as a whole were satisfactory, the blade of the 'Long' sword was not strong enough. He suggested that it should be shortened and the forte strengthened. The matter was referred to Colonel Arbuthnot, at Enfield, who thought that the 'Long' blade was too light and too long, and that the suggestions of the CO of the 1st Life Guards would certainly improve it. In another report, dated 3 June 1886, he went further and now considered, somewhat ironically, that the whole pattern was a bad one on account of the weak blade. He pointed out that the 'Long' pattern weighed virtually the same as the ordinary Pattern 1885 cavalry sword, which was nearly $4^1/2$ inches shorter and from which it followed that the Household Cavalry blade was, in proportion, some 2 ozs too light.[30]

The failure of the ordinary Pattern 1882 Cavalry swords was still fresh in the minds of the authorities at the Horse Guards, and both the Commander-in-Chief (the Duke of Cambridge) and the Adjutant-General (Wolseley) were inclined to be critical of a system that allowed failures of this kind. Cambridge, in particular, felt that the technical officers - notably the Superintendent at Enfield - had been remiss in not having pointed out the defects in the Pattern 1882 Household Cavalry swords before. He refused to allow the Household Cavalry to be equipped with a sword which had been condemned by the officer responsible for its manufacture - and, he might have said, for a large share of its design. But the wretched Colonel Arbuthnot could reasonably claim to have been unfairly criticised. He had been asked to produce copies of the original 1820 pattern; he had nevertheless improved it, albeit not enough; and, given the peculiar position and influence of the Household Cavalry, he obviously felt constrained in the lengths to which he could go in designing a new sword, particularly in relation to the length of the blade. Indeed, it might be said that it was impossible to design a satisfactory blade as long as 38 inches.

Household Cavalry Troopers' Swords

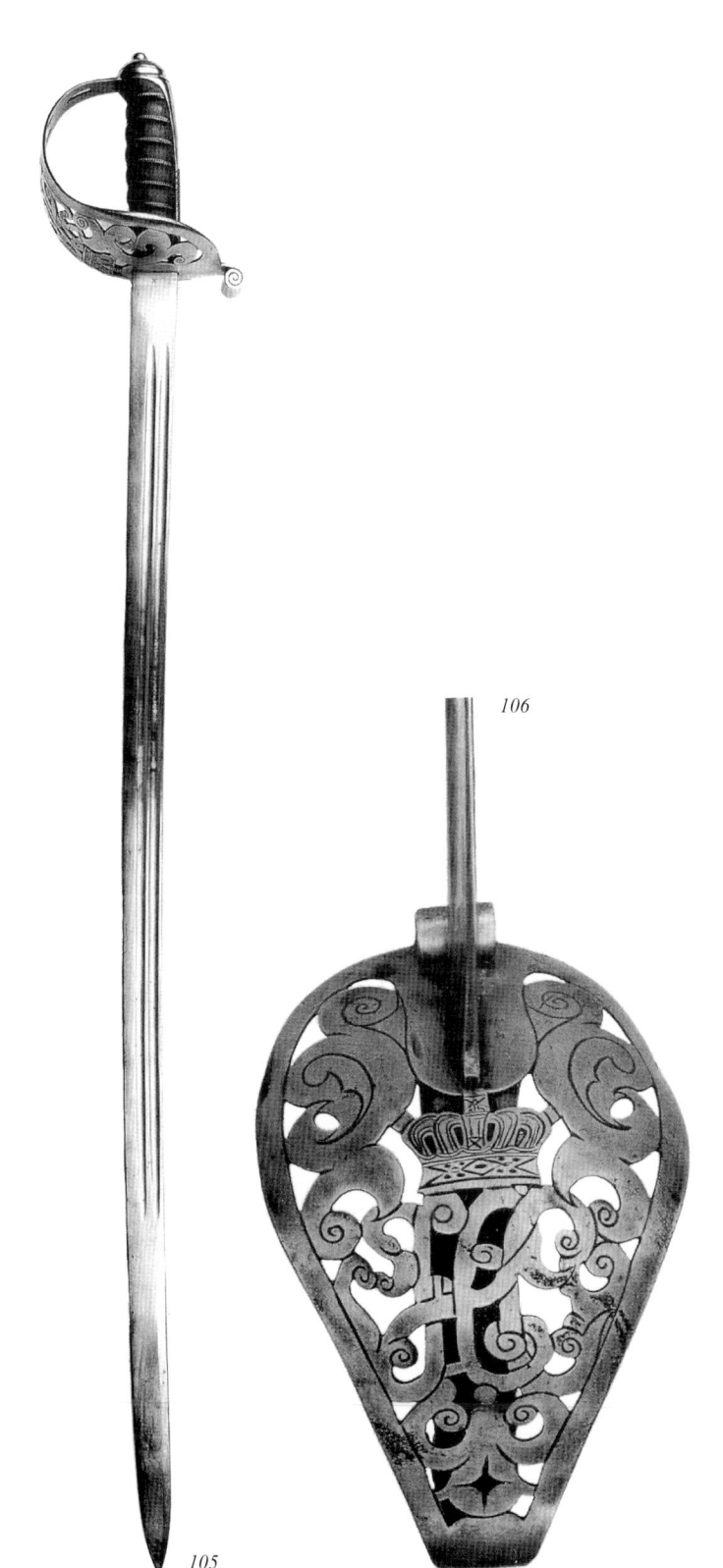

105 Sword, Household Cavalry, Trooper, Experimental, Pattern 1891

Blade length and width: 37in. x 1¼in.
Blade type: straight, round back, double fuller each side, extending from 2 in. from shoulder to 26 in., spear point.
Guard: Household Cavalry, Trooper, Pattern 1888.
Hilt mounts: steel.
Grip: wood, bound with fishkin and German silver wire.
Scabbard: steel, two bands and loose rings.
Note: the unusual double-fullered blade and the fact that the blade is by Wilkinson and the guard by Mole indicates that this is almost certainly one of the experimental swords made up in 1891.

(NAM 6706-40-11)

106 Sword, Household Cavalry, Pattern 1892, Mark 1

Blade length and width: 34½in. x 1¼in.
Blade type: identical with Cavalry, Pattern 1890.
Guard: steel basket, hollow scroll quillon.
Hilt mounts: steel.
Grip: wood, covered with fishskin and bound with German silver wire; inside length 5½in.
Scabbard: virtually identical with Cavalry, Pattern 1885, Mark II, except for an additional loose ring on back, 8½in. from mouth.
Sword weight: 2lb 4¼oz.
Scabbard weight: 1lb 15½oz.
Note: the filled-in spaces in the guard round the blade should be compared with Household Cavalry, Pattern 1888.

(NAM 9508-1)

Household Cavalry Troopers' Swords

No criticism had been made of the hilt of the 1882 Household Cavalry swords so the problem was to design a satisfactory blade. The result of Enfield's efforts was the Sword, Household Cavalry, Long, Pattern 1888, which replaced the two 1882 patterns, (Plate 104).[31] The hilt was virtually identical with the 1882 patterns. The scabbard was similar in general form although curved and shorter and lighter to match the new blade. In September 1891, a Mark II version of this Pattern 1888 scabbard appeared in which the lower band and ring were 1 inch nearer, ($9^3/4$ instead of $10^3/4$ inches), to the mouth; these scabbards are marked 'II'.[32]

The main difference in the Pattern 1888 sword is that the blade, which is slightly curved, has no distinct ricasso and in consequence has a slightly different shaped fuller, starting some 2 inches from the shoulder and finishing some $10^1/2$ inches from the point. It is $1^3/4$ inches ($37^1/8$ against $38^7/8$) shorter than the Pattern 1882 Long blade, but the sword as a whole is 4 ozs heavier and since the hilt was virtually identical most of this extra weight went into the blade which is correspondingly stronger. Even so, this Household Cavalry Pattern 1888 sword was evidently still too light or too long, as becomes evident when compared with the slightly later Pattern 1890 Cavalry sword, which is 3 inches shorter but weighs the same.

The Pattern 1888 Household Cavalry sword had a comparatively short life although never used on active service. In February 1890, it was necessary to procure a further 350 swords and the Adjutant-General agreed a revised specification put up by Enfield which was designed to make the Pattern 1888 sword and scabbard stand up to more stringent proof. This specification was sealed in March 1890 but three months later the Director-General of Ordnance Factories enquired whether steps should not now be taken to produce an entirely new pattern for the Household Cavalry in view of the fact that the ordinary cavalry of the line had just been given a new sword, (the Sword, Cavalry, Pattern 1890). It may have been in his mind that the Household Cavalry should adopt the same sword or that the Household Cavalry blade should be strengthened as the ordinary cavalry blade had been. Be that as it may, the RSAF and Wilkinsons were each asked to make up six blades, each 37 inches long and weighing between 1lb 10ozs and 1lb 12ozs. These twelve blades, fitted with Pattern 1888 Household Cavalry hilts, were completed by May 1891, (Plate 105).

The resulting swords, however, were considered badly balanced and the RSAF was asked to submit modified versions, designed to balance nearer the hilt; whereas the original Enfield and Wilkinson swords had balanced between $7^7/8$ and $7^3/4$ inches from the hilt, the modified swords were to balance between 6 and $6^1/4$ inches. In addition, Enfield was asked to make up a number of swords consisting of the existing Household Cavalry hilt mated to an ordinary Pattern 1890 cavalry blade.

Enfield was of the view that to bring the balance back to between 6 and $6^1/2$ inches from the hilt would require a significant increase in the weight of the blade. In view of this, the Adjutant-General decided that trials should proceed only with the swords mounted with Pattern 1890 cavalry blades.

Trials took place at the Hyde Park Barracks in August 1891 and proved disappointing as regards the cutting power of the swords. The general view was that the hilt was too heavy for the blade and that more weight was needed near the point. A further modified sword to meet these criticisms was produced by the RSAF and submitted again to the three Household Cavalry regiments. While the two regiments of Life Guards were strongly in favour, the Royal Horse Guards favoured thrusting swords and therefore found the trial sword too short. The Inspector-General of Cavalry was of the same opinion.

The Director of Artillery was of the view that the arguments over thrusting versus cutting were never likely to be settled to everyone's satisfaction. He recommended that the pattern arrived at should be adopted. His view was accepted and the pattern was sealed in June 1892 as the Sword, Household Cavalry, Pattern 1892.[33] Except for the tang, the blade was identical to that of the ordinary Pattern 1890 cavalry sword, (see Chapter 3). The tang and the hilt were virtually identical to the Household Cavalry Pattern 1888 sword except that the guard was lighter, four of the open spaces were filled in and the scroll quillon was hollow, (Plate 106). The sword balanced 7 inches from the hilt. The scabbard was basically the same as the ordinary cavalry Pattern 1885, Mark II scabbard except that it had two bands, the lower of which had an unusually large loose ring, while the upper band had a small fixed ring on the back edge and a fixed flat loop or bar on the inside. The sword weight was 2lbs 4$^{1}/_{4}$ ozs and that of the scabbard 1lb 15$^{1}/_{2}$ ozs.

In 1902, a revised version (the Sword, Household Cavalry, Pattern 1892, Mark II) was introduced.[34] It differed from the first version in having a longer grip (5$^{7}/_{8}$ as against 5$^{1}/_{2}$ inches) to allow the thumb to lie flat along the backpiece, while the sword as a whole was some 3 ozs heavier, at 2lbs 7$^{1}/_{4}$ ozs, the extra weight having gone mainly into the blade, although some went into thicker gauge metal for the guard. With the accession of King Edward VII, the crown in the guard was changed from the St Edward's Crown used in earlier versions to the Tudor Crown.[35]

When the Pattern 1908 cavalry sword was introduced, the Household Cavalry retained their Pattern 1892, Mark II swords for ceremonial use but carried the Pattern 1908 on active service, the first issues of the latter sword being made to the Household Cavalry apparently in 1911.

Chapter 5: Notes

1. See F Wilkinson, *Swords and Daggers*, London (1967) Plate 101. From its quality, however, it could be a warrant-officer's or, more improbably, an officer's sword.

2. I am indebted to the late James Rowntree for this reference.

3. See Latham, *op. cit.*, p85, quoting from a pamphlet issued by Thomas Gill in 1790.

4. PRO. WO 3/15, p263. Charles Lennox, 3rd Duke of Richmond, Colonel of the Royal Horse Guards from 1795.

5. PRO. WO 3/29, p158, letter of 2 December 1796.

6. Royal Horse Guards Letter Book, No 42, p2 - Household Cavalry Museum (HCM), Windsor.

7. *Ibid.*, p4.

8. C H Smith, *Costume of the Army of the British Empire*, London (1814-15).

9. Royal Collection No 1789 - reproduced in Miller and Dawnay, *op. cit.*, Vol I, Plate 245.

10. Royal Collection, No 762.

11. See G R Worrall, 'The Household Cavalry Troopers [sic] Sword 1780-c.1820', *Guns, Weapons and Militaria*, Vol I, No 1, 1981, pp40-41.

12. See James Rowntree, 'Some observations on the Household Cavalry Trooper's Sword 1780-c1820 by G R Worrall', *ibid.*, Vol 2, No 9, p14, 1984.

13. 1st Life Guards Record Book No 127, p57 (HCM).

14. See Jenny Spencer-Smith, *Portraits for a King: The British Military Paintings of A-J Dubois Drahonet*, National Army Museum, London (1990) Nos 14 and 12.

15. I am indebted to Mr G R Worrall for pointing this out.

16. Spencer-Smith, *op. cit.*, No 16.

17. 2nd Life Guards Letter Book No 109, p152 (HCM).

18. Including the NAM, the Royal Armouries and the Castle Museum, York. Another specimen was sold by Wallis & Wallis in 1977, marked 'Woolley', an appellation in use until *c*1797: see also Worrall, *op. cit.*, p41.

19. Spencer-Smith, *op. cit.*, Nos 19 and 21.

20. *Ibid.*, No 20.

21. I am indebted to Mr Karl Purdy for these references.

22. 1887, *Royal Commission on War-like Stores* - evidence of E C Nepean, Director of Stores, War Office (Question 1204).

23. NAM 7504-35-74 and -81.

24. *Ibid.*, -45 and -31, for example. Mr G R Worrall informs me that he has noted three of the Pattern 1848 RHG swords marked to the 2nd Life Guards.

25. Lehmann, *op. cit.*, p309.

26. 1887 *Royal Commission*, Questions 5552 and 1210.

27. *Ibid.*, Question 5556.

28. Royal Horse Guards Letter Book No 47, p1 (HCM). Burnaby was killed in January 1885 at the Battle of Abu Klea, defending himself with his sword against Dervish spearmen.

29. *LC* 4052, 1 July 1882 and *LC* 4076, 1 August 1882.

30. Colonel the Hon R A J Talbot, 1st Life Guards, was even more critical in his evidence to the 1887 *Royal Commission* (Question 2828): 'I think the swords are utterly unserviceable. They are lighter in proportion to the length than any sword in the service. They are made of very bad steel, as is proved by the fact that when they are bent at all they do not fly back to the straight position; and, if bent to a great degree, they snap'. See also his response to Question 2835: 'I do not think it is a safe sword to use'. This evidence raises interesting questions as to the unofficial tests that went on in the regiments. Talbot believed that the pre-1882 patterns were better and stronger, which may be doubted.

31. *LC* 5928, 1 March 1890.

32. *LC* 6601, 1 February 1892.

33. *LC* 6859, 1 November 1892.

34. *LC* 11290, 1 November 1902.

35. For a detailed study of the forms of crown used on swords between 1788 and 1914, see N P Dawnay, 'Crowns and Coronets on Military Appointments', *JSAHR*, Museum Supplement No 47, 1961.

6. Household Cavalry Officers' Swords

We have little clear evidence about the precise patterns of sword carried by the officers of each of the three Household Cavalry regiments between 1788 and 1796.

As regards pictorial evidence, a portrait of Lieutenant-Colonel William John Arabin, 2nd Life Guards, painted by A Morris and exhibited at the Royal Academy in 1791, (and now in the Cavalry and Guards Club in London), shows him carrying a straight sword, with a basket guard composed of curved bars and pierced panels, similar to that carried earlier by the 1st Troop of Horse Grenadier Guards. A similar sword appears in a portrait of Captain George Porter, who served in the 1st Troop of Horse Guards from 1780 to 1783; and also in a portrait of an officer of the 1st Troop of Horse Guards by Frederick George Byron, dated 1786, now in the Anne S K Brown Military Collection, Providence, Rhode Island. An actual specimen of this pattern is at Windsor, (Laking 760); it is by Bland and can therefore be dated to 1768-1787/8 but it cannot be linked directly to the Household Cavalry. A sword formerly in the author's possession, dated 1788 and bearing a Garter star on the blade, may possibly be a sword of the Royal Horse Guards, (Plates 107, 108), although it is probable that the hilt is not contemporary with the blade. Similar basket-hilted swords are shown in Hoppner's portrait of the 10th Earl of Strathmore *c*1789, and in Sir Joshua Reynolds' portrait of the Marquess of Granby, one version of which was completed in 1766.

The problem is compounded by the fact of the amalgamation of the various troops of Horse and Horse Grenadier Guards into two regiments of Life Guards in 1788, since it may well be that swords carried before 1788 were retained in service after that date. Two swords at Windsor, (Laking 751, (Plate 109) and Windsor 759 (formerly Laking 749)), and another formerly in the collection of the late W Howarth, (illustrated in F Wilkinson's *Swords and Daggers*, London (1967)) are characterised by broad, single edged, longish blades and bright steel, barred basket hilts of 'Inniskilling' form, with white shagreen-covered grips. The blade of Windsor 759 was made by J F Raab at Hertzberg in 1782 while the scabbard was apparently supplied by John Bland (1767-1787/88). It would appear to be the sword supplied to the Duke of York when he was appointed Colonel of the 2nd Troop of Horse Grenadier Guards in 1782. Laking 751 is not dated, although a note in the Carlton House Catalogue refers to Bland and Foster, (1787/88-1791/92), which may relate only to the scabbard (black leather, with steel locket and chape). The blades of these swords are shorter than the 39 inches prescribed for the Pattern 1788 Heavy Cavalry troop-

Household Cavalry Officers' Swords

108

107

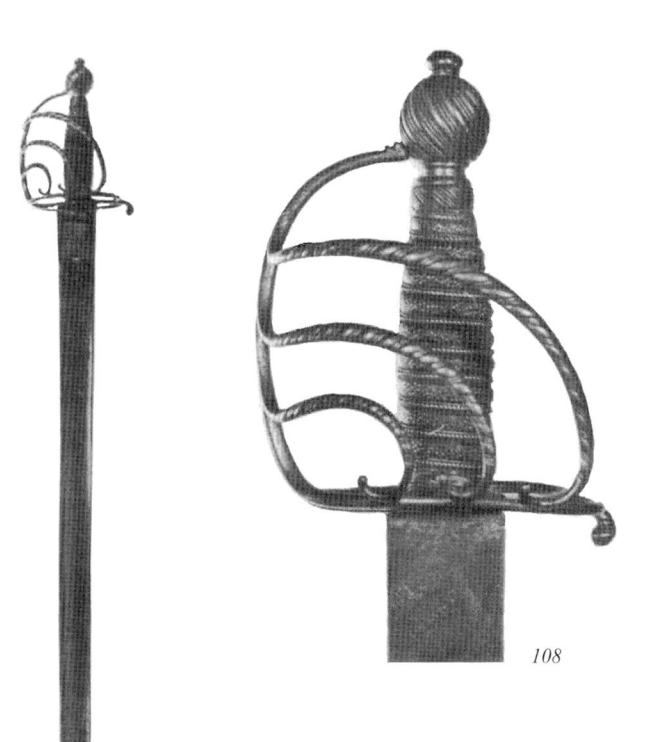

107   Sword, Royal Horse Guards, 1788
Blade length and width: 30¼in. x 1½in. x ⅜in.
Blade type: straight, flat back, broad fuller each side to within ½in. of point; double edged for last 7in.
Guard: steel basket; no provision for sword knot.
Hilt mounts: steel.
Grip: wood, covered with sharkskin and bound with copper wire.
Sword weight: 2lb 0oz.
Note: Made by Gill and marked on back of blade 'Warranted to cut iron'. The blade bears the Garter star, the cypher of George III and the date 1788. There is no scabbard, but by analogy with other swords of the period it could be expected to have been of leather.

(Formerly Author's Collection)

108   Sword, Royal Horse Guards, 1788
 - right side of hilt

(Formerly Author's Collection)

109   Sword, Household Cavalry, *c*1788
Blade length and width: 34½in. x 1⁷⁄₁₆in.
Blade type: straight, flat back, spear point, two broad fullers each side for 9in. from shoulder, becoming one broad and two narrow fullers almost to the point.
Guard: polished steel basket with three faceted outer bars on each side, slotted round blade.
Hilt mounts: polished steel, with ovoid faceted pommel.
Grip: wood, bound with white shagreen or rayskin and copper foil.
Scabbard: black leather, steel chape and locket, with frog stud, and a flat steel loop near mouth.
Note: acquired from Bland & Foster (1787/88-1791/2).

(The Royal Collection © Her Majesty The Queen, Laking no 751)

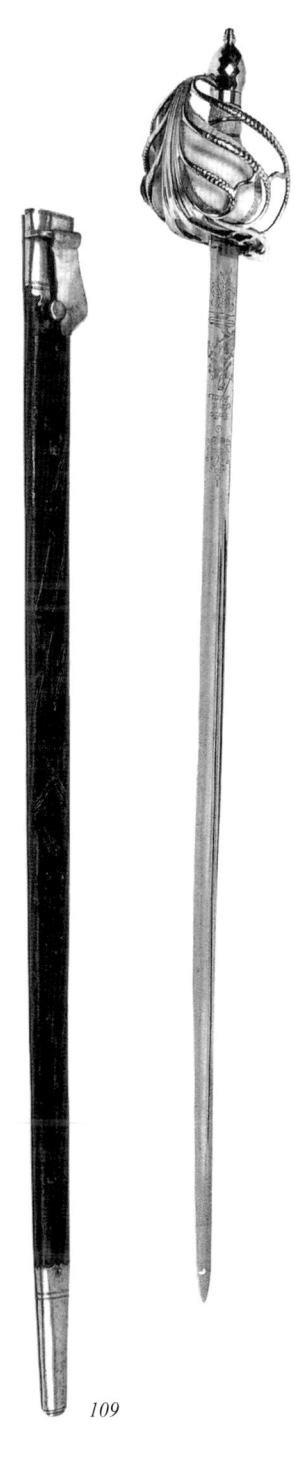

109

125

ers' sword but otherwise the resemblance, albeit in a more elaborate form, is sufficient to suggest that these may be specimens of the swords carried by Household Cavalry officers after 1788. One may at least be tolerably certain that officers of the Household Cavalry carried long, straight-bladed swords, with basket hilts of curved bars, of the same generic pattern as those carried by the heavy cavalry of the line.

There is evidence that, in addition to these heavy service swords, which must have been very unwieldy when dismounted, officers carried a lighter sword known as a 'frock' sword and obviously intended for dismounted and off-duty wear. A letter from Frederick, Duke of York to George, Prince of Wales in April 1782, referring, *inter alia*, to what was probably Windsor 751, refers also to a 'frock' sword[1] and Farmer, in his *Universal Dictionary* of 1810, uses the same term (see page 82).

From 1796, the ground becomes firmer. On 30 December 1796, the officers of the 1st Life Guards were ordered to 'supply themselves with the new pattern broadsword and knot'.[2] A Letter Book of the Royal Horse Guards contains an extract from the General Order, issued by the Adjutant-General on 1 July 1796, announcing the introduction of the Pattern 1796 disc-hilted sword for heavy cavalry troopers.[3] Finally, an Order Book of the 2nd Life Guards of the period contains an extract from an order of 25 September 1797, issued by Major-General Lord Cathcart:

'Swords: Two only are regimental or ever to be worn with Regimentals, the Broad Sword and the Gilt Sword ordered by His Majesty for the Cavalry; the Broad Sword to be worn on all duties with Arms mounted or dismounted, always in the belt and always with the leather sling and Crimson and Gold Tossil. The other sword may be worn at all other times with a frog under the waistcoat to hang just low enough to be quite clear of the Bridle Hand and when on horseback; this sword is always to have a crimson and gold Sword Knot of the pattern approved by His Majesty.[4]

These extracts make it clear that officers of the Household Cavalry regiments followed the ordinary heavy cavalry in carrying the ladder - (or 'first honeysuckle' pattern) hilted broadsword, (Plate 64) and the boatshell-hilted small sword, (Plate 61) introduced in 1796, (see Chapter 4). The ladder-hilted sword is shown in a careful pencil drawing of an officer of the 2nd Life Guards, c1802 by Robert Dighton Junior,[5] and a portrait by the same artist of an officer of the Royal Horse Guards, c1805.

Charles Hamilton Smith's coloured lithograph of an officer of the 2nd Life Guards in Full Dress, dated 1 July 1812, shows a broad straight blade with hatchet point, similar to that of the Pattern 1796 Heavy Cavalry troopers' sword, with a steel guard which might be either a pierced basket or an engraved bowl, the edges of which have either raised studs or pierced holes: the scabbard is of iron or steel. Smith is deemed to be a reliable painter of uniforms and equipment, having been an officer himself, but it seems probable that he was here attempting to portray the ladder-hilted sword. Unfortunately, he did not publish similar drawings of the other two regiments. However, a ladder-hilted Pattern 1796 Heavy Cavalry officers' sword engraved on the guard 'Worn at Waterloo by Capt W T Drake R H Gds' is in the NAM, (8505-26), (Plate 110). (It may be noted, however, that the sword alleged to have been carried at Waterloo by the famous Captain Edward Kelly, and now in the Household Cavalry Museum at Windsor, was, in fact, a Pattern 1796 Light Cavalry officers' sword, suggesting that on active service officers were accustomed to suiting themselves when it came to swords for fighting).

In 1814 another artist who specialised in military paintings, Denis Dighton, painted an officer of the Royal Horse Guards in mounted order.[6] Dighton was a meticulous artist who worked generally from detailed pencil drawings and the accuracy of his portrayal here can be relied upon. The sword shown in this 1814 picture has an ornate gilt hilt of a kind not hitherto seen in British military swords, (Plates 111, 112, 113). The same hilt is shown three years later in a painting by the same artist of officers of the 1st Life Guards, dated 1817.[7]

The origins of this sword are not entirely clear. The long, double-fullered blade is very similar in form to that of the French Cuirassiers' sword, *Modèle AN.XI*, (1802-03), while the hilt, excluding the grip, is reminiscent of the sword of the French *Garde du Corps, Modèle 1814*.[8] The model for this new Household Cavalry sword, however, appears to be a sword at Windsor, (Laking No 766), which is described in the original Carlton House Catalogue as 'after the Pattern of Prussian Gen Darmes'.[9] It is in fact, based upon the Prussian *Kurassierpallasch, Model 1797*, and the actual Prussian sword used as a pattern is Laking 770, which bears the monogram of Frederick William III (1797-1840). Laking 766 differs in the form of the pommel from later Household Cavalry specimens, (Plate 114). This Windsor sword is shown in J S Copley's equestrian portrait of George, Prince of Wales, begun in 1805, completed in 1809 and exhibited at the Royal Academy in 1810.[10] The earliest version of this sword may be that given by the Prince of Wales to the 3rd Earl of Harrington and it has been suggested that this was in 1792 when he took command of the Life Guards. But this date seems unduly early in view of the other evidence and it seems more reasonable to date its introduction into the Household Cavalry to 1810-12, although it could be earlier. Swords with variant pommels exist, including a lion's head and a version shaped rather like a child's spinning top on a sword which may have belonged to Ernest Augustus, Duke of Cumberland, who commanded the 1st Life Guards from 1827 to 1830. But it is clear from actual specimens and paintings that the regulation pommel was the flattened ball with encircling ridge.

Dighton's 1817 picture also confirms that officers of the 1st Life Guards in Dress order were still carrying the Pattern 1796 boatshell-hilted sword.

Household Cavalry Officers' Swords

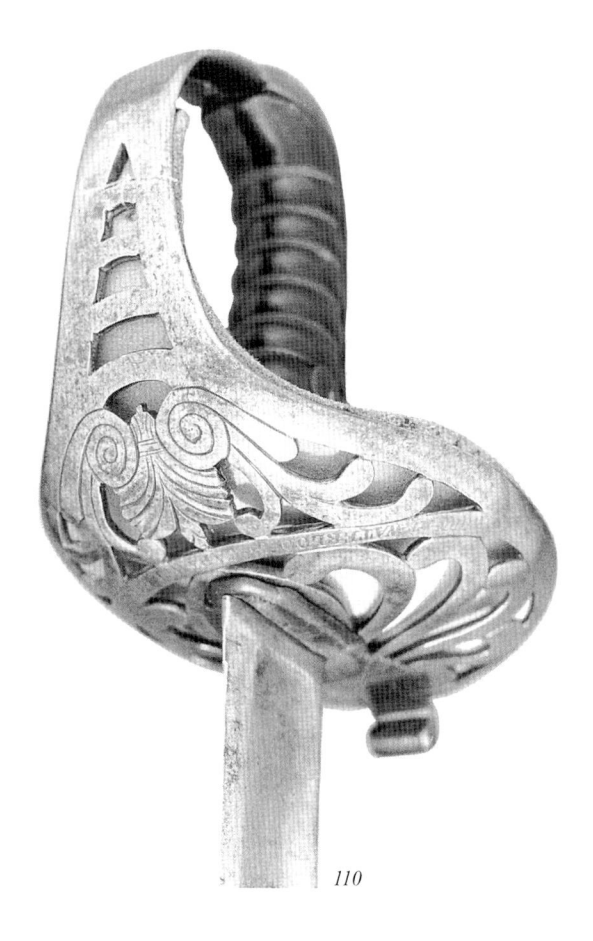

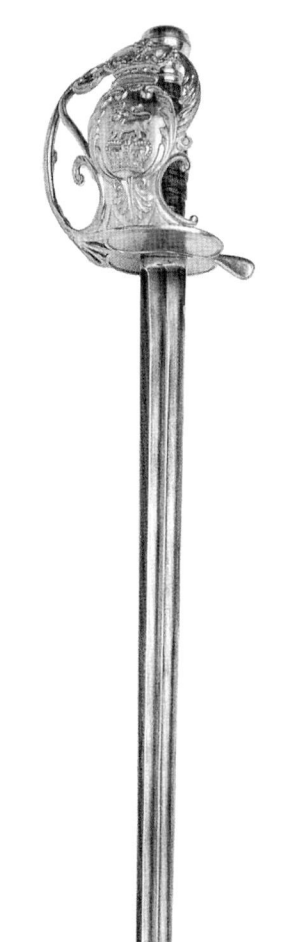

110

110   Sword, Heavy Cavalry, Pattern 1796

Note: Sword carried by Captain W T Drake, Royal Horse Guards, at Waterloo.

(NAM 8505-26)

111   Sword, Household Cavalry, Dress, Pattern 1814

Blade length and width: $37^7/_8$in. x $1^1/_8$in. x $^3/_8$in.
Blade type: straight, flat back, double fullers each side to within 1in. of point.
Guard: gilt brass, no provision for sword knot.
Hilt mounts: gilt brass.
Grip: wood, covered with fishskin and bound with brass wire.
Scabbard: gilt brass with fishskin inserts; loose rings are 3in. and $10^1/_2$in. from mouth.
Sword weight: 2lb 2oz.
Scabbard weight: 1lb 4oz.

(NAM 6912-4)

111

128

Household Cavalry Officers' Swords

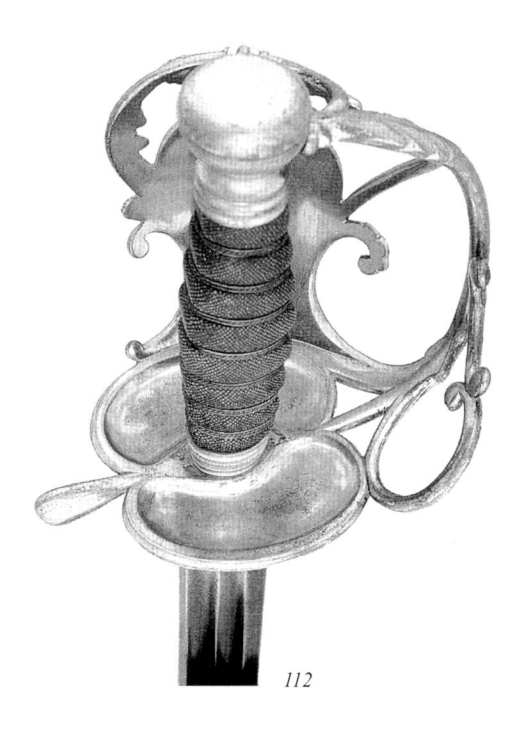

112

113

112   Sword, Household Cavalry, Dress, Pattern 1814 - inside of hilt

(NAM 6912-4)

(See also Colour Plate II)

113   Sword, Household Cavalry, Dress, Pattern 1814 - outside of hilt

(NAM 6912-4)

(See also Colour Plate II)

114   Sword, Model for Household Cavalry, Full Dress, *c*1805

Blade length and width: 34$\frac{1}{2}$in. x 1$\frac{1}{4}$in.
Blade type: straight, single edged, with two narrow fullers each side ending close to spear point.
Guard: gilt brass basket.
Hilt mounts: gilt brass.
Grip: wood, covered with brown leather and bound with steel wire.
Scabbard: wood, covered with black leather, with elaborate gilt brass chape and locket, with frog hook.
Note: the blade appears to be much earlier than the hilt. The scabbard at least was made by Prosser in 1805.

(The Royal Collection © Her Majesty The Queen, Laking no 766)

114

129

Household Cavalry Officers' Swords

The *Dress Regulations* of 1822 specified the patterns of sword to be carried by the officers of the Household Cavalry regiments. For the two regiments of Life Guards, the authorised patterns were described thus:

'Full Dress: gilt guard, pommel and boatshell; black fishskin and silver-twisted wire grip; straight blade, full thirty two inches long, one inch wide at the shoulder. Scabbard - leather, gilt chape and lockets.
Dress: gilt half-basket hilt, guard, pommel and shell; black fishskin grip with gilt twisted wire; straight steel cut and thrust blade, thirty four and a half inches long and full one inch wide at shoulder. Scabbard brass, with two narrow inlets of black fishskin.
Undress: with open shell guard, black fishskin grip - blade a little curved, with round back, thirty six inches long. Scabbard - steel.

No great difficulty arises over the Full Dress and Dress swords. The former is clearly the Pattern 1796 boatshell-hilted sword. Indeed, a Regimental (Gold Stick) Order of 9 August 1828 specifies that for the officers of the Life Guards attending Royal Drawing Rooms; '[the] cavalry small sword to be suspended straight from the hip through a frog and not with slings'. The reference to the frog in particular takes us straight back to the order of 25 September 1797, (see above).

Similarly, the description of the Dress sword, particularly in its description of the scabbard, makes it clear that this was the elaborate sword shown in Denis Dighton's picture of 1814. This is confirmed by a further Dighton portrait in the Royal Collection at Windsor of an officer of the 1st Life Guards, dated 1821, which shows this sword and scabbard quite clearly;[11] and by Dubois Drahonet's portrait of Cornet and Sub-Lieutenant Samuel Marindin, 2nd Life Guards, painted in 1832.[12]

The identification of the sword prescribed for Undress, however, presents difficulties since the description given is sketchy and confusing. The description of the blade as having a 'round back' might suggest a pipe-backed blade since this is also the description given in the same *Dress Regulations* of the Pattern 1822 Infantry Officers' blade, (see Chapter 7 below). The reference to an 'open shell guard' is meaningless by itself and the only clear piece of evidence is the length of the blade. The Household Cavalry Museum at Windsor, however, possesses three swords which belonged to Captain John Trotter, who was an officer in the 2nd Life Guards from 1825 to 1836. One of them, bearing the royal cypher of George IV (1820-30) so exactly matches the scanty description given in the *Dress Regulations* that, taken in conjunction with the date-span established by Trotter's service and the royal cypher, there can be no serious doubt that this is the Undress sword referred to. It is, in fact, identical with the honeysuckle-hilted sword, with pipe-backed blade, authorised for heavy cavalry officers in 1822, (see Chapter 4 and Plate 69). Its date of introduction can be fixed by reference to a Gold Stick Order of the 1st Life Guards of 20 May

Household Cavalry Officers' Swords

1820 which refers to the introduction of a new pattern of sword for officers which can only be the Undress sword, since the Full Dress and Dress swords had been in service for some years.[13]

By comparison, the identification of the swords prescribed in the 1822 *Dress Regulations* for the Royal Horse Guards presents no problems. Only two swords were authorised, one for Full Dress and Undress and one for Dress. The description of

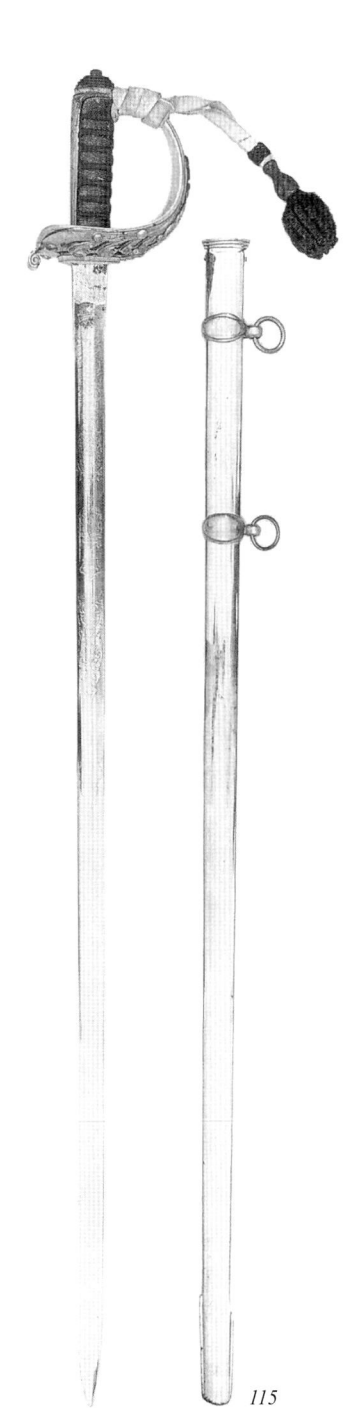

115   Sword, 1st Life Guards, Dress and Undress, Pattern 1834

Blade length and width: 39in. x 1 1/8in.
Blade type: straight, flat back, spear point, single fuller each side.
Guard: nickel-plated steel, with gilt brass ornaments.
Hilt mounts: plated steel but with brass pommel.
Grip: wood, covered with fishskin and bound with German silver wire.
Scabbard: steel, with two brass bands and loose rings and brass shoe.
Note: this is a late specimen, belonging to H M Grenfell, who joined the regiment in 1892. In the original 1834 specification the blade was to have a hatchet point.

(NAM 7701-14)

116   Sword, 1st Life Guards, Dress and Undress, Pattern 1834 - outside of hilt

(NAM 7701-14)

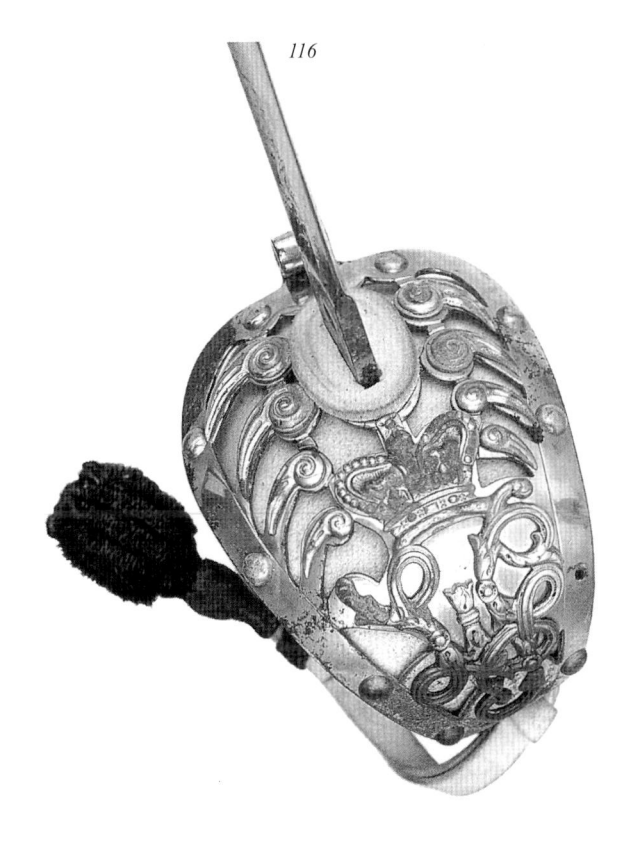

the Full Dress is identical with that for the Life Guards and is therefore the Pattern 1796 boatshell-hilted sword, except that the scabbard was of steel, with a narrow shoe. The description of the Dress sword is again identical with that of the Life Guards and is therefore the gilt-hilted sword, (Plate 111).

In the *Dress Regulations* of 1831, the steel-hilted Undress sword of the Life Guards disappears and the two regiments were then required to carry the boatshell-hilted 1796 sword in Full Dress (for Levées, Drawing Rooms etc) and the gilt-hilted sword for Dress and Undress. In the same *Regulations* the Royal Horse Guards scabbard for the boatshell-hilted sword worn in Full Dress was changed to black leather with gilt mounts, as in the ordinary heavy cavalry, and the Dress scabbard for the gilt-hilted sword was changed from brass, with fishskin inserts, to steel.

The *Dress Regulations* for 1834 introduced new swords for all three regiments. For the 1st Life Guards, the gilt-hilted sword disappears and for Dress and Undress a new sword was prescribed, under the following description:

> '...half-basket, steel pierced hilt, with regimental cipher in brass; the edges of basket ornamented with twelve plain brass studs; lining of white leather, backpiece of plain polished steel, with a brass cap; straight cut and thrust blade with hatchet edge and square back, thirty eight inches long. Scabbard - steel, with plain brass mountings.

This sword, (Plates 115, 116), is a very handsome weapon and, with minor changes, is still in use today in the Household Cavalry. Its great length makes it unsuitable for cutting and the weight in proportion to its length makes the blade somewhat weak, but there is no actual evidence from combat. Indeed, it is doubtful if it ever had much actual use in action. It is shown very clearly in Dubois Drahonet's paintings of Lieutenant Thomas Biddulph and Lieutenant Sidney Parry, both of the 1st Life Guards and both apparently painted in 1833.[14]

The 2nd Life Guards' new sword for Dress and Undress was quite different from any previous British cavalry sword, (Plate 117). The guard was described in the 1834 *Dress Regulations* as, 'half-basket hilt, with three scrolled and chased bars'. In fact, it would be more accurate to describe it as a four-bar hilt. The 'stool' (the flat surface of the guard in front of the hand) was decorated on both sides with a bursting grenade in relief, (Plate 118), a reference to the Horse Grenadier Guard troops abolished in 1788 and incorporated into the new Life Guard regiments. In the specimen that belonged originally to Captain Trotter, the grenade bears an incised rampant horse.[15] This sword is incidentally dated 1832 so its introduction antedates the 1834 *Regulations*, although its precise date of adoption is not as yet known.

The whole appearance of this sword, particularly the ornate pommel and cap, and the way in which the upper part of the grip is bent forwards is distinctly Conti-

Household Cavalry Officers' Swords

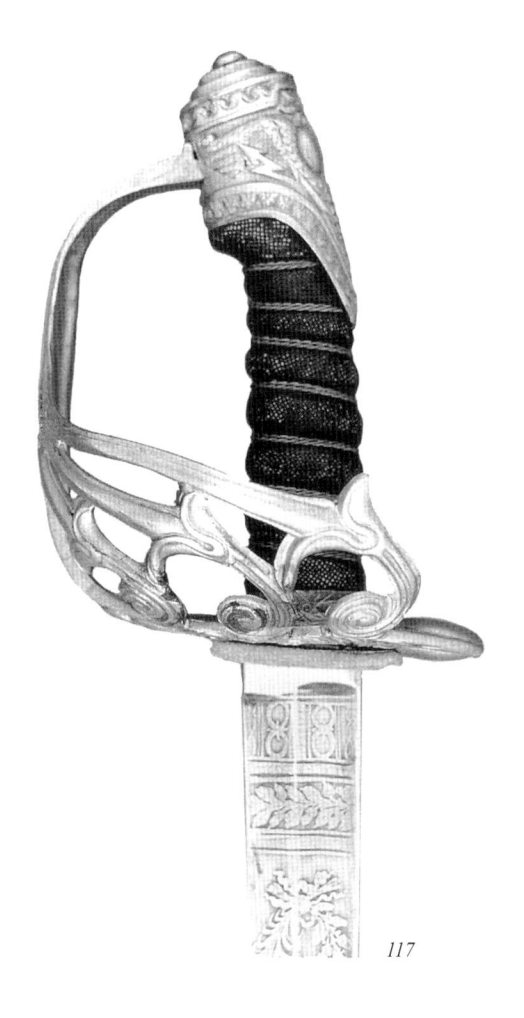

117

117   Sword, 2nd Life Guards, Dress, *c*1832

Blade length and width: 40in. x 1¼in.
Blade type: straight, flat back, fuller each side to within 8in. of spear point, double edged for last 10in.
Guard: brass.
Hilt mounts: brass.
Grip: wood, covered with fishskin and bound with brass wire.
Scabbard: steel, with two brass bands and loose rings, and elaborate brass shoe.
Sword weight: 2lb 10oz.
Scabbard weight: 1lb 8oz.

(NAM 6509-38)

**118   Sword, 2nd Life Guards, Dress, *c*1832
- inside of hilt**

Note: The grenade device on the stool and pommel should be noted. The guard and hilt mounts may originally have been intended to be of gilt brass but this is not stated in *Dress Regulations* and is not readily discernible in existing specimens - for example, Royal Armouries IX-1038 and Household Cavalry Museum HCM 76.

(NAM 6509-38)

118

133

nental and probably based upon a model such as the French *Gendarmerie* officers' sword of the Consulate and Empire periods.[16]

For both regiments of Life Guards, the sword for wear at functions such as Levées and Drawings Rooms continued after 1834 to be a boatshell-hilted sword similar to the Pattern 1796 Heavy Cavalry sword. But there is a good deal of evidence in the way of specimens to show that in the later years of the period, up to 1856, the versions used in the Household Cavalry differed in significant respects from the ordinary heavy cavalry version. Two swords in the Castle Museum at York bear the name of Sir W A Fraser, who served in the Life Guards between 1847 and 1854, (Plate 119). They are characterised by vase-shaped tang buttons, the absence of a cross-bar quillon and by the extension of the rear end of the boatshell along the knucklebow. A number of swords at Windsor - for example, Laking 822 and 919 - share these characteristics although it has not been possible to associate these swords directly with the Household Cavalry. The distinctive shape of the tang button would appear to be derived from contemporary German military designs; a sword in the NAM (7504-90), made by Moore, late Bicknell and Moore, (1838-50) had the same type of tang button and a scallop shell let into the front of the shell, (Plate 120). Household Cavalry Museum AB35 is similar.

There is a considerable number of variants of this pattern of sword, including single and double quillons, folding and fixed shells, the presence or absence of a scallop shell in the front of the shell, and flat, (Plate 121) or sharply curved shells. So far, it has not been possible to assign these variations accurately to particular periods or regiments.

If the 1834 *Dress Regulations* were reasonably precise in their descriptions of the swords of the two Life Guards regiments, they were remarkably obscure and even misleading regarding the swords for the Royal Horse Guards. Moreover, where the 1822 and 1831 *Regulations* had prescribed only two swords, the 1834 *Regulations* prescribed three. For Full Dress (Levées, Drawing Rooms etc), the authorised sword continued to be the Pattern 1796 boatshell-hilted sword. For Dress, the sword was described as: '...gilt guard, pommel and shell; black fishskin grip, twisted with yellow wire; straight, cut and thrust blade, full one inch wide at shoulder, and thirty nine inches long. Scabbard - steel'.

This description is highly misleading since the sword in question is actually a variation of the 2nd Life Guards Dress sword, (Plate 122), the main differences being:

(a) the stool is decorated in relief with a Tudor Crown, (Plate 123);

(b) the pommel is not stepped and bears a Tudor rose;

(c) the cap similarly bears a Tudor rose and tends to be slightly smaller;

Household Cavalry Officers' Swords

119

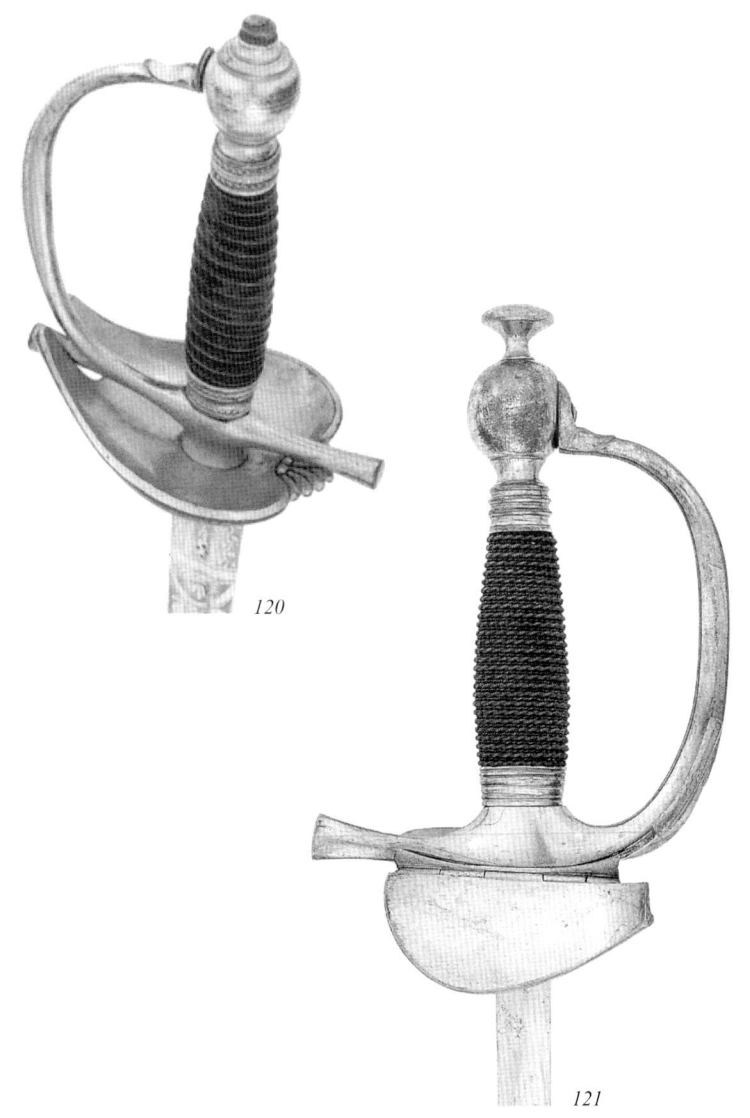

119 Sword, Life Guards, Full Dress, c1850

Guard: gilt brass boatshell.
Hilt mounts: gilt brass.
Grip: wood, bound with silver wire.
Scabbard: black leather, gilt brass locket and chape.
Note: these swords belonged to Sir W A Fraser, who served in the 1st Regiment of Life Guards from 1847 to 1854.

(Castle Museum, York, T738/2 and T737/2)

120 Sword, Life Guards, Full Dress, c1820

Blade length and width: 28 1/4in. x 7/8in.
Blade type: straight, spear point, single fuller each side.
Guard: gilt brass knucklebow, with double shell and straight quillons.
Hilt mounts: gilt brass.
Grip: wood, bound with gilt brass wire.
Scabbard: black leather, with gilt brass chape, locket and band, the two latter with loose ring, and frog stud on locket.
Note: made by Moore, late Bicknell & Moore, with cypher of George III. Note cockleshell design in opening of shells; also on frog stud.

(NAM 7504-90)

120

121 Sword, 2nd Life Guards, Full Dress, c1854 - shell guard folded

Note: the blade is by Wilkinson. Swords of this type were worn with the frock coat in dismounted order until 1856.

(NAM 6310-124)

121

Household Cavalry Officers' Swords

122

123

124

122 Sword, Royal Horse Guards, Dress, c1832
Blade length and width: 39in. x 1¼in.
Blade type: identical with 2nd Life Guards' Dress sword of same date.
Guard: gilt brass.
Hilt mounts: gilt brass.
Grip: wood, covered with fishskin and bound with brass wire.
Scabbard: identical with 2nd Life Guards' Dress sword of same date.
Sword weight: 2lb 7oz.
Scabbard weight: 1lb 12oz.
Note: although the regulations describe the guard as 'gilt', this is not readily discernible in the existing specimens that I have examined.

(NAM 6602-24-3)

(See also Colour Plate III)

123 Sword, Royal Horse Guards, Dress, c1832
- inside of hilt

(NAM 6602-24-3)

(See also Colour Plate III)

124 Sword, 2nd Life Guards (?), c1850
Blade length and width: 33½in. x 1⅛in.
Blade type: almost straight, unfullered, flat back, spear point.
Guard: four-bar in steel, grenade engraved both sides of stool.
Hilt mounts: brass pommel and ferrule, which may have been plated originally.
Grip: wood, covered with fishskin and bound with triple strands of brass wire.
Scabbard: steel, two oval brass mounts with loose rings, steel shoe.

(SUSM 1990-147)

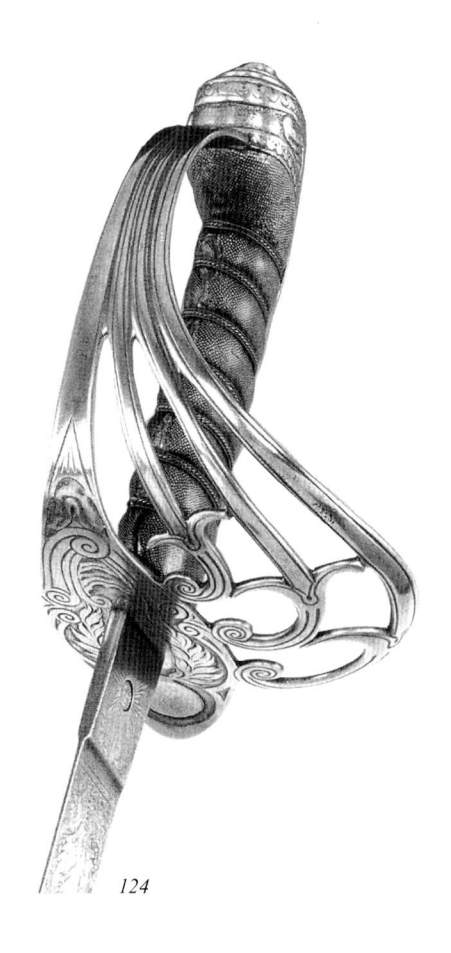

(d) the decoration generally on the hilt is of a different pattern.

Taken as a whole, the hilt is slightly less ornate than that of the 2nd Life Guards sword although clearly derived from the same source.[17] The scabbard is identical.

The real puzzle lies in the third, Undress sword. This was described in the *Regulations* as:

> 'Undress: boatshell, gilt, with silver wire grip; the blade thirty six inches long. Scabbard - thirty seven inches long, of black patent leather, with a gilt shoe, the top locket on the scabbard six inches long, the bottom locket and shoe eight inches and a half.

This description suggests that the sword was intended to be merely a longer bladed version of the Full Dress sword; a sword at Windsor (Laking 822) of this pattern has a $35^{1}/_{2}$ inch blade; other swords of this pattern with blades in excess of 35 inches are known. But it seems a curious complication to prescribe two swords which differ only in blade length. Whether both swords were carried in practice must therefore be open to some doubt. This second boatshell-hilted sword, if that is what it was, disappears in the *Dress Regulations* of 1846, and in the same *Regulations* it was laid down that officers of the Royal Horse Guards in Undress were to carry the Dress sword except in blue frock coat order when they were to carry the Full Dress boatshell-hilted sword. Officers of the 2nd Life Guards were now required to revert to the gilt-hilted sword, (Plate 111) for wear in Dress order but with a steel scabbard.

Eleven years later, the *Dress Regulations* of 1857 recorded further changes for the two regiments of Life Guards. The boatshell-hilted Full Dress sword, which had lasted since 1796 was at last abandoned. For the 2nd Life Guards, the Dress sword and scabbard were now described in terms which were almost identical with those of the Royal Horse Guards' Dress sword in the 1834 *Regulations*, including the length. It would therefore appear that the 2nd Life Guards Dress sword as prescribed in the 1857 *Regulations* was merely the 1834 Dress sword lengthened by 1 inch, a somewhat curious alteration.

The sword illustrated in Plate 124 dates from this period and from the grenade on the stool would seem to be a sword of the 2nd Life Guards. What may be this sword appears in three photographs datable to the period 1857-69.[18] All three photographs show the wearers in dismounted dress and it is possible that this sword was carried as a replacement for the old boatshell-hilted sword. But this must remain speculation until more evidence becomes available.

In the 1860s a major standardisation took place, with all three Household Cavalry regiments adopting one general pattern for all occasions except active service. This sword then became known as the State sword. The change first appears in *Dress Regulations* in 1872 but almost certainly occurred in practice some years before

Household Cavalry Officers' Swords

125 Sword, Royal Horse Guards, State sword, Pattern 1874

Note: the Wilkinson blade number (33016) shows this sword to have been made in 1892.

(NAM 6312-251-137)

126 Sword, 2nd Life Guards, State sword, Pattern 1874

Note: this sword belonged to Osbert Cecil Molyneux, 6th Earl of Sefton, who joined the regiment in 1895.

(NAM 5702-55)

127 Scabbard, 2nd Life Guards and Royal Horse Guards, State sword, c1872

Note: scabbard body plated steel, shoe, bands and rings brass or gilt brass.

(NAM 5702-55)

128 Sword, Royal Horse Guards, Pattern 1912

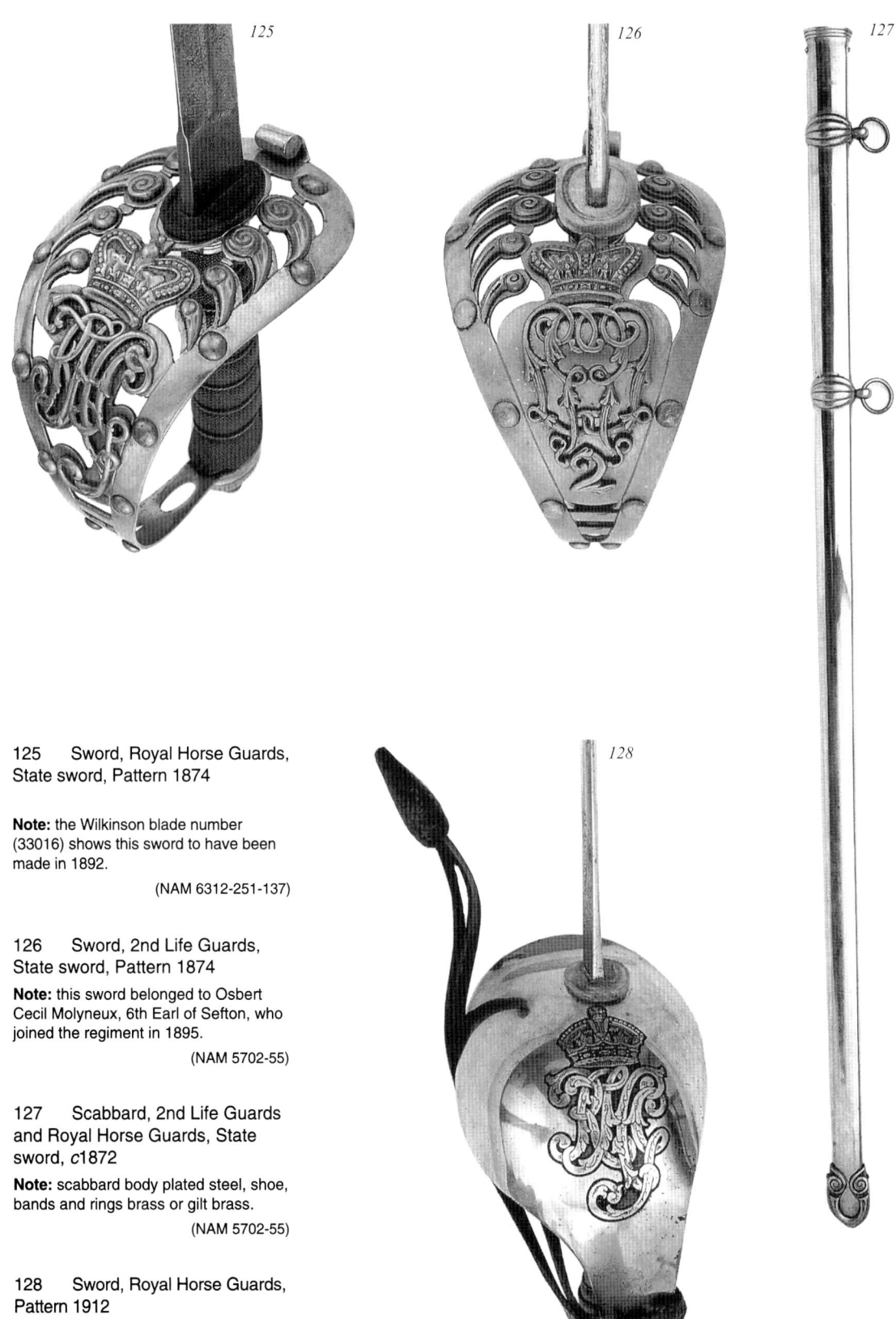

Note: note absence of normal honeysuckle pattern etching on bowl.

(NAM 8110-116)

that; at least one sword of this pattern, (see below) but with a hatchet-pointed blade, marked to the Royal Horse Guards, is known from 1860. Another example, of the 2nd Life Guards, can be dated to 1868.[19]

The basic pattern adopted was the Dress sword of the 1st Life Guards specified in the 1834 *Dress Regulations*, (Plate 115) with a steel pommel instead of brass. The swords bear the respective regimental cyphers in brass on the outside of the guard and the pommel is stepped in the case of the 1st Life Guards, (Plate 115) and a chequered hemisphere in the case of the other two regiments, (Plate 125). The plated steel scabbards also differ in their mounts, the 1st Life Guards retaining the original narrow steel shoe and stepped brass bands, while the other regiments have a decorated brass shoe and reeded bands, (Plates 115, 127).[20] The weight of all three patterns averages 2lbs 7 ozs for the sword and 1lb 4 ozs for the scabbard but since blade lengths vary between wearers the weights also vary slightly.

During the South African War of 1899-1902 the officers of the 1st Life Guards on active service wore their State swords in a brown leather-covered wooden scabbard. The officers of the other two regiments carried the ordinary cavalry sword, (Plate 87), in the standard leather-covered wooden scabbard with steel mounts introduced in 1899, (see page 100). In all cases, the scabbards were worn suspended from a frog on the Sam Browne belt.[21]

With the introduction of the Pattern 1912 Cavalry officers' sword, this pattern was prescribed for the Household Cavalry for active service; the Royal Horse Guards alone of the three regiments had its regimental cypher etched on the outside of the bowl, (Plate 128).

When the 1st and 2nd Life Guards amalgamated in 1922, the pattern of State sword adopted was that of the 2nd Life Guards with hemispherical chequered pommel but with the '2' deleted from the regimental cypher and replaced by a rosette.[22] In recent years, however, the present two regiments have reverted to having the 'LG' and 'RHG' cyphers in brass on the guards.[23]

Chapter 6: Notes

1. I am indebted to Mr A V B Norman for this reference and for information on Windsor 759.

2. 1st Life Guards Record Book No 72, p5 (HCM).

3. Royal Horse Guards Letter Book No 42, p64 (HCM).

4. See Sir George Arthur, *The Story of the Household Cavalry*, Vol II, London (1909) p501.

5. Miller and Dawnay, *op. cit.*, Vol I, Plate 284 (Royal Collection No 762). A typical specimen of this sword is HCM 32, the blade by Runkel.

6. *Ibid.*, Vol I, Plate 302 (Royal Collection No 410).

7. *Ibid.*, Vol I, Plate 303 (Royal Collection No 407).

8. See M Bottet, *De L'Arme Blanche (1789-1870)*, Paris (1959) p23 and Plate XV, 4.

9. See A V B Norman, 'The dating and identification of some swords in the Royal Collection at Windsor Castle' *JAAS*, Vol IX, 1979, pp236-40 and Plate LXXIII, A.

10. Reproduced in J D Prown, *John Singleton Copley in England 1774-1815*, Cambridge, Mass. (1966) p66. I am indebted to Mr A V B Norman for this reference.

11. Miller and Dawnay *op. cit.*, Vol I, Plate 316 (Royal Collection No 408).

12. See Spencer-Smith, *op. cit.*, Plate 15.

13. 1st Life Guards Record Book No 127, p57 (HCM).

14. Spencer-Smith, *op. cit.*, Plates 12A and 12B.

15. HCM 76.

16. Bottet, *op. cit.*, Plate IV, 2.

17. See also HCM 105, made by Wilkinson.

18. These images are:

    (1) a photograph of Colonel L D Williams who commanded the 2nd Life Guards 1854-57, in an album formerly in the United Services Club;

    (2) a lithograph based upon a photograph of the Marquess of Tweedale who commanded the 2nd Life Guards 1863-76;

    (3) a photograph of Captain Sir George Hayes' Troop of the 2nd Life Guards c1867-69, formerly in the possession of the late James Rowntree.

19. Mr G R Worrall informs me that he has in his Collection two swords with guards of similar pattern, with twelve domed studs, sold to an officer of the Royal Horse Guards by Wilkinsons in 1854. The swords differ in important respects from the pattern subsequently standardised but they would seem to show the trend towards standardisation.

20. See, for example, HCM 116, the sword of Prince Edward of Saxe-Weimar, 1st Life Guards, dated 1883, and RA IX-1042, a sword of the RHG, c1902.

21. See, for example, HCM 169.

22. Proceedings of a Board of Officers, held on 29 November 1922, (copy in Uniforms Register of Royal Horse Guards, formerly in Royal United Services Institute, now in the NAM, (6807-495)).

23. See *Illustrated Catalogue of Current Armes Blanches*, published by DGDQA, MoD Central Library, 1986.

1   Sword, Lancers, Officer, Full Dress, Pattern 1822

(See also Plate 79)

II Sword, Household Cavalry, Dress, Pattern 1814

(See also Plates 112, 113)

III Sword, Royal Horse Guards, Dress, *c*1832

(See also Plates 122, 123)

IV Sword, Pattern 1786

(See also Plate 129)

V Sword, Pattern 1796

(See also Plate 132)

VI Broadsword, Officers', Highland Regiments, 79th Highlanders, Pattern 1798

(A variation of the pattern shown in Plate 161)

(NAM 9507-60)

7. Infantry Officers' Swords

The history of the regulation patterns of sword in the British Army can properly be said to have started in 1786, when infantry officers were ordered to lay aside the spontoon and equip themselves with a fighting sword.

Before 1786, the true symbol of authority of the infantry officer was the spontoon (or espontoon) - a staff weapon of the half-pike variety, somewhat similar in form to the partisan still carried by Her Majesty's Yeomen of the Guard.[1] It had little or no value as a weapon but as a badge of authority it was highly distinctive. In addition to the spontoon, however, officers were required under the Clothing Warrant of 1768 to carry a sword. No specific pattern was laid down, the Warrant specifying only that the hilts should be of gilt or silver according to the colour of uniform buttons and that within each regiment all the officers should carry the same pattern of sword. In practice, some regiments carried steel hilts; the Inspection Returns for the 1st (or Royal) Regiment in 1777 and 1779 refer to the officers' swords having steel hilts, and steel hilts were to be specifically allowed under the order abolishing the spontoon.

Even before 1786, the spontoon was increasingly being discarded, particularly on active service outside Europe. What was merely an encumbrance on the formalised, stately battlefields of the Low Countries must have been a dangerous absurdity in the woods of North America or the jungles of Southern India. In 1784, the Inspection Return for the 63rd Foot noted that the regiment had: 'just returned from America where the officers never made use of espontoons; saluted with swords'.[2] The Inspection Returns for the 3rd, 9th, and 22nd Regiments in 1784-85 noted, similarly, that spontoons were not carried by officers of these regiments.

It seems very probable that it was indeed the experience of the American War of Independence between 1775 and 1783 which precipitated the abolition of the spontoon. The order abolishing it and substituting the sword in its place was issued by the Adjutant-General on 3 April 1786:

> 'His Majesty having been pleas'd to order, that the Esponton shall be laid aside, & that, in lieu thereof the Battalion Officers are, for the future, to make use of Swords, it is His Majesty's Pleasure, that the Officers of Infantry Corps, shall be provided with a strong, substantial, Uniform-Sword, the Blade of which is to be straight, & made to cut & thrust; - to be one Inch at least broad at the Shoulder, & 32 Inches in Length:- The Hilt, if not of Steel, is to be either Gilt or Silver, according to the Colour of the

Buttons on the Uniforms - & the Sword Knot, to be Crimson & Gold in the stripes, as required by the present Regulation [the 1768 Warrant].[3]

It will be noted that this order gives no details of the form of the hilt, and the reference to 'Battalion Officers' suggests that the officers of the so-called 'flank' companies - that is to say, the grenadier and light companies - were not necessarily to be included. It will be noted also that only the *minimum* width of the blade was specified.

Old habits die hard and it seems clear that standardisation was not intended at this stage to go beyond the blade. The choice of hilt lay with the regimental colonel, the material varying between silver, gilt metal and steel, depending in the first instance on the colour of the regiment's buttons and lace:

'I believe I sent you over some time since two or three different Hilts for Swords, that you might choose one for the Regiment, but not being quite clear on which you fixed your choice, I must beg the favour of you to send me over a pattern Hilt, by the first favourable opportunity that offers, returning at the same time those, if you have any which you have no longer any occasion for.[4]

A high proportion of authenticated infantry swords from this period, however, have a common form of hilt, consisting of a straight knucklebow guard, with a fluted or reeded grip in ivory, horn or ebony, with a cushion or vase-shaped pommel. There is frequently a horizontal band round the grip, bearing a cartouche on which is engraved the regiment's number or initials. A loose ring through the knucklebow, near the pommel, often exists to take the sword knot. There is frequently a side ring in the plane of the foot of the knucklebow, which may be linked to the foot by a diamond shape or badge. In the commonest form, the middle of the knucklebow and of the side ring (where it exists) is moulded into five balls or beads, and the whole hilt is known as a 'beaded' or 'five-ball' hilt.[5]

Specimens of these hilts exist in all three metals. A steel-mounted specimen, with a black horn grip, by Bland & Foster and datable to 1788, is in the Royal Collection at Windsor, (Laking 698).[6] A gilt version, by Knubley, made for an officer of the 95th Foot is illustrated in Plate 129; from the maker's name, it can be dated to 1794-97. A silver version, by Francis Thurkle, datable to 1792-93, is illustrated in J D Aylward's *The Small Sword in England*; another specimen is NAM, 6607-7 hallmarked for 1797[7].

This type of sword was used extensively in the Royal Navy from about 1790,[8] and a similar pattern in gold or gilt was in use in France from about 1800, where it was described as '*à l'anglaise*'.[9] A similar hilt was adopted for infantry officers in the United States Army between 1812 and 1840.[10]

Infantry Officers' Swords

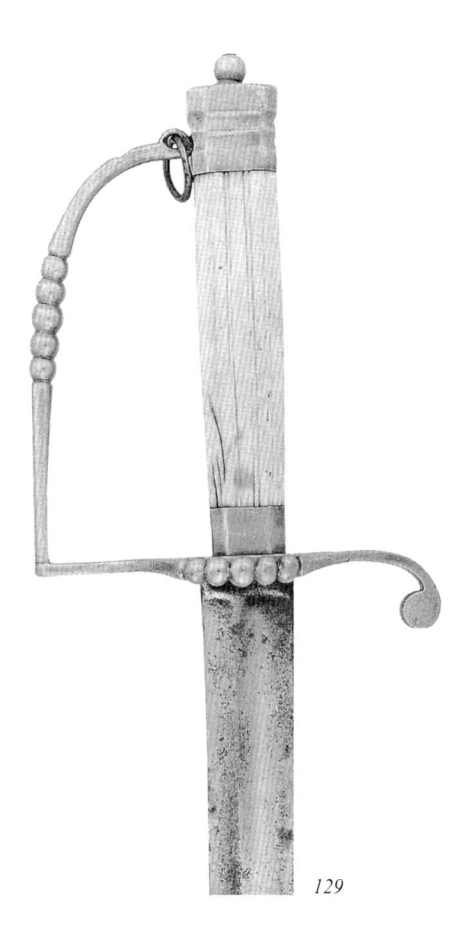

129 Sword, Pattern 1786

Blade length and width: 32in. x 1in.
Blade type: so-called 'spadroon', with flat back, single wide fuller to within 1in. of spear point, single edge.
Guard: 'bead' pattern in gilt brass.
Hilt mounts: gilt brass.
Grip: ivory.
Scabbard: this specimen has no scabbard, but the normal scabbard was of black leather with locket, band and chape of same metal as the hilt.
Sword weight: 1lb 3¹/₂oz.
Note: belonged to an officer of the 95th Foot. Note the loose ring in the guard near the pommel for the sword knot.

(NAM 6305-80)

(See also Colour Plate IV)

130 Sword, Pattern 1786

Blade length and width: 32in. x 1in.
Blade type: straight, double edged, diamond-section, spear point.
Guard: steel knucklebow and rigid shells.
Hilt mounts: steel, pommel decorated with acanthus leaves.
Grip: wood, bound with steel wire.
Scabbard: black leather, steel locket with frog stud, middle band and chape.

(SUSM 1932-126)

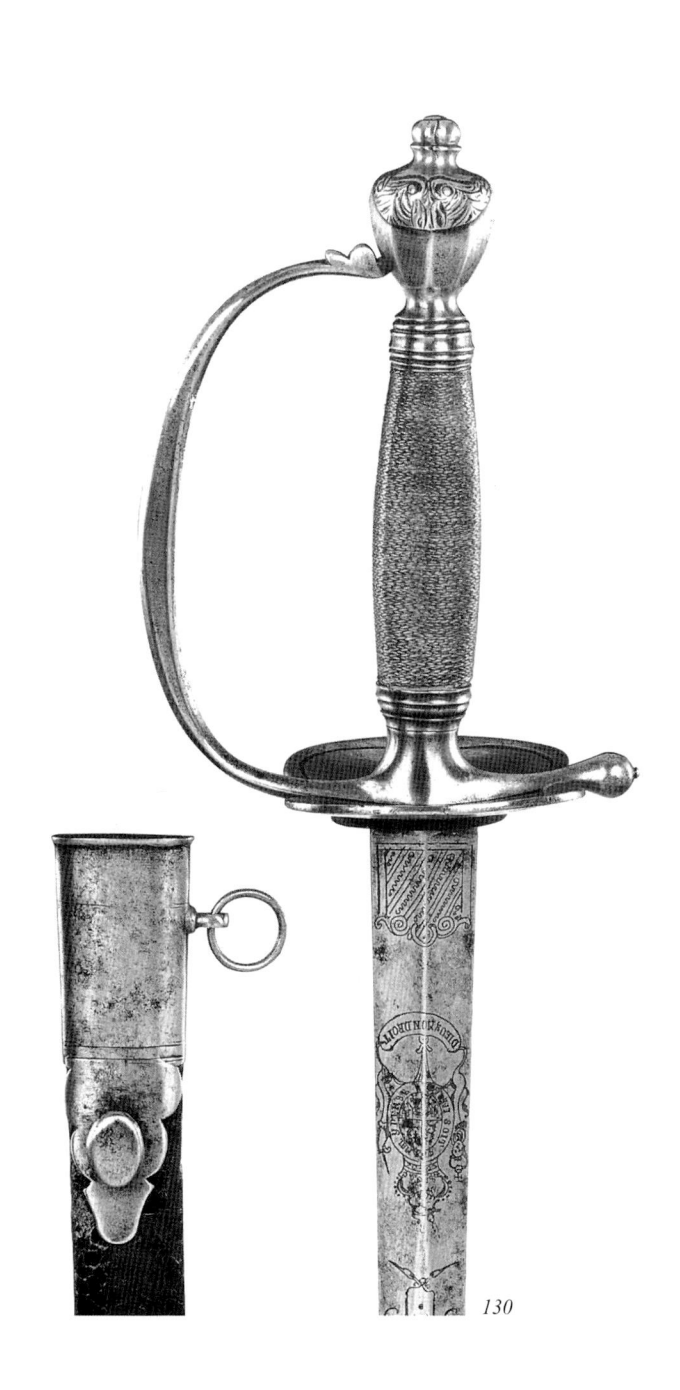

But the beaded or straight knucklebow hilts were not the only form of hilt in use for this type of sword at this time. Edward Dayes' drawings of officers of the Foot Guards, the Royal Artillery and the 2nd Foot, *c*1792, show swords with double-shell guards of the type standardised in 1796, and both gilt brass and steel versions are known at this time, (Plate 130). Another form, in which the knucklebow divides at the base, round the grip - the so-called 'slotted hilt' - was also in use.

As has been indicated, the real element of standardisation in 1786 was in the dimensions and form of the blade, viz. made to cut and thrust, 32 inches long and 1 inch wide minimum at the shoulder. It is clear from the numerous existing specimens that the commonest - perhaps the intended - form was the spadroon blade, straight and single edged, with a single broad fuller to within a few inches of the spear point where it becomes double edged, and with a flat back. Some specimens have diamond section or lenticular blades, and it is clear that, provided they met the specified dimensions, these fell within the specification. In practice, lengths fell between 32 and $32^{1}/_{2}$ inches.

The scabbard was of black leather, with metal fittings according to the metal of the hilt, and a War Office Circular of 22 July 1786 makes it clear that the sword was meant to be worn normally in a frog on a cross-belt,[11] so there is normally a frog stud on the locket for this purpose.

The Pattern 1786 sword was clearly intended as a fighting sword if necessary and the blade was not ill-adapted for the purpose, although rather light, even if the type of usage was perceived as more in the way of an elegant duel between officers rather than with heavy cavalry. The guard, however, whether of bead or other pattern, was flimsy and gave minimal protection. As it happened, the introduction of this pattern coincided with one of the rare periods of peace in Europe in the eighteenth century, which endured up until the outbreak of war with Revolutionary France in 1793, which was to last in one form or another until 1815.

It may have been the experiences of the early years of the war which led, in 1796, to the introduction of a new pattern of sword for infantry officers and others. The General Order introducing this new pattern now specified the sword in some detail:

> 'The sword to have a brass guard, pommel and shell, gilt with gold; with grip, or handle, of silver twisted wire. The blade to be straight and made to cut and thrust; to be one inch at least broad at the shoulder and 32 inches in length, conformably to former orders given out in April 1786.[12]

The Pattern 1796 sword was, therefore, essentially the Pattern 1786 blade, with a standardised, double-shell hilt based on that already in use in some regiments, (Plate 131).[13] As a fighting weapon it was no improvement on its predecessors, such as the beaded-hilt. In theory, the twin-shell guard gave slightly more protection to the hand than a simple knucklebow but in practice the shells are extremely flimsy

Infantry Officers' Swords

and, with the quillon end, easily broken off. In practice, infantry officers' swords were not really intended for serious fighting but, even so, the Pattern 1796 sword seems to have been regarded with contempt by its wearers; General Cavalié Mercer, reminiscing about the Royal Artillery (whose officers carried the same sword, at least in the Foot Artillery), recalled that:

> 'Nothing could be more useless or more ridiculous than the old Infantry regulation [sword]; it was good neither for cut nor thrust and was a perfect encumbrance. In the Foot Artillery, when away from headquarters, we generally wore dirks instead of it.[14]

While it might conceivably have been of some use in hand to hand combat against a French infantry officer, whose regulation pattern was equally flimsy, the 1796 Pattern was clearly of doubtful value against a light cavalry sabre or a cuirassier's long thrusting sword. Many an infantry officer must have lost his life in the Peninsula in consequence.

The twin shells prevented the sword from lying close to the wearer's body and, from the beginning, a high proportion of swords were made with one shell which hinged down in normal wear but which would be hinged upwards to offer protection to that side of the hand in combat, (Plate 132).[15] The normal scabbard was of black leather, with gilt locket, band and chape, with frog stud for carriage in a frog from a cross - and later, a waistbelt. Sir William Beechey's painting of George III reviewing troops, exhibited at the Royal Academy in 1798, however, shows him wearing a steel scabbard suspended from slings.[16]

This Pattern 1796 sword remained the regulation for infantry of the line and other corps for just over a quarter of a century and is therefore among the commonest of British Army swords, although the fragility of the guard makes intact specimens rather rarer. A relatively high proportion of existing blades are marked as being by Runkel but this may simply reflect a concentration by the British swordmakers during the French wars on producing cavalry blades in quantity, or simply the greater productivity of Solingen manufacturers.

Despite its defects, virtually the same pattern was in use c1805 in the United States Engineer Corps, and in 1840 it was adopted for the US infantry officers, with a folding shell. A version in which the shells are fixed and cast integrally with the knucklebow was adopted for United States Army non-commissioned officers, also in 1840.[17]

When it was introduced, the Pattern 1796 sword was intended for all infantry officers but officers of flank companies were already beginning to carry curved sabres, similar in form to those carried by light cavalry officers. As early as 1792, the Inspection Return for the 60th Foot noted that some officers were carrying 'sabres; the latter shorter than the King's orders'. In 1796, the officers of the light company

Infantry Officers' Swords

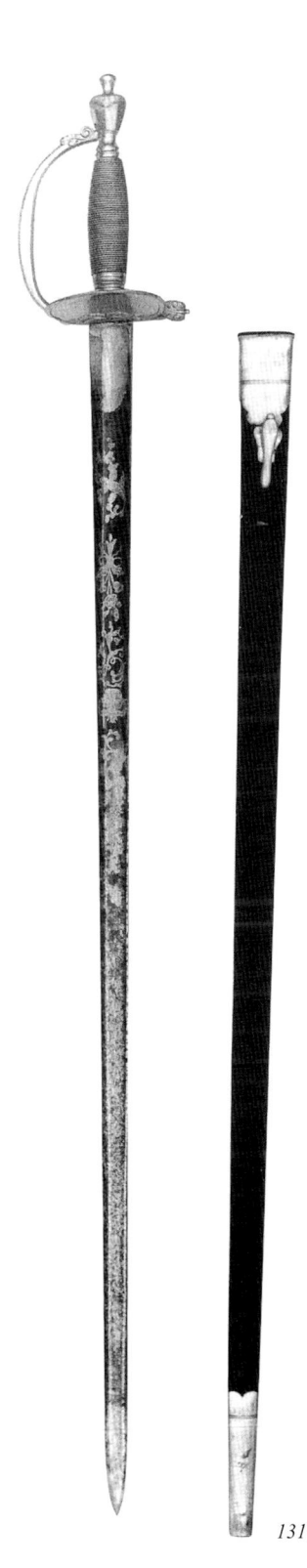

131 Sword, Pattern 1796

Blade length and width: 32in. x 1in.
Blade type: so-called 'spadroon' - straight, flat back, single edged, single fuller each side to within 1in. of spear point.
Guard: gilt brass knucklebow, with two kidney-shaped shells, one of which folds down.
Hilt mount: gilt brass, Adam style pommel decorated with acanthus leaves.
Grip: wood, bound with German silver wire.
Scabbard: black leather, with locket, band and chape of gilt brass.
Note: supplied by Cornthwaite. The majority of blades are decorated in blued and gilt designs but others have simple line engraving or etching.

(NAM 7905-2)

132 Sword, Pattern 1796 - close-up of hilt to show the fall of the folding shell guard

Note: some blades are of flattened diamond section.

(NAM 6509-42)

(See also Colour Plate V)

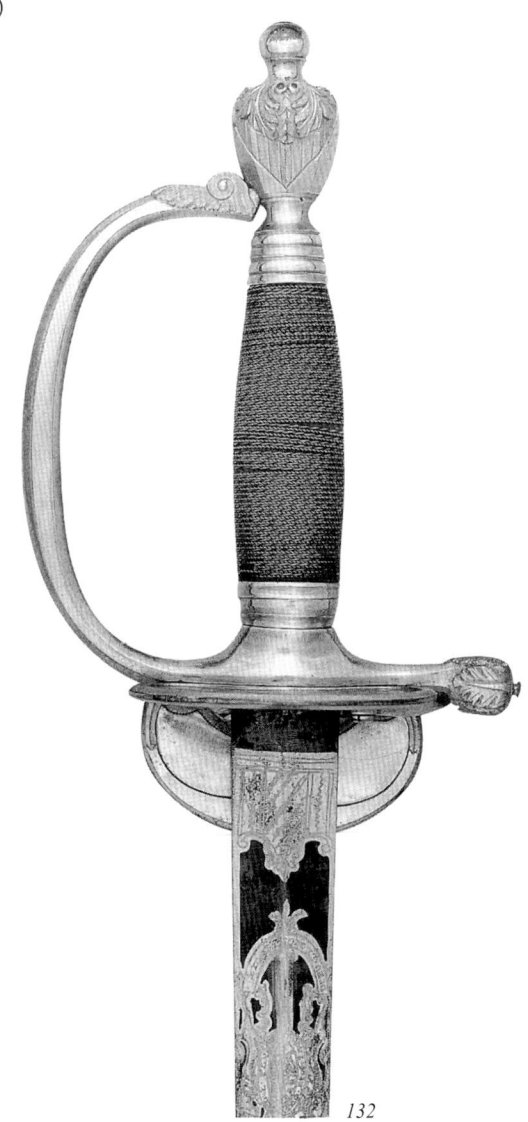

131

132

of the 12th Foot were reported as carrying 'sabres' and it is clear that the custom was widespread by this time among light infantry officers.[18] The swords in question differed in detail among the regiments but the general form consisted of a curved blade, some 30 inches long, with a spear point and a curved knucklebow or stirrup guard, sometimes with an additional curved bar or bars on the outside, (Plates 133, 134).

It seems probable that two separate strands lay behind this particular development. For the light infantry officer, engaged in scouting and skirmishing, a short, curved sword was likely to be handier than the longer, straight regulation infantry pattern, and this, in turn, may have come from experience in close, wooded country in America between 1775 and 1783. It is significant that when rifle regiments began to appear around 1800, the officers invariably adopted curved sabres. But light infantry and rifle regiment officers tended also to adopt other items of light cavalry clothing, such as the helmet and this suggests that the desire to distinguish themselves from the ordinary battalion company officers, as an élite, was another factor which would also explain the adoption of sabres by grenadier company officers.

By 1799, the development had gone so far that the Commander-in-Chief's department was forced to give it official recognition. An Order of 29 August 1799 therefore authorised officers of the flank companies to wear sabres, although no pattern was specified.[19] But it was inevitable that once the development had been officially recognised and authority given, an attempt would be made to standardise the patterns of sword.

Early in 1803, the Adjutant-General (Major-General Harry Calvert) wrote to the Governor of Gibraltar (the Duke of Kent), apprising him of the latest development:

> 'I have the honor to enclose for your Royal Highness's Information, H[is] Majesty's Orders, as they are now preparing for Publication, respecting the Swords, Sword-Knots, Belts, Sashes & Gorgets, to be used by Officers of the Infantry, likewise directing the mode in which these various Appointments are to be worn; but, I beg leave to apprize your Royal Highness that the Com.r in Chief [the Duke of York] has directed Patterns of Swords, with curved Blades to be prepared for His Inspection, and I believe, that HRH has it in Contemplation, to recommend to His Majesty, that Officers of Grenadiers, & Light Infantry, shall be ordered to adopt the use of Swords, of the above description.'[20]

Eight weeks later, Calvert again wrote to the Duke, telling him of the King's decision:

> 'I beg to inform you, that a Pattern Sword for the Officers of Grenadiers & Light Infantry, has been approved by His Majesty, and together with the

Infantry Officers' Swords

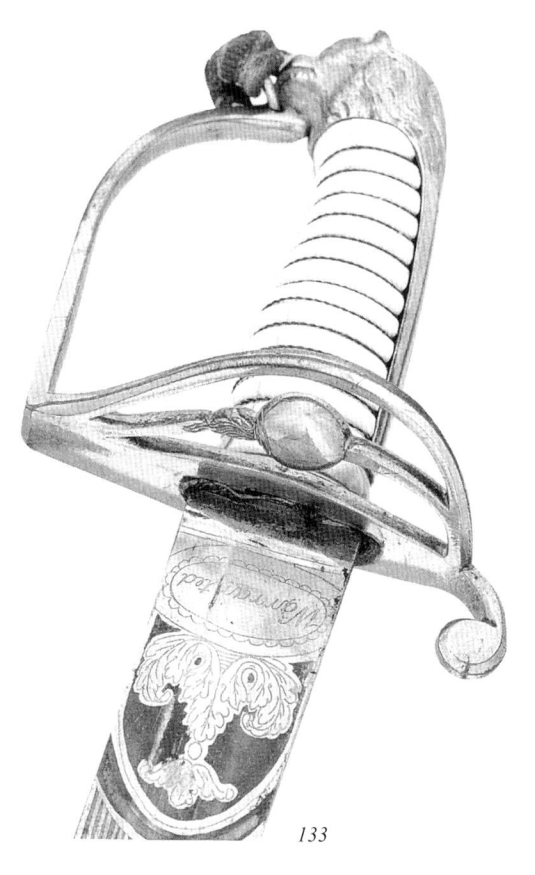

133 Sword, Grenadier Company, 84th Foot, 1809-1818

Note: Made by Dawes, Birmingham. Hilt of gilt brass, scabbard black leather with gilt brass chape and locket (with frog stud). Sword knot gilt and crimson stripes. Blade marked 'Captain Entwhistle'[*sic.*]; Philip Entwistle served in the 84th from 1809 to 1818.

(NAM 8406-50)

134 Sword, Grenadier Company, *c*1802

Note: blade bears initials 'GG' and figure of grenadier with what appear to be pre-1804 epaulettes. Marked as made by 'Osbornes', which is probably Henry Osborne, working in Birmingham from 1785.

(NAM 6310-122)

149

Pattern Sword for Regimental Officers of the Infantry, and that for General Officers and for other Officers on the General Staff of the Army, is lodged in the Office of the Comptrollers of Army Accounts. The Mounted Officers and the Flank Officers use the same Sword Belts and carry their Swords in the same manner, as other Regimental Officers [i.e. from a cross-belt]. The officers on the General Staff of the Army use a waist-belt.[21]

The general form of this sword is shown in Plates 135-138. It is a fairly elaborate weapon and there are numerous variations. The royal cypher in the knucklebow is sometimes moulded but also pierced or chased, and the bugle or grenade is by no means common. Some specimens have a slit for the sword knot in the guard near the pommel; in other cases there is a small loose ring for the knot near the pommel. The normal length of the blade was approximately $30^{1}/_{2}$ inches and the width at the shoulder $1^{3}/_{8}$ inches but these dimensions vary between specimens. These differences reflect the process of individual makers copying from a pattern sword, as well as the preferences of individuals and regiments. Without the bugle or grenade, this sword was frequently carried by field officers (or regimental officers, as they were sometimes confusingly called). Farmer refers to this sword as the 'GR or Guards hilt', claiming that it was first adopted by the flank officers of the Foot Guards, ('GR' clearly refers to the cypher in the guard). There is a sword of this type in the NAM, (7608-42), marked 'GG' (Grenadier Guards) but this title was not awarded until 1815.[22]

The introduction of the Pattern 1803 sword coincided broadly with the conversion of a number of regiments - notably the 43rd and 52nd - into light infantry regiments to provide specialised troops to oppose the French *voltigeurs*. The original intention would seem to have been that the officers of this regiment should carry the Pattern 1803 sword, as indeed the extracts quoted above indicate; Sir John Moore, writing in 1803, explained that: '...the 52nd, as Light Infantry, wear jackets, caps and a sword different from the Battalions but the same as directed for the Light Companies of the Army'.[23]

In practice, the 52nd, like other élite regiments, succumbed to the temptation to be different and adopted a sabre of regimental pattern, (Plate 139).[24] The change would seem to have taken place very shortly after the regiment's transformation into light infantry because Ensign Charles Booth, writing to his brother in 1805, noted that the equipment that he had had to buy on transferring to the 52nd included 'a regimental sabre (different pattern to the Line)' which had cost the large sum of four guineas. This pattern is shown in Charles Hamilton Smith's painting of an officer of the 52nd, published in November 1814. A second pattern, in which the hilt was of gilt brass, was presumably intended for wear by field officers of the regiment.

Infantry Officers' Swords

135   Sword, Pattern 1803

Blade length and width: 31½in. x 1½in.
Blade type: curved, flat back, single wide fuller each side to within 6½in. of spear point, double edged for last 7in.
Guard: gilt brass knucklebow, with sword knot ring near pommel.
Hilt mounts: gilt brass, with lion's head pommel.
Grip: wood, bound with fishskin and brass or copper wire.
Scabbard: black leather, gilt brass chape, locket and band, with loose rings on locket and band, and frog stud on locket for hooking sword up in action.
Note: blade by Runkel (1786-1808).

(NAM 6510-87)

135

136

136   Sword, Pattern 1803 - detail of hilt
(NAM 6510-87)

151

Infantry Officers' Swords

137

138

137   Sword, Grenadier Company, Pattern 1803

Blade length and width: 29in. (across curve) x 1½in.
Blade type: curved, flat back, single broad fuller each side to within 6in. of spear point, double edged for last 7in.
Guard: gilt brass with grenade pinned to outside of knucklebow, sword knot slit near pommel.
Hilt mounts: gilt brass.
Grip: polished wood, with traces of brass or copper wire binding.
Note: the blade has incised floral decoration and 1801 royal arms. It may have been blued and gilt originally but no traces remain.

(Author's collection)

138   Sword, Light Company, Pattern 1803

Blade length and width: 30¼in. (across curve) x 1½in.
Blade type: curved, flat back, single broad fuller each side to within 6½in. of spear point, double edged for last 7in. Blued and gilt.
Guard: gilt brass, with stringed bugle pinned to knucklebow, sword knot slit near pommel.
Hilt mounts: gilt brass.
Grip: wood, covered with sharkskin and bound with copper wire.
Scabbard: black leather, with gilt brass chape, locket and band, with loose ring on locket and band and frog stud on locket.
Note: blade marked 'Osborne and Gunby Warranted' with post-1801 royal arms.

(Author's Collection)

152

Infantry Officers' Swords

139   Sword, 52nd Foot, *c*1803
Blade length and width: 31 1/2in. x 1 1/8in.
Blade type: curved, flat back, no fuller, double edged for last 10in., spear point.
Guard: steel.
Hilt mounts: steel.
Grip: wood, covered with fishskin, secured through tang by two rivets.
Sword weight: 1lb 8oz.
Note: in its original state, the grip had a steel bugle fixed on each side. The scabbard (missing) was probably of steel with two loose rings. The sword knot is red and gold.
(Royal Armouries IX-383)

139

There is a sword of this type in the NAM, (9502-69). A very similar pattern was in use in the 43rd, (Plate 140) and in the 51st, (Plate 141).

Other regiments to adopt their own patterns of sabre for field and flank company officers included the 23rd, (Plate 142). Their pattern would seem to have been in use by about 1809 since the Regimental Museum at Caernarvon Castle contains a distinctive sword which belonged to Lieutenant-Colonel Wyatt, who transferred to the regiment in that year. Other regimental patterns include that of the 95th, (Plate 143).

In the last decade of the eighteenth century yet another type of regiment was introduced into the regular establishment of the British Army - the rifle regiment. The first regular corps of riflemen was the 1st Battalion of the 60th (Royal American) Regiment, re-equipped as a rifle regiment in 1794.[25] Three years later, the 5th Battalion of the same regiment was raised as a rifle battalion, and in 1800 an Experimental Corps of Riflemen, composed of detachments from other infantry regiments, was raised by Colonel Coote Manningham. It became in due course the Rifle Bri-

Infantry Officers' Swords

140

140 Sword, 43rd Foot, *c*1803

Blade length and width: 32in. x 1³/₈in.
Blade type: flat back, unfullered, spear point.
Guard: gilt brass or copper, sword knot slit near pommel.
Hilt mounts: gilt brass or copper.
Grip: wood, covered with fishskin.
Scabbard: black leather, gilt brass or copper locket, band and chape.
Note: this regiment acquired the designation 'light infantry' in 1803.

(By courtesy of Wallis & Wallis, Lewes, Sussex)

141 Sword, 51st Foot, *c*1809

Blade length and width: 31¹/₂ in.x 1¹/₈in.
Blade type: curved, flat back, unfullered, spear point, double edged for last 10in.
Guard: steel stirrup.
Hilt mounts: steel, with shield-shaped langets.
Grip: wood, covered with fishskin or sharkskin, three steel ornamented rivets.
Note: the 51st became light infantry formally in 1809; this sword belonged to Lieutenant H B Hawley, ADC to Lord Hill at Waterloo, who joined the regiment in 1807.

(NAM 6310-110)

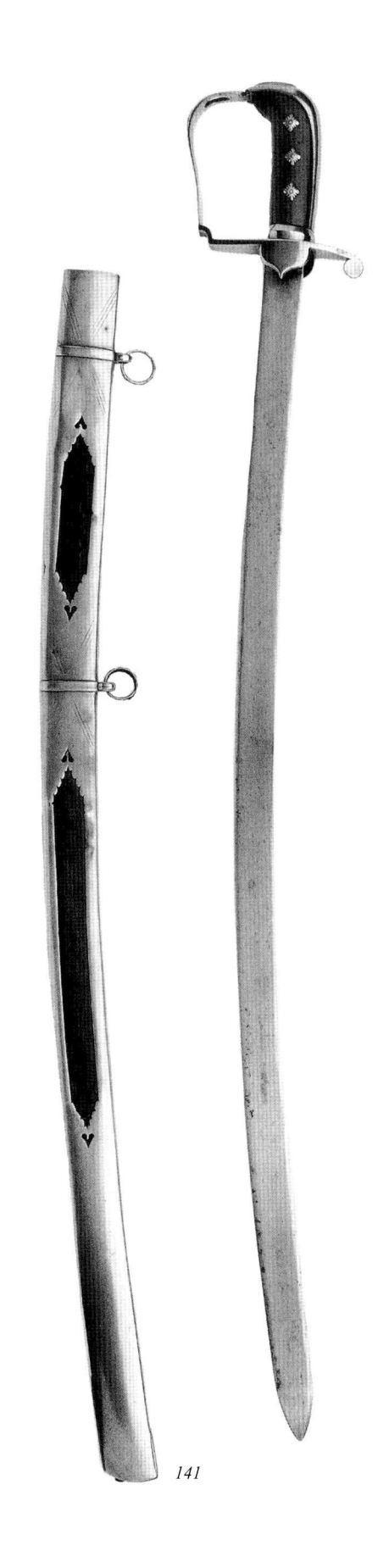

141

Infantry Officers' Swords

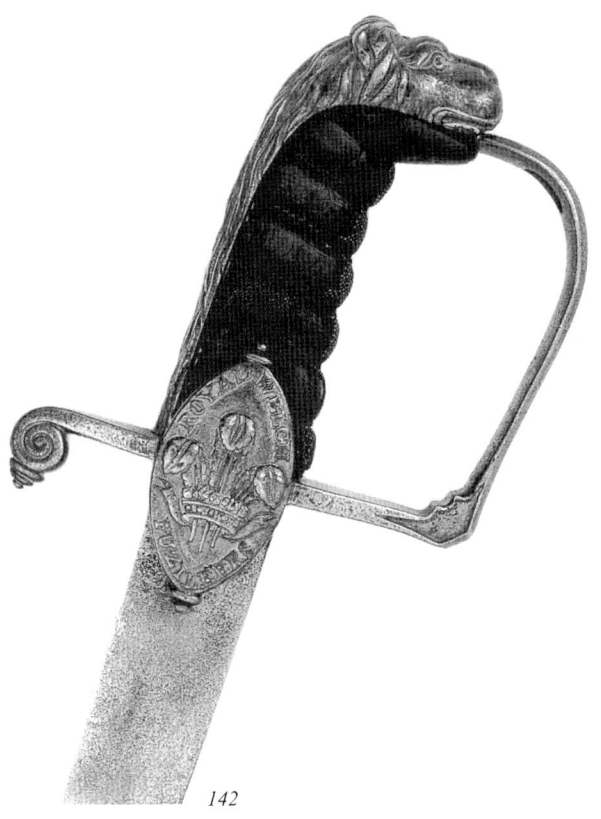

142

142 Sword, 23rd Foot
(Royal Welch Fuziliers), c1803
Blade length and width: 31in. x 1³/₈in.
Blade type: curved, flat back, spear point, double edged for last 11in.
Guard: brass or copper, sword knot slit near pommel.
Hilt mount: gilt brass or copper.
Grip: wood, covered with fishskin and bound with brass or copper wire.
Scabbard: black leather, gilt brass or copper mounts, frog stud on right side of locket.
Note: the most unusual form of the quillon is noteworthy.
(NAM 8001-21)

143 Sword, 95th Foot, c1805
Blade type: curved, flat back, unfullered, spear point.
Guard: steel.
Hilt mounts: steel.
Grip: wood, covered in leather and bound with steel wire.
Scabbard: steel.
Note: made by Brunn, 56 Charing Cross.
(NAM 8105-37)

143

155

gade. From the start, the officers of these regiments carried curved, light infantry type sabres. The rifle battalions of the 60th initially carried a sabre with gilt-brass stirrup hilt, in a black leather scabbard with gilt mounts.[26] The officers of Coote Manningham's Corps carried a similar sabre but with steel mounts; this is well depicted in a print in *The British Military Library*, dated February 1801.[27] Both the 60th and the Experimental Corps carried the sabre in slings from a black leather waistbelt. *The View of the Standing regulations for the Colours, Clothing etc of the Infantry, to which are annexed the Guards, Rifle Corps etc* (1802) specified that the sword for officers of the Rifle Corps was to be 'a sabre similar to the Light Cavalry', carried on a black waistbelt with silver mounts.[28] Clearly, the Pattern 1796 Light Cavalry sword was too long and heavy for infantry use and it is reasonable to assume that 'similar to' in this case meant of the same general form, with stirrup hilt and curved blade, but smaller. In order to emphasise their exclusivity, the rifle regiments adopted other items of light cavalry uniform such as the furred pelisse and the frogged jacket.

The Pattern 1796 and 1803 patterns, as well as the special regimental patterns, endured until the end of the first quarter of the nineteenth century, and longer in some cases. But the issue of the first printed *Dress Regulations* in 1822 introduced a totally new pattern of sword which, with a change of blade, was to remain the standard pattern for infantry officers, as well as for many other departmental corps, until nearly the end of the century. (Indeed, in steel-mounted versions, it is still in use in the Foot Guards and Royal Green Jackets today). This was the so-called 'Gothic-hilted' sword, a term invented by Charles ffoulkes because of a fancied resemblance between the bars of the guard and the shapes of windows in Gothic architecture. The resemblance is perhaps more fancied than real but the term is a convenient one and has been used by writers ever since, although it does not occur anywhere in official documents.

The precise origins of this pattern of hilt, (Plate 144) remain obscure. The copying of French military fashion after 1815, under the influence of George, Prince Regent, leads one to look for a clue in that direction but no French sword of this period resembles the 'Gothic hilt', which may conceivably owe something to Prosser who supplied the Prince Regent with numerous swords and scabbards at this time. In the 1822 *Dress Regulations*, it is described as 'a gilt half-basket hilt, with GR IV inserted in the outward bars'. The reference to 'outward bars' is significant because this guard is, in essence, a three-bar guard, with the bars linked by tracery. In its early form, the inner panel of the guard was hinged to fall down to allow the hilt to lie closer to the wearer's body, (Plate 145), and the scabbard has a small pin which fits into a hole in the guard. The hilt had a black leather lining to protect the wearer's hand and gloves.

The blade was also entirely new in infantry swords, being a slender, slightly curved, pipe-backed design, double edged for the last few inches, (Plate 146). It forms part of the same blade fashion as the Pattern 1821 cavalry swords, (see Chapter 4). The

144 Sword, Pattern 1822 - outside of guard
Note: in this photograph, the inner portion of the guard is not folded down.
(NAM 7501-74)

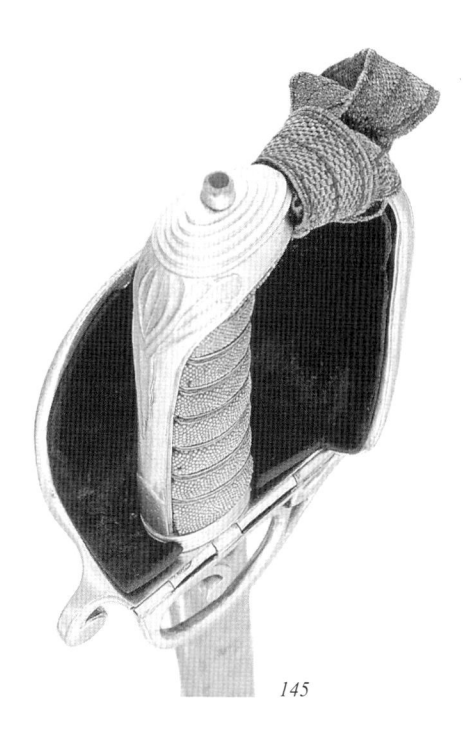

145 Sword, Pattern 1822 - inside of hilt
Note: observe the folding inside portion of guard and the black leather lining.
(NAM 7501-74)

scabbard was black leather with decorated brass mounts, (Plate 147). Field officers carried it in slings and their scabbards had two loose rings; other officers carried it in a frog and these scabbards had a frog stud on the locket; some scabbards have both. The sword weighed approximately 1lb 12ozs and the scabbard 12^{1}/2ozs.

This pattern, called for convenience the Pattern 1822,[29] is an elegant, even beautiful, weapon but both guard and blade are painfully weak. Writing of it in 1863, the well-known swordmaker, John Latham of Wilkinsons, described it as:

> '...the worst possible arrangement of hilt, blade and shape that could possibly be contrived. It is crooked but has no regular curve; it is wrongly mounted for thrusting and wrongly shaped for cutting. The hilt is so flimsy as to be no protection to the hand and it is made of bad metal badly tempered.[30]

The severity of these criticisms reflected, no doubt, the fact that it was not a Wilkinson design but they were basically not unfair. As a fighting sword, the Pattern 1822 must have been almost useless and instances of its failure in battle are not hard to find. Despite this, it was extensively copied in other countries.

Infantry Officers' Swords

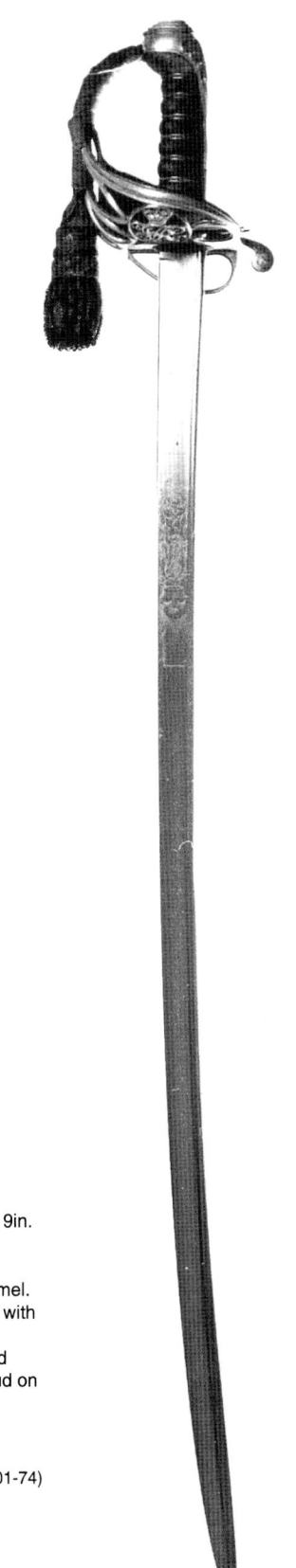

146 Sword, Pattern 1822

Blade length and width: $32^{1}/2$in. x $1^{1}/8$in.
Blade type: pipe back, double edged for last 9in.
Guard: gilt brass, with sword knot slit near pommel.
Hilt mounts: gilt brass, with lion's head pommel.
Grip: wood, covered with fishskin and bound with brass wire.
Scabbard: black leather, gilt chape, band and locket with large shoe, loose ring and frog stud on locket, loose ring on band.
Sword weight: 1lb 13oz.
Scabbard weight: 13oz.

(NAM 7501-74)

147 Sword, Pattern 1822 - close-up of scabbard

(NAM 7501-74)

146
147

158

Infantry Officers' Swords

In 1826, all officers adopted the waistbelt and slings and all scabbards were fitted with loose rings.

The 1822 *Dress Regulations* prescribed the same sword for officers of rifle regiments, but with a steel scabbard in Undress, the black leather scabbard being used for Full Dress and in the evenings. This clearly went against the traditions which the rifle regiments had built up, based on exclusivity, and a Circular Memorandum issued by the Adjutant-General on 17 June 1827 authorised rifle regiments to carry a steel-hilted sword of Gothic pattern but with the royal cypher in the guard replaced by a crown and stringed bugle, (Plate 148). The inner panel of the guard is fixed and had a single spur, (Plate 149) and the bars of the guard are flatter and sturdier. The grip is bound with steel or silver wire, instead of brass wire. The scabbards and blade were unchanged. In the case of the 60th, the surround of the cartouche in the guard is often in the form of a wreath, but in the Rifle Brigade guard the surround is plain. The Royal Welsh Fusiliers carried a version of the Gothic hilt in which the royal cypher was replaced by the Prince of Wales' feathers, (Plate 150).

Another Circular Memorandum from the Adjutant-General, of 30 April 1832 ordered field officers of regiments of the line to carry a brass scabbard and adjutants a steel scabbard except at Levées, Royal Drawing Rooms and in evening dress, when the black leather scabbard was to be worn. The 1834 *Dress Regulations* abolished the steel scabbard for adjutants of the line but introduced the brass scabbard for adjutants of Foot Guards when serving in the field. Both brass and steel scabbards weighed approximately 1lb 3 ozs. The 1834 *Regulations* also abolished the black leather hilt lining for the Foot Guards.

In addition to the normal pattern sword, light patterns of sword, (known as picquet weight swords in the Foot Guards) were introduced in which the blades are narrower (^{3}/4 inch) and the hilts correspondingly smaller and lighter. These were intended for wear off duty, in the evenings and in frock coat order. Although I have not found a specific authority for their introduction, the use was widespread and continued throughout the life of the Gothic-hilted patterns, so it was clearly known and accepted by the authorities at the Horse Guards.

The Pattern 1822 sword continued in use, with these minor modifications, until 1845 when a new blade was introduced, the design of which is generally attributed to Wilkinsons. In a Circular Memorandum of 10 March 1845 from the Adjutant-General the new blade was described thus:

> 'A blade of an improved construction and superior quality having been adopted to the Sword prescribed for officers of infantry, a pattern of the sword thus improved has been sealed and deposited in the Office of Military Boards for the inspection of tradesmen and regulation of future supplies - any deviation from which either as regards form, dimensions or weight as specified in the margin is positively prohibited.

Infantry Officers' Swords

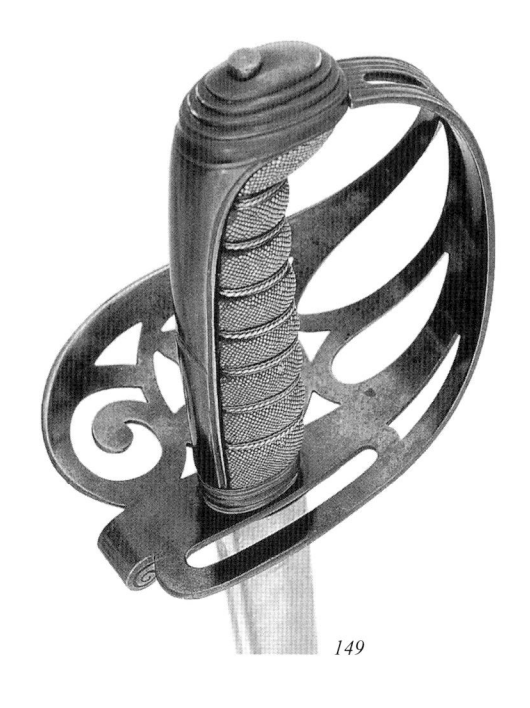

148   Sword, Rifle Regiment, 60th Rifles, Pattern 1827

Blade type: identical to Infantry, Officers', Pattern 1822.
Guard: steel Gothic hilt, but with stringed bugle in cartouche.
Hilt mounts: steel.
Grip: wood, bound with fishskin and steel wire.
Scabbard (Undress): steel, with two bands and loose rings. A black leather scabbard with steel chape, locket and band was worn with Full Dress.
Note: made by Tatham, 37 Charing Cross (1817-60).

(NAM 8106-38)

149   Sword, Rifle Regiments, Pattern 1827 - inside of hilt

(NAM 8106-38)

150   Sword, Pattern 1822, special Royal Welsh Fusiliers Pattern

(NAM 8009-108)

It is to be understood, however, that officers are not required to provide themselves with swords of the improved pattern until those now in possession shall have been worn out.[31]

In the margin of the Memorandum the following dimensions are noted:

'Length (clear of hilt)	32$\frac{1}{2}$ inches
Breadth, at shoulder	1$\frac{1}{8}$ inches
Breadth, 12 inches down	1 inch
Weight	not less than 1lb 15oz without the scabbard [this is clearly the sword weight].

The essential difference between the new and old blades is that the pipe-back has been replaced by a single broad fuller each side, extending from a point roughly 1$\frac{1}{2}$ inches from the shoulder to within 10 inches of the spear point, where it becomes double edged.

At the shoulder, the back of the blade is $\frac{3}{8}$ths of an inch thick, diminishing to $\frac{1}{4}$ inch some 18 inches from the shoulder. There is a solid, flat ricasso, 1$\frac{1}{2}$ inches long, (Plate 151). Weights vary in practice between 1lb 15ozs, as specified, to 2lbs 0$\frac{1}{2}$ oz. As the Memorandum and the specifications indicate, the new blade was very considerably stronger than the previous pattern and to that extent produced a better fighting weapon. It is noticeable also that the guard itself tends to become slightly sturdier, in order to balance the increased weight of the blade, although even in this form the guard cannot be regarded as other than weak. With the new blade, the tang was carried up through the pommel to end in a tang button.

In 1854, the hinged flap of the guard was abolished and the S-shaped insert in the flap was replaced in infantry of the line swords by a single curved spur, (Plate 152). For the Foot Guards, a new hilt was introduced. This is of steel, similar to that of rifle regiments, but the royal cypher was replaced by the regimental badge,[32] (Plates 153, 154); all officers of Foot Guards now carried the sword in a steel scabbard. In the *Dress Regulations* of 1857, the blades of Foot Guards officers' swords were to be embossed (etched, in fact) with the regimental device and battle honours. Light or picquet weight patterns also exist, (Plate 155).

For infantry of the line, the changes were limited essentially to ringing the changes on scabbards. In the same *Regulations* of 1854, adjutants re-adopted the steel scabbards which had been abolished in the 1834 *Regulations*, and in the following year

Infantry Officers' Swords

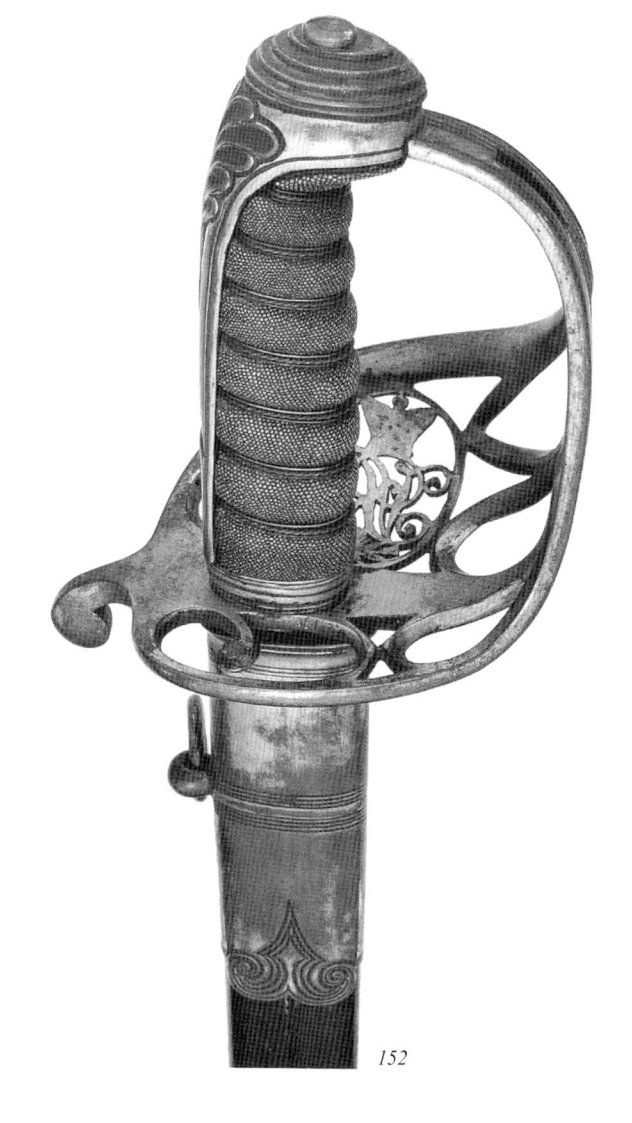

151 Sword, Patterns 1822 (left) and 1845 - comparison of blades
Note: note the tang button in the 1845 blade.
(Author's collection)

152 Sword, Pattern 1845 - inside of hilt
(NAM 8507-53)

162

Infantry Officers' Swords

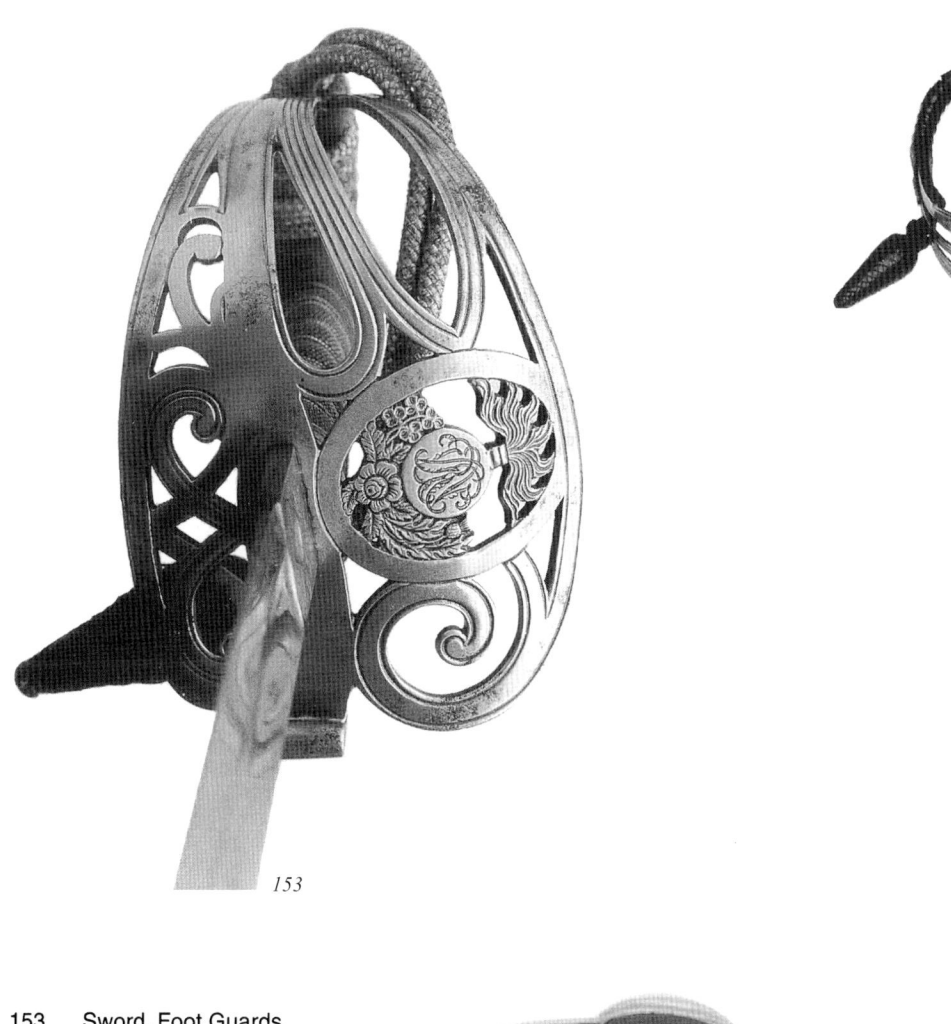

153

153 Sword, Foot Guards, Pattern 1854 - outside of hilt

Note: this is a 1st (or Grenadier) Guards officers' pattern.

(NAM 6503-14)

154 Sword, Foot Guards, Pattern 1854 - outside of hilt

Note: this is the Pattern 1854 hilt of the 3rd (or Scots Fusilier) Guards.

(NAM 6007-90).

155 Sword, Foot Guards, Pattern 1854, light or picquet weight version

Blade length and width: 32$\frac{1}{2}$in. x $\frac{7}{8}$in.
Blade type: identical to Infantry, Officers', Pattern 1845.
Hilt: nickel-plated steel Gothic, with regimental badge of the Grenadier Guards in cartouche.
Hilt mounts: plated steel.
Grip: wood, covered with fishskin and bound with plated steel wire.
Scabbard: plated steel, with two bands and loose rings, and large shoe.

(NAM 6706-2)

154   *155*

163

Infantry Officers' Swords

(1855) the cross-belt was finally abolished and, with it, the need for a frog stud on the locket. Henceforth, all scabbards were to be carried on slings, (which could be hooked up to the waistbelt on parade), until the brown leather scabbard was introduced in the 1890s. In 1864, musketry instructors were authorised to wear steel scabbards.

The old black leather scabbard carried by the majority of infantry officers was a thoroughly unsatisfactory affair for anything except parade wear. It was flimsy, easily cracked or broken, and in tropical climates open to attack from mould and insects. Royal approval was given in November 1866, somewhat belatedly, to all infantry officers below field rank carrying steel scabbards. Officers on the Home Establishment were required to make the change by 1 April 1867; overseas, the timetable was left to the discretion of the local commander.[33]

The *Dress Regulations* of 1872 prescribed two different dimensions of sword for the infantry and other corps using the same pattern. The first version was to have a blade 35 inches long and $1^{1}/8$ inches wide at the shoulder; the overall length of the sword was to be 41 inches and the weight 2lb. The second version was to have a blade of 33 inches, 1 inch wide at the shoulder, and the overall length was to be $38^{1}/2$ inches, with the weight 1lb 12 ozs. The intention behind this somewhat curious innovation remains unknown. What is clear is that these dimensions were never followed in general practice. Indeed, a sword formerly in the possession of the author and made by Wilkinson in 1872 (No 18876) had the normal $32^{1}/2$ inch blade, and while it is true that in many cases officers had swords made to their particular specification the norm remained $32^{1}/2$ inches for the blade.

In the early 1850s, the royal cypher in the guard was altered to incorporate a rose, thistle and shamrock, and at some time between 1872 and 1874 the black leather hilt lining was abandoned for all regiments. No further changes of significance to the Pattern 1845 sword were made before 1891. The Pattern 1845 sword, unsatisfactory as it was as a fighting weapon, thus lasted throughout the great period of Victorian military campaigning - the Second Sikh War, the Crimea, the Indian Mutiny, the Maori Wars, Ashanti, the Zulu War, the Second Afghan War, the Sudan and a host of minor expeditions. By 1890, the case for a better sword was overwhelming and a new design of blade was announced in Army Order 58 of 1892, which announced some amendments to the 1891 *Dress Regulations*.

These amendments, in fact, referred to changes in the infantry sword blade. The new blade was described as straight, $32^{1}/2$ inches long and 1 inch wide at the shoulder, the whole sword now to weigh between 1lb 12 ozs and 1lb 13 ozs. What this bare description concealed was that it was a new and almost revolutionary design. The blade was rounded on back and edge, with a prominent deep fuller both sides, giving it a characteristic dumb-bell cross-section.[34] The last 17 inches to the vicious spear point were double edged, or at least capable of being sharpened thus, as was ordered on the outbreak of war in 1914. It appears that the blade owed its design to

Infantry Officers' Swords

Colonel Fox, the Chief Inspector of Physical Training at the Board of Education, who was later responsible for the design of the grip of the Pattern 1908 cavalry sword, (see Chapter 3) and owed something to his fencing experience.[35]

Announced formally in 1892, the blade had actually been approved in 1891. The new blade was mated with the old Gothic hilt and actually weighed some 2-3 ozs less than its predecessor, (Plate 156).

The new blade cried out for an improved hilt and this arrived in 1895, in the form of a plated steel, three-quarter basket hilt, in a scroll pattern made up of pierced strapwork incorporating a crown and royal cypher, (Plate 157).[36] It gave excellent protection to the hand although a critic might claim that the pierced strapwork might still allow a sword or lance point to penetrate. Nevertheless, taken as a whole, the Pattern 1895 sword, with its excellent guard and its wicked, thrusting blade, was unquestionably the best fighting sword ever prescribed for the infantry officers of the Army, and its theoretical excellence was confirmed in practice. A correspondent, writing in the *Journal of the Society for Army Historical Research* in 1934, recalled that this pattern of sword had served him excellently in hand-to-hand-fighting against the Dervishes in the Sudan, in a way which its predecessor could never have done.[37] One minor modification was introduced in 1897 when the inner edge of the guard was turned down in order to prevent it fraying the clothing, (Plate 158), as had been done with the Pattern 1864 cavalry troopers' sword, (see Chapter 2).

The Army Order No 4 of 1 January 1896, introducing the new hilt, specified that the sword was to be worn by:

(a) Staff officers below the rank of general, (but excluding those officers who then carried the Royal Engineers pattern or the Pattern 1831 mameluke hilt - see Chapter 9);

(b) Infantry officers, excluding Scottish and rifle regiments;

(c) officers of the Army Pay Department;

(d) officers of the Ordnance Stores Department.

Existing swords were to be replaced or re-hilted, and the length of the grip was now to lie between 5 and 5¾ inches, to suit the wearer's hand. This variable length of grip was to apply to all swords, irrespective of pattern.

The rifle regiments and the Foot Guards adopted the new blade but retained their existing steel Gothic pattern hilts.

The Pattern 1895 sword was initially introduced with the existing plated steel scabbard, with two loose rings for use with slings but in 1899, on the eve of the South African War, a brown leather scabbard was introduced for universal use. It

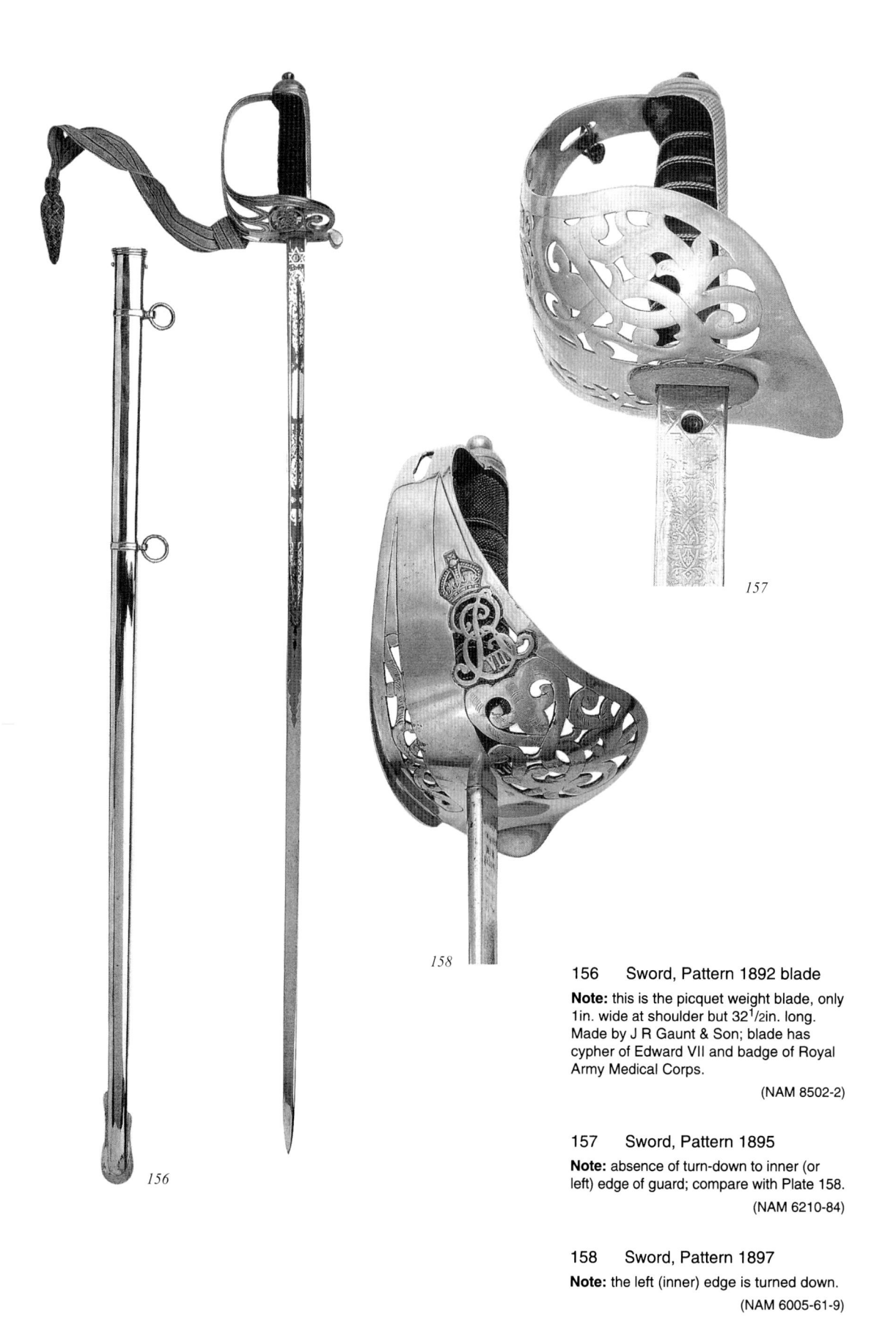

Infantry Officers' Swords

156

157

158

156 Sword, Pattern 1892 blade

Note: this is the picquet weight blade, only 1in. wide at shoulder but 32^{1}/2in. long. Made by J R Gaunt & Son; blade has cypher of Edward VII and badge of Royal Army Medical Corps.

(NAM 8502-2)

157 Sword, Pattern 1895

Note: absence of turn-down to inner (or left) edge of guard; compare with Plate 158.

(NAM 6210-84)

158 Sword, Pattern 1897

Note: the left (inner) edge is turned down.

(NAM 6005-61-9)

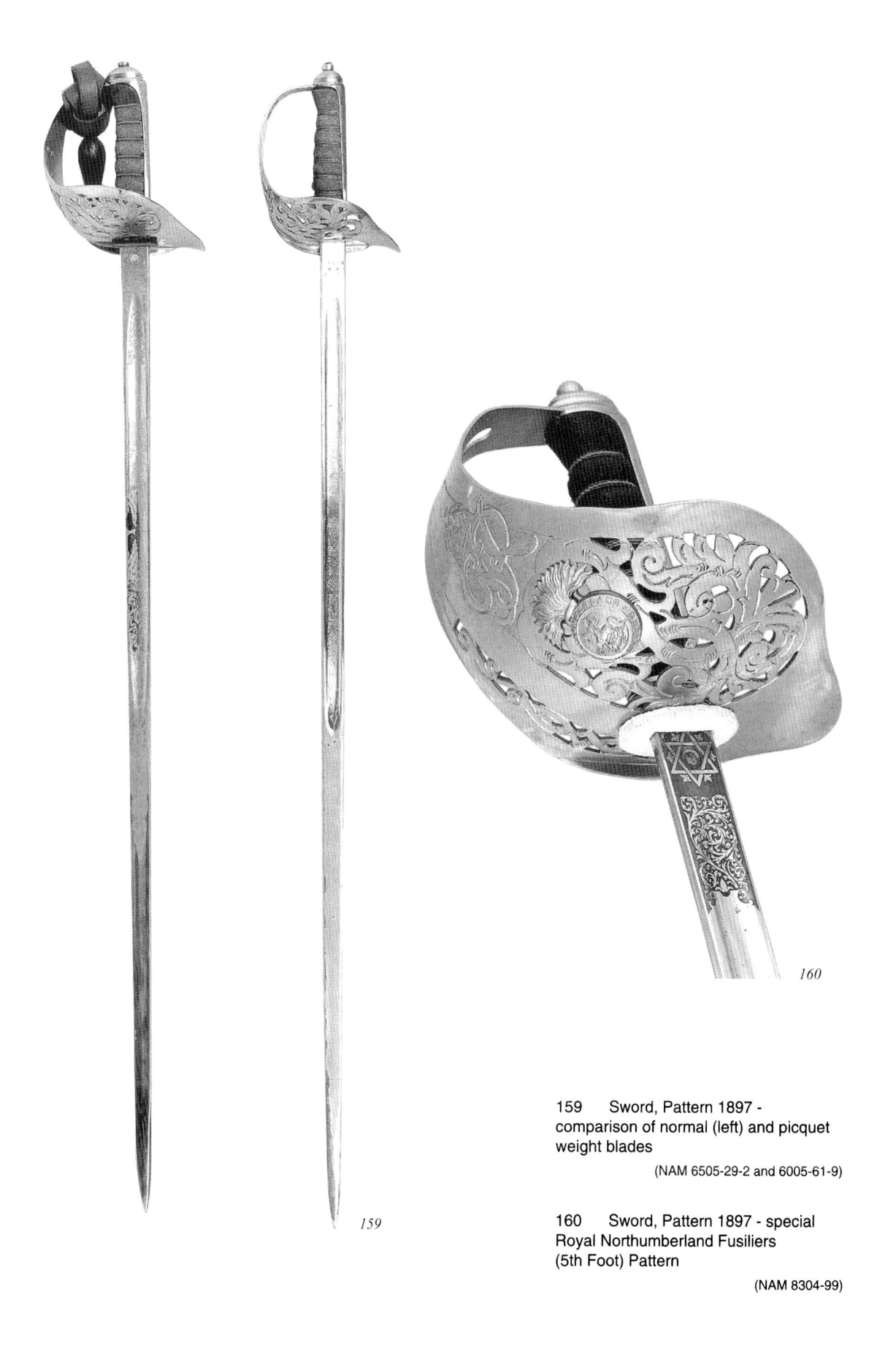

Infantry Officers' Swords

159 Sword, Pattern 1897 - comparison of normal (left) and picquet weight blades

(NAM 6505-29-2 and 6005-61-9)

160 Sword, Pattern 1897 - special Royal Northumberland Fusiliers (5th Foot) Pattern

(NAM 8304-99)

was designed for use by means of a frog attached to the Sam Browne belt. This scabbard had a steel locket and chape, and was wood lined. In 1901, a revised pattern, with a plated steel mouthpiece and without the steel mounts was introduced and this has remained the scabbard for normal use ever since, the plated steel scabbard being worn only in Full Dress or by Directors of Music.

As with the earlier Patterns 1822 and 1845 swords, light or picquet weight versions of the Pattern 1897 sword exist, presumably for the same purposes. The blades are only some $1^{1}/_{16}$ inches wide at the shoulder and the hilts are proportionately smaller also, (Plate 159). These have only a plated steel scabbard and the weights are approximately 1lb 5 ozs (sword) and 12 ozs (scabbard).

Three regimental variations to the Pattern 1897 sword are known:

(a) the Royal Northumberland Fusiliers (the 5th Foot) have a silver grenade, embossed with the regimental badge (St George and the Dragon) and the Roman numeral 'V', pinned to the outside of the guard, (Plate 160);

(b) the Lancashire Fusiliers (the 20th Foot) have the Roman numerals 'XX' inserted in the guard in place of the royal cypher;

(c) the South Wales Borderers (the 24th Foot) have a wreath of immortelles surrounding the royal cypher in memory of the fatal Battle of Isandhlwana (1879).

Chapter 7: Notes

1. See a drawing of a spontoon in *JSAHR*, Vol XXVI, 1948, p30.

2. *JSAHR*, Vol V, 1926, p128.

3. PRO. HO 50/380; also WO 3/26, p166.

4. Adjutant-General to Colonel Myers, 15th Foot, 6 March 1788 - quoted in A V B Norman, *The Rapier and the Small-Sword 1460-1820*, London (1980) p195.

5. See W E May, 'The 5-ball type of sword hilt' *JAAS*, Vol IV, 1964, p153.

6. Bland & Foster appear to have traded under that name between 1788 and 1791; they were succeeded by Robert Foster.

7. A V B Norman has called attention to what may be a silver-hilted version in Raeburn's portrait of Lieutenant-General Hay McDowell as an officer of the 57th Foot 1791-95, now in the possession of the University of Rochester, New York; Norman, 'Notes on some Scottish infantry swords in the Scottish United Services Museum' *JAAS*, Vol V, 1965, p2.

8. See May & Annis, *Swords for Sea Service*, Vol I, HMSO, London (1970) pp22-24.

9. Bottet, *op. cit.*, p63, where the sword is stated to be derived from an English pattern.

10. Peterson, *op. cit.*, pp71-73.

11. PRO. WO 3/8 Circular to Commanding Officers of Infantry Corps; also in WO 3/27, p34.

12. General Order of 4 May 1796, issued by the Adjutant-General. PRO. WO 3/28, p165.

13. An identical type of hilt - the Model 1735 - was in use by Prussian infantry officers from the first half of the eighteenth century - see Wagner, *op. cit.*, p254.

14. See Captain R J Macdonald, *The History of the Dress of the Royal Artillery*, London (1899) p67.

15. Charles Farmer in his *Universal Military Dictionary in English and French*, London (1816), p97 refers to this sword having 'a spring shell', suggesting that by then this had become the normal form.

16. 'King George III and the Prince of Wales reviewing the Third (or the Prince of Wales's) Regiment of Dragoon Guards and the Tenth (or the Prince of Wales's Own) Regiment of (Light Dragoons)', (NAM 7105-30). This is a copy of the original painting destroyed in the fire at Windsor Castle in 1993.

17. Peterson, *op. cit.*, pp13, 81, 144.

18. See a light company officer's sword of the 4th Foot *c*1796 illustrated in L I Cowper, *The King's Own*, Vol I, Oxford (1939) p491; also a sword of a light company officer of the 65th Foot, sold at Wallis & Wallis' sale on 4 December 1972 (Sale 189, Lot 1163).

19. PRO. WO 3/20.

20. PRO. WO 3/35, Letter dated 20 January 1803.

21. PRO. WO 3/35, Letter dated 18 March 1803.

22. Farmer, *op. cit.*, (paginated edition of 1816) p889. More significant evidence comes from a painting by George Romney of Captain Frederick Grey Cooper in the Undress uniform of the 1st Foot Guards. Painted in 1795, it shows Cooper wearing a sword hilt of this distinctive 1803 pattern, thus substantiating Farmer's attribution and indicating that the Pattern 1803 was derived from an existing Foot Guards' officers' sword. I owe this information entirely to Mr A V B Norman. The picture, sold at Christie's in New York on 7 October 1993 (lot 85), is believed to be now in the Far East.

23. See the *Highland Light Infantry Chronicle* for July 1896.

24. A specimen with the bugles on the grip, in a steel scabbard, was sold by Wallis & Wallis in July 1964 (Sale 14, Part II, Lot 291).

25. Individual companies of riflemen had occasionally existed before 1794.

26. See A Terry & S M Milne, *Annals of the King's Royal Rifle Corps*, London (1913) - Annex on uniform, armament and equipment.

27. See also a watercolour of two officers of the Corps reproduced in *JSAHR*, Vol XX, 1941, p38.

28. Copy in MoD Central Library.

29. The precise date of adoption is not known, but a letter from the Adjutant-General of November 1822 refers to it as having been *recently* prescribed for infantry officers - PRO. WO 3/72, p398,

30. John Latham, 'The Shape of Sword Blades' *JRUSI*, Vol VI, 1863, p410.

31. Bound copy in MoD Central Library.

32. The badges were specified as follows: 1st Guards (Grenadiers) - the grenade, with 'VR'; 2nd Guards (Coldstream) - the Garter star and motto; 3rd Guards (Scots Fusilier) - The Thistle star and motto. A steel-hilted version of the ordinary gilt Gothic hilt made for George IV may be an experimental model for the Pattern 1827 Rifle Regiments sword.

33. Circular Memorandum No 389 of 3 December 1866, from the Adjutant-General.

34. There is a story, not necessarily apocryphal, that the blade was intended by Wilkinsons to be double edged but the specimen sent to the War Office for approval in principle had the edges unfinished and was promptly approved as it stood.

35. *JSAHR*, Vol XIII, 1934, p178.

36. Wilkinsons supplied their first sword with this hilt in August 1895.

37. *JSAHR*, Vol XIII, 1934, p178.

8. Scottish Infantry Swords

The authorities in London appear to have exercised a much looser control over the uniforms and equipment of the Scottish and, particularly, the Highland infantry regiments than over those of the other infantry of the line. In consequence, there is a far wider variation in the patterns of sword carried in these regiments than in the ordinary line patterns, for which the specific authority is untraceable, and the dates of introduction and disappearance hazy. Nevertheless, there was a broad pattern of fashion which can be followed and which became narrower and more tightly defined as the nineteenth century advanced, although even up until 1914 there continued to be variations between regiments and even between different battalions of the same regiment.

Officers

In 1788 the Scottish infantry consisted of six Highland regiments (42nd, 71st, 72nd, 73rd, 74th and 75th) and four Lowland regiments (1st, 21st, 25th and 26th).[1]

In the Highland regiments, the officers from the start carried the traditional basket-hilted sword associated with the Highlands as the Full Dress and service sword, as shown in Edward Dayes' painting of an officer of the 42nd (Royal Highlanders or Black Watch), c1790.[2] The basket hilt was either of steel or iron or gilded copper, according to regimental preference, and differed in details between the regiments.[3] The blade was the traditional straight, spear-pointed blade, generally but not invariably, double edged, sometimes fullered but often plain. Numbers of these blades are inscribed 'Andrea Ferrara' (in various spellings), a name which has, in fact, no connection with the real manufacturer but serves usefully on occasion to suggest a Scottish blade.

The first regulation pattern of broadsword appeared in 1798, and its introduction was announced in a letter dated 26 November 1798 from the Adjutant-General to Lieutenant-Colonel McLean of the 4th (Breadalbane) Fencible Infantry:

> 'In reply to your letter of the 9th instant, I have the honour to inform you that it is only within the last few days that His Royal Highness, the Commander-in-Chief [Frederick, Duke of York] has approved a Pattern Sword for the use of the Officers of the Highland Regiments.

Scottish Infantry Swords

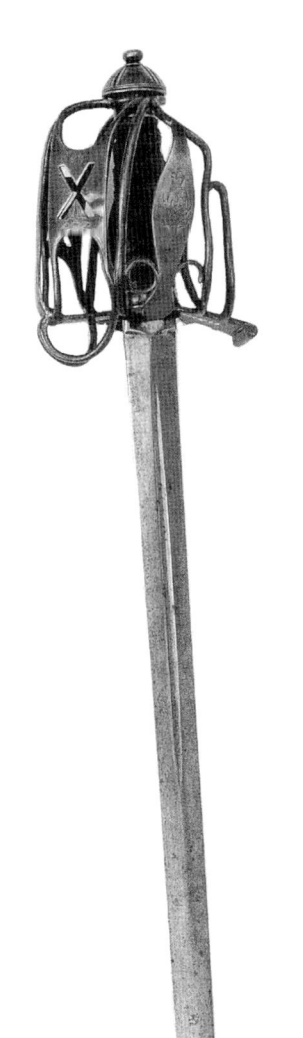

161 Broadsword, Officers',
Highland Regiments,
93rd Highlanders, Pattern 1798

Blade length and width: 32in. x 1¼in.
Blade type: straight, double edged, spear point, single narrow fuller each side.
Guard: traditional Highland basket of brass, with regimental number and St Andrew's Cross on bars.
Grip: wood, covered with fishskin.
Note: the 93rd (Sutherland Highlanders) was raised in 1800 and the sword therefore can be dated to 1800-22.

(NAM 8304-98)

162 Broadsword, Officers',
116th Regiment, 1794

Note: the domed pommel, the slotted form of the steel guard and the single-edged blade.

(SUSM 1938.446)

161

162

173

Scottish Infantry Swords

> The Pattern approved by his Royal Highness was made by Mr Prosser, in Charing Cross, and is lodged in the offices of the Comptrollers of Army Accounts.[4]

A similar letter went a day later to the agents of all the Highland regiments but the pattern sword does not seem to have reached the Comptrollers of Army Accounts (the recognised custodians of sealed uniform and equipment patterns) until 10 December.[5] *The View of the Standing Regulations for the Colours, Clothing etc., of the Infantry* (1802) confirms that the sword for Highland regiments was to be 'according to a particular pattern at the Comptrollers' office'.[6]

No details of this pattern were given but there is a mass of evidence to show that it was in fact a Highland broadsword of traditional form, although it seems to have varied in practice in detail between different regiments. The evidence shows that the hilt and scabbard mounts (locket and chape) were of gilded copper or brass. Numerous portraits, such as J Smith's of an officer of the 42nd in 1808, show this broadsword to have been carried in a black leather scabbard suspended from a crossbelt and frog.[7] This is confirmed directly by the reminiscences of Lieutenant John Ford, who served in the 1st Battalion of the 79th in the Peninsula between 1810 and 1814. He records that the officers of the flank companies carried sabres but that the other officers carried broadswords with gilded copper hilts, worn in a frog suspended from a shoulder belt.[8] The J Smith portrait also shows very clearly the crimson hilt lining, with a fringe round the pommel, characteristic of the regimental Highland broadsword. It may also be noted that, somewhat curiously to modern eyes, some regiments wore sword knots with these swords in the early part of the nineteenth century. Specimens of gilt or brass-hilted broadswords of this pattern exist in some numbers; a typical specimen is NAM 8304-98, belonging to an officer of the 93rd which was raised in 1800, (Plate 161).[9] A number of short-lived Highland regiments were raised during the Revolutionary and Napoleonic Wars, including the 116th (Perthshire Highlanders), raised in 1794 and disbanded shortly thereafter. The broadswords which survive of this regiment embody a basket guard of distinctly different form from that of the other regular regiments, (Plate 162) and similar to those carried by Fencible regiments.[10]

The broadsword is a somewhat bulky weapon and there is evidence that at this period Highland regiment officers in Undress and for evening functions were accustomed to carrying a light sword of ordinary infantry officer pattern. Three specimens of the Pattern 1786 infantry officers' sword, with beaded hilts, (see page 143) belonging to officers of the 71st c1794 are in the Scottish United Services Museum;[11] a similar sword, but without the beads in the hilt and with a black and gold (ebony and gilt brass), longitudinally-striped grip, is shown in Zoffany's portrait of Lieutenant-Colonel Norman McLeod, of the 42nd, painted between 1783 and 1789, now at Dunvegan Castle.[12] The custom would seem indeed to go back even earlier because Major-General David Stewart of Garth in his *Sketches of the Highlanders of Scotland* noted that around 1770 the officers of the 1st Battalion of the 42nd wore broadswords only in Full Dress and on other occasions carried light hangers.[13]

From at least the 1790s, in common with line regiments, the officers of flank companies of Highland regiments carried curved sabres in some forms of dress. While the practice was unofficial, it was nonetheless widespread. It was recorded by John Ford in the 79th (see above) and patterns exist for the period 1793-1817, covering the 42nd, 71st and 78th. These vary in detail between the regiments and between dates but conform to a broad general pattern, with broad curved blades and knucklebow guards, often with one or two outer bars.

A typical sword of this type is that of Captain Duncan MacRae, who served in the 78th between 1793 and 1798, (Plate 163). This has a broad, curved, fullered blade, similar to that of the Pattern 1796 Light Cavalry sword but shorter, with plain gilt brass knucklebow and (originally) two outer bars. The black leather scabbard has a gilt brass chape and locket and was suspended from a frog. A similar pattern, in the SUSM, belonged to an officer of the 42nd and may be the pattern referred to in an Inspection Report on the 1st Battalion in 1807: 'Officers dress correct, except their wearing pantaloons, and the field and flank officers using sabres'.

A number of different patterns of sabre exist from the 71st possibly reflecting its later categorisation as a light infantry regiment. A simple knucklebow hilt, with two curved bars springing from the foot of the guard, the inner one of which carries a somewhat crude grenade, marked '71', (Plate 164) is presumably that of a grenadier company officer and could date from the 1790s. A slightly later sabre of this regiment, which from its markings, is post-1801, is very similar in general form to MacRae's sword, the space between the stirrup and the outer bar being filled with a Union spray of roses, thistles and shamrocks, the stalk of which forms the middle bar of the guard, (Plate 165). The guard of a later sabre of the 71st, datable from the battle honours on the blade to *c*1816-18, is a simple curved knucklebow, with oval langets, the right hand one bearing a bugle horn and the number '71' within a wreath of thistles, (Plate 166). The 71st became a light infantry regiment in 1809 and it is probable that all officers then adopted sabres, of which this may be a specimen. A significant number of patterns exist, even within a regiment, suggesting not merely a wide degree of latitude on the part of regimental colonels, but also that patterns may have differed between grenadier and light companies. Highland regiments appear to have gone their own way in this respect at least until the general tidying-up of sword patterns which took place with the first issue of *Dress Regulations* for the Army in 1822. In the 79th, some attempt had been made earlier to adhere to official regulations, as a Regimental Order of 10 November 1817 makes clear: 'No 5. The flank officers, when in the Highland uniform, are to wear frog-belts and claymores the same as the other officers'. (The use of the term 'claymore' should be noted since there have been attempts to restrict its use to the old, two-handed sword.

Scottish Infantry Swords

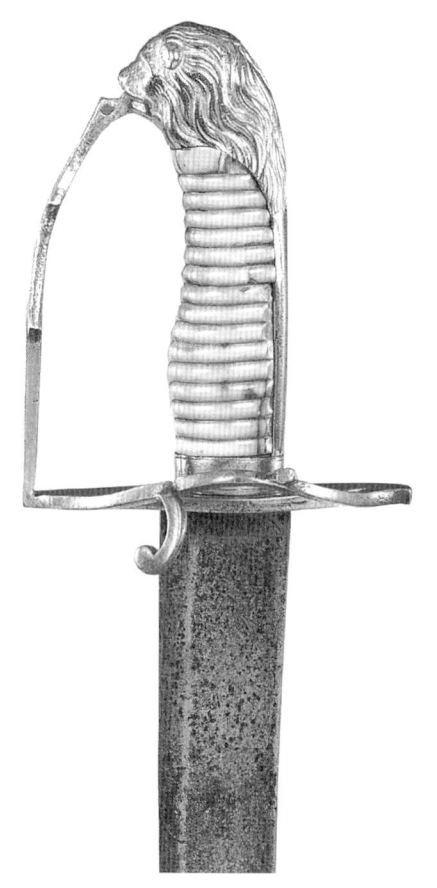

163 Sword, Officers', 78th Regiment, *c*1793
Blade length and width: 32$\frac{1}{8}$in. x 1$\frac{3}{8}$in.
Blade type: curved, flat back, single broad fuller each side to within 7in. of spear point.
Guard: gilt brass knucklebow, originally with two outer bars (broken off).
Hilt mounts: gilt brass pommel, backpiece and ferrule.
Grip: ivory.
Scabbard: tooled black leather, with gilt locket with frog stud and chape.
Note: supplied by Knubley & Co, Charing Cross, London, but blade by Runkel.

(SUSM L1930.94)

164 Sword, Officers', 71st Foot, *c*1800
Blade length and width: 27$\frac{1}{2}$in. x 1$\frac{1}{4}$in.
Blade type: curved, flat back, single wide fuller, spear point.
Guard: gilt brass knucklebow, with two curved bars in plane of stool, with crude grenade between bars, marked '71'.
Hilt mounts: gilt brass, lion's head pommel.
Grip: ivory bound with brass wire, gilt brass lower ferrule.
Scabbard: black leather, gilt brass chape and locket (hole in locket for frog stud).

(SUSM 1990.89)

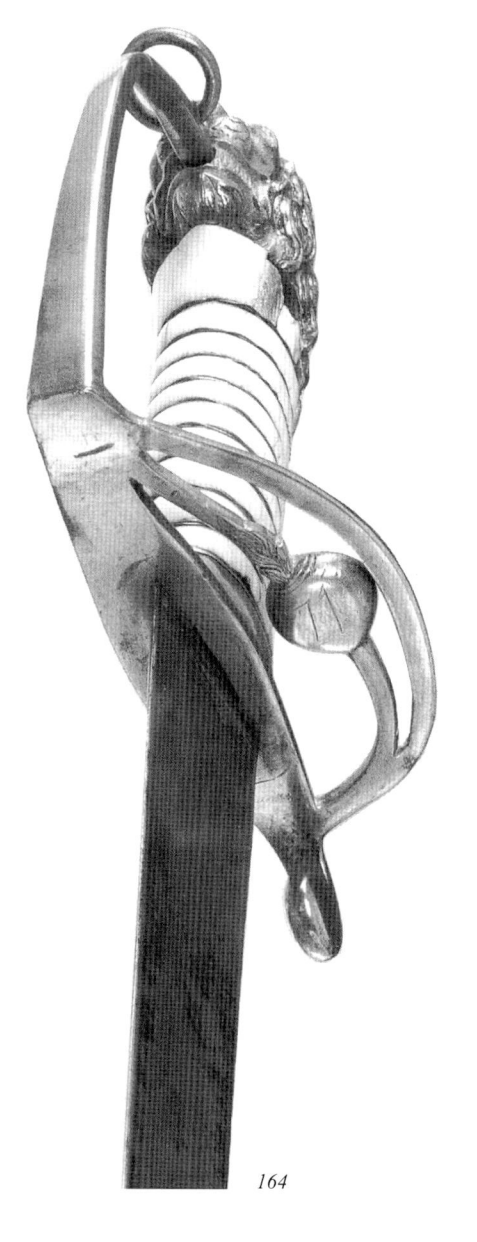

176

Scottish Infantry Swords

165 Sword, Light Company Officers', 71st Regiment, early 19th century

Blade length and width: 30in. x 1¼in.
Blade type: curved, flat back, unfullered, spear point, double edged for last 9½in.
Guard: steel stirrup, with curved outer bar, the intervening space filled with spray of thistles, roses and shamrocks of cast iron.
Hilt mounts: steel.
Grip: wood, covered with black leather.
Note: blade marked with cypher of George III, '71' and stringed bugle. It probably dates from 1800-10. An almost exactly similar sword is SUSM 1953-393.

(NAM 8005-31)

165

166 Sword, Field or Light Company Officers', 71st Regiment, c1817

Blade length and width: 30½in. x 1¼in.
Blade type: curved, flat back, unfullered, spear point, double edged for last 12in.
Guard: steel, simple round knucklebow, ending in straight quillon with finial, in steel.
Hilt mounts: steel. Right-hand langet has a silver badge consisting of a stringed bugle, with '71' below, all surrounded by oval 'Highland Light Infantry'. Left-hand langet has a silver badge of thistle and leaves, surrounded by '*Nemo Me Impune Lacessit*'.
Grip: wood, covered with fishskin and bound with steel or German silver wire.
Note: the blade has battle honour 'Waterloo', awarded in 1816, and is marked with number '43'. The sword was supplied by R Johnston, 68 St James's Street, London, and an almost identical sword, blade marked '20', by the same maker, is in the Royal Highland Fusiliers Museum.

(NAM 7510-22)

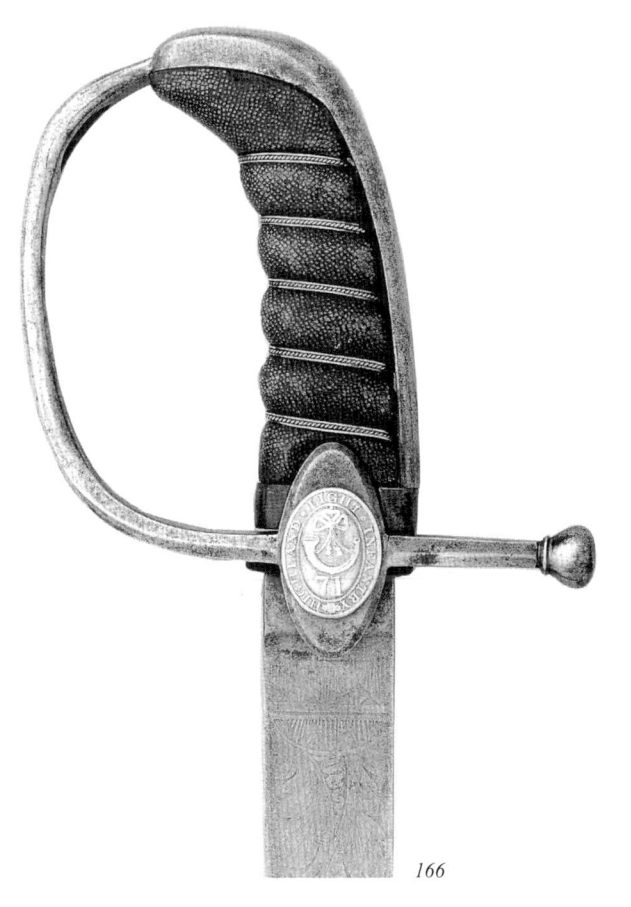

166

177

Claude Blair has, however, shown that the term can properly be applied to the single-handed broadsword although the former term has the longer and better pedigree).[14]

In the 93rd, the use of sabres by flank company officers was apparently abandoned in 1817,[15] and presumably all such sabres were given up in the late 1820s when the introduction of a new pattern of broadsword and of printed *Dress Regulations* made the practice impossible to sustain. Before leaving the subject of flank company sabres, it is worth noting the existence of a broadsword with a silver grenade on the outside of the guard, ascribed to Captain Colin Mackay of the 78th and datable to *c*1805, (Plate 167); this clearly comes from his service in the grenadier company but it may be a purely personal design.

Lowland regiments in the period up to 1822 were closely akin in uniform to the ordinary infantry of the line and carried the same types of sword. A print by Edward Dayes, for example, of an officer of the 1st (or Royal) Regiment, *c*1792, shows him carrying a Pattern 1786 infantry officers' sword.[16] The same regiment used a version of the Pattern 1796 infantry sword in which the inside of each of the two fixed shells carried the badge of the regiment, (Plate 168). The regimental title was changed to 'The Royal Scots' in 1812 and versions of this pattern of sword with both the pre- and post-1812 badges exist in the NAM and SUSM.[17] The blade is usually heavy, broad at the forte and of diamond section. Battalion company officers appear to have carried this sword in the normal black leather scabbard, with gilt brass mounts, but at some point between 1795 and 1810 field officers of this regiment were authorised to carry a brass scabbard with loose rings.[18]

Flank company officers of the 1st Foot adopted a version of the Pattern 1803 Flank Company Officers' sword, in which the guard was modified to incorporate the regimental badge, (Plate 169). Moreover the specimen in the SUSM has an unfullered blade. A sabre of the 25th in the SUSM is evidence that other Lowland regiments followed the fashion of carrying sabres in the flank companies, (Plate 170). The 90th, raised in 1794, also had a sabre of regimental pattern, (Plate 171); the marking 'Egypt' on the blade shows that it was made after 1802 when this battle honour was awarded to the regiments which had taken part in the Egyptian campaign of 1801. Since the 90th seem to have regarded themselves as light infantry from their inception, it is likely that all officers of the regiment carried sabres.

With the publication of the 1822 *Dress Regulations* for officers of the Army, an attempt was made to put the patterns of sword for the Scottish regiments on to a more regular basis. Indeed, the *Regulations* prescribed the ordinary Pattern 1822 sword for all these regiments but this was clearly an oversight because in November 1822, the Adjutant-General's office wrote to General Sir John Hope, Colonel of the 92nd, telling him that the Commander-in-Chief had agreed to the Highland regiments continuing to carry '...the Broad Sword as hitherto in use by Corps of that description'.[19] A similar notification was sent to the commanding officers of High-

Scottish Infantry Swords

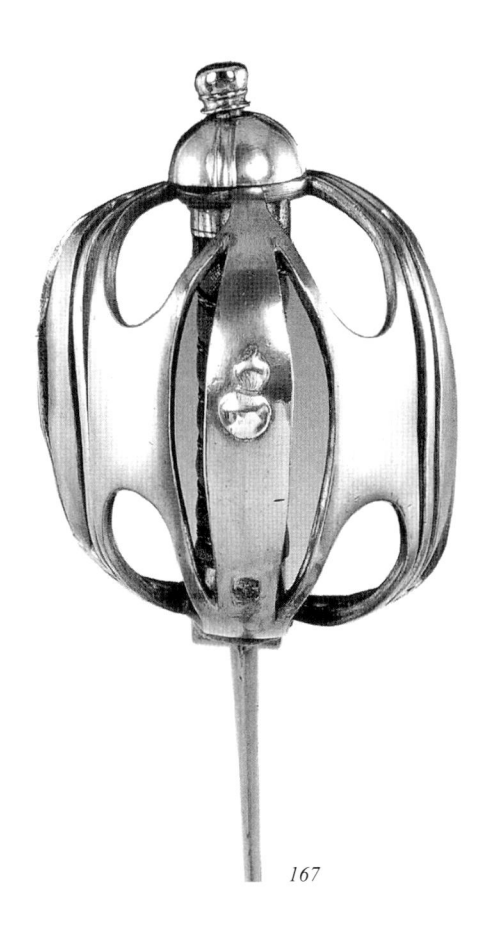

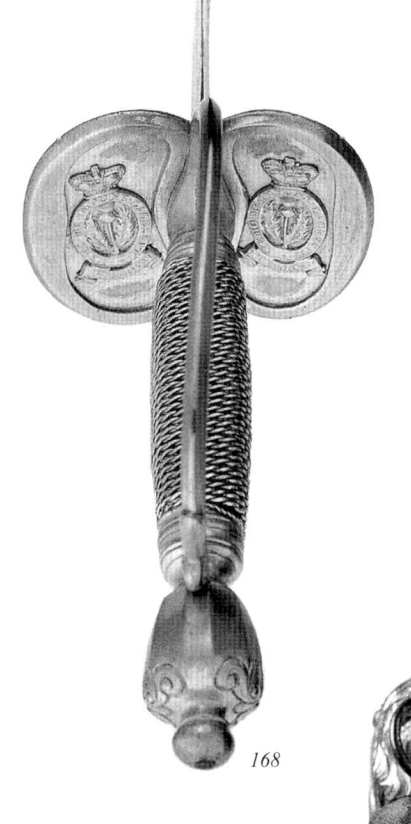

167 Broadsword, Grenadier Company Officers', 78th Foot, c1805

Note: gilt brass basket hilt and blade of traditional form, silver grenade on front of guard. The owner, Captain Colin Mackay of Bighouse, commanded the Grenadier Company of the 2nd Battalion of the 78th from 1805-14.

(SUSM L1932.150)

168 Sword, Officers', 1st (or Royal) Regiment of Foot, c1800

Note: this is a regimental variation of the ordinary Pattern 1796 infantry officers' sword.

(NAM 7203-27)

169 Sword, Officers', 1st (or Royal Scots) Regiment of Foot, c1812

Blade length and width: 28in. x 1½in.
Blade type: curved, flat back, spear point, unfullered.
Guard: gilt brass stirrup, sword knot slit near pommel.
Hilt mounts: gilt brass.
Grip: wood, covered with fishskin and bound originally with brass wire.

(NAM 7811-143)

179

Scottish Infantry Swords

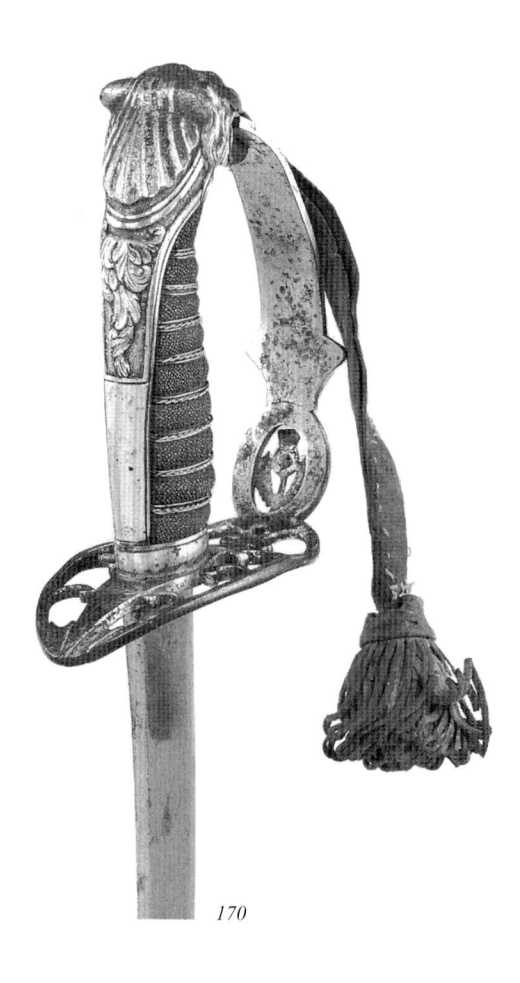

170

170 Sword, ('sabre'), Officers', 25th Regiment, *c*1805

Blade type: curved, unfullered, flat back, spear point.
Guard: steel knucklebow of Pattern 1803 infantry officers' form, with 'Minden' and regimental badge let in.
Hilt mounts: steel backpiece and lion's head pommel.
Grip: wood, covered with fishskin and steel wire.
Scabbard: steel, with two narrow bands and loose rings, narrow shoe.
Note: presumably a flank (light) company officer's sword.

(SUSM M1993.851)

171 Sword, Officers', 90th Regiment, *c*1810

Blade length and width: 31in. x 1⅝in.
Blade type: extremely curved, pipe back, double edged for last 8in., spear point.
Guard: gilt brass.
Hilt mounts: gilt brass.
Grip: wood, covered with sharkskin, secured through tang by three gilt-headed rivets.
Scabbard: black leather, gilt brass reeded locket, band and chape; two loose rings on locket and band; large shoe.
Sword weight: 1lb 15oz.
Note: left side of blade engraved 'Egypt'; right side '90th Light Infantry Regt'. Supplied by Pitter & Fox (1810-29).

(NAM 6312-223)

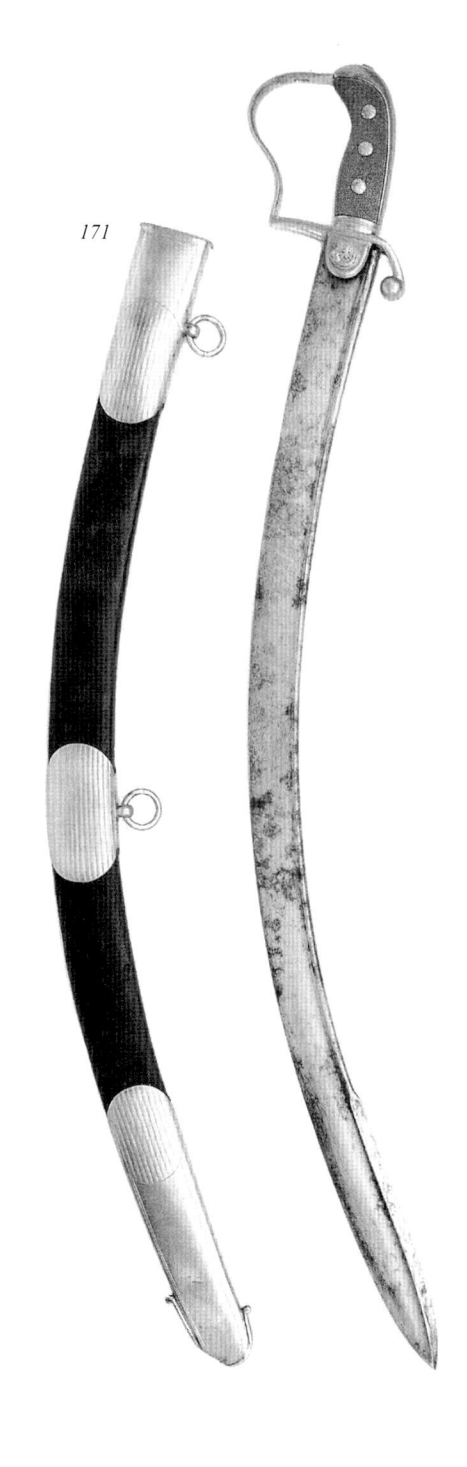

171

land regiments in January 1823. The pattern of broadsword was more closely defined in a manuscript note in a copy of the 1822 *Dress Regulations* corrected up to 25 December 1826, now in the MoD Central Library.[20] This describes the sword as of Highland pattern, with gilt basket hilt and scabbard mounts, with a straight cut-and thrust blade, 33 inches long and 1 inch wide at the shoulder. The scabbard was to be of black leather and the gilt mounts were to have both two loose rings and a frog stud, to enable the sword to be worn either from slings or hooked up. The gilt brass hilt and scabbard mounts are clearly shown in Hull's print of two officers of the 42nd, issued in April 1828.[21] As an exception, the 72nd were allowed to carry a steel hilt and scabbard mounts, with scarlet cloth hilt lining. The 72nd were only slightly premature because in September 1828 the gilt brass hilt was superseded by a steel hilt for all Highland regiments. A Circular of 12 September 1828 to the agents of all Highland regiments announced that a new pattern of broadsword, with a steel hilt, had received royal approval, and was to be adopted as and when existing hilts became unserviceable. This new steel pattern is shown in the Dubois Drahonet painting of Captain James Alexander of the 42nd, painted in 1832.[22] But the gilt brass hilt is shown as late as 1840 in Michael Angelo Hayes' painting of a company of the 78th.[23] The scabbard of the new steel-hilted sword had steel mounts, the chape ending in a ball. Compared with later patterns, the guard of the Pattern 1828 broadsword is usually made of unplated steel and is generally rounder in form; the bars of the guard tend to be round rather than flat and the hilt is not dismountable to take another form of hilt, (Plate 172).

The Lowland regiments adopted first the Pattern 1822, and then the Pattern 1845, infantry officers' sword. But the 21st (the Royal North British Fusiliers, later the Royal Scots Fusiliers) adopted a version of the Gothic hilt in which the royal cypher was replaced by a regimental device consisting of a grenade inscribed '21st', surrounded by thistles, and resting on a scroll bearing the regimental motto *Nemo me impune lacessit*, and surmounted by another scroll bearing the name of the regiment. The pommel had a flattened top, embossed with a thistle, and the backpiece was also decorated with thistles, (Plate 173). The majority of existing specimens have the Pattern 1845 blade and hilts with the title 'Royal Scots Fusiliers', a title not authorised officially until 1877.[24] This special 21st pattern disappeared after 1881 when the regiment adopted Scottish dress.

The steel basket-hilted broadsword remained in essentials unchanged up to 1914. It is, for example, well shown in Roger Fenton's photographs of an officer of the 71st, and of a group of officers of the 42nd, in the Crimea.[25] Its form and that of the scabbard were regulated by a pattern sealed on 7 October 1863. From 1832 onwards successive editions of *Dress Regulations* give the length of the blade as 32 inches. Light patterns, presumably for wear at Levées and evening functions, also exist.[26] Field officers and adjutants were ordered a steel scabbard, with two loose rings, in 1834 but other officers carried the black leather scabbard, with steel mounts, until

Scottish Infantry Swords

172

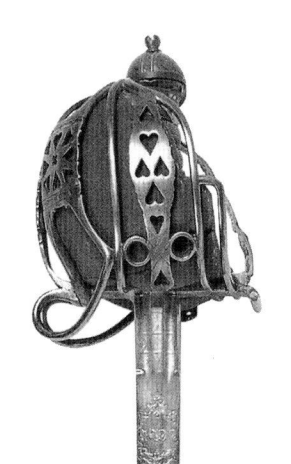

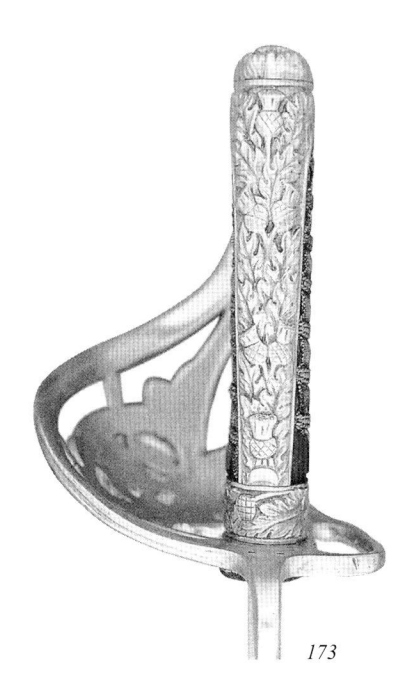

173 *173*

172 Broadsword, Officers', 72nd (Duke of Albany's Own) Highlanders, Pattern 1828
Note: owned by Major Thomas Charles Hardinge Best, 1847-62.

(SUSM 1986.17)

173 Sword, Officers', 21st Regiment, 1868
Blade length and width: 32in. x 1in.
Blade type: identical with Infantry Officer, Pattern 1822.
Guard: gilt brass, sword knot slit near pommel.
Hilt mounts: gilt brass.
Grip: wood, covered with fishskin and bound with brass wire.
Scabbard: black leather, gilt brass locket with frog stud and band (chape missing); loose rings on locket and band.
Sword weight: 1lb 11oz.
Note: although the title 'Royal Scots Fusiliers' was not officially adopted until 1877, the form of the blade and hilt is clearly much earlier.

(NAM 6908-17-2)

1868 when they, too, changed over to steel scabbards. A peculiarity of both of these types of scabbard was that they ended in a ball, rather than a shoe as in other patterns.

The Lowland regiments adopted steel scabbards for all officers in 1866 when they were adopted generally for infantry of the line, (see page 164).

From about 1881 a series of major changes affected the patterns of Scottish regimental swords. The first of these changes was the adoption of elements of Highland dress by all Lowland regiments in 1881. With the change of dress, the regiments concerned, apart from the Cameronians, adopted the Highland broadsword. The second change of consequence was the adoption generally of additional forms of hilt for the broadsword. Despite its long history, the basket guard of the broadsword is not an ideal fighting design. Although it gives very good protection to the hand and wrist, it also restricts the movement of the wrist, particularly when thrusting, for which the modern straight blade was primarily suited. In the early 1880s, therefore, an alternative hilt, in the form of a removable cross-bar, came into general use with the broadsword. Its precise origins are still not wholly clear although it may hark back to the original two-handed Scottish sword. It first appears officially in *Dress Regulations* in 1883, when the Highland Light Infantry were authorised to carry a removable basket hilt for Levées and similar Full Dress functions and a cross-bar hilt for other duties. Two years later, General Order 128 of 1 December 1885 prescribed a cross-bar hilt for all regiments carrying the broadsword. Its origins, however, go back much earlier. A photograph of a group of officers of the 91st in Zululand in 1879 clearly shows a number of cross-bar hilts.[27] Dunn-Pattison, in his *History of the 91st Argyllshire Highlanders*, states that the cross-bar hilt was carried by the 91st from 1865 onwards and includes a reproduction of a painting of the regiment in 1874 by Orlando Norie, showing this hilt.[28] The earliest claim, however, occurs in A N E Brown's *Notes on the Dress of the 71st Regiment* (1935) where it is stated that the 71st adopted the hilt *c*1858 for all purposes; that seems to be supported by a letter from the Horse Guards dated 13 February 1866, informing the regiment that the Commander-in-Chief had no objection to the cross-bar hilt being used by the 71st since it was a light infantry regiment, but that the removable basket hilt was to be used at Levées and similar functions,[29] an instruction which seems to have been ignored in practice since the 71st continued to carry the cross-bar hilt on all occasions. (The 74th, by contrast, carried the basket hilt on all occasions, even after it became the 2nd Battalion of the Highland Light Infantry in 1881).[30] It would appear, therefore, that the *Dress Regulations* were codifying something which was already happening.

Needless to say, the regiments adopted different forms of cross-bar hilt, according to their own predilictions, and in the 1870s and 1880s there was a wide variety of patterns, differing in such details as the presence or absence of langets, and in the shape of the finials of the cross-bar. By 1914 the patterns had been reduced, officially at least, to six, covering all the regiments, (Plates 174-177).[31] In all cases, they

Scottish Infantry Swords

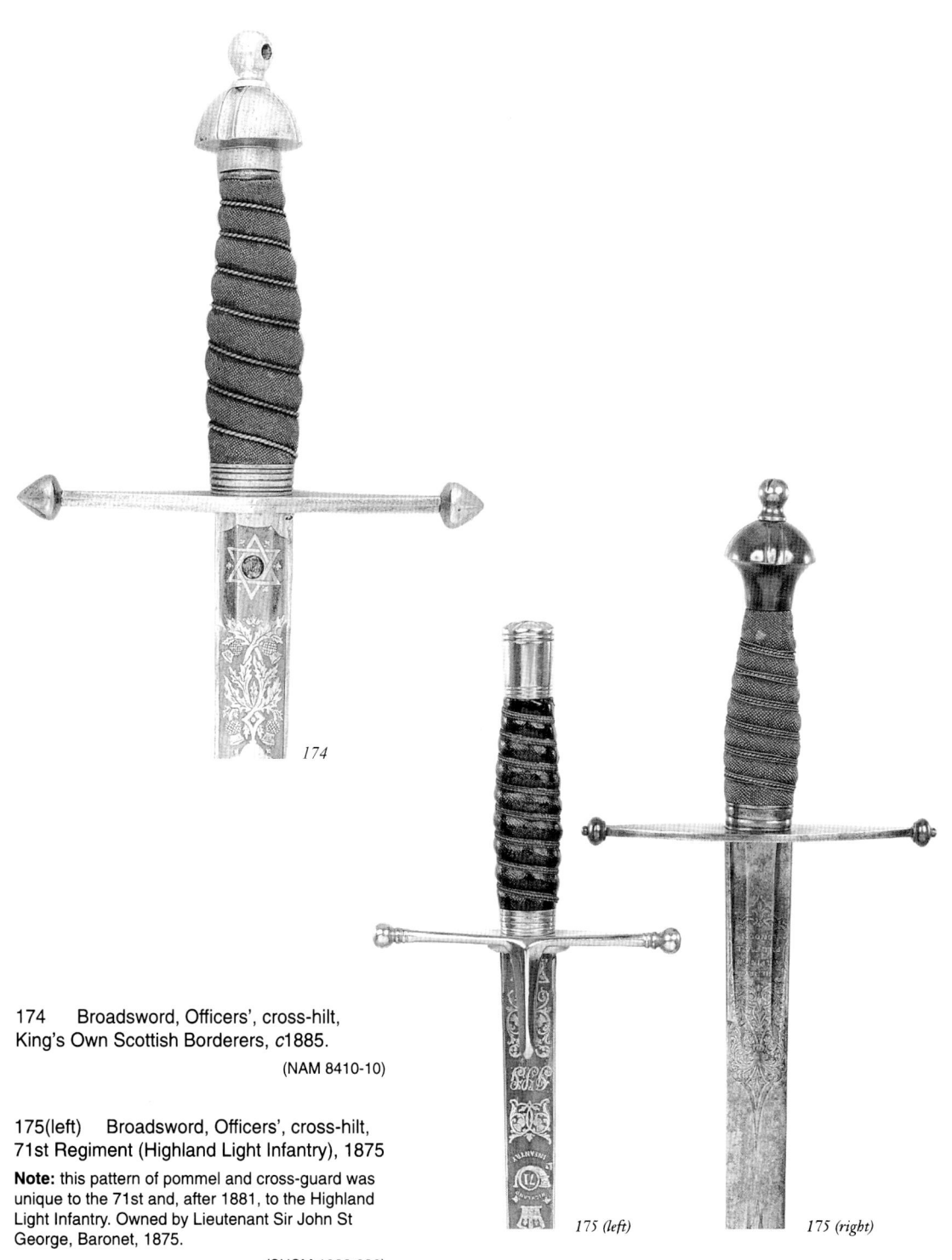

174

174   Broadsword, Officers', cross-hilt, King's Own Scottish Borderers, *c*1885.
(NAM 8410-10)

175(left)   Broadsword, Officers', cross-hilt, 71st Regiment (Highland Light Infantry), 1875

Note: this pattern of pommel and cross-guard was unique to the 71st and, after 1881, to the Highland Light Infantry. Owned by Lieutenant Sir John St George, Baronet, 1875.
(SUSM 1932.686)

175 (right)   Broadsword, Officers', cross-hilt, 74th (Highlanders), 1856.

Note: this pattern of cross-guard appears to be unique to the 74th and is the earliest recorded example of one being fitted to a broadsword blade.
(SUSM 1985.113)

175 (left)   *175 (right)*

Scottish Infantry Swords

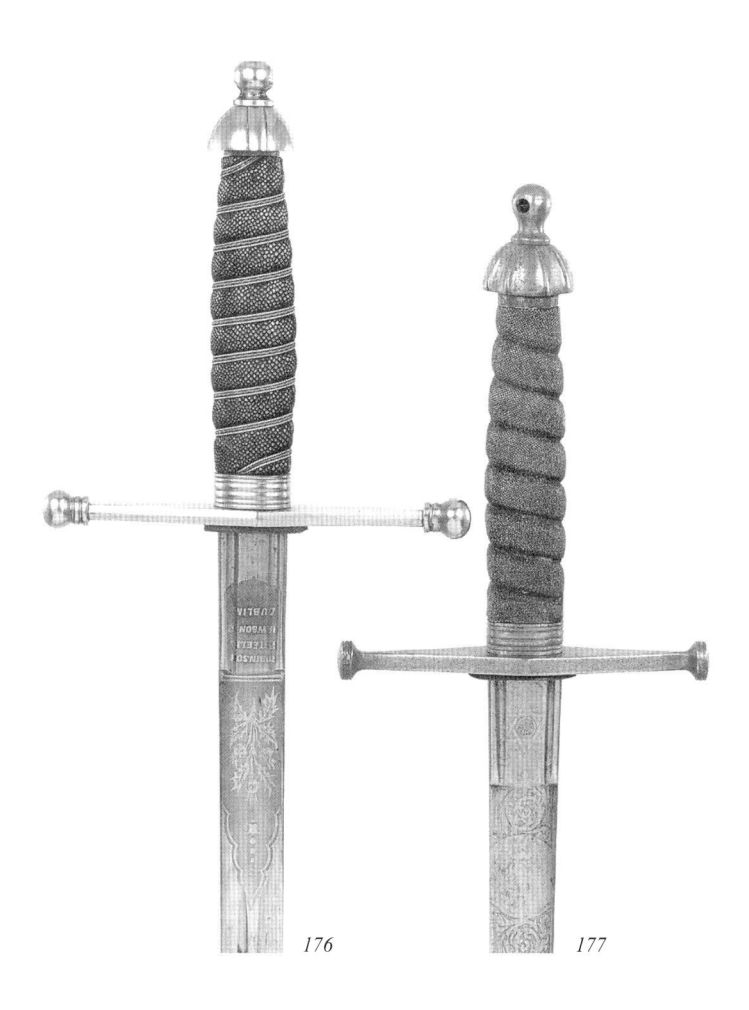

176 Broadsword, Officers', c1914, fitted with a cross-hilt of the pattern associated with the Seaforth and Argyll and Sutherland Highlanders

(SUSM 1993.736)

177 Broadsword, Officers', cross-hilt, 1st Dunbartonshire Rifle Volunteers, c1880

Note: this pattern of cross-guard was associated with The Royal Scots after 1881 and the regiment's adoption of elements of Highland dress.

(SUSM 1985.97)

were interchangeable with the basket hilt by simply unscrewing the tang button or nut and removing guard, grip and pommel. The grip and pommel were used interchangeably. Whereas the basket hilt gave good protection but restricted movement, the cross-bar hilt gave good movement but inferior protection. The balance of advantage is not obvious but was presumably considered to exist by the users. A peculiarity of the cross-bar hilt is that there is no provision for attaching a sword knot.

The cross-bar hilt had in some cases a short life. Some regiments, such as the 42nd (Black Watch), did not adopt them at all. They were discontinued in the Highland Light Infantry as early as 1905, despite the 1911 *Dress Regulations*; and in the 2nd Battalion of the Argyll and Sutherland Highlanders after 1918. It also seems to have been generally discontinued in the Lowland regiments before 1914.

Scottish Infantry Swords

In addition to the cross-bar hilt, other forms of alternative hilt came into existence for field officers and other mounted officers, beginning as early as the 1840s. By 1914 these had become regularised as follows:

Guard	Blade	Regiment
Symmetrical steel basket with pierced thistle design and regimental badge. Removable. Same lining as broadsword, (Plate 178)	Regulation broadsword	RS, RSF, KOSB, GH, HLI
Steel Pattern 1856 RE Removable. Lining as above, (Plate 179).	Regulation Broadsword	BW, A&SH, SH
Pattern 1822 Light Cavalry three-bar. No lining, (Plate 180)	RA officers'	CH

178

179

178 Broadsword, Field Officers', Scottish Regiments, Royal Scots, 1900

Note: the same hilt, with appropriate regimental device, was carried by Royal Scots Fusiliers, Gordon Highlanders, King's Own Scottish Borderers and Highland Light Infantry.

(NAM 8012-61)

179 Broadsword, Field Officers', Highland Regiments - Argyll and Sutherland Highlanders, 1873

Note: this hilt was carried also by Black Watch and Seaforth Highlanders.

(NAM 8007-78)

Scottish Infantry Swords

180

180 Sword, Field Officers',
79th (Queen's Own Cameron Highlanders), c1875

Blade length and width: 33½in. x ⅞in.
Blade type: flat back, single fuller, spear point.
Guard: three-bar in plated steel.
Hilt mounts: plated steel.
Grip: wood, covered with fishskin, bound with silver wire.
Scabbard: plated steel, two loose rings, detachable mouthpiece, medium shoe.
Note: this is a picquet weight sword, Wilkinson blade No.23390.

(SUSM 1985.184)

181   Broadsword, Field Officers',
92nd Highlanders, c1870

Blade length and width: 33in. x 1³⁄₁₆in.
Blade type: normal Highland broadsword blade, straight, double edged, two short fullers each side in ricasso, two long fullers each side to within 9in. of spear point.
Guard: exactly half of a normal Highland basket hilt, in polished steel, removable.
Hilt mounts: polished steel removable pommel, tang nut with slot for unscrewing.
Grip: wood, covered with fishskin and bound with steel wire.
Note: blade etched with battle honours up to 'Waterloo', cypher of Victoria and regimental name and number.

(SUSM M1932.474)

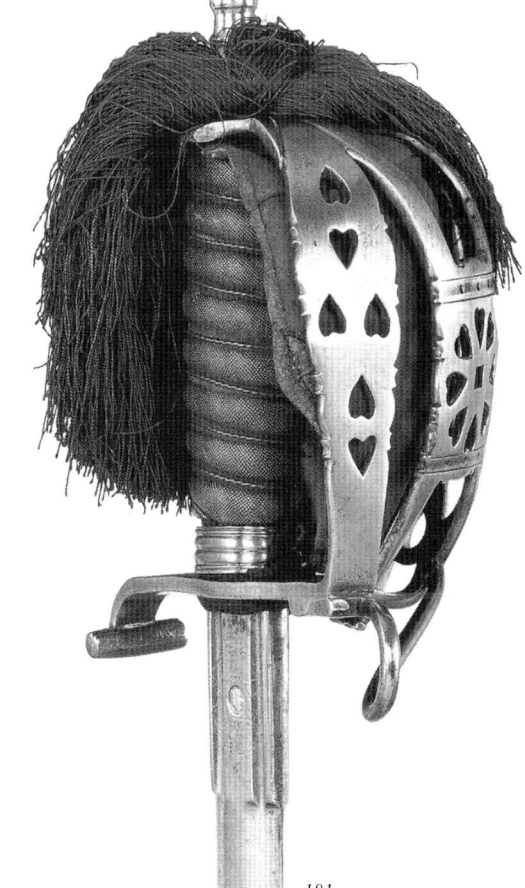

181

187

These hilts were intended to be worn by mounted and field officers when other officers were wearing the cross-hilt or when not in Full Dress. In the 79th, however, all officers wore the three-bar hilt in frock coat order.

In some regiments - for example, the 92nd - at different periods, a halved basket hilt, (Plate 181) was in use, presumably because in certain circumstances, such as evening functions, the full basket was too cumbersome.

The precise origins of these field officers' hilts remains unclear. Daniel Cunliffe's painting 'The 74th in 1846', now in the SUSM, shows the colonel, mounted, carrying a broadsword while the adjutant wears what is clearly a Pattern 1821 Heavy Cavalry officers' sword with a scarlet lining.[32] The three-bar hilt appears to have been in use in both the 42nd and the 79th as early as the 1840s, in the case of the 79th with a standard infantry pipe-backed blade.[33] The fact that in these earlier versions the blade was not always the ordinary broadsword blade, and that the designs of hilt were actually derived from other patterns, - the three-bar hilt, for example, from the Pattern 1822 Light Cavalry officers' sword, and the scroll hilt from the Royal Engineers' officers' pattern of 1857 - suggests strongly that the true origins of these field officers' hilts lies in the fighting swords made up to meet individuals' needs. (It should be noted that although commonly referred to as field officers' hilts and undoubtedly intended in the first instance for such officers, they were also commonly worn by adjutants; in the 79th at one period they were worn by all officers in frock coat order).

One other hilt deserves notice. The regimental amalgamations of 1881 brought the 26th and 90th Regiments together to form a rifle regiment, the Cameronians (Scottish Rifles). As a result, the new regiment adopted the steel, Gothic-hilted, rifle pattern sword, with steel scabbard, (Plate 182). But for a period before and after the First World War, however, the Cameronians hilt had the regimental badge of a five-pointed star surrounded by a wreath of thistles, inserted in place of the more usual stringed bugle.

The changes in hilts appear to have been accompanied by a change in the form of the broadsword blade. Prior to 1881, most blades had two (occasionally three) parallel fullers each side, with two short fullers in the ricasso. But in the early 1880s the twin fullers in the blade were generally replaced by a single central fuller, but retaining the two very short fullers in the ricasso. This is the form generally in use today. In this form, the broadsword, with basket hilt, weighs approximately 2lbs 4 ozs.

In June 1896 a variable length of grip (between 5 and $5^{1}/3$ inches) was permitted, to suit the individual wearer. In 1899 a universal brown leather scabbard with steel mounts was introduced for all regiments and corps, including Scottish units, (see page 168).[34]

182 Sword, Officers', Cameronians, 1926
Note: the sword is identical to the Rifle Regiments officers' sword, Pattern 1892 except for the regimental badge in the hilt. This sword belonged to W A H Forbes, who joined the regiment in February 1926.

(NAM 8210-64)

182

Sergeants

Sergeants of battalion companies of Highland regiments appear to have carried the broadsword from the beginning, along with the officers. The first documentary evidence that has been traced, however, is a Memorandum of 2 March 1799 from the Adjutant-General, ordering the non-commissioned officers of Highland regiments, i.e. the sergeants, and the drummers to carry swords of the same pattern as the officers.[35] This clearly refers to the pattern of broadsword specified in the previous year, (see page 172). Sergeants of battalion companies, at least, continued to carry this broadsword, with a brass hilt, throughout the Revolutionary and Napoleonic Wars, (Plate 183).

When the Pattern 1822 infantry officers' sword was introduced for officers, sergeants and drummers of the line, Highland NCOs and drummers were specifically authorised to continue to carry the broadsword.[36]

Sergeants of light companies ceased to carry swords in 1792 but grenadier sergeants continued to do so, and this applied also to Highland regiments. A sabre in the SUSM (No 1937-15) has been ascribed to Sergeant D Macdonald, of the 42nd, who served in the Peninsula between 1808 and 1814.[37] No evidence has hitherto been found of sergeants of the line carrying sabres and both the grip and the scab-

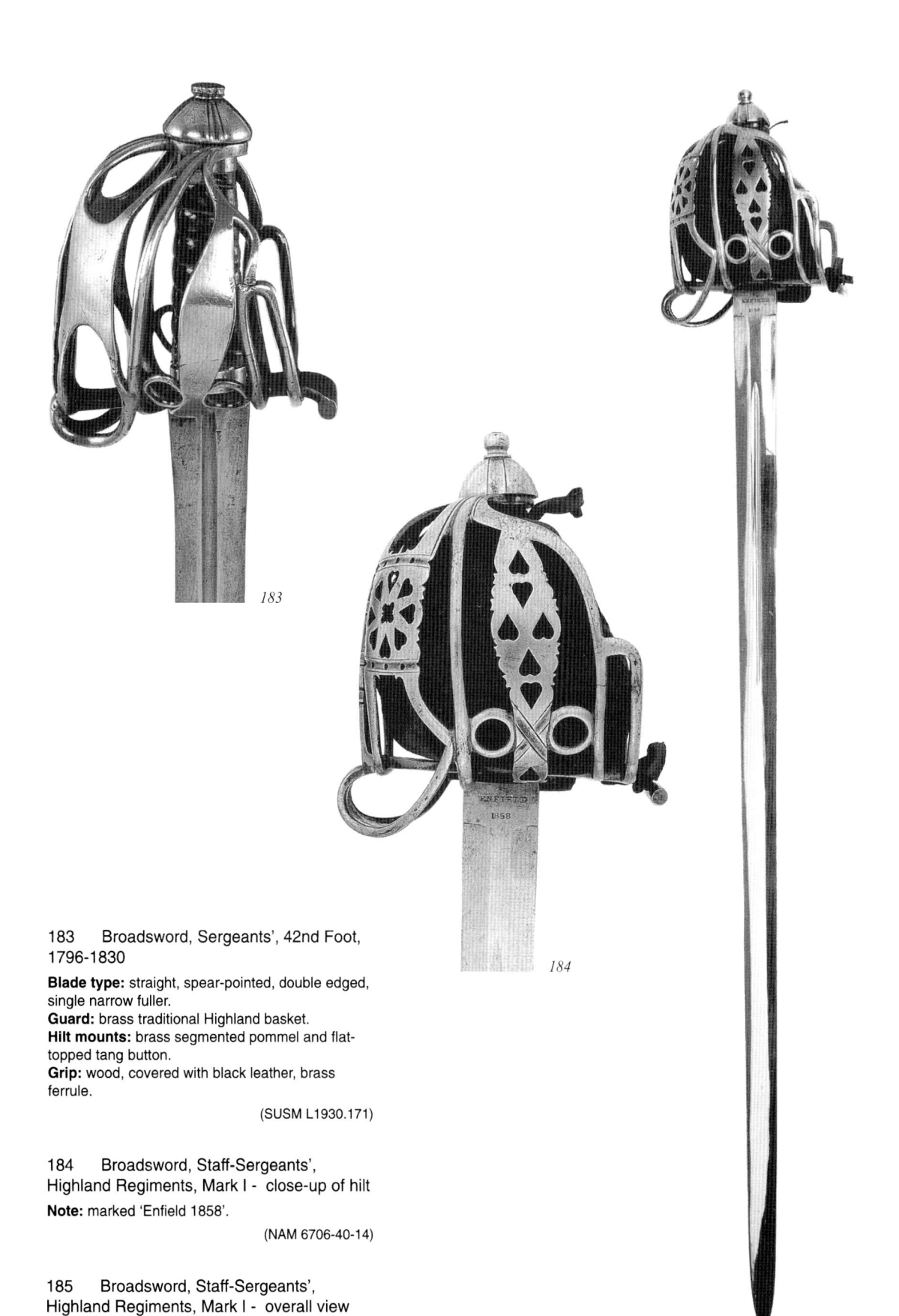

Scottish Infantry Swords

183 Broadsword, Sergeants', 42nd Foot, 1796-1830

Blade type: straight, spear-pointed, double edged, single narrow fuller.
Guard: brass traditional Highland basket.
Hilt mounts: brass segmented pommel and flat-topped tang button.
Grip: wood, covered with black leather, brass ferrule.

(SUSM L1930.171)

184 Broadsword, Staff-Sergeants', Highland Regiments, Mark I - close-up of hilt
Note: marked 'Enfield 1858'.

(NAM 6706-40-14)

185 Broadsword, Staff-Sergeants', Highland Regiments, Mark I - overall view

(NAM 6706-40-14)

190

bard (by Prosser) suggest that this was an officer's sabre. A sabre of similar form in the same museum (No 1964-64) is undoubtedly that of an officer of the 42nd.[38]

Sergeants of Lowland regiments of both battalion and grenadier companies carried the ordinary infantry officers' patterns of sword for this period, but with plain blades and brass hilts.

The steel-hilted broadsword laid down for officers of Highland regiments in 1828 was also adopted, in a plainer version, by sergeants as soon as the old brass - or bronze - hilted swords wore out. A sword of this pattern is shown with great precision in Daniel Cunliffe's painting of a group of NCOs and men of the 79th, painted in 1853-54.[39]

Lowland regiment sergeants adopted the Pattern 1822 Gothic-hilted infantry officers' sword, in a plain version, followed in due course by the Pattern 1845 infantry sword until 1852, when ordinary sergeants of infantry ceased to carry swords. Staff-sergeants of Lowland regiments, who continued to carry swords, used thereafter the same patterns of sword as those of the infantry of the line, (see Chapter 10).

Staff-sergeants of Highland regiments adopted a new pattern of broadsword in April 1857. Known as the Sword, Staff-Sergeants', Highland Regiments, Mark I, it is illustrated in *Army Equipment, Part V - Infantry* (1865).[40] The blade was plain, with a narrow central fuller $10^1/2$ inches long, on each side, and the blade length was $32^1/2$ inches. The hilt, of traditional form, (Plates 184, 185), was of malleable cast iron, lined with buckskin covered in crimson cloth, bound with a blue edging, and with a crimson tassel, exactly as in the officers' sword. The scabbard for this sword was the traditional type, made of black leather, with chape and locket of iron, the latter with a frog stud and the former ending in a rounded end. In January 1861, however, a new scabbard was introduced for staff-sergeants of non-kilted Highland regiments.[41] This had three mounts and two loose rings, like the officers' scabbard, and the chape ended in a large shoe. This is, in fact, the scabbard illustrated in *Army Equipment*. The same scabbard was adopted in 1872 for sergeants of kilted regiments. The sword weighed 2lbs 9 ozs and the Pattern 1861 scabbard 14 ozs.

This pattern was carried through until 1895, being adopted by staff-sergeants of Lowland regiments when they adopted elements of Highland dress after 1881. It was replaced by the Sword, Staff-Sergeants', Highland Regiments, Mark II, approved in July 1895.[42] This was between 2 and 4 ozs heavier and, unlike the Mark I, the hilt lining was removable without dismantling the whole hilt.[43] The blade had a single central fuller, some $10^1/2$ inches long, on each side, starting 2 inches from the shoulder, (Plate 186). The Mark II sword used the Mark I scabbard and was re-designated the No 1, Mark II pattern in 1926.

No further official changes appear to have been promulgated before 1914 except that, in common with some other patterns of sword, the edges of Highland

Scottish Infantry Swords

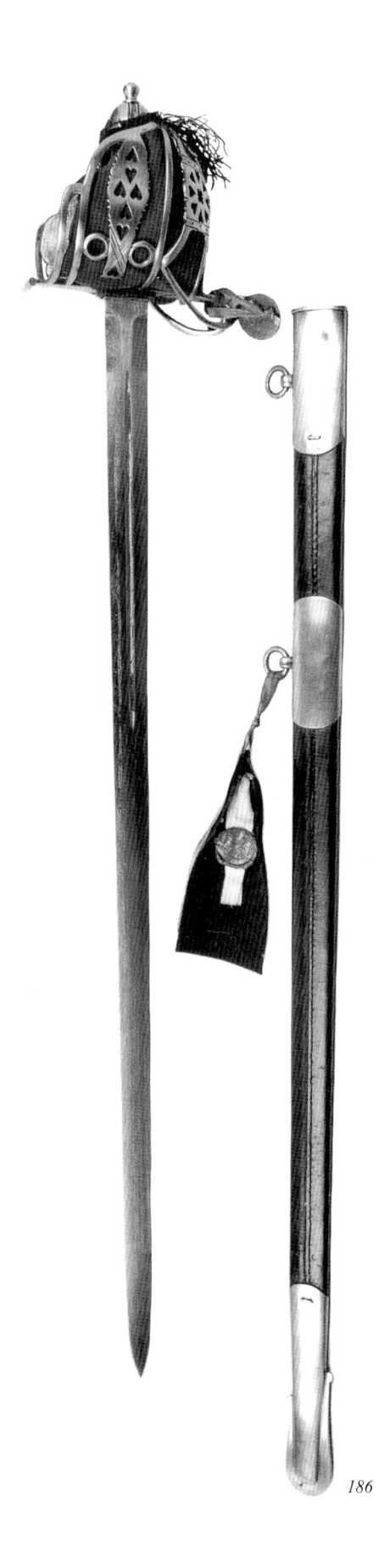

staff-sergeants' swords were ordered in January 1898 to be partially sharpened in manufacture, to a thickness of 0.01 inch, starting 8 inches from the shoulder, and further sharpened regimentally when proceeding on active service.[44]

After the war, with Full Dress temporarily in abeyance, there was clearly a need for a brown leather scabbard for use with Service Dress and the Sam Browne belt. A scabbard of this type was duly introduced in 1922 as the Scabbard, Sword, Sam Browne, Highland Regiments.[45] It heralded a rapid and confusing series of changes. In 1924 an interim pattern of sword was introduced, with a cross-bar hilt similar to previous officers' patterns but using the Pattern 1892 infantry blade; it was designated the Sword, Staff-Sergeants', Cross-bar Hilt.[46] Two years later, in 1926, an extensive re-designation of Highland staff-sergeants' swords took place as follows:

186   Broadsword, Staff-Sergeants', Highland Regiments, Mark II, 1895
Blade length and width: 32^{3}/₁₆in. x 1^{3}/₁₆in.
Blade type: double edged, single fuller each side 10^{1}/₂in. long.
Guard: malleable cast iron.
Hilt mounts: malleable cast iron.
Grip: wood, covered with fishskin and bound with silver wire.
Scabbard: black leather, steel mounts.
Sword weight: 2lb 13oz.
Scabbard weight: 14oz.

(MoD Pattern Room, Nottingham)

	Old Designation	**New Designation**
Sword	Mark I	No 1, Mark I
	Mark II	No 1, Mark II
	Cross-bar hilt	No 6, Mark I
Scabbard	Sam Browne	Sam Browne, No 1 Mark I.

In 1929, all of these patterns of sword and scabbard were declared obsolete and were replaced by an entirely new sword and scabbard, the Sword, Staff-Sergeants', No 1, Mark III and the Scabbard, Staff-Sergeants', No 1, Mark II.[47] This sword was virtually identical with the existing officers' pattern. The blade, however, was narrower (1 inch) and lighter than that of the Staff-Sergeants' Mark II, having a narrow central fuller, $17^{1}/_{2}$ inches long, with two very short fullers in the ricasso. The removable basket hilt was of nickel-plated steel and it differed slightly from the Mark II in its shape and in the piercings. An alternative hilt, a removable nickel-plated steel cross-bar guard, was also provided. The weight, with the basket hilt, was 2lbs 10 ozs and with the cross-bar guard 1lb $10^{1}/_{2}$ ozs. The No 1, Mark II scabbard was of black leather, with nickel-plated steel locket and ball-ended chape; it weighed 12 ozs.

Post-1918 the staff-sergeants of the Cameronians carried the rifle regiments' sword, (Plate 148).

Pipers and drummers

Although pipers, as distinct from drummers, were not officially recognised as part of the battalion establishment until 1854, they existed in Highland regiments from the start and it is equally clear that, from the start, pipers and drummers carried the Highland broadsword. As we have seen, the standardised pattern introduced in 1798 was intended for pipers and drummers, as well as officers and NCOs. When the steel-hilted broadsword was introduced in 1828, however, it was authorised for officers and NCOs only, and pipers and drummers continued to carry the earlier, brass-hilted version until 1857. This pattern is clearly shown, for example, in Joseph Cundall's photograph of a group of the 42nd, taken in 1856.[48] A sword in the SUSM, (Plate 187), which has a half-basket brass hilt and a $26^{1}/_{4}$ inch, diamond-section blade, with Board of Ordnance marks dating it to pre-1855, may be that of a piper or drummer. If so, this would suggest a parallel with the drummers' sword of the infantry of the line between 1822 and 1856, who carried a shorter and lighter version of the normal infantry sword, (see page 252).

Scottish Infantry Swords

187

187 Sword, Pipers'(?), pre-1855
Blade length and width: 26¼in. x 1⅛in.
Blade type: straight, unfullered, diamond section, spear point.
Guard: half of traditional Highland broadsword basket in brass.
Hilt mounts: brass, conical pommel, tang button and ferrule.
Grip: wood, covered with leather and bound with brass wire.
Note: marked 'BO', dating sword to pre-1855 when the Board of Ordnance was abolished. General form suggests a date possibly as early as 1800.

(SUSM 1986.69)

188 Broadsword, Highland Regiments, Drummers', 1857
Blade length and width: 29½in. x 1³⁄₁₆in.
Blade type: narrow fuller each side 8½in. long.
Guard: malleable cast iron.
Hilt mounts: malleable cast iron.
Grip: wood, covered with fishskin and bound with brass wire.
Scabbard: black leather steel mounts, frog stud on the locket.
Sword weight: 2lb 7oz.
Scabbard weight: 9oz.
Note: reissued in 1871 as Sword, Staff-Sergeants', Highland Militia and Volunteers, with a scabbard similar to that of the Staff-Sergeants', Highland Regiments, Mark II.

(MoD Pattern Room, Nottingham)

188

A new regulation pattern for pipers and drummers was introduced in 1857, possibly following the War Office's official recognition of pipers. This was essentially a shorter (29$^{1}/_{2}$ inch blade) version of the Staff-Sergeants', Highland Regiments, Mark I sword, but with a different, hemispherically-ended scabbard, (Plate 188).[49] The sword weighed 2lbs 7 ozs. This weapon had only a short life in the regular regiments and was withdrawn in 1871 and re-issued to staff-sergeants of Highland Militia and Volunteers but with a scabbard similar to that of the Staff-Sergeants', Highland Regiments, Mark II, (Plate 186).[50]

When this sword was withdrawn from the regular units, the pipers and drummers received in its place the Dirk, Mark I and subsequent patterns, (see below).

Pipers and drummers of the 3rd (or Scots) Guards carried the same patterns of sword as the Highland regiments.

Bandsmen

Until 1881, bandsmen of Lowland regiments followed much the same path as the rest of the infantry of the line - that is to say, carrying band swords of regimental pattern until 1856, (Plate 223), and thereafter the Sword, Drummers', Mark I, (Plate 217). A particularly fine example of the pre-1856 regimental patterns is that of the 21st (Royal North British Fusiliers) which is noteworthy for the length of the blade - at 30 inches, more typical of a cavalry band sword - and for the fact that it was carried on slings, (Plate 189). Moreover, there exists a particularly fine photograph of the band of the regiment playing in camp before Balaclava in 1856, showing the sword very clearly.[51]

With the adoption of some elements of Highland dress, the Lowland bands adopted the Dirk Mark I, and subsequent patterns (see below), with the exception of the Cameronians which, on becoming a rifle regiment at that time, adopted as its band sword the Sword, Buglers', Mark I, with steel or iron hilt, and then subsequently the Buglers' Mark II sword.

Bandsmen of Highland regiments carried the broadsword until 1871,[52] when it was replaced by the Dirk Mark I. This was of traditional form, with a 12 inch blade with scalloped back, decorated and inscribed with the regiment's name. The grip was of ebony or black wood, and the black leather scabbard had four iron mounts, (locket, chape and two middle bands) engraved with a thistle design.[53] It was superseded in 1879 by the Dirk Mark II, (Plate 190) which had steel scabbard mounts and omitted the name of the regiment from the blade.[54] In November 1902, this was modified in that the Tudor Crown replaced the St Edward's Crown on the pommel cap.[55] This was succeeded by the Dirk Mark III in 1913 which had a plain, undecorated blade, without scalloping along the back edge; the scabbard mounts were of nickel-plated steel, (Plate 190).[56]

Scottish Infantry Swords

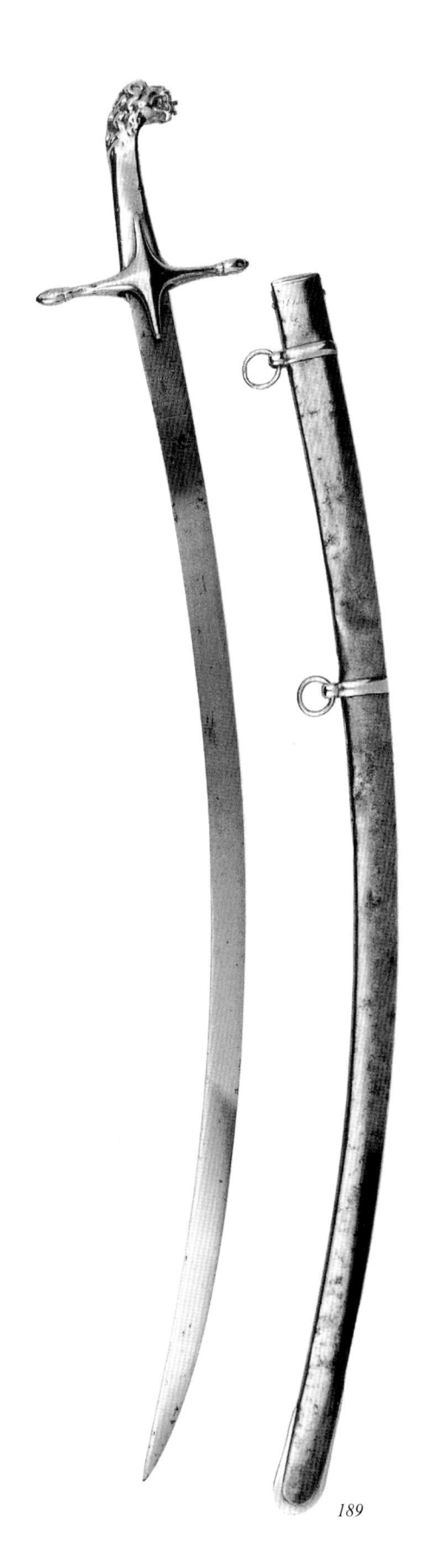

189 Band sword, 21st Regiment
(Royal North British Fusiliers), pre-1856
Note: hilt and scabbard are polished brass.

(NAM 8404-129)

190 Dirks, Marks II, 1879 and III (left), 1913
Blade length and width: 12 1/8in. x 1 1/4in.
Grip: ebony with malleable iron cap and German silver ferrule.
Scabbard: wood, covered with black leather, with iron (Mark II) or plated steel (Mark III) mounts.
Dirk weight: 14 1/2oz.
Scabbard weight: 6 1/2oz.
Note: the Dirk Mark I is identical with the Dirk Mark II except that the Dirk Mark I has the name of the regiment etched on the blade. (Sealed Patterns Nos.588 and 1316).

(MoD Pattern Room, Nottingham)

Chapter 8: Notes

1. Between 1782 and 1805, the 25th, as 'The Sussex Regiment', was technically an ordinary regiment of the line. It reverted to being a Lowland regiment in 1805, as 'The King's Borderers'.

2. See *JSAHR*, Vol XVII, 1938, p1 (facing page 1).

3. For a detailed, scholarly discussion of the origins of the Scottish basket hilt, see Claude Blair, 'The Early Basket-Hilt in Britain', in David Caldwell (ed.), *Scottish Weapons and Fortifications 1100-1800*, Edinburgh (1981) pp153-252.

4. PRO. WO 3/19, p81. The 4th were disbanded in 1799.

5. PRO. WO 3/19, p106.

6. Copy in MoD Central Library, London.

7. Other illustrations include that of a sergeant of a Highland regiment in P J de Loutherbourg's painting 'The Battle of Alexandria', 1803, and an un-named print of an officer of the Princess Charlotte of Wales's Loyal McLeods, a regiment which existed only between 1798 and 1802.

8. 'Military Scraps from the Notebook of Lieutenant John Ford, Half-Pay, 3rd West Indian Regiment, late of the 79th Regiment or Cameron Highlanders'; manuscript volume, (NAM 6807-71) formerly in the RUSI Library, pp132-34. See also the specimens of this period recorded in *Historical Records of the Queen's Own Cameron Highlanders*, Vol II, Edinburgh (1909) p292. There is no doubt that at this period the broadsword was carried in a frog; slings for the carriage of the broadsword came in *c*1830.

9. Others are SUSM 1938-62, 1985-20-1 and L1930-171; they differ in minor details.

10. Fencible regiments were, in effect, regular regiments raised for service in the UK only.

11. See A V B Norman, 'Notes on some Scottish infantry swords in the Scottish United Services Museum', *JAAS*, Vol V, 1965, pp1-2. A sword in the SUSM, (1990-24), with a Pattern 1786 infantry blade, a straight knucklebow hilt and marked '78' on one langet, may be an example of this fashion.

Scottish Infantry Swords

12. See *JSAHR*, Vol XLV, 1967, p222. A very similar sword, with an ebony grip, with longitudinal brass strips, bearing the regimental number '64' (2nd Staffordshire), is in the Royal Armouries, RA IX-1231.

13. Third edition, Edinburgh, (1825), Vol II, p373.

14. Claude Blair, 'The word Claymore' in Caldwell, *op. cit.*, pp378-87.

15. Brigadier-General A E J Cavendish, *The 93rd Sutherland Highlanders, 1799-1927*, (Privately printed), Frome (1928) p37.

16. Reproduced in Hew Strachan, *British Military Uniforms, 1768-1796*, London (1975) Plate 52.

17. SUSM Acquisition Nos 1930-473A, 1958-6 and 1958-7.

18. The Inspection Return for the 4th Battalion in 1810 records that the mounted officers carried brass scabbards by special permission of the Commander-in-Chief. A steel scabbard, with a regimental badge pinned on the outside, is in the Royal Scots Museum, Edinburgh Castle.

19. PRO. WO 3/72, p398.

20. MoD Central Library C.8.c.

21. E Hull, *Costume of the British Army*, London (1828-30).

22. Spencer-Smith, *op. cit.*, No 73.

23. See *JSAHR*, Vol XL, 1962, p88.

24. There are a number of variations, the result presumably of this not being a strictly regulation pattern. The principal variations which may be encountered are: (a) use of the title 'Royal Scots Fusiliers', in place of 'Royal North British Fusiliers'; (b) a variation in the number of langets from nil to two; (c) the backpiece may or may not be decorated with a thistle design; (d) the top of the pommel may be decorated with one or three thistles, or none at all. Specimens are Royal Armouries IX-381; SUSM L1930-26, L1930-48, 1934-642, 1951-738; NAM 6908-17-2.

25. See *JSAHR*, Vol XXXV, 1957, p78 and Vol XVII, 1938, p224.

26. For example, NAM 5907-47-7.

27. Reproduced in Michael Barthorp, *The Zulu War: A Pictorial History*, Poole (1980) p93.

28. See R P Dunn-Pattison, *History of the 91st Argyllshire Highlanders*, Edinburgh (1910) p344.

29. Brown, *op. cit.*, pp 20, 69.

30. A cross-hilted sword of the 74th exists in the SUSM (No M1985-113), with a blade made by Wilkinsons in 1856. The hilt is not made to remove, and it is not clear whether hilt and blade are contemporary or whether the blade has been re-hilted. Either way, the fixed hilt suggests that this is an individual fighting sword.

31. In practice, there remain wide variations in the precise form of the finials and of the pommel, and the combinations thereof, even between battalions of the same regiment.

32. See *JSAHR*, Vol XXXIII, 1955, p143.

33. See SUSM 1984-40.

34. Army Order, 1 June 1896.

35. PRO. WO 3/19, p231

36. PRO. WO 3/399, p256, Memorandum of 10 January 1823 from the Adjutant-General to the officer commanding 42nd Regiment.

37. see Norman, *op. cit.*, p8.

38. *Ibid.*, p7.

39. Reproduced in *JSAHR*, Vol LX, 1962, p190.

40. Copy in NAM.

41. *LC* 250, 1 April 1861.

42. *LC* 7954, 1 October 1895.

43. *LC* 7954 gives the difference as 2 ozs, but other documents - for example, the *Table of Arms*, 1910 - give the difference as 4 ozs.

44. *LC* 9206, 1 October 1898.

45. *LC* 25210, 30 September 1922.

46. *LC* A47, 31 January 1924. The sealed pattern is in the Pattern Room, Nottingham.

47. *LC* A4034, 31 January 1929. The sealed pattern, No 1793, is in the Pattern Room, Nottingham.

48. See *JSAHR*, Vol XXVI, 1948, p77.

49. See the pattern sword in the Pattern Room, Nottingham.

50. This is apparent from subsequent War Office *Tables of Arms*; *LC* 6017 of 1 June 1890, introducing a new leather scabbard with iron mounts for this sword, refers to it as a 'pipers' sword' - see Appendix 4.

51. See *JSAHR*, Vol XXIX, 1951, p182.

52. See, for example, a depiction of the band of the 93rd at the Duke of Wellington's funeral in 1852 - Cavendish, *op. cit.*, p343.

53. *LC* 2299, 1 August 1872; see also the sealed pattern, No 587, in the Pattern Room, Nottingham.

54. *LC* 3504, 1 April 1879; see also the sealed pattern, No 588, in the Pattern Room, Nottingham. *LC* 3707, 1 May 1880, authorised its issue to pipers, drummers and bandsmen of Highland regiments.

55. *LC* 11290, 1 November 1902.

56. *LC* 16582, 1 November 1913; see also the sealed pattern, No 1316, in the Pattern Room, Nottingham.

9. General and Staff Officers' Swords

Identifying the patterns of sword authorised to be worn by general officers at different times is complicated by the tendency of such officers to be a law unto themselves and to wear whatever pattern of sword, regulation or non-regulation, appealed to them. A notorious offender in this respect was the Duke of Wellington himself. Never over-fussy about the dress of his soldiers, provided that they turned out with clean muskets and 100 rounds in their pouches, he habitually wore a mameluke-hilted scimitar, of Oriental type (presumably as a result of his Indian service) long before such a pattern became the regulation. Staff officers, by contiguity and familiarity, tended to imitate their masters in adopting non-regulation patterns as it suited them. It follows therefore that, in the case of general and staff officers, the use of pictorial or statuary material to identify regulation patterns of sword requires extreme caution but, equally, documentary evidence is sparse for the earlier period.

No regulations covering the swords to be worn by such officers exist before 1796. In May of that year, a General Order from the Commander-in-Chief laid it down that general officers and officers on the staff were to carry the sword prescribed at this time for infantry officers:

> 'All Generals and other Officers on the Staff, are in future when employed on military duty, to wear a crimson and gold cord round their hats, with crimson and gold rosettes or tufts brought to the edge of the brims...
> The sword to be worn on the same occasions is to have the guards, pommel and shell gilt with gold, and the grip, or handle, of silver twisted wire. The blade is to be straight and made to cut and thrust; to be one inch at least broad at the shoulder and thirty two inches in length conformably to His Majesty's former orders, given out in April 1786.[1]

This is, of course, the Pattern 1796 infantry officers' sword, (see Plate 131). A sword of this type is shown in the print of George, Prince of Wales in general's uniform in *The British Military Library*, issued in 1799.

The same sword is prescribed in *View of the Standing Regulations for the Colours, Clothing etc. of the Infantry*, issued in 1802:

'The uniform sword for general officers, officers on the staff, officers of the Guards, and of regiments or corps of Infantry is to be the same. It is to have a brass guard, pommel and shell, and gilt, with the grip or handle of silver twisted wire. The blade straight and made to cut and thrust, one inch at least broad at the shoulder, and to be strong and substantial. The scabbard black with gilt mounting...The sword knot to be crimson and gold in stripes.[2]

It was to be worn from a white leather waistbelt.

There is, nevertheless, a good deal of pictorial evidence to suggest that throughout the period 1796-1802 and beyond, a gilt boatshell-hilted sword, similar to that authorised in 1796 for heavy cavalry officers for Dress, (Plate 62) was widely carried by general officers.[3]

The regulations which introduced a new pattern of sword for officers of flank companies of infantry in 1803, (see page 150), have been interpreted as introducing the same type of sword for general and staff officers. A careful reading makes it clear, however, that the sword for these officers was different:

'I beg to inform you, that a Pattern Sword for the Officers of Grenadiers and Light Infantry, has been approved by His Majesty, and together with the Pattern Sword for Regimental Officers of the Infantry and that for General Officers and for other Officers on the General Staff of the Army...[4]

This might, indeed, suggest that a new and specific pattern of sword for general and staff officers was being introduced at the same time and that it was, by implication, different from either of the two infantry officers' swords. The wording is undoubtedly ambiguous but there is no evidence to support the idea of a new sword at this time for generals and staff and it seems almost certain that the Pattern 1796 infantry sword continued to be the regulation, even if, in practice, such officers tended to please themselves. There is, indeed, evidence to suggest that, in this period, the heavy cavalry boatshell-hilted sword continued to be popular wear.[5]

In December 1816, the Adjutant-General issued a Memorandum on the Dress of the General Staff Officers, which was presumably intended to bring the dress of these officers back to some measure of uniformity after the excesses of the previous twenty years of war.[6] The pattern of sword to be worn was specifically described as that established for infantry officers, and the description given is that of the Pattern 1796 infantry officers' sword. For Full Dress, the scabbard was to be of black leather, but for Dress and Undress it was to be of steel. Whether the steel scabbard was carried in practice is not clear.

General and Staff Officers' Swords

The Pattern 1796 infantry officers' sword remained the regulation until 1822, when general officers, and staff officers of certain grades, were ordered to wear a version of the Gothic-hilted sword introduced in the *Dress Regulations* of that year for the infantry:

'General Officers
Staff Sword - With gilt three-quarter basket hilt with staff device inserted; straight sabre [*sic.*] blade with rounded back, 34 inches long.
Scabbard - steel.

The general and staff officers' version differed from the Pattern 1822 infantry version in four respects:
(a) a crossed sword and baton (the so-called 'staff device') replaced the royal cypher in the cartouche in the guard, (Plate 191);[7]
(b) the prescribed blade length was 34 inches;
(c) the Dress and Undress scabbard was to be steel, the Full Dress scabbard being of black leather with gilt mounts, (Plate 192);
(d) the decoration of the scabbard mounts is sometimes more ornate, in a leaf design as opposed to geometric.

Again, there seems to have been some discrepancy between regulation and practice since the overwhelming majority of swords of this pattern have $32^{1}/2$, rather than 34 inch blades. And indeed it is difficult to see any logical reason for the increased length other than the fact that staff officers were invariably mounted.

Swords of this pattern are commonly assumed to be those of generals although statistically the chances are that such swords, when encountered, are actually those of staff officers.[8]

An amended version of this sword appeared in 1845 with the fullered, so-called Wilkinson blade in place of the Pattern 1822 pipe-backed blade, (Plate 193).

For general officers and equivalent a completely new pattern appeared in 1831, which has remained the regulation ever since. As has been suggested, the new pattern, (Plate 194) was almost certainly influenced by the Duke of Wellington, who was Commander-in-Chief from 1827 until 1828 and again from 1842 until his death in 1852. It followed closely the type of mameluke-hilted sword which he had carried since his Indian days and of which a number of specimens still exist.[9] Equally, swords of this type had been fashionable in various quarters since the Egyptian expedition of 1801; it is of interest that the same type of sword was in use in the United States Marine Corps from at least 1825, apparently as a direct result of the United States

General and Staff Officers' Swords

191

192

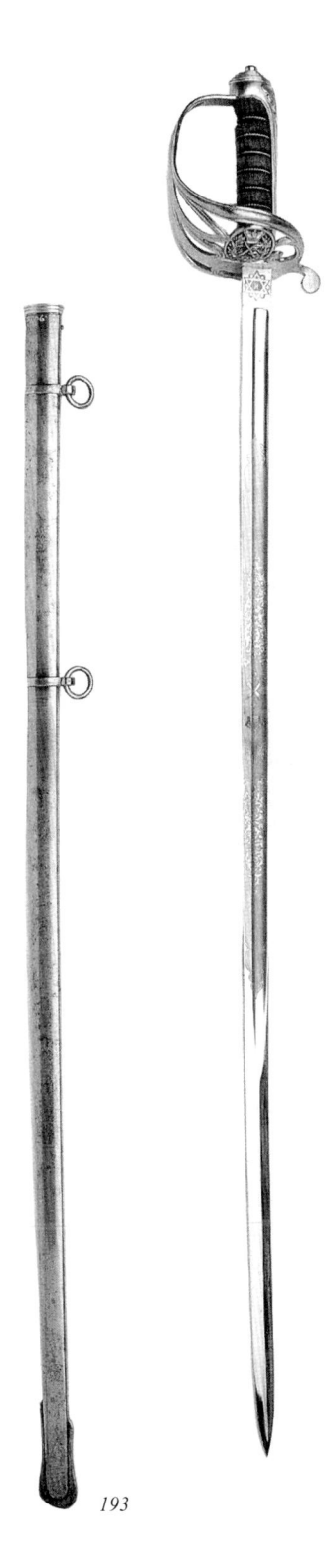

191 Sword, General and Staff Officers', Pattern 1822

Blade length and width: 34in. x 1in.
Blade type: identical with Infantry, Officer, Pattern 1822.
Guard: gilt brass.
Hilt mounts: gilt brass.
Grip: wood, covered with fishskin and bound with brass wire.
Scabbard: (Full Dress) similar to Infantry, Officer, Pattern 1822; (Undress) steel, with two loose rings on narrow bands.
Note: although the regulation blade length was stated to be 34in., in practice the great majority of existing blades have a length of 32 to $32^{1}/2$in.

(NAM 6311-36)

192 Scabbard, General Officers', Pattern 1822

Note: scabbard of General Sir David Baird GCB, Baronet, (1757-1829).

(SUSM 1943-149)

193 Sword, Staff Officers', Pattern 1845

Note: virtually identical with infantry officers' sword, Pattern 1845, except for crossed sword and baton in cartouche in the guard.

(NAM 6706-69)

193

205

General and Staff Officers' Swords

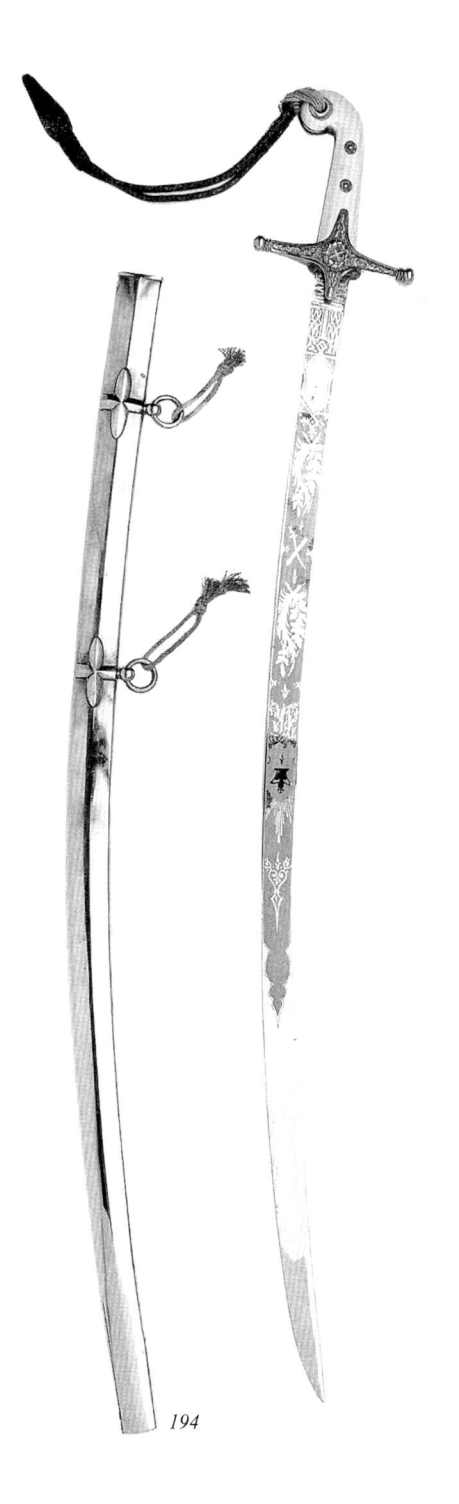

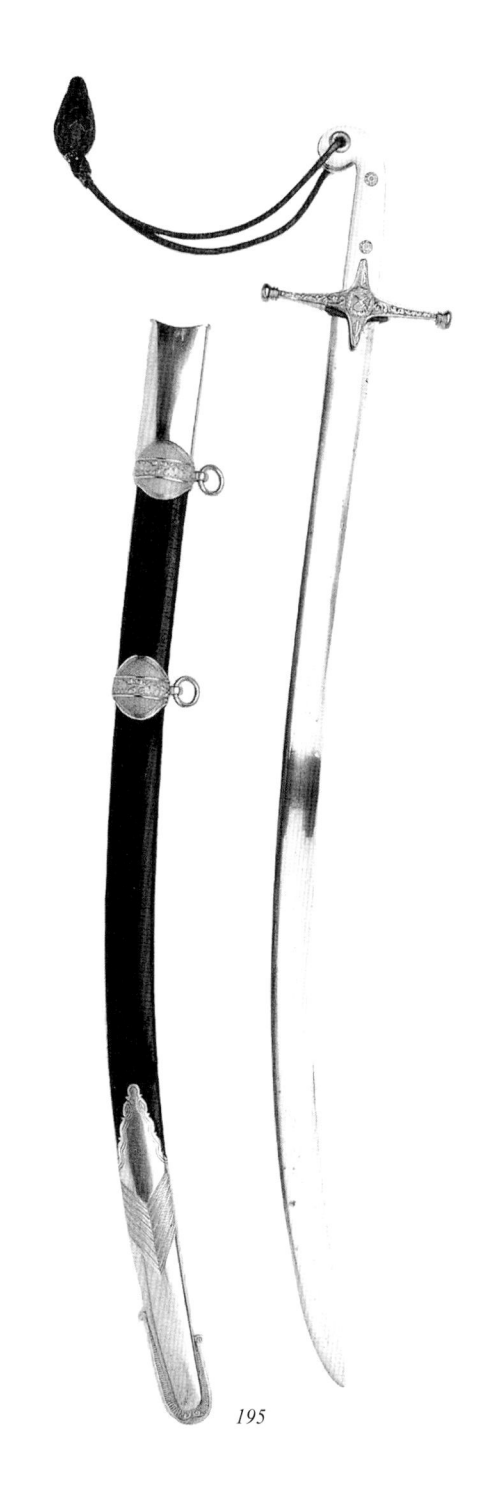

194 Sword, General Officers', Pattern 1831
Blade length and width: 31in. x 1in.
Guard and hilt mounts: gilt brass.
Grip: ivory, with gilt brass floral-headed rivets and gilt brass bushed hole for sword knot.
Scabbard: gilt brass.

(NAM 9410-63)

195 Scabbard, General Officers', Pattern 1831
Note: black leather scabbard with elaborate gilt brass mounts, originally prescribed for Levées, Drawing Rooms and evening occasions.

(NAM 7105-34-2)

General and Staff Officers' Swords

196 Sword, Indian Political Service, c1925

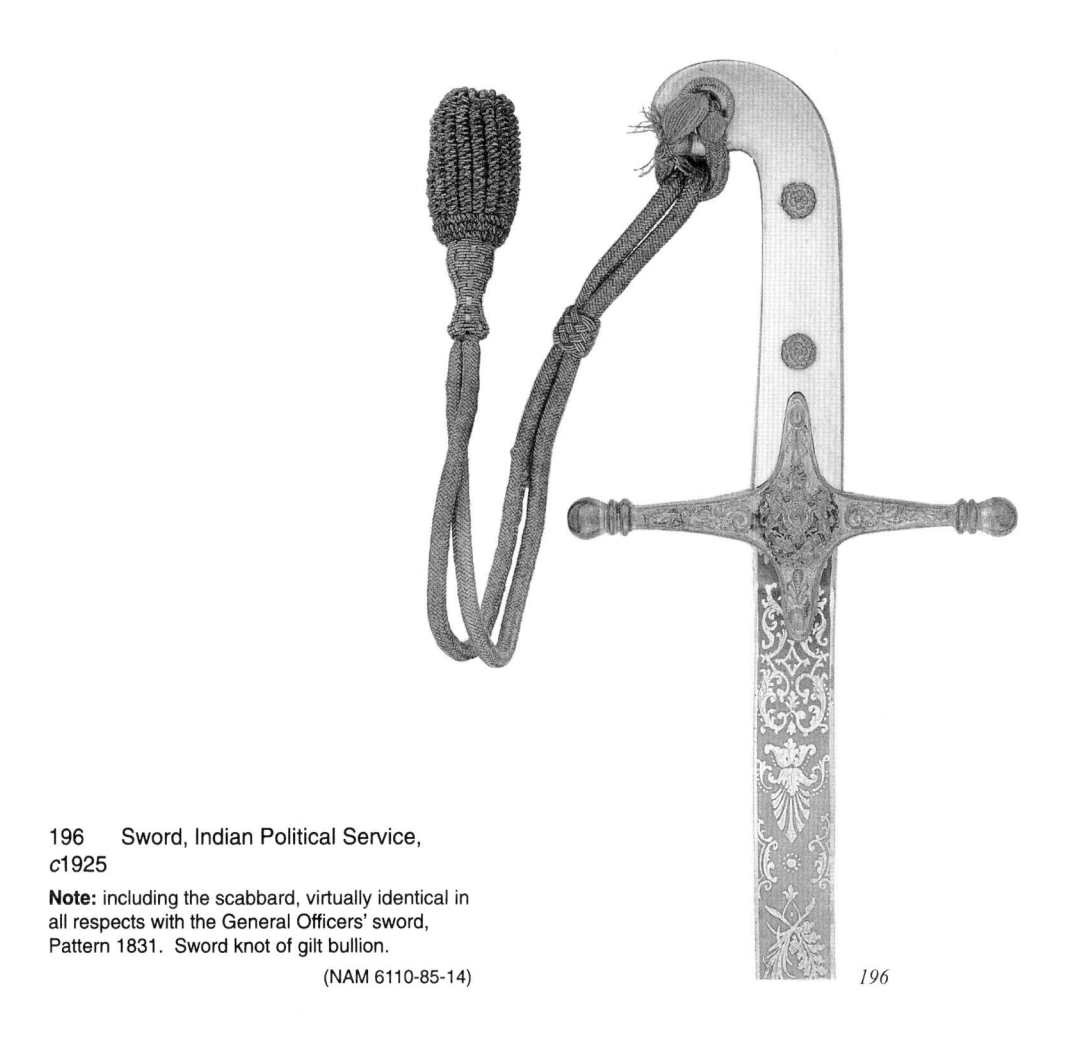

Note: including the scabbard, virtually identical in all respects with the General Officers' sword, Pattern 1831. Sword knot of gilt bullion.

(NAM 6110-85-14)

196

expedition against the Barbary pirates in 1801-05.[10] The new 1831 pattern was therefore the product of two strands of historical development.

Two patterns of scabbard were originally authorised - a black leather scabbard for Levées, Drawing Rooms and evening occasions, and a brass scabbard for all other occasions. This black leather scabbard, (Plate 195) is of distinctly Oriental form; the loose rings are attached to circular gilt bands with a transverse ornamental decoration of leaf design and the elaborate chape has an incised chevron design.[11] Again there are variations in the scabbard mounts, depending upon maker and individual taste. In practice, this scabbard soon disappeared and the wood-lined brass scabbard became the standard wear. It had a square toe, with a vestigial shoe and two loose rings on cruciform bands.

This pattern of sword, (with a change of scabbard in 1898), has remained the regulation pattern for general officers ever since. It was also adopted for royal equerries and Lords Lieutenant of counties. The equerries' swords had the royal cypher on the écusson in place of the crossed sword and baton; a particularly rare

207

variant is that of the equerries to Prince Albert, where the écusson has a simple letter 'A'.[12] In the case of Lords Lieutenant, the écusson has a silver rose in the case of English counties, a thistle for Scottish, a shamrock for Northern Ireland and the Prince of Wales' feathers for Welsh counties.

The same pattern of sword, but with the royal arms on the écusson, was also worn by members of the Indian Political Service (in effect the Diplomatic Service of the Indian Government), (Plate 196).[13]

Field Marshals were not given a specific regulation pattern until 1831. Before that, they would seem to have followed the custom of the generals and carried either the Pattern 1796 infantry sword or the Pattern 1796 Heavy Cavalry boatshell-hilted sword. A painting of a Field Marshal in 'full-dress uniform' in 1812, by Charles Hamilton Smith, who was then the Deputy-Assistant-Quarter-Master-General, shows the boatshell-hilted sword; and a sword at Windsor (Catalogue 767), with the same type of hilt and a straight pipe-backed blade, is described in the accompanying bill from Prosser as a 'Fine large Boatshell Field Marshals Sword'.[14] In 1831, Field Marshals were ordered to wear the Pattern 1831 General Officers' sword, but with crossed batons on the écusson. It has remained the regulation pattern ever since.

In 1898, the brass scabbard was replaced by a plated steel scabbard for both generals and Field Marshals,[15] and in the following year a brown leather scabbard was introduced for use with the Sam Browne belt in Undress. On active service, where the 1831 pattern was of no value as a weapon, general officers tended to carry the sword of their original arm or corps, and this practice was regularised in the *Dress Regulations* of 1900.

Staff officers continued to carry the Pattern 1845 sword until 1892 when they were officially required to replace the blade with the new, straight, Pattern 1892 infantry blade. When the Pattern 1895 infantry officers' sword came in, (Plate 157), this replaced the staff officers' sword entirely. Some discussion took place at this time on introducing a new pattern of staff officers' sword, which would have been identical with the infantry sword except for the insertion of the traditional crossed sword and baton into the strapwork of the guard in place of the royal cypher.[16] A sample specimen was produced by Mole & Son but, in the event, it was not proceeded with.

Chapter 9: Notes

1. PRO. WO 3/28 p169, General Order of 3 May 1796.

2. *View of the Standing Regulations.*

3. See, for example, the portrait of Major-General Sir Alured Clarke, by Sir William Beechey, exhibited at the Royal Academy in 1797 and now in the possession of Mrs Hugh Heaton. Also, James Northcote's portrait of Sir John Moore, c1801-02, now in the National Portrait Gallery of Scotland; and a portrait of George III, c1800, in the National Portrait Gallery in London, (Catalogue 2502).

4. PRO. WO 3/35, Adjutant-General to the Duke of Kent, 18 March 1803.

5. For example, Sir Thomas Lawrence's portrait of George, Prince Regent in Field Marshal's uniform, exhibited at the Royal Academy in 1815, and now in the collection of the Marquess of Londonderry. A sword formerly at Windsor (Laking 875) and now in the Royal Armouries (XVI-58) is of this type and is referred to in the Carlton House Catalogue (no 390) as 'a staff sword'. A similar sword (Laking 767) is described in a bill of 1816 from Prosser as 'a large Boatshell Field-Marshal's sword'. I am indebted to Mr A V B Norman for these references.

6. Bound copy in the MoD Central Library.

7. This was the first official use of this device on a regulation pattern sword. The earliest use on an unofficial pattern appears to be on a sword carried by the Earl of Uxbridge, c1815 which has the device on the langets. This sword is in the collection of the Marquess of Anglesey.

8. The precise grades of staff officer authorised to carry the staff officers' pattern sword are given in *Dress Regulations*, and varied from time to time.

9. A sword of this type, attributed to Wellington, was formerly in the Royal United Services Institution. It closely resembled the Pattern 1831 sword, except that the brass scabbard had a prominent shoe. Although basically of Persian origin, it was commonly in use in India during Wellington's time there (1797-1805). From Persia, it had also spread to Turkey and Egypt - see P S Rawson, *The Indian Sword*, Copenhagen (1967).

10. See Harold L Peterson, *The American Sword*, revised edition, Philadelphia (1965) pp166-72.

11. An early record of this scabbard in use is in Robert McInnes's portrait of Major-General Sir James Kempt, painted apparently in 1836, and now in the Royal Collection (No 935) - see Miller and Dawnay, *op. cit.*, Plate 256.

12. There are two specimens of this rare pattern in the Royal Artillery Regimental Museum at Woolwich.

13. Members of the Indian Political Service were primarily employed as agents to the native states of India, but also occupied some diplomatic posts outside India; a high proportion was seconded from the Indian Army.

14. See note 5 above.

15. Sealed pattern 304 in the Pattern Room, Nottingham, sealed on 4 May 1898.

16. See J W Latham, *op. cit.*, Plate 6.

10. Sergeants' Swords
(excluding Scottish Regiments)

Until 1768 all ranks of infantry carried swords, but supply had become erratic and in that year the military authorities took heed of the situation and arranged for the issue of a Royal Warrant stating that: 'All Sergeants and the whole Grenadier Company are to have swords, the corporals and men of the Battalion companies, except the Regiment of Royal Highlanders (42nd), to have no swords'.[1] In July 1784 the process went a stage further when the sword was abolished for all infantry except sergeants.[2]

It is not known with absolute precision what swords were carried by infantry sergeants between 1788 and 1796. As we have seen, the sword introduced for the officers in 1786 had a straight blade, with a relatively flimsy hilt in gilt brass, silver or, more uncommonly, steel. It is possible that the infantry sergeants continued for a time to carry the old Pattern 1751 hanger, and hangers of this type were certainly in use in the Militia as late as 1800. But it is more probable that in the majority of cases sergeants of infantry were issued with a stouter and plainer version of the officers' sword. A sword in the NAM with a plain blade and a simple brass knucklebow hilt, marked 'Royal Fusiliers' is very possibly a sergeant's sword of this period, (Plate 197), but may alternatively be a band sword.

From 1792, sergeants of light companies ceased to carry swords, a move dictated by their new, more active role as skirmishers.[3]

From 1796 onwards, however, the ground is firmer. In that year, the first, fully standard pattern of sword for infantry officers was introduced, (see page 145 and Plate 131), and it is clear that a plainer version was adopted then for the sergeants, other than Highlanders or rifle corps. This sword is described in the 1802 *View of the Standing Regulations for the Colours, Clothing etc of the Infantry*:

> 'The swords for sergeants of the Guards and of the Infantry throughout except the Rifle Corps to be the same. They are to have a brass hilt and the grip or handle to be of brass twisted wire, which with the blades are to be in the same dimensions and form exactly similar as stated for the officers.....The sergeants of Light Infantry not to wear swords.[4]

These swords, as the *View* makes clear, were altogether plainer than the officers' version. In particular, the blades were of plain steel, without decoration, and the guard was of plain, not gilded, brass. It will be noted that the grip used brass wire

Sergeants' Swords (excluding Scottish Regiments)

197

197   Sword, Sergeants'(?), Royal Fusiliers (7th Foot)
Note: hilt is brass alloy and the grip of ridged ebony. Blade of diamond form, 32in. long and 1³⁄₈in. wide at shoulder.
It was, however, more usual at this period to use the spelling 'FUZILEERS'.

(NAM 8905-76)

198   Sword, Sergeants', *c*1830
Blade length and width: 32¹⁄₂in. x 1¹⁄₈in.
Blade type: slightly curved, flat back, single fuller each side to within 9in. of spear point, then false edge to point.
Guard: brass Gothic with fixed inner guard and 'GR IV' cypher.
Hilt mounts: brass, stepped pommel, upper part of backpiece decorated with leaf design.
Grip: solid brass, ridged to simulate wood bound with wire.
Note: Made by Osborne. Other specimens in Royal Armouries have cypher of Victoria.

(Royal Armouries IX-2184)

198

Sergeants' Swords (excluding Scottish Regiments)

rather than the silver wire of the officers' version. Indeed, some specimens have a grip of solid brass, moulded or cast to give the impression of wire binding.

Although the *View* says nothing about scabbards, later evidence shows that these were almost identical with those of the officers, that is to say, of black leather, with brass mounts and suspended from a frog. A scabbard of this pattern may be seen in Charles Hamilton Smith's print of a sergeant and private of the 1st Foot Guards, dated 1st May 1812.[5] His print of a sergeant and privates of the 87th Foot, dated 1st January 1813, shows the same sword and scabbard.

This Pattern 1796 sword was carried by sergeants of the Guards and the line until *c*1822. In that year, the familiar Gothic-hilted sword, (see page 156 and Plate 144) was introduced for infantry officers and a virtually identical version, with plain blade, was brought in for sergeants, except those of Highland regiments. This is clearly stated in a letter of November 1822 from the Deputy-Adjutant-General to General Sir John Hope, then Colonel of the 92nd Foot (Highlanders): 'I am to add, that the adoption of the Sword of the Pattern prescribed in recent Regulation for Officers, Serjeants and Drummers, of the Infantry of the Army, will be dispensed with in the case of Highland Regiments...'[6]

The sergeants' version was, initially, indistinguishable from the officers' sword except for having a plain blade and a brass, as opposed to a gilt, hilt. But there also exist a number of Pattern 1822 swords in which the grip is of solid moulded brass and the blades are of an intermediate form between the original pipe-backed blades and the fullered, Wilkinson, design adopted in 1845, (Plate 198). The royal cyphers date these swords to the period 1822-1852 but their scarcity suggests that they could not have been introduced on a large scale and their use remains unclear.

In 1852, swords were abolished for ordinary infantry sergeants and carried thereafter by staff-sergeants of infantry - that is to say, battalion, as opposed to company, sergeants - and by sergeants of Departmental corps, such as the Ordnance and Commissariat.

A new pattern of sword for staff-sergeants of infantry of the line, Militia, Volunteers and Army Hospital Corps was introduced in October 1861. It had a $32^{1}/_{2}$ inch blade similar to the Pattern 1845 infantry officers' sword and was generally indistinguishable from that sword apart from the plain blade. The scabbard was black leather with brass mounts and the gilt brass guard had no hinged flap. The back of the blade was flat.[7]

This pattern was replaced in September 1866 by the Sword, Staff-Sergeants', Line Regiments, Pattern 1866, in which the back of the blade is round.[8] The pattern sword at Nottingham also shows minor differences in the decoration of the scabbard mounts. The pommel had a prominent tang button. The weight of the sword was 1lb $14^{1}/_{2}$ozs, and that of the scabbard 10 ozs. Otherwise, the 1861 and 1866 swords are virtually identical.

Sergeants' Swords (excluding Scottish Regiments)

It does not seem to have occurred to anyone in official circles that this sword was too light and flimsy to be an effective fighting weapon until May 1884 when the Superintendent of the Royal Small Arms Factory inspected the weapons of the 1st Battalion, the York and Lancaster Regiment, just returned from Sir Gerald Graham's first expedition to Suakin against the Dervish leader, Osman Digna. He noted, *inter alia*, on the staff-sergeants' swords: 'They are useless as weapons of offence, and of very little use for defensive purposes, but as the staff sergeants are armed with pistols, possibly the uselessness of their swords is not of much consequence'.[9]

This damning criticism was referred to the Equipment Committee at Aldershot. It took the somewhat relaxed view that since these swords were basically the same as those of the officers it was essentially a personal matter and there was therefore no sound reason for change - in other words, the sword was useless but if staff-sergeants wanted to buy themselves a better one then that was up to them!

Matters rested there until July 1887 when the Superintendent at the RSAF Enfield was asked to review the specifications of all swords. Again, he took an extremely critical view of the various swords for staff-sergeants, and not merely those of the infantry:

> 'Under no conditions could I think that any of the swords supplied to Staff Sergeants fairly take rank as weapons. It seems a pity, that when in 1856 the blades of the Staff Sergeants' swords were assimilated, the blade was not a new and efficient one. I don't think a good blade of 2ft.8½ inches long, which seems a reasonable length, ought to weigh less than, say, 2lb.2oz., and up to 2lb.4oz. [This clearly refers to total sword weight].

He was accordingly directed to submit a suitable pattern of blade, which he did in October 1887. This blade was similar in general form to its predecessors but it was 32¾ inches long and the whole sword weighed 2lbs 5¼ ozs, some 6 ozs more than any of the previous staff-sergeants' patterns. The hilt appears to have been that of the existing Staff-Sergeants', Royal Engineers, Mark III, Pattern 1872 (see below). Most of the extra weight had therefore gone into the blade. The Director of Artillery, then responsible for patterns of small-arms, asked for it to be modified by substituting the three-bar hilt of the existing Staff-Sergeant's, Royal Artillery sword, introduced in 1856 (see below) but made slightly larger to provide the same protection as the Royal Engineers' guard. In submitting this sword to the Adjutant-General (Wolseley), the Director of Artillery pointed out the wastefulness in having no less than five patterns of sword for staff-sergeants, with four patterns of hilt, two different weights of blade and three different weights of scabbard, requiring separate methods of manufacture, separate contracts and separate reserve stocks. He therefore proposed that the sword now submitted should be issued, with a steel scabbard, to all dismounted units except Highland regiments. Wolseley directed that the sword should be sent to the Engineers, Artillery and Army Medical Department for comments; it was not apparently sent to the infantry who might have been expected to have had the greatest interest.

None of the Corps consulted liked the sword, which they thought too heavy and badly balanced, although one is tempted to think that these objections owed more to familiarity with the old than objective analysis of the new. Both the Assistant-Adjutant-General and the Director of Artillery, however, were clear in their own minds about the desirability of one, universal pattern, although only the latter seems to have grasped the fact that the fundamental question was whether the sword was to be for actual fighting use or merely ornamental. When the matter went to the Commander-in-Chief (the Duke of Cambridge) he accepted the argument for a universal pattern blade but wanted alternative Gothic hilts in steel and gilt brass (or yellow metal). To work out the detailed specifications, a small committee, consisting of the Chief-Inspector of Small Arms (Colonel King-Harman), the Inspector of Gymnasia at Aldershot (Lieutenant-Colonel Onslow) and Major Anstruther, Royal Artillery, was set up.

It reported in April 1888 that the proposed blade was too curved, too heavy and the balance too far from the hilt; it disliked the proposal to use ebonite (a form of plastic) for the grip, and felt that the hilt should approximate more to the rifle regiments' staff-sergeants' sword of 1866, (see page 218); the scabbard should have a frog stud as well as fixed loops. Two new swords, with gun-metal and gilt brass hilts, were prepared to meet these criticisms, and approved by the Committee in October 1888. The pattern was finally sealed in November 1888 as the Sword, Staff-Sergeants', Pattern 1888, in two versions: gilt hilt for dismounted Engineers, Infantry (except Rifles and Highlanders) and Medical Staff Corps, (Plate 199); steel hilt for dismounted Artillery, Rifles and other Department Corps. The scabbard was the same for both versions.

The blade, at $32^{3}/4$ inches, was basically a straight version of the original Pattern 1845 blade and the sword weighed 2lbs $2^{1}/2$ ozs in both versions. The scabbard, (Scabbard, Staff-Sergeants', Pattern 1888, Mark I), weighed 1lb $4^{1}/2$ozs; it had two fixed loops like the existing cavalry scabbard but no frog stud.[10] Although sealed in 1888, the sword was not introduced via the *List of Changes* until 1 February 1889 and in subsequent official lists it is referred to as the Pattern 1889. Before manufacture commenced, it was agreed that the 'steel' version should actually be made of malleable cast iron, which was considered just as strong and much cheaper than steel. The formal designation of this version was changed accordingly in April 1889.[11]

The new sword, with its straight, heavier blade, was ironically a better fighting weapon than the contemporary officers' sword, although that situation was about to change. If it had a defect, it was in the weight of the scabbard and a new, lighter scabbard - the Pattern 1889, Mark II - was introduced in January 1892[12] but that also was not entirely satisfactory and a lightened (1lb $2^{3}/4$oz) version of the original Mark I scabbard was brought in in July 1892.[13] It was re-designated the Scabbard, No 3, Mark I in the general re-numbering in 1926.

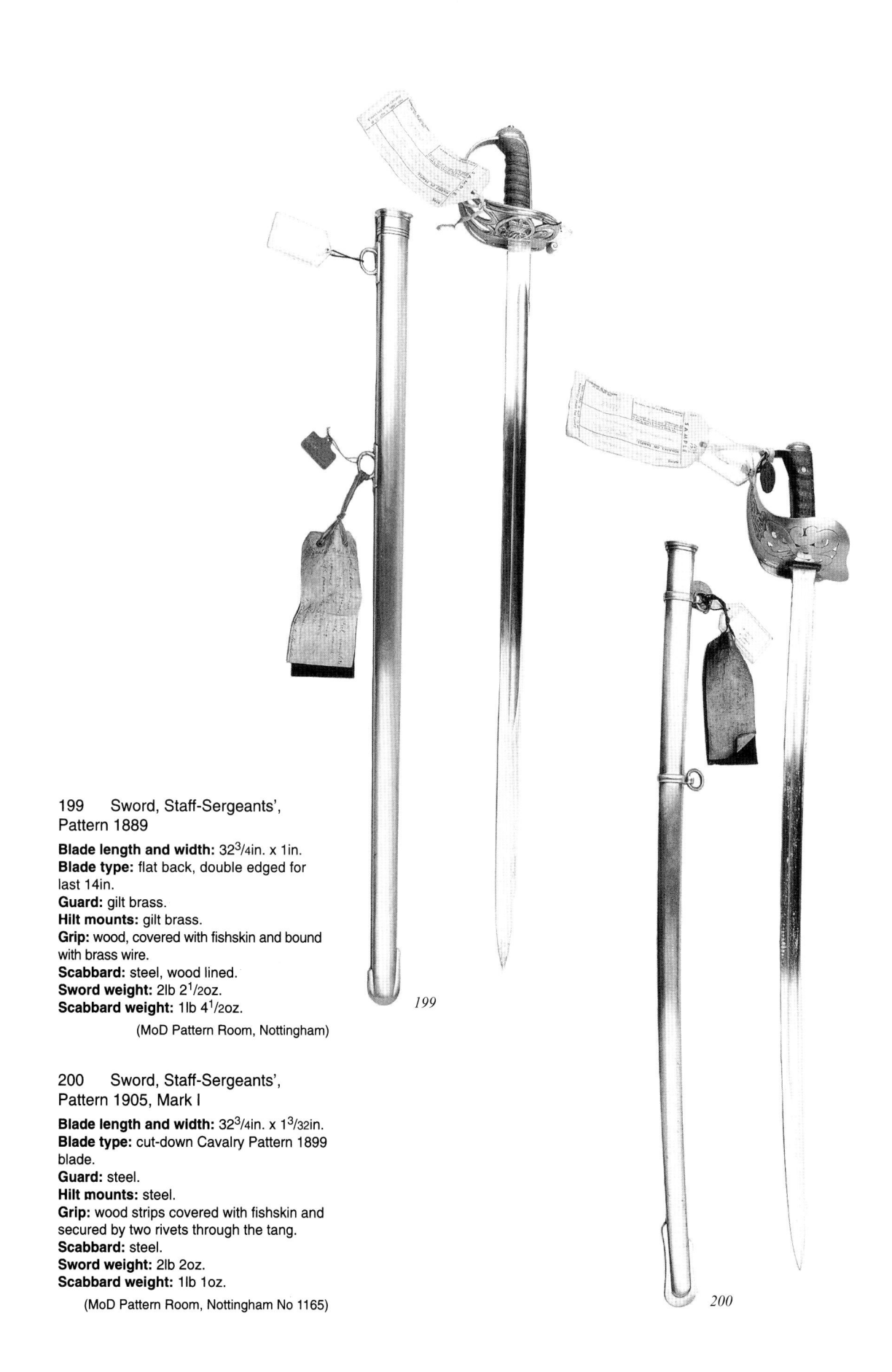

Sergeants' Swords (excluding Scottish Regiments)

199 Sword, Staff-Sergeants', Pattern 1889

Blade length and width: $32^{3}/_{4}$in. x 1in.
Blade type: flat back, double edged for last 14in.
Guard: gilt brass.
Hilt mounts: gilt brass.
Grip: wood, covered with fishskin and bound with brass wire.
Scabbard: steel, wood lined.
Sword weight: 2lb $2^{1}/_{2}$oz.
Scabbard weight: 1lb $4^{1}/_{2}$oz.

(MoD Pattern Room, Nottingham)

199

200 Sword, Staff-Sergeants', Pattern 1905, Mark I

Blade length and width: $32^{3}/_{4}$in. x $1^{3}/_{32}$in.
Blade type: cut-down Cavalry Pattern 1899 blade.
Guard: steel.
Hilt mounts: steel.
Grip: wood strips covered with fishskin and secured by two rivets through the tang.
Scabbard: steel.
Sword weight: 2lb 2oz.
Scabbard weight: 1lb 1oz.

(MoD Pattern Room, Nottingham No 1165)

200

Sergeants' Swords (excluding Scottish Regiments)

As already noted (page 165), an entirely new design of dismounted officers' sword was introduced in 1895-97, and the same design was adopted for all sergeants of dismounted corps (except Highland) in October 1897 as the Sword, Staff-Sergeants', Pattern 1897.[14] The plain blade is 32^{9}/16ths inches long, with the single fuller both sides starting about 1^{3}/4 inches from the shoulder and finishing about 18 inches from the spear point. The 5^{1}/4 inch hilt is identical with that of the officers' sword and the scabbard (Pattern 1897) is of plated steel, wood lined, with two bands and loose rings. The mouthpiece is detachable and secured by two small screws.

This was a somewhat light sword at 1lb 14^{3}/4 ozs - almost exactly the same as the 1866 sword which had been criticised for that reason, although undoubtedly the blade because of its dumb-bell form is stiffer. It was rapidly replaced by the Sword, Staff-Sergeants', Pattern 1898 in November 1898[15] which had a heavier and stiffer blade, the sword weighing 2lb 1^{1}/2 ozs, (roughly the weight suggested by the Superintendent at Enfield back in 1887) and the blade was designed to withstand a testing pressure of 30lbs as against 22lbs for the 1897 pattern. The blade was ordered to be ground to a thickness of ^{1}/100th of an inch for a distance of 3 inches from the point along the back edge and for 15 inches along the front edge. Both the Pattern 1897 and Pattern 1898 had the turned-over inner edge to the guard introduced into the officers' sword in 1897.

A slightly modified version of the sword - the Sword, Staff-Sergeants', Pattern 1898, Mark I - was introduced in 1902. It differed only in having a Tudor Crown in the guard instead of a St Edward's Crown and the cypher of Edward VII in place of that of Queen Victoria.[16]

A curious hybrid pattern was introduced in July 1905 for all dismounted corps except Highland.[17] This consisted of a cut-down Cavalry Pattern 1899 blade mated with the Pattern 1897 hilt, (Plate 200). It can only be assumed that this makeshift design was introduced in order to make up losses in the South African War. It is doubtful if many were made or issued and in 1912 both the 1898 and 1905 patterns were modified to substitute the cypher of George V for that of Edward VII.

Rifle Regiments

When the first corps of riflemen were formed at the end of the eighteenth century, the sergeants appear not to have carried swords as such but only the sword-bayonets issued with the rifles. The 1802 *View of the Standing Regulations* specifically excluded rifle corps from carrying the sword prescribed for sergeants of the line and this seems to have remained the case until 1827. By that time, the rifle corps had assumed many of the characteristics of the ordinary infantry battalions and, as we have seen, the officers had been prescribed a steel-hilted version of the Pattern 1822 infantry officers' sword, (see page 159 and Plate 148). Sergeants of rifle regiments appear to have adopted a plainer version of the Rifle Officers' Pattern 1827 sword.

Sergeants' Swords (excluding Scottish Regiments)

This sword was carried by staff-sergeants of rifles until a new sword - the Sword, Staff-Sergeants', Rifle Corps, Pattern 1866 - was introduced.[18] This was essentially the same as the previous sword, but with the Pattern 1845 blade. The scabbard was black leather with steel mounts and loose rings. The fishskin on wood grip was bound with German silver wire. The weights of sword and scabbard were the same as those of the 1866 pattern for infantry staff-sergeants, (see above).

This pattern was replaced by the Sword, Staff-Sergeants', Steel Hilt, Pattern 1889 (see above), subsequently re-named the Sword, Staff-Sergeants', Iron Hilt, Pattern 1889. The subsequent changes up to 1914 followed those of the infantry of the line.

Dismounted Royal Artillery

Sergeants of Royal Artillery battalions, (as opposed to the Horse Artillery) carried the infantry sergeants' version of the Pattern 1786, and then the Pattern 1796 infantry officers' sword (see above) until after 1822, when they adopted the infantry sergeants' version of the Pattern 1822 infantry officers' sword. The hilt of this sword is well shown in a portrait of a colour-sergeant of the Royal Artillery c1846 by an unknown artist.[19]

An entirely new pattern of sword for dismounted staff-sergeants of the Royal Artillery and Conductors of Stores was introduced in January 1856.[20] It had a plain blade of Pattern 1845 form (see page 159) with a three-bar steel guard similar to that of Royal Artillery officers, (Plate 205), a fishskin-covered, wooden grip, bound with German silver wire and a steel scabbard with two loose rings. The sword weight was 1lb 14^{1}/$_{2}$ozs and the scabbard weight 1lb 1^{1}/$_{2}$ozs. This sword was replaced by the Sword, Staff-Sergeants', Steel Hilt, Pattern 1889, (see above). Thereafter, dismounted staff-sergeants of the Royal Artillery followed staff-sergeants of the infantry of the line.

Royal Engineers

The progenitors of the Corps of Royal Engineers, the Royal Military Artificers and Labourers were raised in England in 1787. The sergeants carried the Pattern 1786 infantry officers' sword but with plain blade and brass hilt and brass mounted scabbard, as worn by sergeants of the Royal Artillery at that date.[21] In 1797, the Royal Military Artificers were amalgamated with the Soldier Artificer Companies, originally raised in Gibraltar and stationed there ever since. Although there is at present no direct evidence, the presumption must be that in due course the sergeants adopted the Pattern 1796 sword worn by infantry sergeants. In 1812 the Royal Military Artificers added the suffix 'or Sappers and Miners', and in the following year they became simply 'The Royal Sappers and Miners', a title which remained until 1856 when they amalgamated with the Corps of Royal Engineers (hitherto the officer branch) to form the present Corps of Royal Engineers. From 1822 the sergeants appear to have carried the ordinary infantry sergeants' sword,[22] (see above) but in 1843 the ordinary

Sergeants' Swords (excluding Scottish Regiments)

sergeants ceased to carry swords which were henceforth carried only by staff-sergeants (and in due course warrant officers).

A specific new pattern of sword for RE staff-sergeants was approved in October 1861. This was essentially the Pattern 1845 infantry sergeants' sword, with plain blade, 34 1/2 inches long, but with the Royal Engineers officers' sword hilt of scroll pattern in brass, (see above and Plate 211). The brass pommel was chequered and the sword weighed 2lbs 7 ozs. What appears to be the pattern sword, made by J B Watts & Co, Birmingham, is in the Pattern Room at Nottingham[23] but the pattern was not promulgated in the *List of Changes* and it seems unlikely that any significant number of these swords was either made or issued since it was replaced by a new pattern in May 1862. This was essentially the same sword but with a blade 2 inches shorter, which suggests that the 34 1/2 inch blade of 1861 was an official aberration. The new sword, the Sword, Staff-Sergeants', Royal Engineers, Pattern 1862, weighed 1lb 14 1/2 ozs and the brass scabbard 1lb 3 ozs.[24]

In 1868, Mole & Son submitted a new design in which the guard was slightly smaller and more symmetrical; the sword was otherwise the same as its predecessor. It was adopted as the Sword, Staff-Sergeants', Royal Engineers, Pattern 1869 in February 1869.[25] It was subsequently known as the Sword, Staff-Sergeants', Royal Engineers, Mark II. The Mark III version which followed it in April 1872 differed only in having a slightly enlarged sword knot slit in the guard, as in the Royal Artillery Pattern 1856 Staff sword.[26]

When the Sword, Staff-Sergeants', Pattern 1889 was introduced, in two forms, the Royal Engineers adopted the version with gilt hilt. Thereafter, the history of the Royal Engineers' staff-sergeants' sword is the same as that of the infantry of the line.

Army Hospital Corps

The ancestor of this Corps was the Army Conveyance Corps, organised in 1854 to provide stretcher-bearers and nursing attendants in the Crimea. The men seem to have been largely pensioners, too feeble or alcoholic, or both, to have been of much value and the Corps disappeared within a matter of months, to be succeeded in June 1855 by the Medical Staff Corps, which in turn was reorganised between 1857 and 1861 into the Army Hospital Corps. Somewhat curiously to modern eyes, all ranks of this Corps carried swords.[27] The Sword, Staff-Sergeants', Army Hospital Corps, Pattern 1861, approved in October 1861, was a slightly lighter version, at 1lb 12 ozs, of the Royal Engineers' Mark III sword, with a very light black leather, brass-mounted scabbard weighing only 12 ozs.[28]

This sword was carried until 1889 when the Corps, (which had reverted to its former title of Medical Staff Corps in 1884), adopted the gilt-hilted version of the Pattern 1889 Staff-Sergeants' sword. In 1898, the Corps amalgamated with the Army Medical Department (the doctor element) to form the Royal Army Medical Corps and thereafter the staff-sergeants carried the same swords as the infantry of the line.

Sergeants' Swords (excluding Scottish Regiments)

Sergeants of the original Army Hospital Corps had carried a short (29$^{1}/_{2}$ inch blade) version of the staff-sergeants' Pattern 1861 sword, weighing only 1lb 8$^{1}/_{2}$ ozs. The black leather scabbard had no middle band or loose rings but a frog stud on the locket, and weighed 8 ozs. This was the same pattern sword and scabbard as that carried by infantry drummers between 1822 and 1856[29] and it seems probable that these were issued to the Army Hospital Corps because there were now surplus stocks of them as a result of the introduction of the Mark I Drummers' sword in 1856, (see page 252). These swords were carried until 1888, when they were declared obsolete and, as they came up for replacement, the sergeants were issued with the Bayonet, Sword, B[reech] L[oading], Snider carbine, Lancaster O[val] B[ore], Non-interchangeable.[30]

Foot Guards

During the period c1822 - 1852, sergeants of at least two of the three regiments of Foot Guards appear to have carried patterns of sword peculiar to those regiments.

The 1st (or Grenadier) Guards sword consists in its first version of a pipe-backed blade similar to that of the Pattern 1822 infantry officers' sword but only 27$^{1}/_{2}$ inches long, a brass knucklebow guard into which is let the regimental badge of a grenade, and a lion's head pommel. The grip is the standard fishskin-covered wooden grip of the period, bound with brass wire. A second, presumably succeeding, version has a standard 32$^{1}/_{2}$ inch, Pattern 1845 infantry blade, (Plate 201). Since the grenade badge was awarded after Waterloo, this suggests that these swords were introduced in the 1820s and worn until 1852, when sergeants ceased to carry swords.[31]

The 3rd (or Scots) Guards version is virtually identical except for the regimental badge in the guard, (Plate 202). The only specimens seen by the author have the standard, 32$^{1}/_{2}$ inch, Pattern 1845 infantry blade, and the maker's (or retailer's) name (Hebbert & Hawkes) suggests a date in the period 1850-60.[32] But it is entirely possible that an earlier version, with pipe-backed blade, existed, as in the 1st Guards.

No version of this sword for the 2nd (or Coldstream) Guards has yet been firmly identified. A curious sword, with a brass cruciform hilt of trefoil form, with a very narrow, unfullered blade, and a Garter cross on the écusson, (Plate 203), has been claimed to be the sergeants' sword of this regiment. But it has also been claimed to be that of the Military Knights of Windsor and the case remains unproven in the absence of pictorial or documentary evidence.

A remarkably similar sword to that of the 1st Guards exists for the Welsh Regiment, (Plate 204). It has a 28$^{1}/_{2}$ inch blade, of diamond section, and the specimen illustrated was supplied by Firmin & Sons, of 153 Strand and 13 Conduit Street, London, which suggests a date of around 1850.[33] It is possible that some other infantry regiments adopted a similar pattern in the first half of the nineteenth century,[34] although they were clearly never a regulation pattern and may have been worn only off parade.

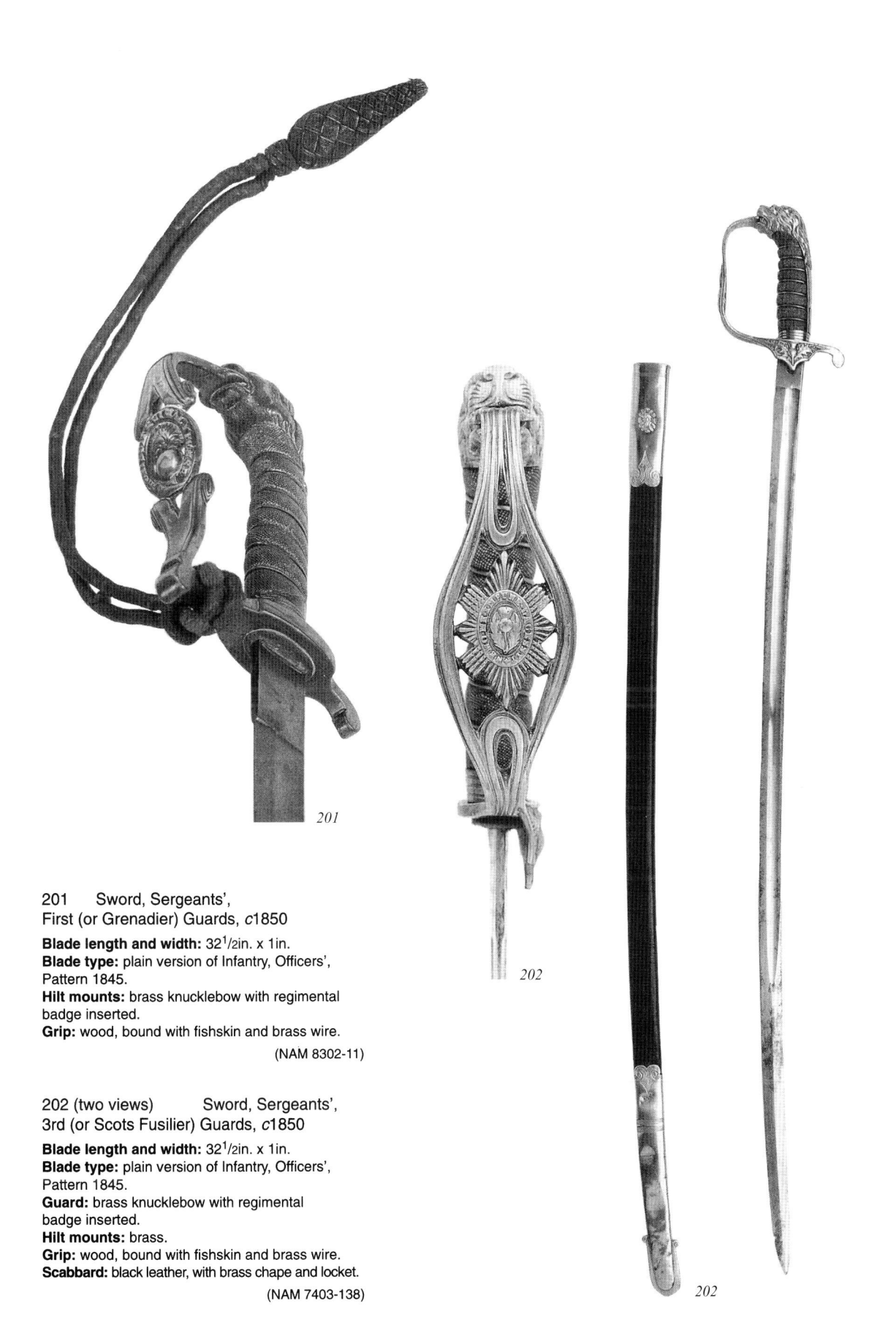

Sergeants' Swords (excluding Scottish Regiments)

201

202

202

201   Sword, Sergeants',
First (or Grenadier) Guards, c1850

Blade length and width: 32½in. x 1in.
Blade type: plain version of Infantry, Officers', Pattern 1845.
Hilt mounts: brass knucklebow with regimental badge inserted.
Grip: wood, bound with fishskin and brass wire.

(NAM 8302-11)

202 (two views)   Sword, Sergeants',
3rd (or Scots Fusilier) Guards, c1850

Blade length and width: 32½in. x 1in.
Blade type: plain version of Infantry, Officers', Pattern 1845.
Guard: brass knucklebow with regimental badge inserted.
Hilt mounts: brass.
Grip: wood, bound with fishskin and brass wire.
Scabbard: black leather, with brass chape and locket.

(NAM 7403-138)

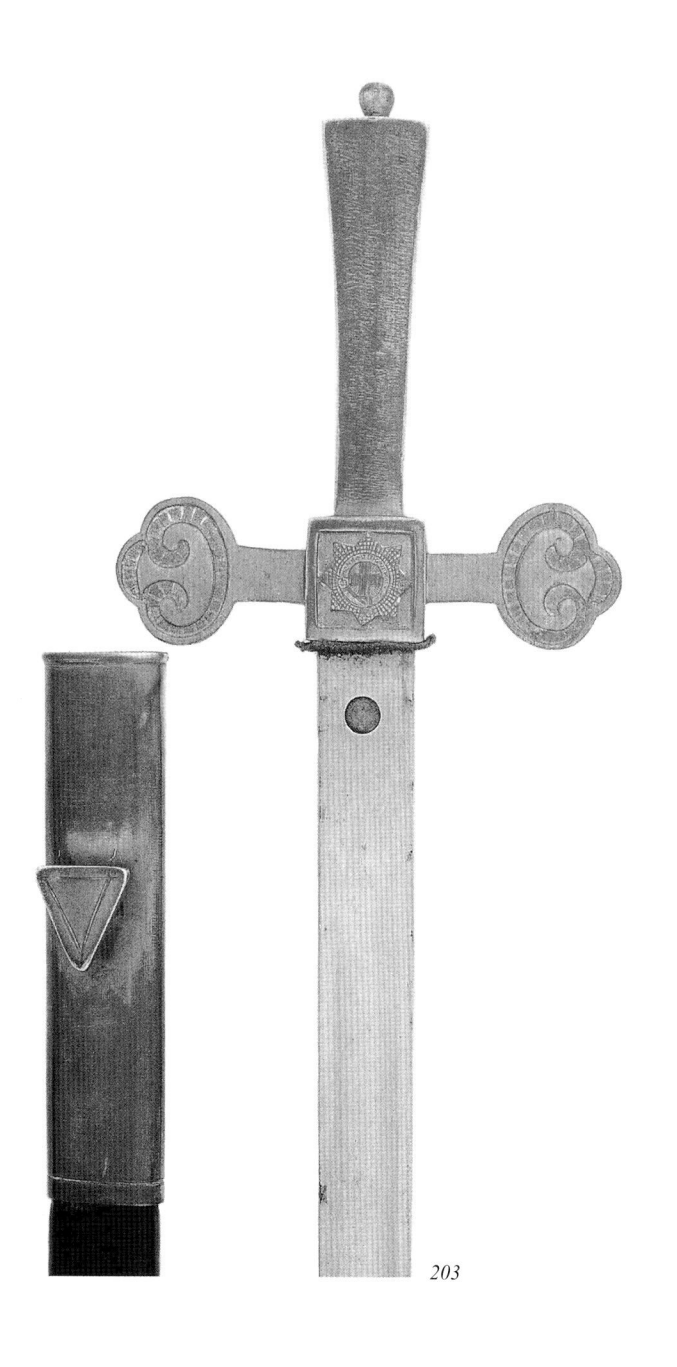

Sergeants' Swords (excluding Scottish Regiments)

203 Sword, possibly Sergeants',
2nd (or Coldstream) Guards

Note: hilt and scabbard mounts in brass. The Garter badge is equally applicable to either the 2nd Guards or the Military Knights of Windsor.

(NAM 8302-41)

204 Sword, Sergeants', The Welsh Regiment, *c*1850

Note: the normal spelling today is 'Welch'. Apart from the badge, similar in all respects to the Sergeants' sword of 3rd Foot Guards (Plate 202).

(NAM 7306-31-1)

222

Chapter 10: Notes

1. PRO. WO 30/13B, p16.

2. PRO. WO 4/373, p235.

3. PRO. WO 3/10, Order dated 17 February 1792.

4. There is a copy of these regulations in the MoD Central Library.

5. Hamilton Smith, *op. cit*.

6. PRO. WO 3/72, p398.

7. Sealed patterns 417, 162, in the Pattern Room, Nottingham.

8. *LC* 1377, 1 January 1867. Sword No 621 in the Pattern Room, Nottingham.

9. The material in this, and the next four paragraphs, comes from a War Office printed précis, *Staff Sergeants' Swords*, dated June 1889.

10. *LC* 5629, 1 February 1889; see also the specimen sword in the Pattern Room, Nottingham.

11. *LC* 5672, 1 April 1889.

12. *LC* 6581, 1 January 1892.

13. *LC* 6763, 1 July 1892.

14. *LC* 8823, 1 October 1897; see also the sealed pattern, No 957, in the Pattern Room, Nottingham.

15. *LC* 9243, 1 November 1898.

Sergeants' Swords (excluding Scottish Regiments)

16. *LC* 11290, 1 November 1902; the sealed pattern is in the Pattern Room, Nottingham.

17. *LC* 12825, 1 July 1905; the pattern sword, made by Mole & Son, is in the Pattern Room, Nottingham.

18. *LC* 1377, 1 January 1867. The pattern sword at Nottingham, made by Mole & Son, is marked as approved November 1866.

19. Reproduced in *JSAHR*, Vol XXXVII, 1959, p64.

20. *Staff Sergeants' Swords, op. cit.*, p1.

21. The Proceedings of the Board of Ordnance for 8 November 1788 record the procurement of 24 swords and cross-belts for sergeants of the Corps of Royal Military Artificers and Labourers to the same pattern as those issued to sergeants of the Royal Regiment of Artillery, PRO. WO 47/112, p512.

22. *Regulations for Provision of Clothing, Necessaries, etc for the Royal Regiment of Artillery and Corps of Sappers and Miners*, London (1824) make it clear that swords were carried by sergeants and staff-sergeants of the Royal Sappers and Miners, and other evidence suggests that they were of the infantry pattern.

23. *Staff Sergeants' Swords, op. cit.*, p1 and the pattern sword in the Pattern Room, Nottingham.

24. *LC* 560, 1 July 1862.

25. *LC* 1761, 1 April 1869.

26. *LC* 2333, 1 October 1872.

27. The patterns of sword are illustrated in Plate IV of *Army Equipment, Part VII - Hospital Service*, London, (1865). Both ffoulkes and Latham, *op. cit.*, confuse the sergeants' and the privates' swords.

28. *Staff Sergeants' Swords, op. cit.*, p2.

29. See Chapter 12, note 3.

30. *LC* 5627, 1 February 1889.

31. See also Inventory No T897, in the Castle Museum, York.

32. One in the NAM (7408-138), two in the Royal Armouries (Nos IX-392 and XXV-20) - all by Hawkes - and one in the SUSM (No 1930-1238), by Hebbert.

33. NAM 7306-31-1.

34. See, for example, a similar sword in the NAM (8601-92) bearing the badge of the 56th or 58th Regiment, which may be a sergeant's sword.

11. Corps and Departmental Swords

Royal Artillery: Officers

In 1788 the Royal Regiment of Artillery consisted of 40 companies, making up four battalions. The companies were deployed in the United Kingdom, the West Indies, Canada and Gibraltar and they fulfilled the functions of what later came to be designated field, garrison and coastal artillery, changing from one role to another as occasion demanded. Until 1794, the Regiment did not have its own horses and drivers but relied upon hiring them from private contractors as required. In addition to the 40 active companies, there were also ten companies of invalids who were normally stationed in the United Kingdom and served only as garrison and coastal artillery.[1]

It will be seen from this that at this time the artillery was more closely akin to the infantry than to the mobile corps it became later or to the cavalry, and the evidence shows that the officers and NCOs carried the pattern of infantry blade introduced in 1786. Garrison Orders of 8 August 1794, by Lieutenant-Colonel A Farrington, are clear in this respect: 'The sword has a straight blade and the length of it as established by His Majesty's regulations; it is to be worn with a gold and crimson sword knot'.[2]

As we have seen, the regulation introducing the Pattern 1786 infantry sword was not specific as to the hilt, and although many swords had the so-called five-ball or beaded hilt, some certainly had a twin-shell guard of the pattern specified in 1796. A watercolour drawing by Edward Dayes of a Royal Artillery officer *c*1792 shows him carrying an infantry pattern sword with straight, tapering blade and what appears to be a twin-shell guard.[3]

In 1793, the British Army followed Continental practice and raised its first four troops of horse artillery. Since a majority of the men and all the officers were mounted, and the basic function was to accompany the cavalry, the Horse Artillery from the outset adopted uniform and equipment based on that of the light cavalry regiments. (In interesting contrast, the Horse Artillery of the Indian armies adopted helmets derived from the heavy cavalry style). From 1793 until 1796, the officers and men of the Horse Artillery (excluding drivers, who never wore swords) carried the Pattern 1788 Light Cavalry sword.

In the Royal Artillery companies, the custom of carrying the infantry sword continued after the introduction of the Pattern 1796 infantry officers' sword, (Plate 131). A Regimental General Order of 12 October 1796 required Royal Artillery officers to 'conform to the uniform sword and hat, as established by His Majesty for the Army'.[4] General Cavalié Mercer of the Royal Artillery, reminiscing later about the swords of this period, remarked that 'Nothing could be more useless than the old Infantry regulation; it was good neither for cut nor thrust and was a perfect encumbrance. In the foot artillery, when away from Headquarters, we generally wore dirks instead'.[5]

From its introduction, the Horse Artillery carried the Pattern 1796 Light Cavalry sword, (see Plate 59). This can clearly be seen in the portraits of the period - for example, catalogue numbers 1995 and 1996 in the Royal Collection at Windsor[6] - and it is also vouched for by Mercer in his reminiscences: 'In the Horse Artillery, besides the large, regulation sabre, we had a small undress one but in the form of this we were not particular'.[7]

As anyone who has handled one can testify, the Pattern 1796 Light Cavalry sabre and scabbard is a heavy and cumbersome weapon, particularly when dismounted, and it was almost inevitable that officers should look for a lighter sword to wear off-duty and at social functions. As has been seen, the Egyptian campaign of 1801 and the example of Sir Arthur Wellesley combined to make the so-called mameluke-hilted sabre popular among light cavalry officers, and the fashion quickly spread to the Horse Artillery. A Regimental General Order of 1 November 1806 for the Royal Horse Artillery specified that: 'When officers are dressed for a ball, evening party or dine out, they are to wear the jacket open, white pantaloons, plain white waistcoat (with sash over it), light sword, regulation sword-knot, black belt, with cocked hats and feather'. A mameluke-hilted sabre is shown in Hull's print of an officer of the Royal Horse Artillery, published in September 1828.

In 1822 new patterns of sword were authorised for both infantry and light cavalry in the first printed *Dress Regulations*. The infantry pattern was the well-known Gothic-hilted sword, with pipe-backed blade, (Plate 144). This sword is depicted in Hull's 1828 print mentioned above which shows also the regulation black leather scabbard with gilt mounts.[8] It is also shown exceptionally clearly in a portrait of Captain Henry Baynes c1826.[9] The *Dress Regulations* of 1822 do not, in fact, cover the Royal Artillery but special dress regulations for the Regiment were issued in 1833. These state that the sword for officers of the Royal Artillery (excluding the Horse Artillery) was to be 'gilt half-basket as established for infantry'.[10] Regimental field officers were to have brass scabbards, other mounted officers steel scabbards and company officers not attached to field batteries, as well as all ranks at Court, were to have black leather scabbards with gilt mounts. This was broadly in line with infantry practice. Thus it is clear that after 1822 Royal Artillery officers continued to carry the infantry pattern sword.

Similarly, officers of the Horse Artillery continued to follow light cavalry practice, adopting the Pattern 1821 Light Cavalry officers' sword, with three-bar hilt, (Plate 78), The Royal Artillery *Dress Regulation* of 1833 actually refer to the sword

Corps and Departmental Swords

for Royal Horse Artillery officers as 'Regulation Cavalry' but this is clearly inaccurate since there was no 'Regulation Cavalry' sword but rather a heavy and a light cavalry pattern. Dubois Drahonet's painting of Lieutenant Arthur Gossett, RHA, in the Royal Collection at Windsor, shows the three-bar hilt quite clearly.[11]

But a Regimental General Order of 1 June 1833 perpetuates the imprecision by stating that: 'On no occasion will a Royal Horse Artillery officer appear, whether in jacket, pelisse or frock coat, without his sword which shall be Regulation Cavalry with steel scabbard'.

At some point not determined in the late 1840s, the officers of the Royal Artillery battalions gave up the infantry pattern sword and adopted the Pattern 1821 Light Cavalry officers' sword, bringing them into line with the Horse Artillery. The change appears to have been made in 1846-47; a Martens print of 1846, published by Ackermann, shows a Royal Artillery officer with the infantry pattern sword whereas prints of 1847 and 1849 show a steel hilt of light cavalry pattern.[12] The change had certainly taken place by 1857, when the standard *Dress Regulations* include the Royal Artillery for the first time and describe the sword for all artillery officers as 'Regulation, Light Cavalry'.

The Pattern 1822 Light Cavalry sword was succeeded by a new pattern in the 1850s in which the pipe-backed blade was replaced by a fullered blade, (Plate 205 and Chapter 4). This pattern of sword has been carried by Royal Artillery officers ever since. Royal Horse Artillery officers however changed to the Pattern 1912 Cavalry Officers' sword and continue to carry it in the King's Troop. With the abandonment of the sword as a fighting weapon, the three-bar-hilted Royal Artillery sword has tended to become narrower and lighter in the blade, being now only 1 inch at the shoulder. In 1896, along with all other officers' swords, the length of the grip was made variable between 5 and $5^{1}/_{2}$ inches to suit the individual hand. With minor changes - and one exception - this sword has been carried by Royal Artillery officers (except Royal Horse Artillery) ever since.

The exception referred to was the introduction in April 1896 of a special pattern of sword for all ranks of mountain artillery batteries. Mountain guns had been used in the British Army since 1813 when Wellington employed the equivalent of a battery in the Pyrenees campaign. Thereafter, they were used from time to time, as occasion required, being manned from the ordinary artillery battalions; there were no permanent mountain batteries until 1889. The Indian Army, by contrast, had permanent mountain artillery units from 1850 onwards, when the Hazara Mountain Train was formed, followed by the Peshawar Mountain Train in 1853. They quickly established themselves as an invaluable weapon in mountain and other difficult country and by 1889 there were eight batteries. From the beginning, these units had carried a short, curved sword as being less cumbersome in their activities than a longer, straighter sword. (The small size of mountain guns meant that much of the firing drill was carried out on bended knee where a short, curved sword fitted very

Corps and Departmental Swords

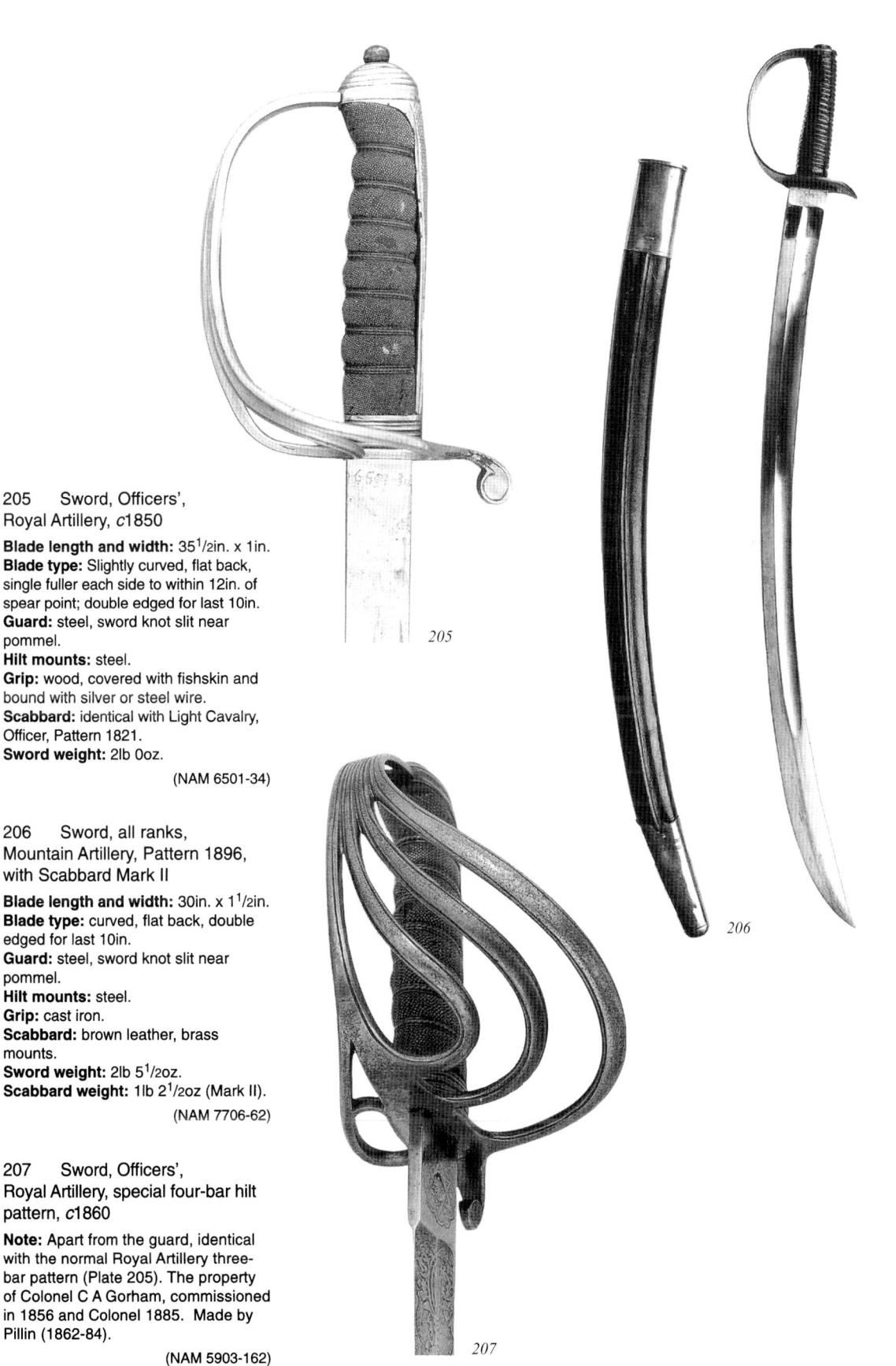

205 Sword, Officers', Royal Artillery, c1850

Blade length and width: 35½in. x 1in.
Blade type: Slightly curved, flat back, single fuller each side to within 12in. of spear point; double edged for last 10in.
Guard: steel, sword knot slit near pommel.
Hilt mounts: steel.
Grip: wood, covered with fishskin and bound with silver or steel wire.
Scabbard: identical with Light Cavalry, Officer, Pattern 1821.
Sword weight: 2lb 0oz.

(NAM 6501-34)

206 Sword, all ranks, Mountain Artillery, Pattern 1896, with Scabbard Mark II

Blade length and width: 30in. x 1½in.
Blade type: curved, flat back, double edged for last 10in.
Guard: steel, sword knot slit near pommel.
Hilt mounts: steel.
Grip: cast iron.
Scabbard: brown leather, brass mounts.
Sword weight: 2lb 5½oz.
Scabbard weight: 1lb 2½oz (Mark II).

(NAM 7706-62)

207 Sword, Officers', Royal Artillery, special four-bar hilt pattern, c1860

Note: Apart from the guard, identical with the normal Royal Artillery three-bar pattern (Plate 205). The property of Colonel C A Gorham, commissioned in 1856 and Colonel 1885. Made by Pillin (1862-84).

(NAM 5903-162)

229

Corps and Departmental Swords

well). When permanent batteries were formed in the British Army, it is not surprising that the same sort of sword was adopted. The Mountain Artillery Pattern 1896 sword is one of the rarest of all regulation patterns, (Plate 206).[13] The scabbard has a frog stud only so the sword was designed to be worn from a Sam Browne belt and hence only on exercises or in the field; personnel who wore swords presumably reverted to their normal patterns of sword in other circumstances. It is a fairly heavy sword at 2lbs 6 ozs. The original Mark I scabbard had a square end to the chape but this was replaced in 1899 by the Mark II scabbard, which had a rounded end,[14] presumably because this was more useful where men were kneeling and the tip of the scabbard trailed on the ground. This sword was still in use in 1910 but it is assumed that it fell into disuse for British units in 1914 and was not carried after that, even though mountain (or pack) batteries continued after the First World War.

Before leaving the subject of Royal Artillery officers' swords, it is necessary to glance at a group of swords which, from the dates of the known owners and/or the makers, appear to date from the period c1850-60. These swords, (Plate 207) have the normal Royal Artillery blade and a four-bar steel hilt - effectively an ordinary three-bar hilt with an extra, outer bar. These are clearly not a regulation pattern and were presumably designed as private fighting swords. As such, they are extremely handsome weapons, giving good protection to the hand and being very well balanced; indeed, it is difficult to understand why this pattern was not adopted as the regulation. At least five specimens are known, made by different makers, and it is tempting to think that they were made for the Indian Mutiny except that at least one sword was apparently made for an officer who retired in 1849.

Royal Artillery: Other Ranks

Other ranks of the Royal Horse Artillery (excluding drivers) replaced the Pattern 1796 Light Cavalry sword with the Pattern 1821 Light Cavalry sword, (Plate 21), but as with the cavalry itself the changeover was slow - Dubois Drahonet's portraits of a sergeant and a gunner of the Royal Horse Artillery in 1832 show them still carrying the Pattern 1796 sword[15] and the sword may not actually have appeared in the hands of RHA gunners until the late 1830s or even early 1840s. A specimen of the Pattern 1821 sword, dated 1842, and marked 'C44RHA' (C Troop, Royal Horse Artillery, Sword No 44) is in the Royal Armouries, (RA IX-345).

The Pattern 1821 sword was replaced in due course in the Royal Horse Artillery by the Pattern 1853 Cavalry sword and then by the Pattern 1864 sword, (Plate 24). This latter was disliked by gunners because the sharp inner edge of the guard rubbed and frayed the clothing, as well as being uncomfortable. Following representations, the War Office agreed in 1876 to the Royal Horse Artillery reverting to the Pattern 1853 sword.[16] The fact that reverting to the three-bar hilt of the Pattern 1853 sword gave greater uniformity with the officers' sword may also have been a factor.

The Pattern 1853 sword was carried by all ranks of the Royal Horse Artillery (excluding drivers) and by mounted ranks of the ordinary Royal Artillery until *c*1891 when it was replaced by the Pattern 1890 Cavalry sword, with the Pattern 1885, Mark II scabbard, (Plate 32). This sword was replaced in turn by the Pattern 1899 Cavalry sword and scabbard, (Plate 33).[17] Drivers and dismounted men, except staff-sergeants, carried sword-bayonets. Clearly as part of the general reforms after the South African War, Army Order No 242 of 1 December 1901 laid it down that: 'swords and sword-bayonets shall no longer form part of the equipment of non-commissioned officers and men of the Royal Horse and Royal Field Artillery'.[18] But it was partially relaxed by Army Order No 259 of 1 October 1910 which reintroduced the sword for other ranks of the Royal Horse Artillery (excluding drivers) for ceremonial purposes only: 'In future, non-commissioned officers and men, other than drivers, of the Royal Horse Artillery will be equipped with swords and sword-belts, which will be worn on all occasions when full dress is worn'.

The sword taken back into use was the Pattern 1899 Cavalry sword, of which there were beginning to be large reserves as a result of the introduction of the Pattern 1908 Cavalry sword. The Pattern 1899 swords went into store in the First World War and when swords were reintroduced into the Royal Horse Artillery in the early 1920s the sword issued was the Pattern 1908, Mark I*,[19] still carried today by the King's Troop, with, however, a plated hilt.

The swords carried by the ordinary artillerymen between 1788 and 1855 present difficult problems of identification. It seems reasonably clear that in the 1790s and very early 1800s, they were equipped with a short sword, with a brass knucklebow hilt, with black leather scabbard with brass locket and chape, suspended from a frog. This type of sword is shown in a painting by Denis Dighton, in the Royal Collection at Windsor, entitled 'Royal Artillery dislodging French Cavalry'[20] and in Charles Hamilton Smith's aquatint of two privates of the Artillery, dated 1815, in his *Costumes of the Army of the British Empire*.[21] This may well be the sword referred to in the *Report* of the Select Committee on Artillery in 1819: 'The Sub-Committee beg to remark that the sword with which the Artillery-men are now armed is in itself a very inefficient weapon for any purpose'.[22]

The situation then becomes much less clear. The only direct documentary evidence is contained in the report of the *Select Committee on Artillery Equipment* in 1855:

> 'The sword worn in 1820 was the Spanish pattern hangar, it continued to be worn by all gunners and drivers attached to field guns down to 1826. In the expedition to Portugal the men received the curved Cavalry light sword, with a sling belt, and its use was continued until 1843, when a peculiar sword, with a saw back was tried for a short time. The musket was given up by the Battalion artillery in 1845, and the Victoria carbine introduced in its

place, as the arm of Artillerymen not attached to guns. This carbine had an ordinary Infantry bayonet, but the men attached to field guns wore, instead of a bayonet, and in the same belt, a sword proposed by Colonel Dundas, having a steel scabbard and a brass handle. At about the same time the Light Cavalry sword of the pattern of 1822 was given to the Horse Artillery. The Victoria carbine was replaced by the Artillery carbine in 1853, of the Enfield-Pritchett construction, to which is attached a sword bayonet.[23]

This summary indicates that between 1820 and 1853 four distinct patterns of sword were carried by other ranks:

(a) a hanger of 'Spanish' pattern;

(b) the Pattern 1796 Light Cavalry sword, to 1843;

(c) a saw-backed sword, between 1843 and 1845;

(d) a sword designed by Colonel W B Dundas, from 1845 to 1853.

This sequence is by no means clear since it does not indicate whether the Pattern 1796 Light Cavalry sword was issued only to those men going on the Portuguese expedition and then only to Horse Artillery, or whether, as the report seems to suggest, it was issued to all gunners and drivers, which seems slightly improbable.

What the 'Spanish pattern hangar' was is by no means clear. Morrison and Reeder in their interesting article 'Short Swords of the Foot Artillery'[24] appear to confuse the Spanish pattern with the saw-backed sword, although it is quite clear from the extract quoted that they were distinct patterns. They predicate instead a so-called 'Prussian' pattern, with a short 22 inch blade and a straight brass knucklebow hilt. A number of swords exist which meet this specification, (Plate 208) and to this author, at least, it seems probable that the 'Spanish' hanger is that shown in the Hamilton Smith picture mentioned above and identical with Morrison and Reeder's 'Prussian' pattern. Its introduction and origin may be connected with the Peninsular War.

The saw-backed sword is very probably that identified by Morrison and Reeder of which a significant number of specimens exist in the Royal Armouries, the Museum of Artillery in the Rotunda, the NAM and in private hands, (Plate 209). It is of the same form as contemporary pioneer swords and probably copied from them since the function was exactly the same - cutting down light timber and brushwood, in the case of the artillery to make gun platforms and gabions and to clear a line of sight. None of the swords concerned, however, bear identifiable Royal Artillery markings and makers' names suggest manufacture rather earlier than 1843.[25]

Corps and Departmental Swords

208 Sword, Foot Artillery, Private, *c*1820

Blade length and width: 26 1/8in. x 1 1/2in.
Blade type: straight, unfullered, flat back, spear point.
Guard: brass, straight knucklebow.
Hilt mounts: brass shield-shaped langets, curled quillon.
Grip: ridged wood but may have been fishskin or leather covered and bound with brass wire.
Note: made by J H Reddell & Co, viewing mark crown over '2'. This is probably a specimen of the so-called 'Spanish pattern hangar'.

(SUSM 1987-47)

209 Sword, Pioneer and possibly Royal Artillery Other Ranks, *c*1820

Blade length and width: 22in. x 1 1/2in.
Guard: brass.
Grip: brass.
Sword weight: 2lbs 7oz.
Note: made by T Craven (1818-20).

(NAM 5608-57)

210 Sword, possibly Royal Artillery Other Ranks, *c*1850 - the so-called 'Dundas' sword

Guard: iron.
Grip: iron.
Scabbard: wrought iron.

(NAM 7910-65)

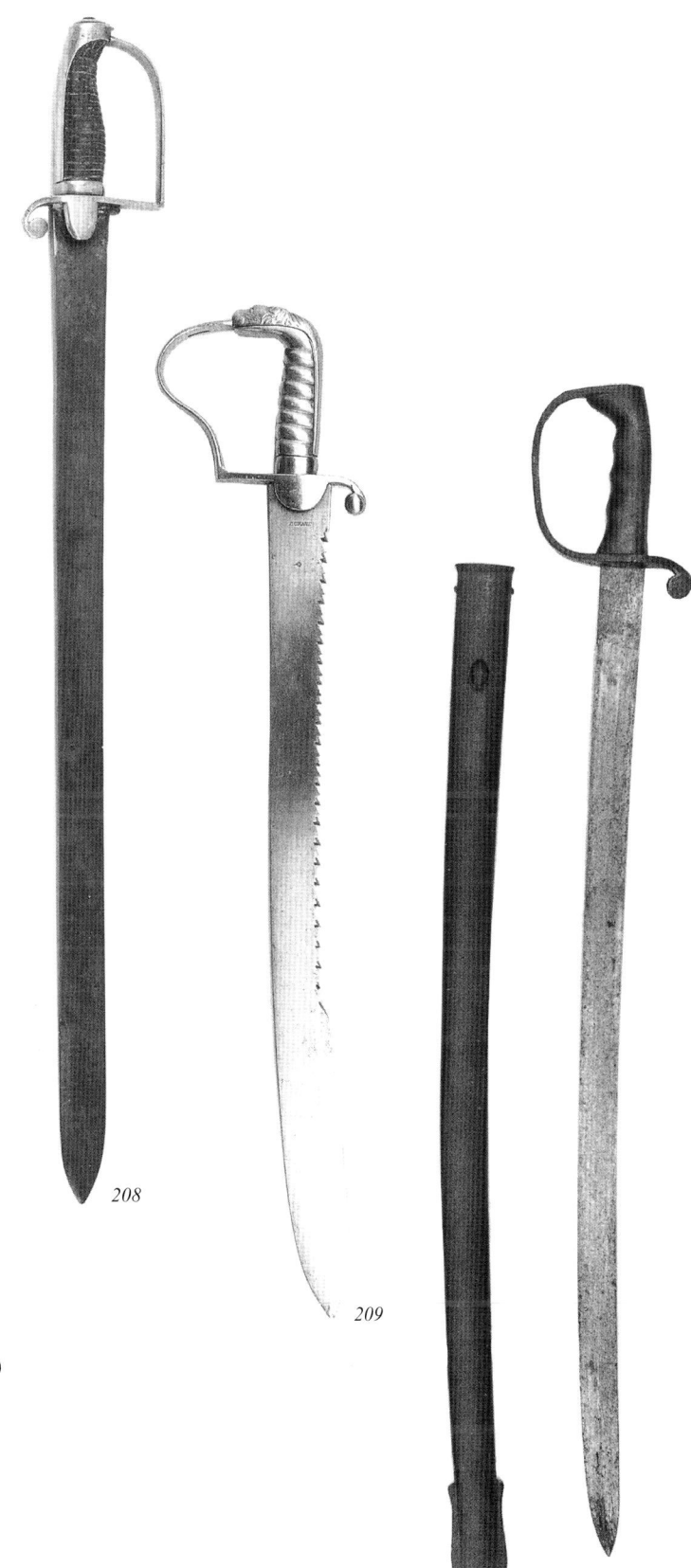

208

209

210

233

Corps and Departmental Swords

The sword designed by Colonel Dundas has not been positively identified but from contemporary illustrations it appears to have been a conventional design with a shortish, slightly curved blade and a plain brass stirrup hilt. Morrison and Reeder identified three specimens of this description, with 28 inch blades, although without specific Royal Artillery markings, and other specimens exist in the NAM and SUSM, (Plate 210), although again none can be directly linked to the Royal Artillery. The *Dress Regulations* for 1855 state that drivers were to carry no arms at all and the Dundas sword presumably became obsolete at this period.

Royal Engineers: Officers

By 1788, the engineer officers who had originally been part of the Ordnance Department, along with the Artillery, had achieved separate status as the Corps of Engineers, although still under the control of the Master-General of the Ordnance. The Corps consisted at this time solely of officers, the other ranks comprising the Royal Military Artificers, (see note 32).

There is no clear evidence as to the pattern of sword carried by officers of the Corps between 1788 and 1796. A Garrison Order at Gibraltar in February 1790, referring to engineer officers, stated that: 'The officers are to appear in boots, plain cocked hats with black buttons and loops and black stocks - sashed and with regimental swords'.

This might be taken to mean that engineers had their own special pattern of sword. The uniform of this period, however, was very similar to that of the Artillery, whose officers carried the Pattern 1786 infantry officers' sword, and it seems very probable that engineer officers did the same. This view is strengthened by the evidence of the later period. In November 1796 a Corps Order for the Royal Engineers described the officers' sword in terms which make it obvious that it was the infantry officers' pattern introduced a few months earlier:

> 'The sword to have a brass guard, pommel and shell, gilt with gold, with the grip of silver twisted wire. The blade to be straight and made to cut and thrust, one inch broad at the shoulder and 32 inches in length according to former orders. The sword knot to be crimson and gold in stripes.[26]

A pattern was to be available at Knubley's, at Charing Cross.

The first printed *Standing Orders* for the Royal Engineers' establishment at Chatham, issued in 1817, described the officers' sword as 'army regulation', with a steel scabbard for mounted duties and black leather scabbard for other occasions.[27] Again, this was clearly describing the Pattern 1796 infantry officers' sword.

In 1824, dress regulations were issued for the Engineers for the first time. The sword was described thus: 'Sword. The new sabre for Infantry, as described in the

Corps and Departmental Swords

Army Regulations'.[28] This was, of course, the Pattern 1822 infantry officers' sword, (Plate 144). The Full Dress scabbard for the Engineers was to be the black leather scabbard with gilt mounts and the sword knot a crimson and gold strap, with bullion tassel, as for the infantry. For Dress and Undress, the scabbard was to be of steel. The sword is shown exceptionally clearly in the Dubois Drahonet portrait of Second Captain L A Hall, Royal Engineers, in 1832.[29]

In *Revised Orders* issued in May 1835 field officers were authorised to wear a brass scabbard, thus bringing them into line with the infantry and artillery. Other officers continued to carry the steel and black leather scabbards.[30]

In 1845 the Pattern 1822 infantry blade was replaced by a new, fullered pattern, (the so-called Wilkinson - see page 159). This was adopted by the Royal Engineers at the same time; *Revised General Orders* in September 1845 refer to the sword as 'The new Regulation pattern for Infantry'. The scabbards remained the same.

This sword remained in use in the Royal Engineers until 1857 when, for the first time the Corps adopted its own pattern, (Plate 211). The new sword was described in the standard *Dress Regulations*, and in the *Regulations for the Dress and Appointments of the Corps of Royal Engineers* (April 1857) in almost identical terms: 'Regulation pattern blade for Infantry, $32^{1}/2$ inches long by $1^{1}/8$ inches wide, hilt of rolled metal, gilt, scrolled pattern, pierced and engraved'.

The scabbard was to be brass for field officers and steel for the remainder; the black leather scabbard disappeared for engineers. The sword knot was henceforth to be a braided gold cord with gold acorn. The link with the infantry was thus broken.

This Pattern 1857 sword was carried until some time between 1897 and 1900. It gives reasonably good protection to the hand; Latham's assessment in 1873 was that it was a 'very good guard but overbalanced', i.e. heavier on one side than the other.[31] While this is obviously true in a literal sense, the sword does not feel noticeably over-balanced and it was one of the best guards available among the regulation patterns until superseded by the Pattern 1895 infantry guard. The *Dress Regulations* of 1874 introduced a minor change inasmuch as field officers serving with engineer units in the field were to carry steel, instead of brass, scabbards; this was a purely utilitarian measure since steel was less easily damaged than brass.

The new straight infantry blade introduced in 1892 was adopted in due course by the Royal Engineers; but the new plated steel guard introduced for infantry in 1895 was not; Army Order 4 of 1 January 1896, announcing the introduction of this new hilt, specifically excluded the Royal Engineers, except that, along with all other Corps and Departments, the length of the grip was in future to be variable between 5 and $5^{3}/4$ inches, to suit the wearer. This largely regularised something which had always happened in practice.

Dress Regulations for 1900 prescribed the Pattern 1897 infantry hilt for the Royal Engineers so that the date of changeover evidently took place some time between 1897 and 1900. In 1899 the Engineers, along with all other branches of the Army

Corps and Departmental Swords

211 Sword, Officers', Royal Engineers, Pattern 1857
Blade length and width: 32$\frac{1}{2}$in. x 1$\frac{1}{8}$in.
Blade type: identical with Infantry, Officer, Pattern 1845.
Guard: gilt brass, sword knot slit near pommel.
Hilt mounts: gilt brass, with chequered hemispherical pommel.
Grip: wood, covered with fishskin and bound with brass wire.
Scabbard: steel, with two loose rings on bands; large shoe.
Sword weight: 2lb 6oz.
Scabbard weight: 1lb 2oz.
Note: the gauge of metal in the guard is thicker than normal.

(NAM 6306-13)

212 Sword, Drummers', Royal Sappers and Miners, c1843

(NAM 8310-145)

236

had adopted a brown leather scabbard with steel mounts for use with the Sam Browne belt and Service Dress; the steel mounts, however, disappeared in 1900. There were no further changes to the Royal Engineers' sword after 1900.

Royal Engineers: Other Ranks[32]

The notes made by T J W Connolly for his *History of the Royal Sappers and Miners* (1855) refer to the drummers carrying, from 1788, a short, broad-bladed sword, with brass knucklebow guard and a black leather scabbard with brass mounts.[33] From 1822, drummers and buglers appear to have carried the short Gothic-hilted sword carried by infantry drummers, (page 251) but Connolly indicates that this was replaced in 1843 by a brass-hilted, straight-bladed sword in which the ends of the quillons of the cross-hilt were of trefoil form. This sword, of which there are specimens in the NAM and the Royal Armouries, had a $25^{1}/2$ inch blade and the écusson had a moulded grenade and thistles, (Plate 212). A virtually identical sword appears in a portrait of a group of the 68th Regiment, c1846. The Royal Engineers' sword was clearly the model for the first regulation drummers', buglers' and band sword introduced in 1856, (see page 252 and Plate 217).

The Royal Sappers and Miners band was not officially recognised until 1856 although it had been in existence before then, on a private basis. Bandsmen then adopted the regulation Pattern 1856 band sword with a bugle on the écusson. The band-master appears to have had a short, curved sword, with scimitar blade, straight quillons and a brass grip ornamented with masks and foliage, ending in a lion's head pommel, with a loose chain connecting the pommel to the end of one quillon. This type of musicians' sword was common in the first half of the nineteenth century, (see Chapter 12).

The Pattern 1856 drummers' sword is illustrated in the *Dress Regulations for Royal Engineers* of 1868 but with the somewhat unusual, although not unique, feature of a decorated blade. It presumably continued in use until replaced in 1895 by the Mark II Drummers' (and Buglers') sword, (Plate 218). This was abolished in 1904 and not replaced.

Connolly's notes refer also to a special sword carried by Royal Engineers' drivers in the 1850s.[34] This was described as: 'a light Prussian sword, having half-basket hilts and buff leather tassels. The grip was partly of japanned wood ridged; all else, with the Scabbard, steel'. It was carried on slings from a buff leather waistbelt.

Until recently, this sword had not been identified but since 1980 a group of swords has been identified in Germany and England, whose characteristics very closely match the description given by Connolly, (Plates 213, 214).[35] These swords appear to have been produced in the first instance by Schnitzler & Kirschbaum, of Solingen, for trial in the Prussian Guard Hussar Regiment in 1849-50. The trials would appear not to have been successful because the regiment was re-equipped fully with new, regulation pattern swords, (probably the Prussian Cavalry Pattern 1852). The swords

Corps and Departmental Swords

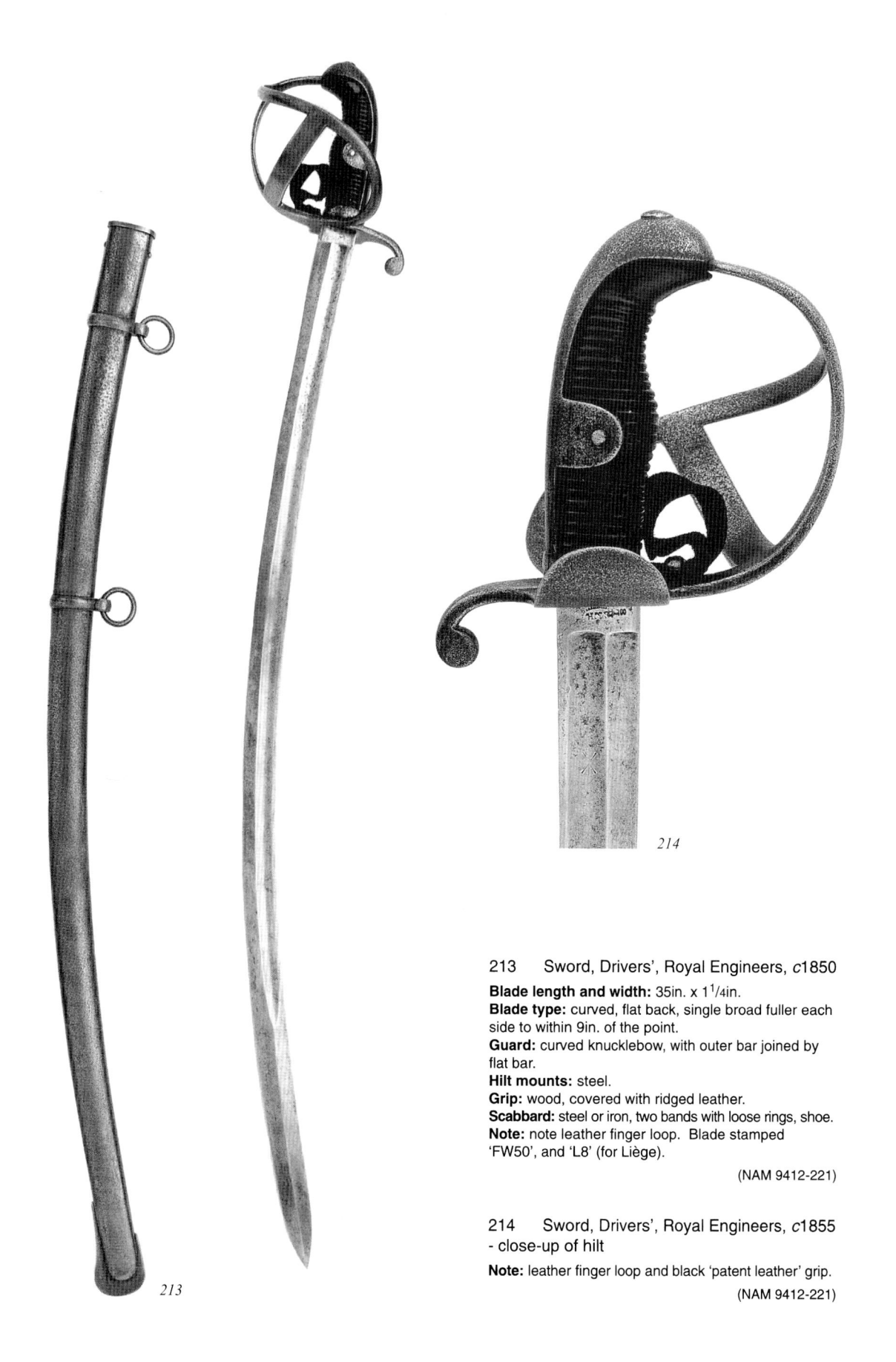

213

214

213   Sword, Drivers', Royal Engineers, *c*1850
Blade length and width: 35in. x 1¼in.
Blade type: curved, flat back, single broad fuller each side to within 9in. of the point.
Guard: curved knucklebow, with outer bar joined by flat bar.
Hilt mounts: steel.
Grip: wood, covered with ridged leather.
Scabbard: steel or iron, two bands with loose rings, shoe.
Note: note leather finger loop. Blade stamped 'FW50', and 'L8' (for Liège).

(NAM 9412-221)

214   Sword, Drivers', Royal Engineers, *c*1855
- close-up of hilt
Note: leather finger loop and black 'patent leather' grip.

(NAM 9412-221)

in question all bear the viewing marks of the British Board of Ordnance inspectors stationed at Liège in the 1850s, and the presumption must therefore be that the trials swords were disposed of through the Liège market and purchased by the British Government for issue to the Royal Engineers. Some at least bear the additional Ordnance mark of opposed broad arrows signifying that the weapon had been sold out of service, although there is no evidence as to the date on which this was done.

As will be seen from the illustrations, (Plates 213, 214), these swords closely match Connolly's description, even including the leather finger loop which is a highly unusual feature in British Swords. One at least has a black painted grip although the others have leather grips. Although the identification of this group of swords with Connolly's Royal Engineers drivers' sword falls short of absolute proof, it carries a high degree of probability.

Royal Staff Corps

Until the end of the Crimean War there were, in effect, two 'British Armies' - that commanded by the Commander-in-Chief, at the Horse Guards, comprising essentially the cavalry and the infantry, and that commanded by the Master-General of the Ordnance, in Pall Mall, comprising the Artillery and the Engineers. This dichotomy, as was pointed out earlier, was a recipe for friction and confusion and, in a number of cases, plain duplication of effort. In the campaign in North Holland in 1799 the expeditionary force found itself inadequately provided with engineers and, in exasperation, the Commander-in-Chief created his own corps of military artificers, known as the Royal Staff Corps, whose memorial is the Royal Military Canal in Kent and Sussex. The officers of this Corps carried first the Pattern 1796 infantry officers' sword and subsequently the Pattern 1822 sword.[36] The Corps was disbanded in 1838.

Royal Army Service Corps

Before the outbreak of the war against Revolutionary France in 1793 there was no organised military system of transport in the British Army. In emergency, a transport corps was extemporised by the simple expedient of hiring civilian horses, waggons and drivers. This system received a heavy blow in the Flanders campaign of 1793-95 and in 1794 a Royal Warrant authorised the creation of a small uniformed transport corps to be known as the Royal Waggoners. It was to consist of five companies, comprising 600 men in all. From its uniform and its generally infamous behaviour, it quickly became known as 'The Newgate Blues'. There is no clear evidence on the sword carried by the Waggoners' officers but since it was a mounted unit, and from later analogies, it is probable that it was the Pattern 1788 Light Cavalry sword, (Plates 2-4). The Corps seems to have disappeared as a unit following the disastrous retreat to the River Ems in the winter of 1794-95 but it was revived in August 1799 as the Royal Waggon Corps and, in 1802, re-designated the Royal

Corps and Departmental Swords

Waggon Train. The pictorial evidence makes it clear that the officers carried the Pattern 1796 Light Cavalry sword until 1822[37] when *Dress Regulations* for that year required them to carry the Pattern 1822 Light Cavalry sword. This remained the authorised pattern until the Train was disbanded in 1833.[38]

The outbreak of the Crimean War again found the Army without any organised system of transport and the breakdown of its supply arrangements in the dreadful winter of 1854-55 led to the hasty creation of the Land Transport Corps early in 1855. Its officers carried the Pattern 1822 Light Cavalry sword and continued to do so when the Corps was re-formed as the Military Train towards the end of 1856;[39] a sword of this pattern, marked 'Military Train' is in the National Army Museum, (NAM 8212-44).

There is no evidence that the other ranks, including sergeants, of the Royal Waggoners, the Royal Waggon Corps or the Royal Waggon Train carried a sword, and this would not be surprising since their work was essentially non-combatant and the men effectively civilians in uniform. But in the case of the Land Transport Corps, it has been accepted in the past, on the authority of ffoulkes and Hopkinson, that the other ranks were armed with a replica of the French infantryman's sword, Model 1831 (known vulgarly in the French Army as a 'cabbage cutter'), (Plate 215).[40] This had a 19 inch blade in two forms - a broad, straight, parallel-sided blade, roughly 1 1/2 inches wide at the shoulder and ending in a spear point, and a broad, leaf-shaped blade. Both forms are clearly modelled on the Roman short stabbing sword (*gladius*). The cruciform hilt was made of solid brass and was a push-fit over the tang being secured by a large brass tang button. The scab-

215

---

215 Sword, Land Transport Corps, *c*1856
Blade length and width: 22 1/2in. x 1 1/2in.
Blade type: double edged.
Guard: brass.
Hilt mounts: brass.
Grip: brass.
Scabbard: black leather, brass locket with frog stud, and chape.
Sword weight: 2lb 1oz.
Note: Made by Kirschbaum, Solingen. Marked 'WD' (a post-1855 mark) and 'V/CPA 4/74' (Cinque Ports Volunteer Artillery, a unit disbanded in 1814 and re-raised in 1859).

(Royal Armouries IX-414: Nos IX-1226 and -1292 are similar)

bard is of black leather, with brass chape and locket, the latter with a frog stud.

There are indeed a number of swords of these two patterns in the Royal Armouries with British Army markings but I have found no documentary evidence for the carriage of this sword by the Land Transport Corps, nor have I seen any so marked. The attribution must therefore be treated with some caution.

We are on firmer ground with the Military Train, where the sergeants, trumpeters, farriers and armourers (all mounted ranks) were authorised the light cavalry troopers' sword, first the Pattern 1853 and then the Pattern 1864, (Plates 22, 24).[41] In the Indian Mutiny, because of a shortage of regular cavalry, soldiers of the Military Train performed creditably as light cavalry.

In 1869, the officers of the various corps and departments that were involved in the supply and transport of the Army were brought together in a single organisation, the Control Department, the main constituents being the Military Train, the Military Store Department and the Commissariat Staff. The last-named had existed since the eighteenth century when it was a civilian department under the direct control of the Treasury, its officials wearing uniform on active service and carrying the infantry officers' sword but not holding the King's commission; field officers followed the infantry in having a brass scabbard.[42] In 1854 control of what had then become the Commissariat Department was transferred from the Treasury to the War Office and five years later, in 1859, it was militarised, the officers then forming the Commissariat Staff and the other ranks the Commissariat Staff Corps. Officers carried the appropriate infantry sword, (see Chapters 7 and 10), field officers having brass scabbards, other officers a steel scabbard. Commissariat generals, who ranked as general officers, carried the Pattern 1831 General Officers' sword, (Plate 194).[43] The buglers carried the infantry drummers' sword of pre-1856 (see page 251). Staff-sergeants and conductors of stores, as in the other stores departments, carried the Pattern 1856 Artillery Staff-Sergeants' sword, (see above).

The officers of the new Control Department carried the infantry officers' sword with a blue and gold sword knot, field officers continuing to wear a brass scabbard and other officers a steel one. The Controller carried the Pattern 1831 General Officers' sword.[44]

To carry out the actual work of supply, particularly in the field, a number of working units were formed in 1869, the officers coming from the Control Staff and the other ranks from a mixture of the former Military Train, the Commissariat Staff Corps, the Military Store Staff Corps and the Purveyor's Branch of the Army Hospital Corps. These new units were known collectively as the Army Service Corps.

The officers came from the Control Department and carried the ordinary infantry officers' sword when dismounted; the senior NCOs continued to carry the Pattern 1856 Artillery Staff-Sergeants' sword when serving in dismounted units but there is some pictorial evidence to suggest that when serving mounted in transport units these NCOs carried the ordinary cavalry troopers' sword, following the example of the Royal Artillery.[45]

The marriage of the various elements of the Control Department was not a happy one and in 1876 the organisation split into two parts - the Commissariat and Transport Department and the Ordnance Stores Department (the old Military Store Department). It is clear evidence that the War Office was still floundering over the proper organisation of the logistics branch of the Service. More complication was to follow when in 1880 the Commissariat and Transport Department was re-named the Commissariat and Transport Staff while the Army Service Corps, having lost the Ordnance Store element in 1877, became the Commissariat and Transport Corps in 1881. The officers throughout continued to wear the same swords as the infantry, while the dismounted senior NCOs continued with the Pattern 1856 Artillery Staff-Sergeants' sword and mounted NCOs continued to carry cavalry troopers' patterns.[46]

Finally, in 1891, the Commissariat and Transport Department (officers) and the Commissariat and Transport Corps (other ranks) amalgamated to form the Army Service Corps, reviving the name abandoned in 1877. On its creation the officers of the new Corps adopted the three-bar-hilted sword already worn by Royal Artillery officers, (Plate 205), which they have carried ever since.[47] The dismounted staff sergeants, however, carried the Pattern 1889 Staff-Sergeants' sword with the steel (later, cast iron) hilt (see page 215), while mounted senior NCOs carried the Pattern 1890, then the Pattern 1899 and finally the Pattern 1908 cavalry troopers' sword.

Royal Army Ordnance Corps

> 'The English Ordnance Department goes back into older history than the army, of which it has since become a part. There were Master Generals and Boards of Ordnance centuries before there were Secretaries of State for War or Commanders-in-Chief.

This extract from a War Office committee report of 1889 on ordnance services points to the fact that the Royal Army Ordnance Corps can lay some claim to being the oldest corps in the British Army. Its history is also probably the most complex and only a bare summary can be given here.

Until 1857 the business of supply to the Army in peacetime was in the hands of the Board of Ordnance and, in particular, of the Storekeeper-General. He was a civilian official and to assist him he had a staff of civilian storekeepers located at all the principal bases at home and overseas. Although the organisation was essentially a civilian one, the storekeepers wore uniform and carried the infantry pattern sword. In the field, however, armies had naturally to procure a good deal of their food and stores on the spot, and for this purpose there existed a quite separate civilian organisation, under the direct control of the Treasury, the Commissariat, (see above).

This curious, duplicated system began to founder in the organisational storms aroused by the maladministration of the Crimean War. In 1857 the storekeepers were formed into the Military Stores Department and in 1861 they were granted Queen's commissions, thus becoming a military formation. They continued to carry the Pattern 1845 infantry officers' sword with brass scabbards for field officers and steel for the rest.[48] Four years later, in 1865, a Military Stores Staff Corps was created to provide an 'other ranks' component. The senior NCOs of this corps wore the Pattern 1856 Artillery Staff-Sergeants' sword.

In 1869, as we have seen, the two Military Stores corps were merged into the new Control Department, along with the Commissariat but this lasted only until 1876 when it was again divided. The original Military Store components then became a separate department again under the title of the Ordnance Stores Department, under a Commissary-General, the officers carrying infantry pattern swords with brass scabbards for field officers and steel for the rest, with the Commissary-General, as a general officer, carrying the Pattern 1831 General Officers' sword.[49] The senior NCOs continued to carry the Artillery staff-sergeants' sword.

In 1889 the senior NCOs adopted the Pattern 1889 Staff-Sergeants' sword, with steel (later cast-iron) hilt. Thereafter, they followed the infantry patterns.

The officers of the corps adopted the Pattern 1895 infantry officers' sword, with steel and, later, leather scabbards for all ranks, except for the Commissary-General.

In 1896 the Ordnance Stores Department was reorganised into the Army Ordnance Department (officers) and the Army Ordnance Corps (other ranks). The two Corps survived the First World War, being amalgamated into the Royal Army Ordnance Corps (RAOC) in 1918. Patterns of sword remained unchanged and the Principal Ordnance Officer wore a general officer's sword.

Royal Army Medical Corps

The creation of the Royal Army Medical Corps (RAMC) in 1898 brought together a number of disparate elements.

By the end of the eighteenth century the medical officers of the Army fell into two main groups; the regimental surgeons of the individual units, and the staff surgeons attached to the higher formations. The regimental surgeons did not normally carry swords but when they did they would have been of the appropriate regimental pattern. The staff surgeons, when they carried swords, carried the appropriate infantry pattern.

This situation was regularised in the inaugural *Dress Regulations* of 1822, when regimental surgeons were required to carry the pattern of sword appropriate to the unit to which they were attached; all other surgeons - on the Staff, in hospitals etc - were to carry the new Pattern 1822 infantry officers' sword, with black leather scabbard.

Corps and Departmental Swords

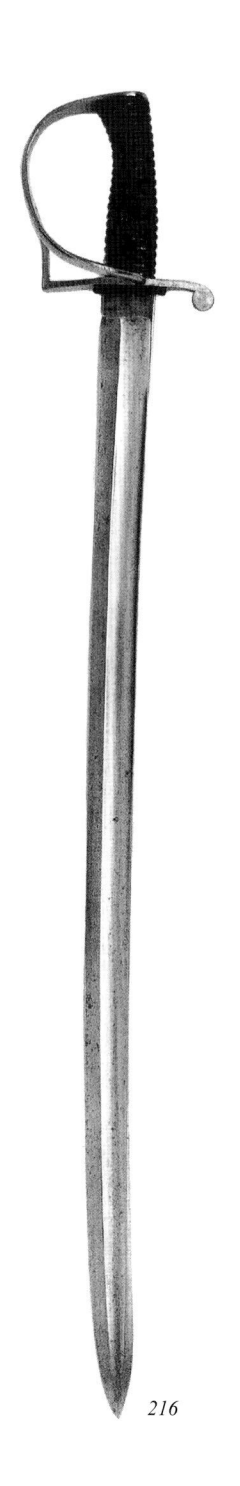

In addition to the surgeons who carried out strictly medical duties, there were in existence from the end of the eighteenth century a class of medical storekeepers, known as purveyors. They were of officer status, and carried out storekeeping and accounting duties, and were responsible for the domestic economy of the various general hospitals. They are not mentioned specifically in the 1822 *Dress Regulations* but they appear to have carried the appropriate infantry sword. Purveyors were abolished in 1830 but reinstated in 1854 just in time to share in the scandals of the hospital arrangements of the Crimean War. They formed part of the Army Hospital Corps when that was formed but in 1869 the Purveyors' Branch disappeared into the new Army Service Corps.

The Crimean War had forced the creation of a corps of other ranks to act as stretcher-bearers and nursing attendants and this led to the formation of the Army Conveyance Corps in 1854. It seems to have consisted mainly of pensioners, too feeble or alcoholic for serious work, and it disappeared in a matter of months. It was replaced in June 1855 by the Medical Staff Corps, which was reorganised and reformed into the Army Hospital Corps between 1857 and 1861.

Somewhat curiously, it might be thought, all ranks of the Army Hospital Corps carried swords.[50] The staff-sergeants had their own pattern, the Sword, Staff-Sergeants', Army Hospital Corps, Pattern 1861. This had the Pattern 1845 infantry blade, with a gun-metal hilt of honeysuckle pattern, with a grip of fishskin on wood, bound with brass wire. The scabbard was of black leather, with two loose rings and gilt mounts. The sword weighed 1lb 12 ozs and

216

216 Sword, Army Hospital Corps, Private, *c*1861
Blade length and width: 27in. x 1in.
Blade type: straight, flat back, spear point, fuller both sides.
Guard: brass.
Grip: cast iron.
Scabbard: black leather, brass belt hook and chape.
Sword weight: 1lb 12oz.
Scabbard weight: 9oz.

(Royal Armouries IX-8140)

the scabbard 12 ozs. The sword knot was of buff leather with cylindrical plaited 'acorn'. The sergeants carried a shorter sword, with a 29$^{1}/_{2}$ inch, curved blade, weighing 1lb 8$^{1}/_{2}$ ozs. The black leather scabbard had a brass chape and locket with frog stud on the locket, and weighed 8 ozs. This was, in fact, the infantry drummers' sword carried between 1822 and 1856 and it seems probable that this pattern was issued to the Army Hospital Corps simply because there was a surplus of them following the introduction of the Pattern 1856 drummers' sword.

The privates of the Army Hospital Corps carried a most curious pattern of sword which is, with the possible exception of the Pattern 1896 Mountain Artillery sword, the rarest of all regulation patterns, (Plate 216). The straight blade is 27 inches long, with a broad fuller running almost to the spear point. The grip is of moulded cast iron and the stirrup guard with outside bar is of brass. The scabbard is the usual black leather with brass chape but no locket or band, but with an elongated frog stud and hook. The sword is actually quite heavy for its length, at 1lb 12 ozs, but this is due to the grip. It is identical to the sword issued originally to the Coast Guard and it is possible that it was issued from surplus stocks when the Coast Guard gave up carrying weapons earlier in the nineteenth century. This sword does not appear in the 1887 *Table of Arms* and was presumably obsolete some time previously.

Until 1873 the Army Hospital Corps lacked a cadre of officers but when that was provided the officers carried the Pattern 1845 infantry officers' sword.

In the *Dress Regulations* of 1861 the Director General of the Medical Department and the Inspectors General of Hospitals were authorised to wear the Pattern 1831 General Officers' sword. Other medical officers continued to carry the Gothic-hilted infantry officers' sword - Pattern 1822, Pattern 1845 and, finally, the Pattern 1892 - until 1934 when the RAMC finally changed over to the Pattern 1897 infantry pattern. Any sword of the infantry Pattern 1892 made in the reigns of Edward VII and George V is therefore likely to be that of an RAMC officer. Between 1857 and 1902, medical officers of field rank carried brass scabbards while more junior officers carried black leather scabbards until 1874 when they were replaced by steel scabbards, which were adopted by field officers in 1902.

Royal Army Veterinary Corps

Until 1796, veterinary work was carried out by the regimental farriers of the various mounted units who naturally carried the pattern of sword appropriate to their regiment. In 1796, qualified veterinary surgeons were ordered to be attached to the cavalry regiments and to other mounted units such as the Royal Waggoners. They were commissioned officers[51] and again carried the pattern of sword appropriate to officers of their regiments or corps.[52]

In 1859, a Royal Warrant established the grade of Staff Veterinary Surgeon, thus beginning a move away from the purely regimental veterinary system. These staff veterinary surgeons were employed in staff and administrative appointments and their uniform included the Pattern 1822 Light Cavalry officers' sword.[53] In the *Dress Regulations* of 1872 however the staff surgeons were required to change over to the heavy cavalry officers' sword, (see page 87). Four years later the system of regimental surgeons was abolished for all units except the cavalry. The former regimental surgeons henceforth formed part of the Veterinary Department, which included the former staff surgeons as well. In 1881 the veterinary surgeons in the cavalry regiments followed suit and all veterinary personnel became part of an Army Veterinary Department. From this point on officers of field rank and below carried the Pattern 1822 Light Cavalry officers' sword while other ranks carried the ordinary cavalry troopers' sword.[54]

Under the *Dress Regulations* of 1891 however, the Principal Veterinary Surgeon and the Inspector of Veterinary Services were to carry the ordinary infantry officers' sword. Five years later the Director General, (successor to the Principal Veterinary Surgeon) and all veterinary lieutenant-colonels were authorised to carry the infantry sword. In 1896, with the introduction of a common pattern of sword for both light and heavy cavalry, the same sword was prescribed for all veterinary officers, who also adopted the Pattern 1912 Cavalry pattern.

Other ranks through the period carried the successive patterns of cavalry troopers' sword.

The Army Veterinary Department became the Royal Army Veterinary Corps (RAVC) in 1906 in recognition of its work during the South African War, 1899-1902.

Royal Army Pay Corps

The Royal Army Pay Corps evolved in a somewhat similar manner to the RAVC inasmuch as paymasters originally formed part of the regimental establishment and carried their regiment's sword. The tiny handful of pay staff officers - the various grades of paymaster-general - carried the ordinary infantry officers' sword.[55] The paymasters were departmentalised in 1875, becoming the Army Pay Department, with officers and staff-sergeants carrying the appropriate infantry pattern swords.

Other Corps and Departments

The Royal Corps of Signals, the Royal Army Educational Corps, the Royal Electrical and Mechanical Engineers, the Royal Pioneer Corps and the Royal Army Dental Corps, although their creation lies somewhat outside the strict parameters of this book, all carried the infantry officers' sword from their inception.

Chapter 11: Notes

1. There was, in addition, a corps of Royal Irish Artillery which in peacetime served only in Ireland. Between 1793 and 1801, some companies served outside Ireland but the corps was disbanded in 1801. So far as can be discovered, its uniform and equipment was similar in all important respects to that of the Royal Artillery.

2. Quoted in Captain J R Macdonald, *The History of the Dress of the Royal Regiment of Artillery*, (Privately printed), (1899), p41.

3. Reproduced in *JSAHR*, Vol XXXVII, 1959, p47.

4. PRO. WO 55/677.

5. Macdonald, *op. cit.*, p67.

6. See Miller and Dawnay, *op. cit.*, Plates 195 and 196. See also Sauerweid's portrait of a private and farrier of the RHA, 1816, *op. cit.*, Plate 249.

7. Macdonald, *op. cit.*, p.67.

8. Hull, *op. cit.*

9. I am indebted to Mr W Y Carman for a photograph of this painting in his possession.

10. *Regulations for the Dress and Appointments of General, Staff and Regimental Officers, and the Non-Commissioned Officers and Men of the Royal Regiment of Artillery*, Woolwich (1833) p20.

11. Spencer-Smith, *op. cit.*, No 47.

12. I owe this information to Mr W Y Carman.

13. *LC* 8368, 1 September 1896. A sword of this general type in the Rotunda at Woolwich (Class 14, No 199) is labelled as 'Mountain Artillery, Pattern 1861'. The only date stamps on it are for 1896 and it seems likely that it is an Indian Army pattern.

14. *LC* 9359, 1 February 1899.

Corps and Departmental Swords

15. Spencer-Smith, *op. cit.*, Nos 48 and 49.

16. *LC* 2870, 1 March 1876.

17. See *Regulations for the Equipment of the Regular Army, Part 2, Section XI*, War Office, (1896 and 1901).

18. The organisation of the Royal Artillery has a complex history. In 1859, the existing Company and Battalion system was altered to one of Batteries and Brigades, of which six Brigades were field and eight garrison artillery (the Royal Horse Artillery remained in batteries); the remnants of the old Invalid Battalion were organised into a Coastal Brigade. In 1889, the Brigades were abolished, leaving the battery as the primary unit, but in 1891 the garrison artillery batteries reverted to being companies. In 1899, the Artillery was reorganised into three distinct branches - Horse Artillery, Field Artillery and Garrison Artillery, the first two comprising the mounted and the latter the dismounted part of the corps. The Royal Field and Royal Garrison Artillery were reunited in 1924 to form the Royal Artillery. Between 1822 and 1858, men were enlisted as gunner-drivers; after 1858, as gunners or drivers.

19. *Regulations for the Equipment of the Regular Army, Part 2, Section XI(a)*, War Office (1925).

20. Catalogue 15044.

21. Plate 46, issued 1 February 1815.

22. *Proceedings of the Royal Artillery Institution (PRAI)*, Vol I, 1963, p94.

23. *Ibid.*, p186.

24. *JSAHR*, Vol LVI, 1978, pp112-118.

25. *Ibid.*, p115.

26. Quoted in *Royal Engineers Journal*, Vol 48, 1929, p192. Knubley is mistakenly transcribed as 'Kimbley'.

27. *Ibid.*, p195.

28. General Orders, Corps of Royal Engineers, 16 March 1824.

29. Spencer-Smith, *op. cit.*, No 53.

Corps and Departmental Swords

30. *Revised General Orders relative to the Uniform of the Corps of Royal Engineers*, 18 May 1835.

31. See Chapter 4, note 28.

32. The Royal Military Artificers and Labourers were raised in England in 1787. In 1797 they absorbed the Soldier Artificer Companies, raised in Gibraltar in 1772, and in 1812 the Royal Military Artificers added the sub-title 'or Sappers and Miners'. In 1813 they became simply the Royal Sappers and Miners and in 1856, they amalgamated with the Royal Engineers (the officer branch) to become the present Corps of Royal Engineers.

33. *Royal Engineers Journal, op. cit.*, p405. This may have been the same as the Royal Artillery privates' sword of the same period, (see page 231).

34. *Ibid.*, p412.

35. See Brian Robson, 'A Royal Engineer's Driver's Sword?', *Army Museum '82*, National Army Museum, London (1983) pp42-44.

36. *Dress Regulations*, 1822 and 1833. The Royal Staff Corps should not be confused with the Staff Corps of Cavalry, formed by Wellington in 1813 as mounted military police, who wore cavalry uniforms and light cavalry swords.

37. See Hamilton Smith, *op. cit.*, print of an officer, private and driver, published in 1815.

38. The three-bar light cavalry hilt is clearly shown in a print by Hull of an officer of the Royal Waggon Train published in September 1828 - Hull, *op. cit.*. See also *Dress Regulations*, 1831.

39. See *Dress Regulations*, 1857.

40. See Bottet, *op. cit.*, Plate II, No 3.

41. *Army Equipment - Part IV - Military Train* London, HMSO (1865).

42. Memorandum from the Adjutant-General 'comprising the Regulations for the Dress of the General and Staff Officers' 20 December 1816 (copy in MoD Central Library). Deputy-Commissary A L Schaumann, *On the Road with Wellington*, London (1924), refers several times to wearing uniform and a sword.

43. *Dress Regulations*, 1861.

Corps and Departmental Swords

44. *Dress Regulations*, 1872.

45. I am indebted to Mr John Thomson for drawing this point to my attention.

46. *Dress Regulations*, 1883.

47. *Dress Regulations*, 1891.

48. *Dress regulations for the officers of the Military Stores Department* - War Office Circular No 120, of 1 August 1857.

49. *Dress Regulations*, 1883.

50. The various patterns are illustrated in *Army Equipment, Part VII-Hospital Services* London, (1865), Plate IV. Both ffoulkes and Hopkinson and J W Latham confuse the sergeants' sword with that of the privates.

51. Veterinary surgeons in the Royal Artillery, however, achieved commissioned status only in 1805.

52. See, for example, *Dress Regulations*, 1822.

53. See *Dress Regulations*, 1861.

54. See *Dress Regulations*, 1883.

55. See Note 42 above.

12. Drummers', Band and Pioneer Swords

Drummers, fifers and buglers were always enlisted soldiers. In consequence, attempts were made from a fairly early date to regularise the patterns of sword carried by drummers and fifers (and, later, by buglers and trumpeters). The 1768 Royal Warrant laid it down that drummers and fifers should have a short sword with 'a scimitar blade',[1] and in 1770 an Inspection Return for the 30th Foot noted that the drummers carried non-regulation pattern swords. In this context, 'scimitar blade' probably meant little more than that it was curved as opposed to straight.

Robert Hinde, in his *The Discipline of the Light Horse*, published in 1778, says that the arms of trumpeters were a pair of pistols and a sword with 'a scymiter blade' - that is to say, a curved blade. Even earlier, Captain Bennett Cuthbertson, in his *A System for the Compleat Interior Management and Oeconomy of a Battalion of Infantry*, published in Dublin in 1768, with a second edition in 1776, had laid it down that the swords for drummers and fifers should be 'short and light sabre blades, with a neat brass mounting, as that is easiest to keep bright'. He was, in fact, merely repeating what was stated in a Royal Warrant of the same year for regulating the Colours, Clothing, etc of the Marching Regiments of Foot: 'All Drummers and Fifers to have a short sword with a scimetar blade'.

Swords of this type which can confidently be ascribed as being those of drummers and fifers pre-1780 are extremely difficult to find but it may well be that some of the swords which are nowadays ascribed to bands (see below) are in fact those of drummers from the late eighteenth century although this is no more than an hypothesis.

In the *Standing Regulations* of 1802 for the colours and clothing of the infantry, drummers' swords were specified in the following terms: 'The swords of the drummers to have a straight blade 24 inches in length, with the hilt, grip and mounting similar to the sergeants'. (In the same *Regulations*, the sergeants' sword - except in rifle regiments - was described as identical to the Pattern 1796 infantry officers' sword except that the metal was plain, not gilded, brass and the grip was bound with brass, not silver, wire).[2]

This pattern appears to have remained the regulation for drummers, and, we may assume, for fifers, until 1822, when the Gothic hilt and curved, pipe-backed blade was introduced for infantry officers and sergeants. The same Gothic hilt was then adopted for infantry drummers. A Memorandum of 10 January 1823 from the Adjutant-General to the commanding officer of the 42nd (Black Watch) Regiment indirectly makes this clear: 'The Commander-in-Chief has been pleased to dispense with the Sword prescribed by recent Regulations for Officers, Sergeants and Drummers of Infantry being adopted by the Highland Regiments'.[3]

There is, however, later evidence that the drummers' sword had only a $29^{1}/_{2}$ inch blade, as opposed to the officers' and sergeants' $32^{1}/_{2}$ inches.[4] This Gothic-hilted sword is shown clearly in A J Dubois Drahonet's portrait of Drummer William Cann, of the Scots Fusilier Guards, entitled 'Night Rounds' and painted in 1832, in the Royal Collection at Windsor.[5]

This sword appears to have remained the regulation pattern until 1856. In that year, it was replaced by a completely new and wholly ornamental pattern, the Sword, Drummers' (or Sword, Buglers'), Mark I, (Plate 217). The hilt was of cruciform shape, the quillons ending in trefoils and the écusson having the cypher of Queen Victoria; it was of brass for drummers and iron for buglers. The blade was straight and parallel-sided, ending in a spear point. It was 19 inches long and $1^{3}/_{8}$ inches wide at the shoulder, of diamond section, with a prominent medial ridge. The scabbard was of black leather with brass or steel chape and locket, the latter with a frog stud. The solid metal hilt made this a heavy weapon for its size - the sword itself weighing 1lb 14 ozs in the case of the brass-hilted version, intended for drummers, and 1lb 13 ozs in the malleable cast iron version intended for buglers. The scabbards weighed $9^{1}/_{4}$ and $8^{1}/_{2}$ ozs respectively. The number of the regiment is normally stamped on the back or front of the grip in existing specimens.

Although adopted as the standard regulation pattern in 1856, this pattern of sword seems to have appeared in certain regiments and corps at least as early as the 1840s. It is very clearly shown, for example, in the painting of a group of the 68th Regiment, known as the Paulet group, painted about 1846.[6] A specimen, with a $25^{1}/_{2}$ inch blade marked 'Royal Sappers and Miners', and dated 1843, is in the NAM; in this pattern, the écusson has a grenade in place of the later 'VR' cypher, (Plate 212).[7] It would seem therefore that the Mark I sword was not basically a new design but an adaptation of an existing design already in service.

Although introduced in 1856, the Mark I pattern was not actually taken into use in some regiments until some years later - the 31st Foot, for example, adopted it only in 1863, presumably when the old swords were worn out.

The Mark I pattern was carried by all dismounted corps, including the Royal Artillery, until 1895 when it was replaced by a new standard pattern, the Sword, Drummers' (or Buglers'), Mark II. This was a smaller, more refined weapon, (Plates 218, 219).[8] The blade, though of similar form to the Mark I, was only $13^{1}/_{8}$ inches long and $^{7}/_{8}$ inch wide; the hilt was similar, except that the grip was oval and smooth. The scabbard was a smaller version of the Mark I scabbard.

As with the Mark I, the hilt and scabbard mounts were in brass or iron. The brass hilt was intended for drummers and bandsmen of the infantry of the line and dis-

Drummers', Band and Pioneer Swords

217

217 Sword, Drummers', Mark I, 1856
Blade length and width: 19in. x 1³/₈in.
Blade type: straight, unfullered, double edged, spear point; prominent medial ridge.
Guard: brass.
Grip: brass.
Scabbard: black leather, brass locket with frog stud and chape.
Sword weight: 1lb 14oz.
Scabbard weight: 9¹/₂oz.
Note: Buglers', Mark I identical except that hilt and scabbard mounts are of iron and sword and scabbard each weigh 1oz less.

(NAM 5112-34)

218 Sword, Drummers', Mark II, 1895
Blade length and width: 13¹/₈in. x 1in.
Blade type: double edged.
Guard: brass.
Grip: brass.
Scabbard: black leather, brass mounts.
Sword weight: 15³/₄oz.
Scabbard weight: 4¹/₂oz.
Note: Buglers', Mark II identical except that the hilt and scabbard mounts are iron and the sword weighs ³/₄oz less and the scabbard ¹/₂oz less.

(NAM 6312-251-135)

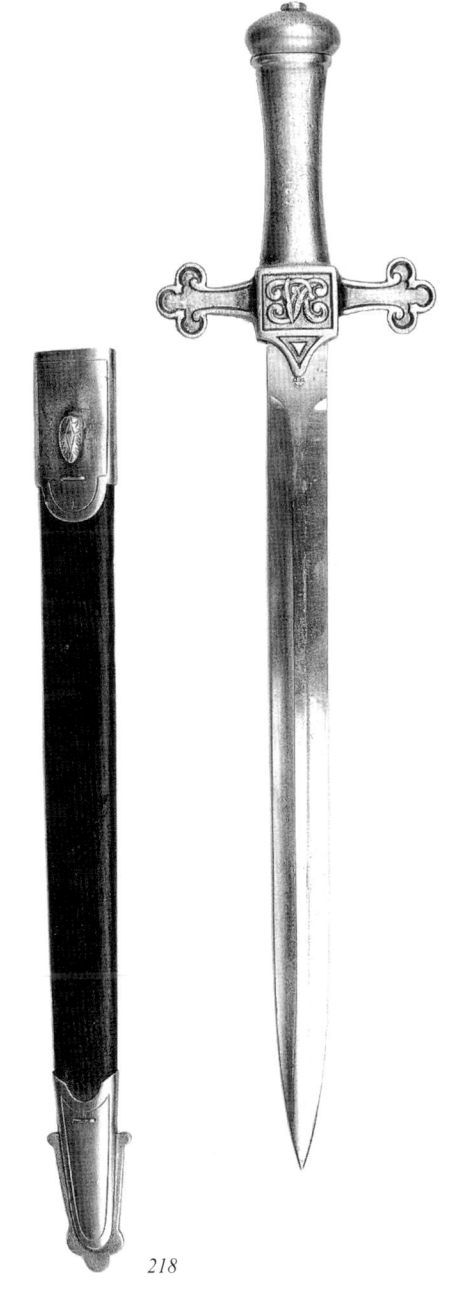

218

Drummers', Band and Pioneer Swords

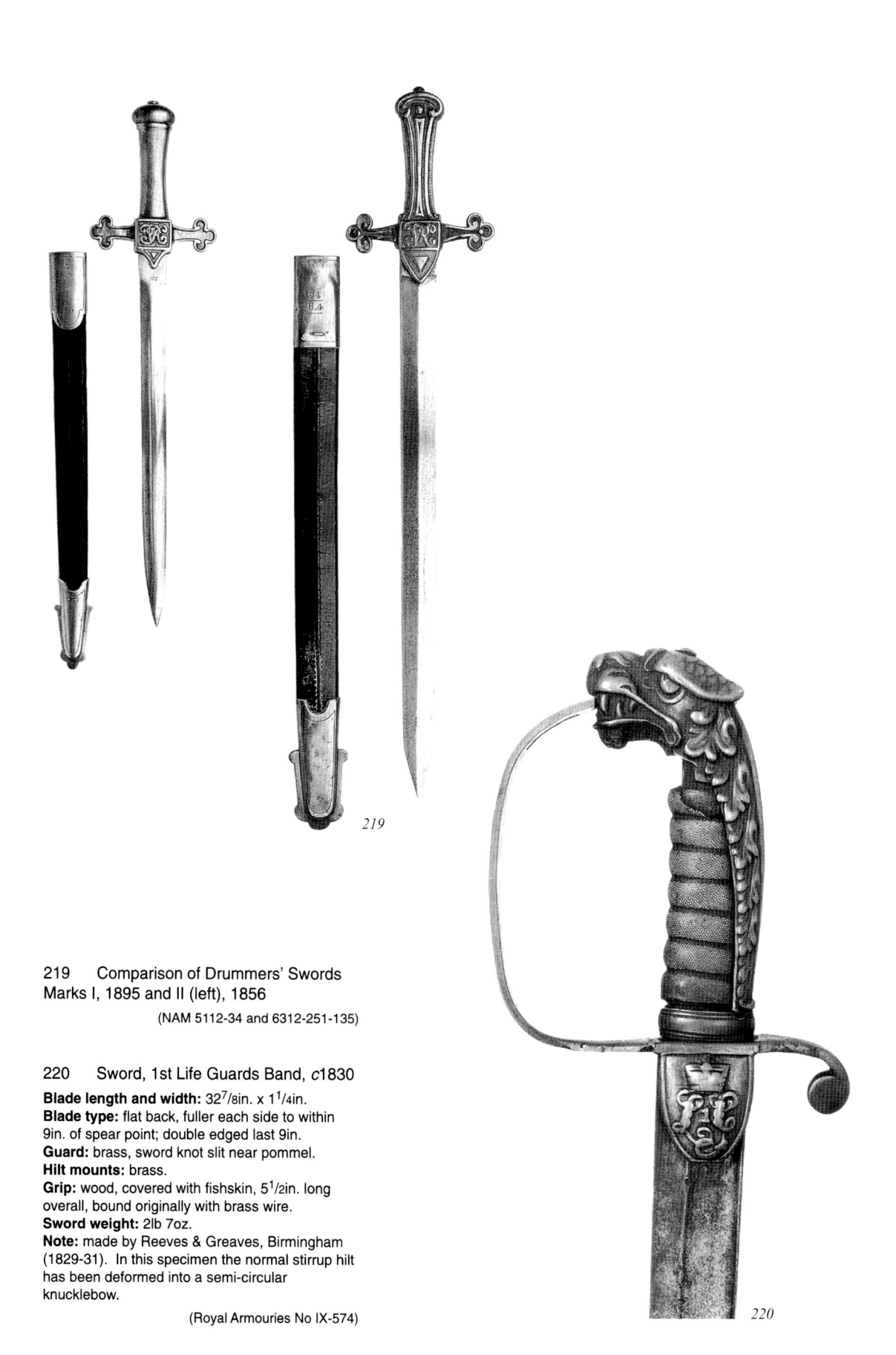

219 Comparison of Drummers' Swords Marks I, 1895 and II (left), 1856

(NAM 5112-34 and 6312-251-135)

220 Sword, 1st Life Guards Band, *c*1830

Blade length and width: 32⁷/₈in. x 1¹/₄in.
Blade type: flat back, fuller each side to within 9in. of spear point; double edged last 9in.
Guard: brass, sword knot slit near pommel.
Hilt mounts: brass.
Grip: wood, covered with fishskin, 5¹/₂in. long overall, bound originally with brass wire.
Sword weight: 2lb 7oz.
Note: made by Reeves & Greaves, Birmingham (1829-31). In this specimen the normal stirrup hilt has been deformed into a semi-circular knucklebow.

(Royal Armouries No IX-574)

254

Drummers', Band and Pioneer Swords

221

221 Sword, Band, 6th Dragoon Guards, mid-19th century

Blade length and width: 30in. x 1 1/8in.
Blade type: curved, flat back, single broad fuller each side to within 1 1/4in. of spear point.
Guard: solid brass cross, with counter-curving quillons.
Grip: of solid brass, elaborately decorated in acanthus design, loose ring for sword knot in lion's head pommel.
Scabbard: brass, with two bands and loose rings, marked near mouth 'VIDG'.

(NAM 9109-55)

222 Sword, Band, Cavalry, possibly 2nd Life Guards, mid-19th century

Blade length and width: 35 1/4in. x 3/4in.
Blade type: narrow fuller 18in. long, starting 4 1/2in. from shoulder.
Guard: gilt brass cross, with grenade on écusson, and crosses on quillon ends.
Grip: wood, covered with fishskin and bound with brass wire.
Scabbard: steel.
Note: made by Andrews, Pall Mall and labelled '2nd Life Guards band 1821-68'. From the length of the blade, this is clearly a cavalry sword and the grenade suggests the 2nd Life Guards. Andrews frequently supplied swords to the Household regiments.

(NAM 8105-36)

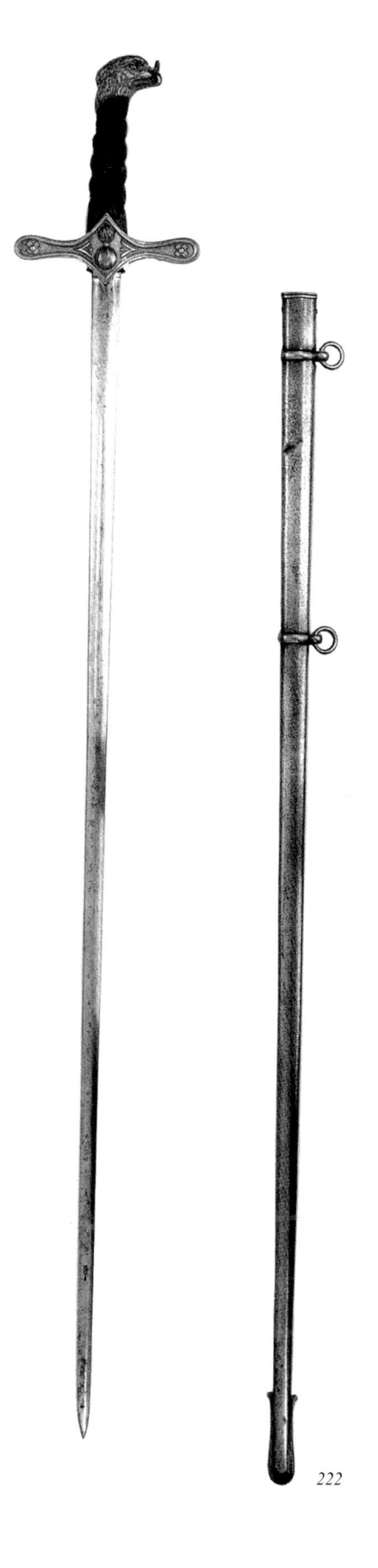

222

mounted corps, while the iron hilt was for buglers and rifle regiments.[9] The weights of the two versions were:

	Sword	Scabbard
Drummers', Mark II	15¾oz	4½oz
Buglers', Mark II	15oz	4oz

The regimental number or abbreviation was usually stamped on the top of the pommel.

This sword was, of course, even less of a fighting weapon than its predecessor; nevertheless, an order was solemnly issued in 1901 that it was to be sharpened for active service.[10] The order was rescinded in 1905.

The Buglers', Mark II version was abolished in 1904[11] but the Drummers', Mark II remained in service in some regiments until comparatively recently. Later specimens have a leather buff-piece and the appropriate royal cypher.[12]

As far as mounted troops were concerned, there were no special regulation patterns for trumpeters, but regimental patterns were in use from an early stage. A bill of 11 November 1803 records the payment of £22 13s 2d to Prosser for twelve trumpeters' swords for the 15th Light Dragoons.[13] At a time when ordinary troopers' swords were costing only about eighteen shillings these were obviously fairly decorative swords.

These cavalry patterns carried on well into the nineteenth century. The best known example is that of the 1st Life Guards, (Plate 220); this particular pattern appears to have been made for the regiment by Charles Reeves & Co, of Birmingham, who were in business under that name from 1829 to 1855.[14] This sword is shown in the portrait of Trumpeter Thomas Jagger, 1st Life Guards, painted by Dubois Drahonet in 1832-33 and now at Windsor.[15] It can be seen also in photographs of the 1st Life Guards c1872-74.[16] It clearly remained in service until 1882 when it was replaced by the Household Cavalry Pattern 1882, Short sword, which was designed specifically for trumpeters and band.

The NAM possesses a band and/or trumpeters' sword of the 6th Dragoon Guards (Carabiniers) which from its general form, can probably be dated to 1820-30, (Plate 221). What may be a trumpeters' sword of the 2nd Life Guards, with a long (35½ inch) blade and a grenade on the écusson is also in the NAM, (Plate 222) although, so far, other examples have not been encountered.

Band or Musicians' Swords

Throughout the eighteenth and most of the nineteenth centuries, bandsmen occupied a somewhat anomalous position in the British Army. They formed part of the recognised unit establishment (although in the eighteenth century at least, not all units had bands) but the upkeep of the band was largely borne by the officers. Some bandsmen were enlisted soldiers; a General Order of 5 August 1803 laid it down that: '...in regiments with bands not more than one private soldier per troop or company is permitted to act as musicians and one Non-Commissioned Officer to act as Master of the Band. [They are] To be trained and fall in for active service as ordinary soldiers'. The remainder were civilians, frequently foreigners, specially enlisted for their appearance (hence the popularity of black musicians) or for their musicianship, and they frequently took their discharge in the event of war or overseas service. Band-masters could be enlisted soldiers but were often civilians, up until the end of the nineteenth century, and frequently transferred or resigned when the regiment went on active service or to an unpopular overseas posting.[17]

The major consequence of this curious situation was that regiments had a very wide discretion as to the uniform and accoutrements of their bands. In particular, since bandsmen were not intended in the first instance to be fighting soldiers, their swords were chosen primarily for decoration rather than effectiveness as weapons, and a major factor was the need for the swords not to interfere with marching and playing. This is probably the reason why band swords from the beginning tended as a class to be relatively short and curved, although there were always exceptions.

A bill of December 1790 records the delivery of swords for the band of the 7th Foot (Royal Fusiliers) at a cost of £46 13s 6d.[18] These swords, presented by the Duke of Kent, seem to have had a very long life, lasting into the twentieth century.

Swords of this general type are therefore relatively common from the end of the eighteenth century but they are difficult to date with any exactness. Since most bandsmen were not hired to fight, their swords were at least as ornamental as those of the trumpeters, where they were not indeed the same.

By 1800, a certain broad uniformity of style had begun to emerge. The typical infantry band sword of the early part of the nineteenth century had a solid brass, mameluke hilt, with a short, curved blade and a brass scabbard, (Plates 223-226).[19] The grip usually ended in a beast's or bird's head, the lion, tiger, horse and eagle being the most popular. The quillons could be straight or S-shaped, plain or ornamented, and the écusson frequently carried a regimental number or device. A common and distinctive feature, almost unique to band swords, was the provision of a loose chain joining the top of the grip to the end of one quillon, intended to protect the knuckles. Where there is only one hole or ring, in the pommel, it was intended for a sword knot. Straight, as well as curved blades are found, although less common, and seem to be more prevalent in the second quarter of the nineteenth century. Although this type of highly ornamental band sword was overtaken in the regular Army by the standard patterns first introduced in 1856, they continued in use in Militia and Volunteer units until at least the 1860s[20] and this further complicates firm unit identification and dating.

Drummers', Band and Pioneer Swords

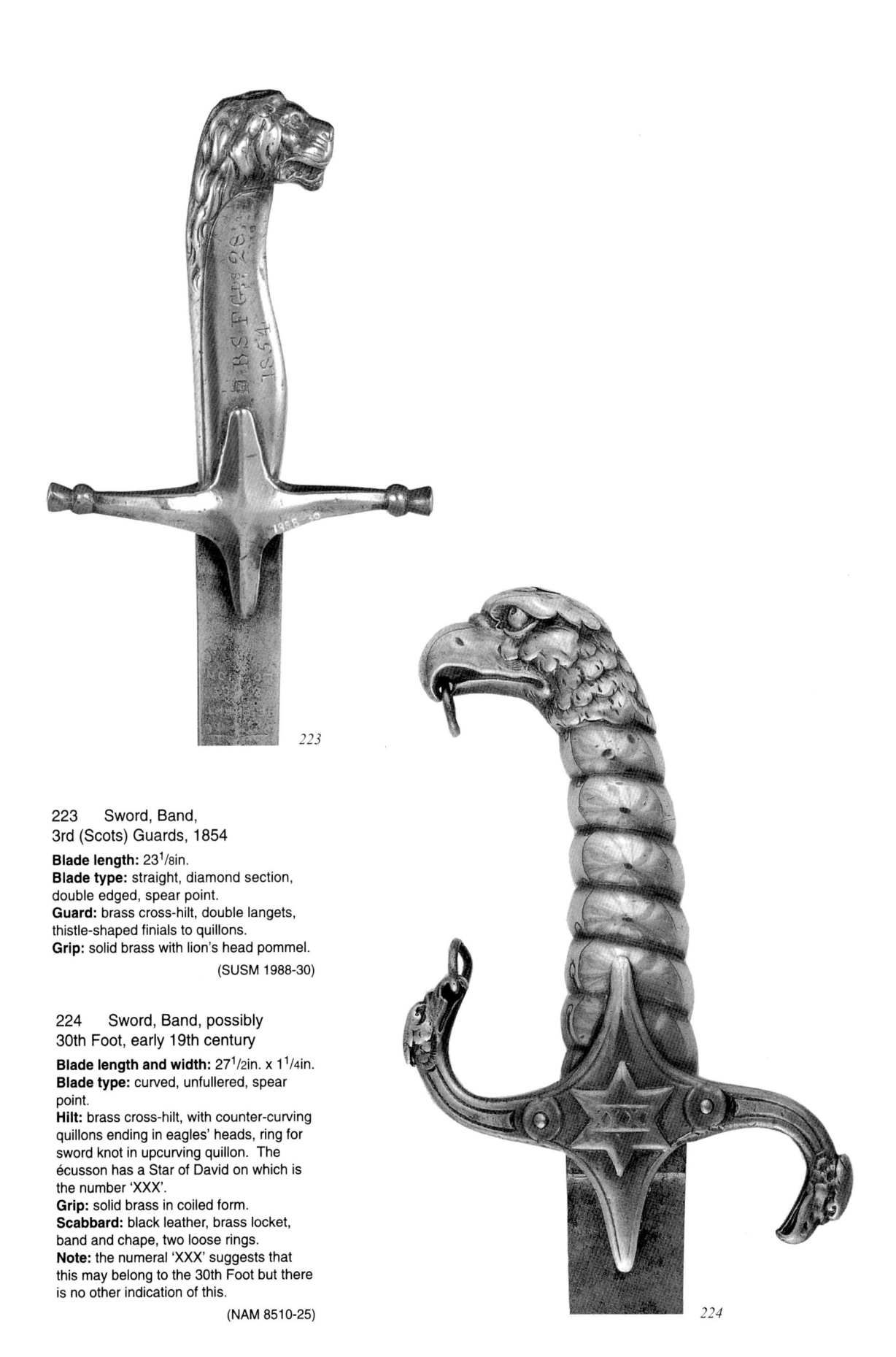

223

**223 Sword, Band,
3rd (Scots) Guards, 1854**

Blade length: 23 1/8in.
Blade type: straight, diamond section, double edged, spear point.
Guard: brass cross-hilt, double langets, thistle-shaped finials to quillons.
Grip: solid brass with lion's head pommel.

(SUSM 1988-30)

**224 Sword, Band, possibly
30th Foot, early 19th century**

Blade length and width: 27 1/2in. x 1 1/4in.
Blade type: curved, unfullered, spear point.
Hilt: brass cross-hilt, with counter-curving quillons ending in eagles' heads, ring for sword knot in upcurving quillon. The écusson has a Star of David on which is the number 'XXX'.
Grip: solid brass in coiled form.
Scabbard: black leather, brass locket, band and chape, two loose rings.
Note: the numeral 'XXX' suggests that this may belong to the 30th Foot but there is no other indication of this.

(NAM 8510-25)

224

Drummers', Band and Pioneer Swords

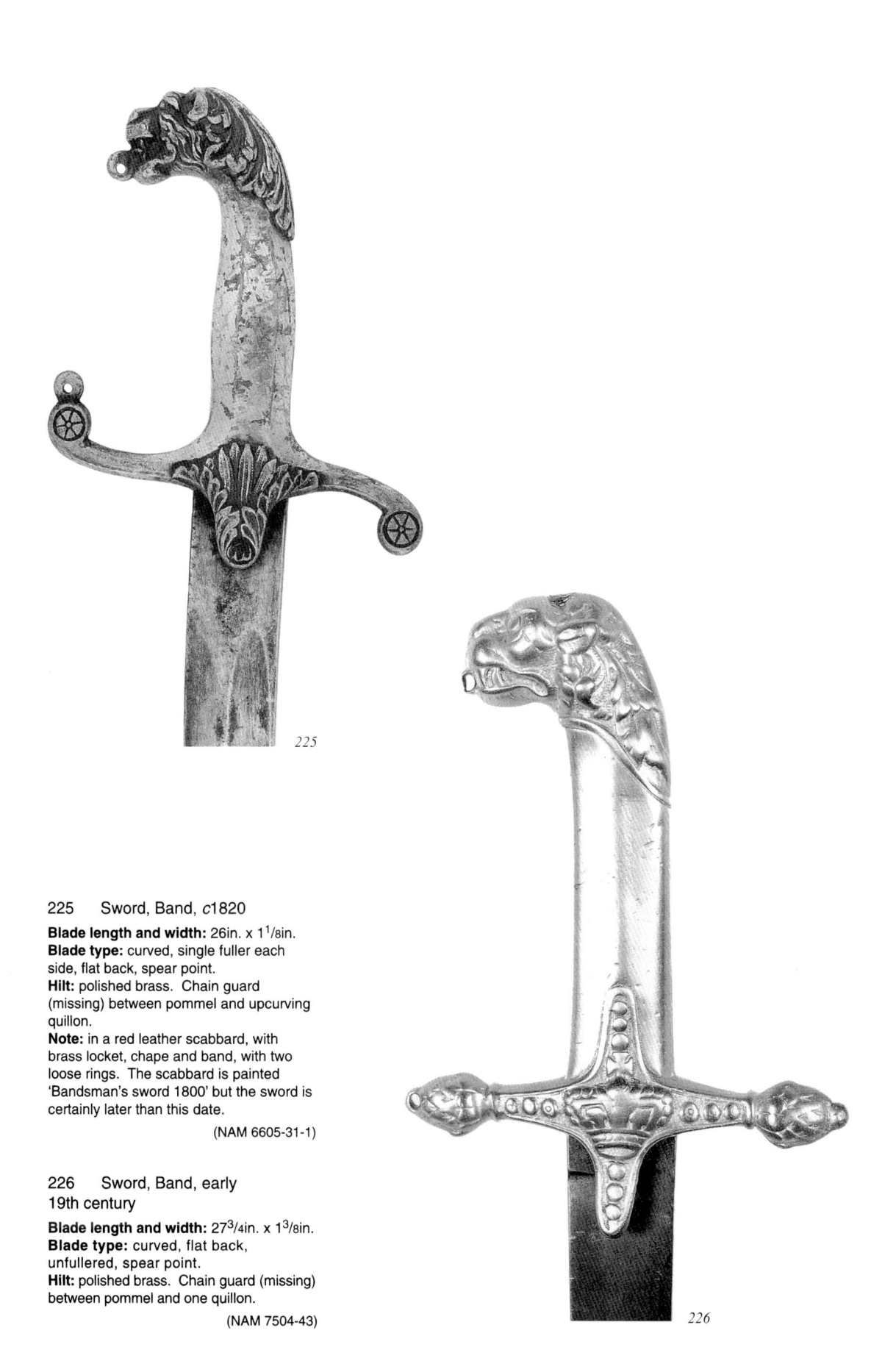

225 Sword, Band, *c*1820

Blade length and width: 26in. x 1 1/8in.
Blade type: curved, single fuller each side, flat back, spear point.
Hilt: polished brass. Chain guard (missing) between pommel and upcurving quillon.
Note: in a red leather scabbard, with brass locket, chape and band, with two loose rings. The scabbard is painted 'Bandsman's sword 1800' but the sword is certainly later than this date.

(NAM 6605-31-1)

226 Sword, Band, early 19th century

Blade length and width: 27 3/4in. x 1 3/8in.
Blade type: curved, flat back, unfullered, spear point.
Hilt: polished brass. Chain guard (missing) between pommel and one quillon.

(NAM 7504-43)

Drummers', Band and Pioneer Swords

227 Sword, Band-masters' (?), 30th Foot, mid-19th century

(NAM 8005-30)

228 Sword, Pioneers', c1820

Blade length and width: 22in. x 1 1/2in., swelling to 1 3/4in. at widest.
Blade type: curved, spear point, saw-toothed back.
Guard: brass knucklebow with 'GR', of Infantry, Officers', Pattern 1803.
Hilt mounts: brass, lion's head pommel.
Grip: wood, covered with fishskin and bound with brass wire.
Scabbard: black leather, brass locket (hole for frog stud) and chape.

(SUSM 1935-258)

229 Sword, Pioneers', Pattern 1856

Blade length and width: 22 1/2in. x 1 3/8in.
Blade type: double edged for last 6in.
Guard: brass, sword knot slit near pommel.
Grip: brass.
Scabbard: black leather, brass mounts.
Sword weight: 2lb 4 1/2oz.
Scabbard weight: 13oz.

(NAM 6702-3)

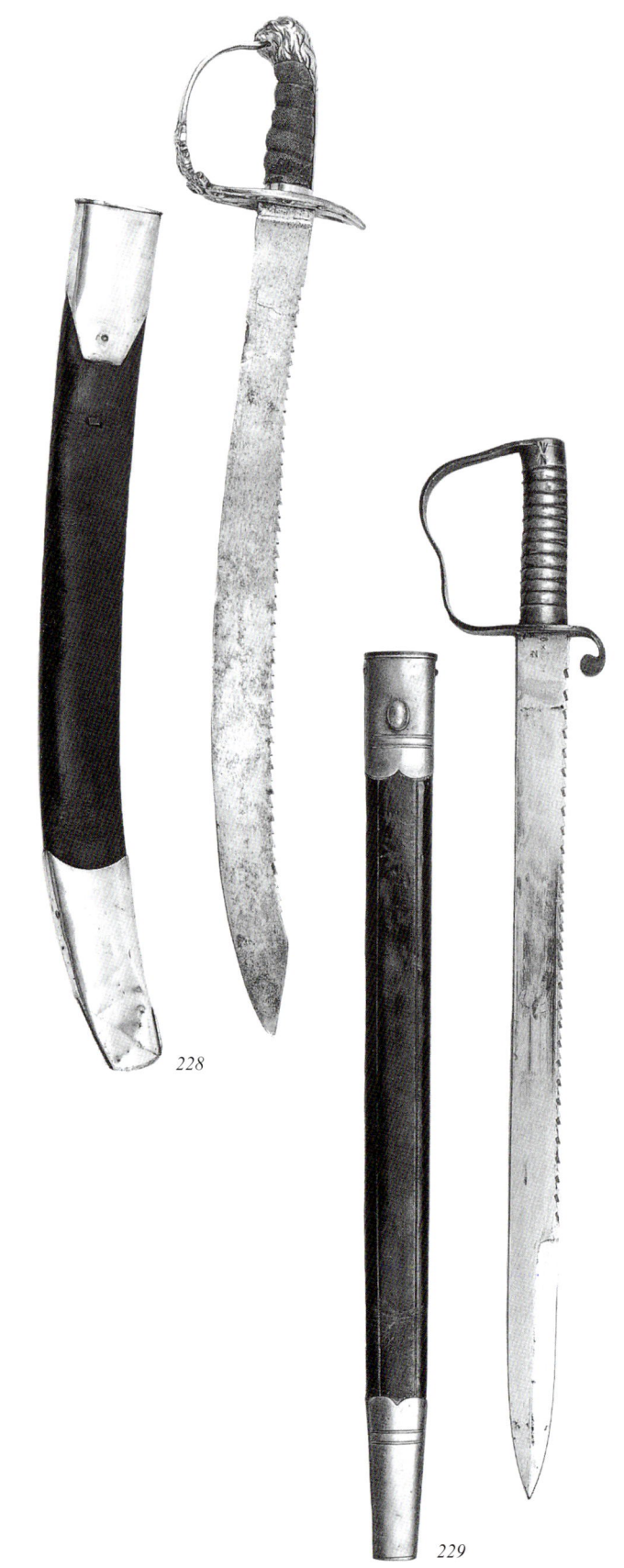

As noted earlier in this chapter, a new type of band sword with a straight broad blade and brass cruciform hilt was coming into fashion in the 1840s in dismounted units. And from 1856, a regulation pattern of this type was prescribed for bandsmen of all dismounted units (except Highland regiments, where the broadsword was worn until officially replaced by the dirk in 1871, (see Chapter 8)). Thereafter, bandsmen followed drummers and buglers, line regiments adopting the brass-hilted drummers' patterns and rifle regiments taking the iron-hilted buglers' versions.

Band-masters might have been expected to have carried even more decorative swords than the bandsmen. But equally they are likely to be even rarer although the sword illustrated, (Plate 227) may be that of a band-master.

Pioneers' Swords

By 1780, pioneers had become an integral part of every infantry regiment. The basic tools of their trade were saws and axes for cutting down trees and erecting obstacles and living accommodation. They were fighting men as well - indeed, the later Indian Army had pioneer regiments - and they therefore carried weapons, including at times swords and muskets.

When swords were withdrawn from infantry privates in 1784, they would seem also to have disappeared from the equipment of pioneers, who then carried muskets and bayonets only. But at roughly the same time, a new type of short sword, with a saw-back to the blade, was appearing among sappers and pioneers on the Continent. It was adopted by Austrian engineer troops as early as 1764[21] and by Prussian pioneers around 1810.[22] This type of sword was intended obviously to be both a weapon and a working tool. It is difficult to regard it as particularly effective in either role but its popularity continued to spread so it may have been more effective relatively than modern critics might think.

This type of sword was adopted in the Russian Army in the middle 1820s,[23] and as early as 1820 in the British Army, (Plate 228).[24] The first and only regulation pattern - the Sword, Pioneers', Brass Hilt - was introduced in 1856, (Plate 229).[25] This had a brass hilt, with stirrup guard with a sword knot slit near the pommel. The grip consisted of a ribbed brass strip on each side of the tang, fastened with four iron rivets through the tang. The almost straight blade was $22^{1}/_{2}$ inches long and $1^{3}/_{8}$ inches wide at the shoulder. From a point about $1^{1}/_{8}$ inches from the shoulder to within $5^{1}/_{2}$ inches of the point, the back of the blade was saw-toothed with a double row of teeth. The scabbard was of black leather, with brass locket and chape, the locket having a frog stud. The sword weighed 2lb $4^{1}/_{2}$ ozs and the scabbard 13 ozs. The sword was declared obsolete in 1904.[26]

Chapter 12: Notes

1. PRO. WO 3/405, p234.

2. See page 211.

3. See also Chapter 8, note 19.

4. The evidence is in *Army Equipment 1865- Part VII - Hospital Service*, where there is a drawing of this sword, described as being 'of the pattern carried by infantry drummers prior to 1865'. The dimensions of this sword are given under the heading 'Sergeants, Medical Staff Corps' in the War Office *Table of Arms 1893*.

5. Spencer-Smith, *op. cit.*, No 65.

6. By David Cunliffe, reproduced in *JSAHR*, Vol XLVI, 1968, p63.

7. See also RA IX/406; other undated specimens are RA XXV/47 and NAM 8310-145.

8. *LC* 7953, 1 October 1895.

9. The Sword, Buglers', Mark II is less common than the Sword, Drummers', Mark II, but specimens are RA IX/539, belonging to the Royal Irish Rifles, and NAM 6312-25-135.

10. *LC* 10559, 1 July 1901.

11. *LC* 12058, 1 March 1904.

12. *LC* 15812, 1 February 1912.

13. *JSAHR*, Vol XVII, 1938, p100.

14. See G R Worrall, 'The First Life Guards Trumpeters Sword' *Antique Arms and Militaria*, Vol IV, 1981, p16.

15. Spencer-Smith, *op. cit.*, p24 and No 13.

16. NAM 7504-35 -12 and -64.

17. The last civilian band-master was engaged in 1905.

18. *JSAHR*, Vol XVII, 1938, p143.

19. This type of sword is well illustrated by Hull, *op. cit.* - see, for example, his illustrations of the Grenadier Guards band (dated July 1829) of a 3rd Foot Guards bugleman (dated August 1828) and of the band of the 17th Foot (dated 1830). There are numerous specimens in the NAM and Royal Armouries.

20. See, for example, NAM 8009-106 (Nottinghamshire Rifle Volunteers), NAM 8704-24 (Gloucestershire Engineer Volunteers).

21. For example, the *Sapeur-säbel, Model 1769*, and the *Pontonier und Tschaikisten -säbel, Model 1764*.

22. See Wagner, *op. cit.*, p272.

23. See NAM 6501-184-1.

24. See a pioneer sword, (NAM 5608-57) by Thomas Craven, who was in business in Birmingham apparently from 1818 to 1820. But see also Chapter 10 for the association of this type of sword with the Foot Artillery.

25. General Order of 11 November 1856.

26. *LC* 12058, 1 March 1904.

13. Practice Swords

The effective use of the sword as a weapon requires much training and practice. In turn, the type of exercise determines whether or not a special practice weapon is required.

Until the second half of the nineteenth century, sword training in the British Army consisted largely of going through a formal sequence of cuts, parries and thrusts, varied occasionally by cutting or thrusting at dummies. For this type of training the regulation issue sword could be used since there was little risk of damage.[1] It may have been the experience of the Crimean War, followed closely by that of the Indian Mutiny, which led in the second half of the century to an emphasis on training more on the lines of fencing, which in turn produced a need for specialised training weapons.

In 1856 a special practice sword was introduced for the cavalry.[2] This consisted of a Heavy Cavalry Pattern 1821 hilt fitted with an unfullered blade, double edged, with a rounded tip, 34$\frac{1}{4}$ inches long. In 1869, matters were taken a stage further when cavalry regiments were ordered to provide themselves with practice swords by casting - that is to say, condemning - 30 of the worst of the troopers' swords in the regiment;[3] presumably these then had their edges blunted and the points rounded by the regimental armourer. This was followed in 1870 by the introduction of the Sword, Practice, Cavalry, Pattern 1856, Converted, which was similar to the Pattern 1856 except that it had a Cavalry, Pattern 1853 hilt.[4] This was followed in 1886 by the Sword, Practice, Mounted Corps, Pattern 1886, Mark II, which was essentially a Cavalry Pattern 1885 sword with blunted edges and rounded point, and with the blade length reduced to 33$\frac{3}{8}$ inches.[5]

A practice sword for dismounted corps was introduced in 1891.[6] It was in fact the Sword, Staff-Sergeants', Pattern 1889, for dismounted corps, with a gilt or iron Gothic hilt, but with the point rounded off, reducing the blade length to 31$\frac{3}{4}$ inches. It was declared obsolete in 1898, presumably because the blade no longer corresponded to that of the new straight infantry blade introduced in 1892, but possibly also because it was realised that staff-sergeants were not likely in future to find much use for a sword for fighting.[7]

In parallel with these practice swords, which all approximated to the actual fighting patterns, a parallel series of swords were introduced for use in the gymnasium. These were akin to the traditional fencing sabre. The first of this series was the Sword, Practice, Gymnasia, Pattern 1864, which had a plain, black japanned bowl

Practice Swords

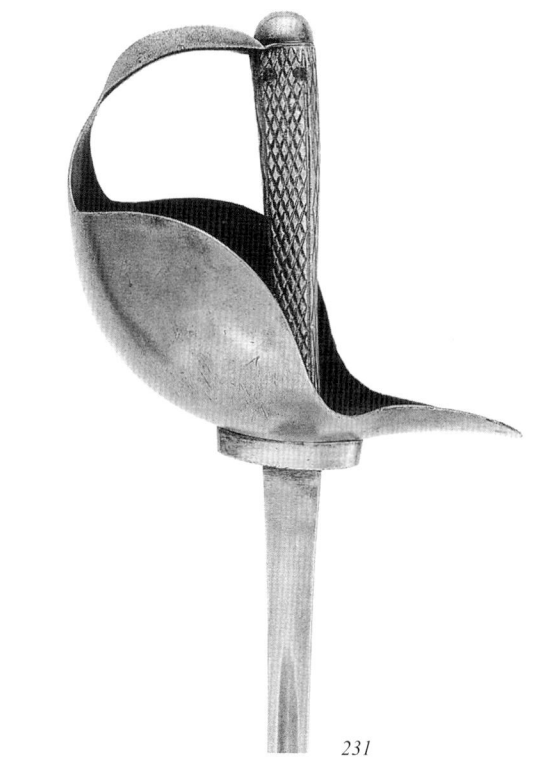

230

231

230   Sword, Practice, Gymnasia, Pattern 1899

Blade length and width: 33in. x ⁵⁄₈in.
Blade type: detachable, straight, flat back, single fuller each side, button tip.
Guard: sheet steel.
Grip: wood, covered with fishskin and bound with steel wire.

(MoD Pattern Room, Nottingham)

231   Sword, Practice, Gymnasia, Pattern 1907, Mark I

Blade length and width: 34in. x ⁵⁄₈in.
Blade type: similar to Pattern 1899.
Grip: aluminium, removable by unscrewing pommel cap.

(NAM 8004-77-2)

232   Sword, Practice, Gymnasia, Pattern 1911, Mark I

Note: steel bowl, aluminium grip, removable blade.

(NAM 7205-7-33)

232

Practice Swords

guard, similar to the Cavalry Pattern 1864 guard, but without the 'Maltese Cross'.[8] The blade was slightly curved, with a single fuller and rounded point, 34 3/4 inches long but only 7/8 inch wide; it was replaceable by unscrewing the pommel cap. This sword was declared obsolete in 1892 and replaced by the Sword, Practice, Gymnasia, Pattern 1895.[9] This was very similar to an ordinary fencing sabre, with a narrow, straight blade, cut off square at the tip, and with a deep bowl guard. The tang of the blade was secured through the grip by a pommel nut, enabling a broken blade to be easily replaced. The blade length was 33 7/8 inches and the sword weighed only 1lb 2 ozs. It was succeeded by the Sword, Practice, Gymnasia, Pattern 1899[10] and the Sword, Practice, Gymnasia, Pattern 1895, Converted.[11] These two swords are practically identical and differed only from the Pattern 1895 in having perforated bowl guards, (Plate 230). The blade of the Pattern 1899 sword was 33 inches long and 5/8 inch wide; that of the Pattern 1895, Converted was 33 inches long and 7/8 inch wide.

The series of gymnasia practice swords continued with the Sword, Practice, Gymnasia, Pattern 1904, Mark II, which had a slightly stiffer blade and an unperforated bowl.[12] This was replaced in turn by the Swords, Practice, Gymnasia, Pattern 1907, Marks I and II, approved in November 1907[13] and December 1909[14] respectively. These were practically identical, (Plate 231). They differed from the Pattern 1904 mainly in having thin, hollow aluminium-alloy grips, the pommel cap having a screwdriver slot to enable the blade to be replaced very quickly. The blades were 34 inches long and ended in a button. Upon the introduction of the Mark II version, with its slightly stiffer blade, the Mark I was relegated to dismounted corps use only.

Both marks were abolished in 1912 and replaced by the Sword, Practice, Gymnasia, Pattern 1911, Mark I which differed essentially in having an aluminium grip similar to the famous Cavalry Pattern 1908,[15] (Plate 232). (The introduction of the 1908 pattern had already led in 1910 to the abolition of the 1886 Mounted Corps practice sword which no longer remotely corresponded to the service weapon).[16]

No further patterns of practice sword were produced before 1914.

Lead-cutting Swords

There remains the curious phenomenon of the lead-cutting swords which every serious student of the subject will have encountered at some stage. They are characterised by very wide, heavy blades and cutlass-type hilts.

The practice of cutting through bars of lead in order to develop strength in the arm, as well as to acquire the most effective cutting technique, appears to date back at least to the fifteenth century among the Arabs, whose scimitars were legendary for their sharpness.[17] It may well, however, go back even earlier, to the eleventh century, since the feat of cutting a lead bar in two was sometimes called the '*Coeur de Lion*' after King Richard I, who had allegedly performed this feat in front of Saladin.

Practice Swords

The use of this form of practice in the British Army in the nineteenth century is described in detail in a now rare book by John Musgrove Waite - *Lessons in Sabre, Singlestick, Sabre and Bayonet, and Sword Feats* - published in London 1880.[18] Waite, who had been a corporal-major in the 2nd Life Guards, stated that the sword generally used for this purpose was a somewhat longer and heavier version of the naval cutlass, the best size for an average man having a blade about 31 inches long and 1³/₄ inches wide, the sword weighing about 3¹/₄ lbs.

Waite appears in fact to be describing the first and only regulation pattern of lead-cutting sword - the Sword, Lead-cutting, No 1, Pattern 1870, with mould for casting the lead bars, introduced in September 1870, (Plate 233).[19] But he goes on to say that the size and weight depend upon the individual's strength so that a very powerful man would find a larger sword more suitable; and indeed there exist lead-cutting swords of different sizes and weights, marked 'No.1', 'No.2', 'No.3' and 'No.4', made by Wilkinsons.[20] The last of these, (Plate 234) weighs nearly 4lbs, and to cut horizontally and accurately requires an exceptionally powerful forearm and wrist. These numbered patterns follow the same general form as the Pattern 1870 sword, with cutlass-type hilts, iron grips (some covered with leather),[21] very wide blades and leather scabbards. The introduction of these numbered patterns is not recorded in the *Lists of Changes* and they would appear to have been a private venture by Wilkinsons; they may have preceded the official 1870 pattern and provided the model for it. But is is also worth noting that whereas the Pattern 1870 has a guard very similar to the Pattern 1845 naval cutlass, some of the numbered patterns have turned-down hilts of the same form as the Pattern 1859 cutlass. Whether these differences are significant is not clear.

The lead bar used was ideally about 12 inches long, of triangular form, and the cut was made against one edge. Initially, the faces of the bar would be about 1 inch wide but as strength and proficiency increased the bar should be increased in size until a man could cut one with faces of 1¹/₂ inches. At that point, the swordsman should move on to cutting at a sheep's carcass or a leg of lamb. The bar of lead could either be suspended or placed upright on a stool, or even thrown in the air and cut; finally it could be supported horizontally and cut with a downward chop. Waite also recommended that the blade should be greased with tallow to provide some lubrication to the cut but also to show which precise section of the blade actually made contact, the aim, of course, being to strike the bar at the exact point of percussion of the blade (the equivalent of the 'sweet spot' in a tennis racquet).

It is not clear, however, whether this form of practice was adopted universally in the British cavalry, and how long it lasted - or, indeed, whether all men in a regiment used this form of practice or whether it was limited only to certain crack swordsmen.

Linked to these lead-cutting swords, in terms of curiosity only, are the swords labelled as 'Handkerchief Cutters'. Three of these swords have come to the atten-

Practice Swords

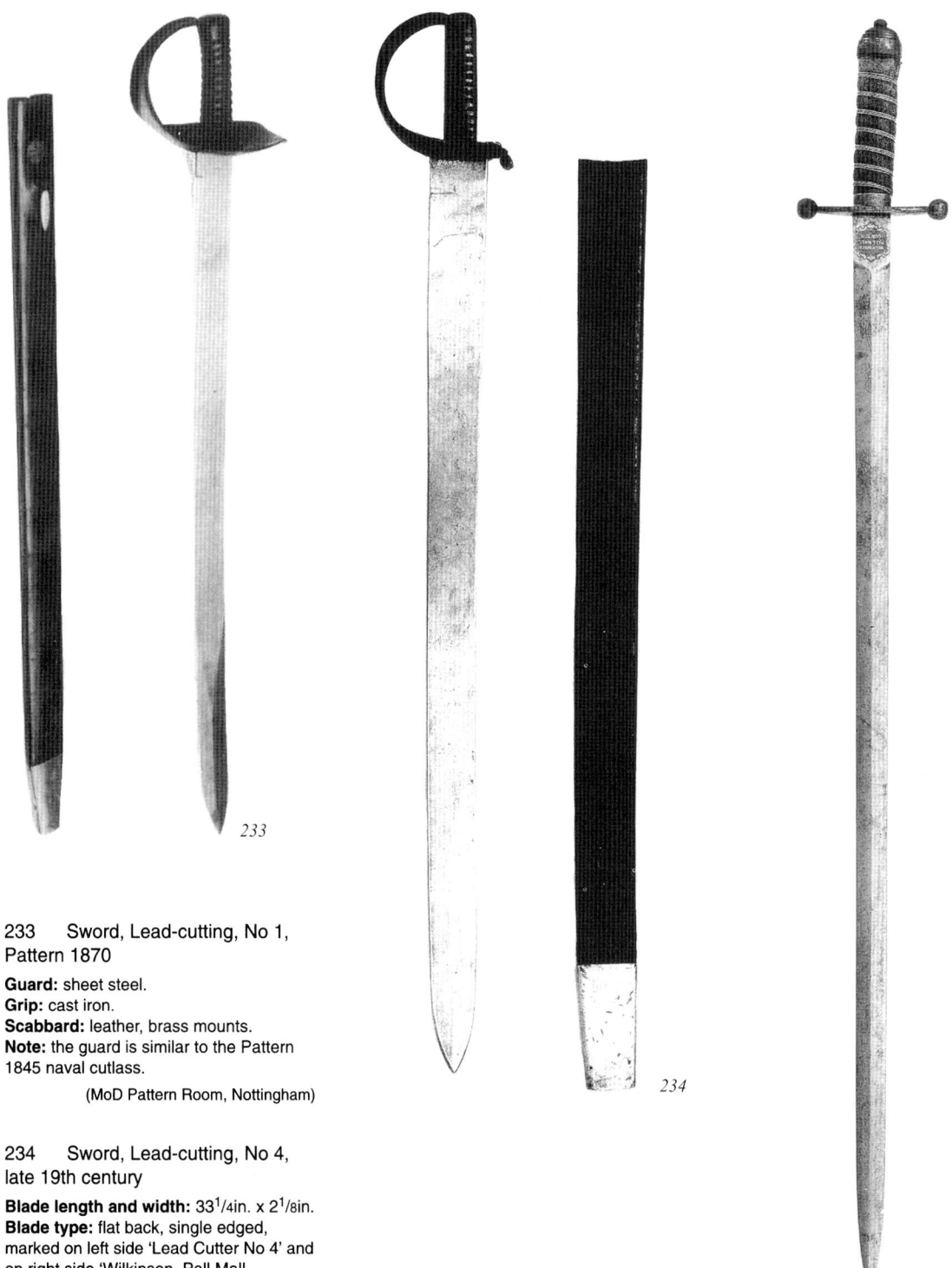

233

233 Sword, Lead-cutting, No 1, Pattern 1870

Guard: sheet steel.
Grip: cast iron.
Scabbard: leather, brass mounts.
Note: the guard is similar to the Pattern 1845 naval cutlass.

(MoD Pattern Room, Nottingham)

234 Sword, Lead-cutting, No 4, late 19th century

Blade length and width: $33^{1}/_{4}$in. x $2^{1}/_{8}$in.
Blade type: flat back, single edged, marked on left side 'Lead Cutter No 4' and on right side 'Wilkinson, Pall Mall, London'.
Hilt: cutlass guard in sheet steel, black japanned iron grip.
Sword weight: 3lb 12oz.
Scabbard: black leather, with steel chape only.
Note: the fourth in a series of four such swords, increasing in weight with number.

(NAM 8405-1)

234

235 Sword, 'Handkerchief cutter'

Note: the long, diamond-section blade. The guard and pommel are of steel, and the grip is wood, covered with fishskin and bound with steel wire.

(RA IX-1487)

235

268

tion of the author, viz. a sword in the Royal Armouries (RA IX-1487), a sword in the Guards Museum (Accession No 359) and one formerly in the possession of a Dr Allen in South Africa. The first and third of these swords are identical and consist of a straight, diamond section blade, 32 inches long, with a simple cross-hilt in steel, (Plate 235). The sword in the Guards Museum has an identical blade but a plain brass knucklebow hilt; it is engraved with the name of Quarter-Master-Sergeant Glynn, of the Grenadier Guards. All three swords were made by Wilkinsons but the blades are not numbered and they were clearly made to special order. One assumes that they were made for that trick of swordsmanship which consists of throwing up a handkerchief and slicing it in two in mid-air, in the same way that Oriental scimitars were reputed to be tested against a silk scarf. What is curious is that these 'Handkerchief Cutters' have straight, not curved, blades.

Chapter 13: Notes

1. In the Royal Armouries are two wooden replica swords $c1800$, found at Alnwick Castle and apparently made for a local volunteer corps of cavalry. It seems likely also that the old singlestick was used on occasion for teaching the preliminaries of swordsmanship.

2. See the specimen in the Pattern Room, Nottingham, labelled 'Sword, Practice, Cavalry, Model 1856'.

3. General Order 89, 1 September 1869.

4. Sealed pattern in the Pattern Room, Nottingham, SP 278.

5. *LC* 5092, 1 December 1886; sealed pattern 681 in the Pattern Room, Nottingham.

6. *LC* 6528, 1 October, 1891; sealed patterns 801 and 800 in the Pattern Room, Nottingham.

7. *LC* 9207, 1 October 1898.

Practice Swords

8. *LC* 1026, 1 January 1865; sealed pattern 865 in the Pattern Room, Nottingham, approved 21 December 1864.

9. *LC* 7848, 1 July 1895.

10. *LC* 9984, 1 January 1900.

11. Specimen in the Pattern Room, Nottingham.

12. *LC* 12328, 1 September 1904.

13. *LC* 13993, 1 January 1908.

14. *LC* 15152, 1 August 1910.

15. *LC* 15813, 1 February 1912.

16. *LC* 14972, 1 March 1910.

17. See the chapter by Professor Edmund Bosworth in Bernard Lewis, ed., *The World of Islam*, London (1976)

18. I am indebted to Mr Percy Wood for drawing my attention to this book.

19. *LC* 1948, 1 September 1870.

20. In the Royal Armouries are specimens of the No 1 (IX-315) and No 2 (IX-1454 and 1460) swords weighing 3lbs 1oz and 3lbs 7ozs respectively. The Guards Museum has another lead-cutting sword but with no number on it; it is engraved for Quarter-Master-Sergeant Glynn, Grenadier Guards. It has a scroll hilt in brass and was clearly a special order although it approximates to a No 4.

21. Mr G R Worrall informs me that some, at least, of these swords had the iron grips covered originally with leather.

Appendix 1. Sword Knots

Officers' sword knots to 1914

In the shock of combat a sword could be easily knocked out of, or could fall from, the user's hand. The original purpose of a sword knot was therefore to attach the sword to the user's wrist so that even if the sword was knocked out of his hand he could still retrieve it. In the course of time, this practical purpose gradually lost its importance, and the sword knot is now purely an ornament.

Sword knots were originally looped round some convenient point of the guard or grip - as, for example, in the Pattern 1796 infantry sword. Towards the end of the eighteenth century, specific provision began to be made for them, either in the form of a small loose ring inserted through the top of a knucklebow guard or, more commonly, in the form of a slot in the guard itself - as in the Pattern 1796 light cavalry sword. A variation was the hole through the top of the grip in the Pattern 1831 general officers' sword. Double slots appeared in the Pattern 1864 cavalry troopers' sword, which was unique in this respect among British regulation patterns although double slots appeared in some Continental swords, for example, the Austrian cavalry sabre Models 1850 and 1869.

There were three basic types of British sword knots: woven ribands, leather straps and plaited cords. These could end in a simple fringe, a bullion (gold-plated wire) tassel, or a plaited 'acorn'. With the introduction in 1899 of the brown leather scabbard for use in the field with all swords, a universal pattern of sword knot - consisting of a brown leather strap with brown leather acorn - was also introduced for use with it. In dismounted corps, sword knots were normally worn wound round the upper part of the guard; but in the cavalry they were normally worn loose, presumably because of the difficulty of unwinding the knot when mounted.

Finally, it must be emphasised that sword knots - being easily interchangeable - are not a reliable guide to the identification or dating of a particular sword. But on the other hand, no sword can be properly regarded as complete without its appropriate knot.

Appendix 1. Sword Knots

General Officers (and Field Marshals from 1831)

1796-1831   Crimson and gold cord, bullion tassel.

1831-1914   Crimson and gold cord and acorn.

1st Life Guards

1796-1822   White leather strap, crimson and gold bullion tassel.
Undress: crimson and gold riband, bullion tassel.

1822-31   Crimson and gold riband, gold bullion tassel.

1831-57   Dress: white leather strap, crimson and gold bullion tassel.
Levées etc: crimson and gold riband, gold bullion tassel.
Undress: white leather strap and tassel.

1857-72   Dress: crimson and gold leather strap, crimson and gold bullion tassel.
Undress: white leather strap and tassel.

1872-1914   Dress: white leather strap, crimson and gold bullion tassel.
Undress: white leather strap and bullion tassel.

2nd Life Guards

1796-1872   As 1st Life Guards

1872-1911   Dress: crimson and gold leather strap, crimson and gold bullion tassel.
Undress: white leather strap and tassel.

1911-14   Dress: gold and crimson embroidered riband, gold and crimson bullion tassel.
Undress: white leather strap and bullion tassel.

Royal Horse Guards

1796-1822   As Life Guards.

1822-31   Dress: crimson and gold embroidered strap and bullion tassel, with crimson velvet slide embroidered with royal cypher and crown. Levées etc: as Life Guards.
Undress: white leather strap and tassel.

1831-72   Unchanged, except that velvet slide disappeared in early part of this period.

1872-1911   As 2nd Life Guards.

1911-14   Dress: crimson leather strap, gilt embroidered, crimson and gold bullion tassel.
Undress: white leather strap and bullion tassel.

Appendix 1. Sword Knots

Heavy Cavalry

1822-31	Dress: crimson and gold riband, bullion tassel. Undress: white leather strap, crimson and gold tassel.
1831-83	White leather strap, crimson and gold tassel.
1883-98	White leather strap, gold acorn.
1898-1914	Dress: white leather strap and gold acorn, except: 3rd and 6th Dragoon Guards, 1st Dragoons - gold cord and acorn. 7th Dragoon Guards - gold and black cord and acorn. Royal Scots Greys - gold cord and thistle end. 6th Dragoons - gold and crimson cord and acorn. Undress: white leather strap and gold acorn, except that 2nd and 7th Dragoon Guards, 1st and 6th Dragoons had a white acorn.

Light Dragoons

1796-1822	Gold cord, bullion tassel.
1822-31	Crimson and gold cord, gold bullion tassel.
1831-55	Gold cord and acorn.
1855-60	Dress: gold cord and acorn. Undress: regimental pattern.

Hussars

1822-31	As Light Dragoons
1831-55	Crimson and gold cord and acorn.
1855-83	Dress: as above. Undress: regimental pattern.
1883-1900	Gold and crimson cord, gold acorn.
1900-14	As above, except that 13th and 14th Hussars had a gold cord and acorn, and 10th Hussars had a crimson leather strap embroidered with gold wire.

Lancers

1822-1914	Crimson and gold cord, gold acorn.

Royal Artillery

1788-1857	Gold and crimson riband and tassel.
1857-1914	Gold cord and acorn.

Appendix 1. Sword Knots

Royal Engineers

1788-1824	Crimson and gold riband.
1824-57	Crimson and gold riband, bullion tassel.
1857-72	Gold cord and acorn.
1872-1914	Dress: gold cord and acorn. Undress: white leather strap and gold acorn.

Foot Guards

1788-1855	Crimson and gold riband, bullion tassel.
1855-83	Dress: gold cord and acorn. Undress: white cord, gold acorn.
1883-1914	Dress: gold cord and acorn. Undress: white leather strap, gold acorn.

Infantry of the line (including light infantry and fusiliers)

1788-1822	Crimson and gold riband, fringed end or tassel.
1822-57	Crimson and gold riband, bullion tassel.
1857-74	Crimson and gold riband, gold acorn.
1874-1914	Dress: crimson and gold riband, gold acorn. Undress: white leather strap and gold acorn. 43rd Regiment *c*1805-81 black leather cord with tassel. 52nd Regiment *c*1805-81 black leather strap with acorn. Oxfordshire Light Infantry 1881-96, 1st Bn - as for 43rd; 2nd Bn - as for 52nd. 1896-1908 both Battalions as for 43rd. Oxfordshire and Buckinghamshire Light Infantry 1908-14 - as for 43rd.

Rifle regiments

From
formation
to 1914   Black leather strap or plaited cord, and acorn.

Departmental Corps

Royal Staff Corps
1799-1838   As for infantry of the line.

Commissariat
*c*1796-1869   As for infantry of the line.

Royal Waggon Train
1799-1833   White leather strap, crimson and gold bullion tassel.

Appendix 1. Sword Knots

Land Transport Corps and Military Train
1855-69   Gold cord and acorn.

Control Department
1869-76   Blue and gold cord and acorn.

Commissariat and Transport
1876-89   As Control Department

Army Service Corps
1889-1914   As Control Department

Storekeeper-General's Staff
1788-1857   As for infantry.

Military Stores Department
1857-69   As for infantry.

Ordnance Store Department
1876-96   As for infantry.

Army Ordnance Department
1896-1914   Colonel: gold and crimson cord and acorn. Below colonel: as for infantry.

Medical Department
1796-1883   As for infantry.
1883-98   Gold and black cord and acorn.

Medical Staff Corps and Army Hospital Corps
1855-98   Officers: as for infantry of the line.

Royal Army Medical Corps
1898-1914   Gold and cherry riband and acorn.

Veterinary Department

1859-1906   Gold and crimson cord, gold acorn.

Royal Army Veterinary Corps
1906-11   Dress: gold and crimson cord and acorn.
            Undress: white leather strap and acorn.
1911-14   Gold and crimson cord and acorn.

Royal Army Pay Corps

Paymasters-General
1796-1875   As for infantry.

Army Pay Department
1875-81   Crimson and gold riband and acorn.
1881-1914   Yellow and gold cord and acorn.

Appendix 2. Markings on Swords

1. Officers' swords

Officers invariably purchased their own swords prior to 1914 from private makers or retailers. Some manufacturers, such as Thomas Gill and James Woolley, in the earlier period, and Henry Wilkinson & Son, in the later one, sold direct to the customer. In many - perhaps most - cases, however, the manufacturer sold to military outfitters, who then sold on to the customer; in this case, the name appearing on the sword is usually the name of the retailer, rather than the actual maker. Wilkinsons did both.

A special case is that of John Justus Runkel, whose name is perhaps the commonest to be found on late eighteenth century blades. The blades, usually marked 'Solingen', were sometimes made up into swords and sold by Runkel as such; in other cases, the blades were sold on to English firms who then had them made up into complete swords. Whether Runkel ever made blades himself or whether, as is generally supposed, he was simply an importer is not as yet clear. Runkel was certainly admitted to the Cutlers' Company in 1796 and in 1806 took an apprentice; his name is not recorded in the Company's records after that.[1]

Some swords are dated; the majority are not. Some makers, notably Mole and Wilkinson, numbered their blades but the only known record of such numbers is that of Wilkinsons. It goes back only to 1854 and even then starts only at 5000. In the absence of date or number, the maker's or retailer's name can provide a useful indication of dates although seldom with absolute precision. A useful, although not wholly accurate, list of cutlers and retailers is contained in Volume II of W E May and P W G Annis, *Swords for Sea Service*, London, HMSO (1970); it covers Scottish and Irish firms only sketchily. A fuller and more accurate list is greatly to be desired.

Officers' blades commonly carry the cypher of the reigning monarch but in the case of George III and Victoria this does not give much useful help with dating because of their long reigns. Blades from the second half of the nineteenth century frequently, (in Wilkinsons' case, invariably), have a circular or polygonal, indented proof mark on the ricasso, often enclosing the maker's initial or symbol - an innovation which Henry Wilkinson claimed to have introduced in 1854 to certify the quality of the blade. In practice, these proof marks rapidly ceased to be real guarantees of quality (except perhaps in the case of Wilkinsons) and became simply a form of advertising, bearing the initial or symbol of the retailer, rather than the maker. There

Appendix 2. Markings on Swords

is a very useful list of such proof marks in May and Annis, *Swords for Sea Service*, Vol II, pp338-341.

These marks are not found on eighteenth or early nineteenth century blades but some makers were fond of putting a written guarantee on their blades - Thomas Gill, for example, inscribed some of his later blades 'Warranted Never to Fail', and some of his earlier blades are marked 'Warranted To Cut Iron'. Osborne and Gunby also marked some of their blades 'Warranted'.

Blades may carry the original owner's family crest or motto, or even, later in the nineteenth century, the actual initials or name. Crests and mottoes can, of course, be easily checked in heraldic dictionaries, such as James Fairbarn's *Crests of the Families of Great Britain and Ireland*, 2 Vols, Edinburgh (1860), and subsequently revised. Names, once known, can be checked against the official *Army List* or *Hart's Army List*.

Apart from the name or initials of the owner's regiment, the other mark commonly encountered is that which marks the percussion point of the blade - that is to say, the point at which a cut with the sword exerts its maximum effect. It is sometimes marked on the back of the blade by an arrow, thus:

$$C \gg \!\!\!\longrightarrow P$$

or by a simple letter P - or even on some eighteenth century blades by a floral knot or similar device. But most swords - and particularly those with rounded backs - do not have a percussion mark.

Generally, the decoration on officers' blades was not standardised although from time to time certain things had to be included, such as crossed lances in the case of the Pattern 1822 Lancers Dress sword, and battle honours in the case of the Foot Guards after 1857. Decoration was intended to be viewed with the point uppermost. It is the reverse with hilt decoration. Battle honours, where they appear, can be checked in N B Leslie's *Battle Honours of the British and Indian Armies*, London (1970) for the date of award and thus provide useful evidence on dating.

2. Other Ranks' swords

(a) Production markings

Before 1788, there was no system of quality control for other ranks' swords. They were purchased privately by the colonel of the regiment and he was responsible not only for the pattern but the choice of supplier, and, by implication, for the quality. There can be little doubt that in some cases quality was sacrificed to cheapness, and there was in any case little understanding of what swords should be designed to do. Thus, the only production marking on pre-1788 swords is likely to be the maker's name, although even this is missing in most cases.

Appendix 2. Markings on Swords

In 1788, as part of their recommendations on cavalry swords, the Board of General Officers laid down certain tests which all cavalry swords should, in future, be required to meet, (see Chapter 2). This implied that swords would in future need to be marked in some way to show that they had passed the regulation tests, either by a government viewer or by a viewer certified by the manufacturer. In September 1788, therefore, Joseph Witten was paid by the Board of Ordnance for punches for the application of view marks; these included the figures 1, 3, 4, 6, and 8 with a crown above (interestingly enough, the figure 9 does not seem to have been included although it became a very common mark).[2] From 1788, view marks begin to appear on cavalry blades although a large proportion, perhaps the majority, do not show such marks. This suggests that initially these marks were only applied to swords specifically ordered by the government.

The viewing marks of a crown over a single digit appear from an examination of swords in the Royal Armouries to have been linked to manufacturers, rather than, as later, to individual viewers. Thus, a crown over the figure '9' was used apparently exclusively for military swords made by Thomas Gill, while the figures '4' and '6' appear on blades submitted by James Woolley (although these numbers differ on naval weapons).

Viewing was done initially at the Tower but in 1797 a Viewing House was established at Birmingham for the convenience of the manufacturers there. Inevitably, accusations of unfair treatment and corruption arose from time to time from disappointed manufacturers, whose blades had been rejected, and it would be surprising if some of the accusations were wholly false. And as we have seen, (Chapter 2), John Gaspard Le Marchant was critical of the quality of some of the swords used in the Low Countries in 1793-94. While the viewing tests were carried out by hand to start with, by 1800, at least, they were done on a simple machine which could be adjusted to the required pressures. A letter from the East India Company in 1805 announced the purchase of three machines (one for each Presidency in India) similar to those used by the Board of Ordnance in England for testing.[3] Interestingly enough, the Company's test was more severe than that of the home authorities, its light cavalry blade being shortened by 6 inches in bending, as opposed to $5^{1}/_{2}$ inches for the British Army. That may have been a precaution against the quality of Indian manufacture.

From about 1820, an increasing proportion of swords were made at the Royal Small Arms Factory at Enfield, as a check upon the private manufacturers, and were invariably marked either 'ENFIELD' or 'EFD', followed by the last two numbers of the year of manufacture, thus 'EFD '39'.

By 1844, indeed, the number of makers in England had greatly decreased, the most prominent then being the Birmingham firms of Mole & Son and Charles Reeves

Appendix 2. Markings on Swords

& Co. The number was increased in 1849 by the appearance in the field of Henry Wilkinson & Son. Between them, Mole and Wilkinson absorbed many of the smaller firms, and others simply ceased to trade, so that by 1914 only Mole and Wilkinson remained, together with the RSAF Enfield. On occasions, English capacity had to be augmented by ordering from Solingen firms such as Weyersburg, Kirschbaum & Co.

Six other types of mark commonly appear on other ranks' swords:

(a) before 1855, swords obtained by the Board of Ordnance were often stamped with the Board's mark - a broad arrow and the letters 'BO'. After the abolition of the Board in 1855, this marking was replaced by a broad arrow and the letters 'WD', standing for 'War Department'. Swords made in England for the Indian Government bore the letters 'ISD' (India Stores Department);

(b) starting in 1855, cavalry swords have the pattern number stamped on the blade and, usually, the guard and scabbard, thus:

'/85 - Pattern 1885.
'/90 - Pattern 1890.
'/99 - Pattern 1899.

The Pattern 1908 sword, however, has the pattern mark in the form 'P '08' (or 'IP '08' for the India pattern).
Where there is more than one mark, then this is also stamped in Roman numerals - 'II' = Mark II;

(c) to avoid overstraining a blade, it was laid down after 1885 that after the initial bending tests to both sides, subsequent bending tests must be confined to one side only. Blades were then marked with an 'X' to show the side to be used;

(d) swords condemned as unfit for further service were marked with two letter Rs, back to back;

(e) swords still fit for service but obsolete or to be sold out of the service were marked with two broad arrows facing each other;

(f) finally, there were the proof marks put on by the Board of Ordnance inspectors after about 1788. Initially, these were in the form of a crown over a single number. From about 1820, this mark assumes the form of a crown over a letter

Appendix 2. Markings on Swords

over a one or two figure number. The number identified the individual viewer while the letter indicated the place of viewing:

B = Birmingham
BR = Birmingham Repair
E = Enfield
L = Liège
S = Solingen
W = Wilkinson

By 1914, the number and place of viewing marks had become elaborately systematised. As an example, the manufacturing specification for the Pattern 1892 Household Cavalry sword specified that marks were to be stamped as follows:

(i) A viewing mark on the ricasso on the left side of the blade and the bending mark 'X' on the right side when the blade was in its initial set and stiffened state;

(ii) after inspection in its polished state, a further view mark above the first;

(iii) after assembly of the sword, a third view mark on the right side of the ricasso, below the initials of the place of manufacture and above the broad arrow mark. The date of manufacture was to be placed on the left of the ricasso;

(iv) a view mark was also to be put on the guard, below the broad arrow and the place initials;

(v) on the scabbard, the view mark was to be put on the mouthpiece, together with broad arrow, date and place initials. These marks were also to be put on the inner loop.

To add to the complication, a fresh date mark was applied after re-hilting, re-testing, re-issue or in a variety of other circumstances; the old date mark was supposed to be obliterated by a diagonal line. The resulting proliferation of marks can sometimes be very difficult to 'read'.

(b) Regimental markings

There is no evidence of the existence of any standardised system of regimental markings before 1796. Some Pattern 1788 swords, as well as even earlier specimens do have regimental markings but they follow no uniform pattern and were clearly peculiar to the regiments themselves. This is what one would expect under a system in which colonels of regiments were responsible for the pattern and purchase of equipment. From 1796 onwards, regimental markings on swords become more

Appendix 2. Markings on Swords

common although the majority of surviving swords from this period do not carry such marks. The Standing Orders of the 5th Dragoon Guards issued in 1797 specify that all 'necessaries and appointments' were to be numbered with the troop letter over a consecutive troop number e.g. $\frac{A}{5}$ and it is probable that swords were intended to be marked in the same way. The Standing Orders of the 11th Light Dragoons issued in 1807 specify that swords and scabbards were to be marked with the troop letter and the man's own number.

A General Order issued on 1 January 1812 stated that arms and accoutrements were to be marked with the number or appellation of the regiment, together with the number or letter of the troop or company. This appears to have been the first attempt to impose a standard system of markings. By 1835, however, the Standing Orders of the 3rd Dragoon Guards were specifying that arms were to be marked with the regimental mark, the troop letter and the troop number, thus: $\frac{A}{50}$ 3.D.G.

Other cavalry and artillery swords of this period have the same form of marking and it is possible that this system was meant to be generally applicable to all mounted units at least, but no General Order to this effect has yet been discovered.

With the appearance in 1865 of the first volumes of *Army Equipment*, the matter was finally put upon a clear, uniform basis. These volumes set out in detail and, in many cases, with drawings, the types of equipment and scales of issue, together with instructions on maintenance, accounting, disposal and marking. Volume I, on cavalry equipment, specified that all arms would be issued already stamped with the year of issue. Regiments were required then to stamp these arms with the regimental number or letters, together with an individual number, starting with 1 and covering consecutively all men on the establishment. Thus '2 D Gds 50' meant sword No 50 belonging to the 2nd Dragoon Guards. No comprehensive list of regimental numbers or initials was given, however, nor was the size of the markings or their placement specified. Volume V, for the infantry, contained the same instructions for infantry swords, thus, '1Bn 24th Regt 29'.

These volumes were followed in 1870 with a single volume of equipment regulations which repeated the same instructions on markings. This volume was reissued in 1876 with significant changes as regards marking weapons. The year of issue was to be stamped thus: $\frac{WD}{76}$

and the regimental marks were to be in the form '1/GG' (1st Battalion, Grenadier Guards) or '2/4' (2nd Battalion, 4th Foot) or '3/DG'. For the first time, the size of the letters and numbers was specified.

Appendix 2. Markings on Swords

The reissue of 1881 made further changes. The size of letters and numbers was slightly increased, the form of regimental appellation was revised, the oblique stroke being replaced by a full stop - '1.GG' - and the consecutive number was to be placed underneath - 1.GG. Sword number 20 of A Battery, A Brigade, Royal Horse Artillery 24 would be marked, somewhat confusingly, A.A.R.H.A. Commissariat and Transport 20 swords for mounted men were to be marked with the company number and sword number: T6 but dismounted company arms were simply marked with an O or a T 36 over a consecutive Corps number - O . 24

For the first time, the locations of these markings was laid down. Swords, generally, were to be marked on the bottom of the guard. Drummers' and buglers' swords were to be marked along the edge of the grip. Scabbards with flat mouthpieces were to be marked on the top of the mouthpiece but scabbards with curved mouthpieces or no mouthpiece would be marked on the back of the mouth. Drummers' and buglers' scabbards would be marked on the frog stud which was to be filed smooth for the purpose.

The 1890 issue made further changes to take account of the fact that the infantry had now received territorial names, and the Commissariat and Transport Corps was now the Army Service Corps. Thus, the form '2,Lan' (2nd Battalion, King's Own (Royal Lancaster) Regiment replaced '2.4', the 5th Lancers became '5L' and swords for the mounted part of the Army Service Corps were marked 'ASC' over the company number over the company sword number. Ordnance Staff Corps and Medical Staff Corps swords were marked similarly. The size of letters and numbers remained at $1/8$ inch except on leather scabbards where it was reduced to $5/64$ of an inch. The locations remained much the same except in the case of the Cavalry Pattern 1882 scabbard where the marking was to be on the lower loop plate, and in the case of the Cavalry Pattern 1885 scabbard - which had fixed and opposite loops, the marking was to be on the front loop plate, the regimental appellation above the loop and the number below.

The position on markings was set out in elaborate detail in the 1912 *Instructions to Armourers*, which is reproduced as Appendix 3.

Appendix 2: Notes

1. I am indebted to Mrs Bridget Clifford, of the Royal Armouries for this information.

2. PRO. WO 52/34, p135 - quoted in May and Annis, *op. cit.*, Vol II, p334.

3. Mr Anthony Bennell kindly drew my attention to this letter, dated June 1805.

Appendix 3. The Marking of Arms, 1912

1. - MARKING OF ARMS ISSUED FROM STORE FOR OTHER THAN ORDINARY SERVICE

(i) EXTRA SERVICE ARMS	Will be marked by the A.O.D. with the distinctive letters of the issuing depot (*see* paragraph 416), and with consecutive numbers. They will receive no corps marks, except in the event of their being taken on active service, when they will receive corps marks and consecutive numbers. The size of the marks and the implements to be used for marking will be as detailed hereafter for arms issued for ordinary service.
(ii) ARMS ISSUED ON LOAN FOR TEMPORARY PURPOSE	Will not be marked.
(iii) ARMS SOLD TO THE ADMIRALTY	Will only be marked as arranged for by the Admiralty.
(iv) ARMS SOLD TO THE INDIAN GOVERNMENT	Will not be marked.
(v) ARMS HELD FOR MOBILIZATION	Will only be marked, on mobilization, with corps marks and consecutive numbers.
(vi) ARMS ISSUED TO CIVILIAN RIFLE CLUBS	Will be marked as per Appendix XXI, Part I, Equipment Regulations.
(vii) ARMS ISSUED ON PREPAYMENT TO OFFICERS OF THE REGULAR FORCES, OFFICERS, NON-COMMISSIONED OFFICERS, AND MEN OF THE SPECIAL RESERVE AND THE TERRITORIAL FORCE.	Will be marked as per Appendix XXI, Part I, Equipment Regulation.
(viii) ARMS SOLD TO ANY PURCHASER, EXCEPT AS IN (iii), (iv), (vi), AND (vii) ABOVE	Will be marked with the sale mark, ↓↑ carbines and rifles being marked on both barrel and body, near the proof marks. (This does not refer to issues to replace lost and damaged arms that have been paid for, as, in such cases, it is the lost or damaged arm, not the new one, that is paid for.)

2. - MARKING OF ARMS ISSUED FROM STORE FOR ORDINARY SERVICE

ARMS ISSUED FOR ORDINARY SERVICE will be marked as detailed below. For a full detail of the authorized abbreviations of corps titles, *see* Lists I, II, and III of this Appendix. Some illustrations of the proper juxtaposition of corps marks and consecutive numbers are given at the end of this Appendix. *The marking should be no deeper than is necessary.*

Arms, &c.		Ordnance marks	Corps marks.	Position of marks.	Letters.	Figures.	Dash lines.	Implements with which marking is to be done.	Remarks.
Carbines and rifles.	(1.) With disc embedded in butt.	Number of month and year of issue.	Corps marks and consecutive numbers.	On the disc	$\frac{5}{64}$	$\frac{5}{64}$	...	Stamps, steel, for metal.	Disc to be removed for the purpose of being marked.
	(2.) Without disc, with brass butt plate.	,, ,,	,, ,,	A.O. marks and corps marks on strap of butt plate.	...	$\frac{5}{64}$	...	Hammers, stamping.	Arms held by Reserve battalions for:- (a) Regular establishment posted for a tour of duty, and (b) advanced recruits, to be marked with the letter D in addition to corps marks and consecutive numbers.
				A.O. marks in centre of butt on right side, 2 inches from butt plate.	$\frac{5}{64}$	$\frac{5}{64}$	...	Stamps, steel, for metal.	
	(3.) Without disc, with iron butt plate.	,, ,,	,, ,,		...	$\frac{5}{64}$	...	Hammers, stamping.	
				Corps marks between A.O. marks and butt plate, close to the former.	$\frac{7}{84}$	$\frac{5}{82}$	$\frac{1}{2}$	Stamps, steel, for wood.	
	M.T.	,, ,,	,, ,,	As at (1), (2), or (3)	$\frac{5}{64}$	...	...	,, ,,	
	A.T. for .22-inch R.F. cartridges.	,, ,,	,, ,,	,, ,,	...	...	...	,, ,,	
	D.P. (issued to O.T.C contingents).	,, ,,	,, ,,	,, ,,	...	...	...	,, ,,	
	D.P. (except as above).	As for extra service arms.	Nil.	,, ,,	...	...	...	,, ,,	
Pistol, Webley		Number of month and year of issue.	Corps marks and consecutive numbers.	On upper part of strap of stock.	$\frac{5}{64}$	$\frac{5}{64}$	...	Stamps, steel, for metal.	
Lance		,, ,,	,, ,,	On shoe, above collar; marks to be in an upright position.	$\frac{5}{64}$	$\frac{5}{64}$	...	,, ,,	
Bayonets, triangular		None	Consecutive numbers only.	Across blade, close to neck.	...	$\frac{5}{64}$	...	,, ,,	
Sword-bayonets		,, ,,	Corps marks and consecutive numbers.	On pommel, the marks to be on that side which is away from the body when worn.	$\frac{5}{64}$	$\frac{5}{64}$	...	,, ,,	
Dirks		Number of month and year of issue.	,, ,,	On band at bottom of hilt.	$\frac{1}{8}$ and $\frac{5}{64}$	$\frac{1}{8}$	...	To be engraved	
Sword, drummers'	Mark I	,, ,,	,, ,,	Lengthways, on edge of hilt.	$\frac{5}{64}$	$\frac{5}{64}$	...	Stamps, steel, for metal.	
	,, II	,, ,,	,, ,,	At bottom of hilt.	$\frac{5}{64}$	$\frac{5}{64}$	...	To be engraved.	

Appendix 3. The Marking of Arms, 1912

MARKING OF ARMS — *Continued*

Arms, &c.	Ordnance marks	Corps marks.	Position of marks.	Letters.	Figures.	Dash lines.	Implements with which marking is to be done.	Remarks.
Swords, other kinds (except naval).	,, ,,	,, ,,	On termination of guard at back of hilt.	$\frac{5}{64}$	$\frac{5}{64}$	...	Stamps, steel, for metal.	
Scabbards. { bayonet	None	Consecutive numbers only.	On the stud	...	$\frac{5}{64}$	...	Stamps, steel, for metal.	
sword-bayonet, leather.	,, ...	,, ,,	On top of mouthpiece ...	...	$\frac{5}{64}$	...	,, ,,	To be held in vice by locket steel between wooden clams which the armourer must make.
sword-bayonet, steel.	,, ...	,, ,,	On the stud	...	$\frac{5}{64}$	...	,, ,,	
APPURTENANCES, &c								
Rods, cleaning, M.H. ...	,, ...	Consecutive numbers only.	About 2 inches from the thick end.	...	$\frac{5}{64}$	...	Stamps, steel, for metal.	
Actions, skeleton, and waster.	,, ...	None	... ...	...	...	...	... ...	
Aim-correctors (magazine arms).	,, ...	,, ...	... ...	...	...	...	... ...	
Scabbards. { dirk, for all services except Scots Guards.	Number of month and year of issue.	Corps marks and consecutive numbers.	On locket above loop ...	$\frac{1}{8}$ and $\frac{5}{64}$	$\frac{1}{8}$	...	To be engraved.	
dirk, for Scots Guards.	,, ,,	Corps marks and consecutive numbers and the letters "S.G."	Letters "S.G.": in centre thistle in front of locket. Other marks: on locket above loop.	$\frac{3}{8}$ $\frac{1}{8}$ and $\frac{5}{64}$	$\frac{1}{8}$	...	,, ,,	
sword, with flat mouthpiece.	Number of month and year of issue.	Corps marks and consecutive numbers.	On top of mouthpiece ...	$\frac{5}{64}$	$\frac{5}{64}$	...	Stamps, steel, for metal.	When holding locket in vice, care to be taken not to unduly compress sides. The mouthpiece should be removed and held on a mandril for the purpose of being marked. The mouthpiece should be removed and a mandril inserted into the scabbard.
sword, with curved mouthpiece with band.	,, ,,	,, ,,	On that side of band of mouthpiece which is worn next to the body when worn.	$\frac{5}{64}$	$\frac{5}{64}$	...	,, ,,	
sword, with curved mouthpiece without band.	,, ,,	,, ,,	Immediately below mouthpiece, on that side of scabbard which is next to the body when worn.	$\frac{5}{64}$	$\frac{5}{64}$	...	,, ,,	
drummers'	,, ,,	,, ,,	On reverse side of locket ...	$\frac{1}{8}$ and $\frac{5}{64}$	$\frac{1}{8}$	...	To be engraved.	
Barrels, with or without body.	Number of month and year of issue.	None	Side of barrel on the left of Knox form.	...	$\frac{5}{64}$	...	Stamps, steel, for metal.	
Bottles, oil (M.L.-M. arms).	None	Consecutive numbers only.	On top of stopper	...	$\frac{5}{64}$	...	,, ,,	
Gauges, action	,, ...	None	... ...	...	...	...	... ...	
Implements, action, { M.L.-M. arms ...	,, ...	Consecutive numbers only.	On flat part of shoulder ...	...	$\frac{5}{64}$	...	Stamps, steel, for metal.	
Martini-Henry arms	,, ...	,, ,,	On the drift	...	$\frac{5}{64}$	...	,, ,,	
Jags (.45-in. arms). { steel	,, ...	,, ,,	On shoulder, close to the swell.	...	$\frac{5}{64}$	...	Stamps, steel, for metal.	
brass	,, ...	,, ,,	On iron part	...	$\frac{5}{64}$	...	,, ,,	
Protectors, front sight (all arms).	,, ...	,, ,,	On cylindrical portion, just above the sight guard.	...	$\frac{5}{64}$	...	,, ,,	A mandril to be used, to keep form of cylinder perfect.
Protectors, front sight, steel.	,, ...	,, ,,	On cylindrical portion, below sight guard.	...	$\frac{5}{64}$	...	,, ,,	
Pull-throughs (.303-in. arms).	,, ...	,, ,,	About centre of weight ...	...	$\frac{5}{64}$	...	,, ,,	
Reflectors (magazine and Martini-Henry arms).	None	None	... ...	...	...	...	... ...	
Sights, auxiliary (Martini-Henry arms).	,, ...	,, ...	... ...	...	...	...	... ...	
Tubes, aiming	,, ...	,, ...	... ...	...	...	...	... ...	
Cuirasses	Number of month and year of issue.	Corps marks and consecutive number.	On the leather lining ...	$\frac{1}{2}$	$\frac{1}{2}$	...	Stamps, copper, inlaid with marking ink.	

Appendix 3. The Marking of Arms, 1912

LIST I.

The following are the abbreviations to be used for the titles of the undermentioned services. Examples of the mode of combining abbreviations of titles common to several corps, with the numerals, &c., that are necessary to distinguish each individual corps bearing the common title, are given at the end of the appendix.

Services.	Abbreviations
REGULAR FORCES.	
Life Guards	L.G
Royal Horse Guards	R.H.G.
Royal Horse Artillery	R.H.A.
Dragoon Guards	D.G.
Dragoons	D.
Lancers	L.
Hussars	H.
Royal Field Artillery	R.F.A.
Royal Garrison Artillery	R.G.A.
Royal Artillery Staff	R.A.S.
Royal Engineers	R.E.
Grenadier Guards	G.G.
Coldstream Guards	C.G.
Scots Guards	S.G.
Irish Guards	I.G
West India Regiment	W.I.
Army Service Corps	A.S.C.
Army Service Corps, Mechanical Transport Branch	M.T., A.S.C.
Royal Malta Artillery	R. MTA.A.
Royal Army Medical Corps	R.A.M.C.
Army Ordnance Corps	A.O.C.
Armament Articifers, Army Ordnance Corps	A.A., A.O.C.
Armourer Section, Army Ordnance Corps	A.S., A.O.C.
Army Pay Corps	A.P.C.
Military Mounted Police	M.M.P.
Military Foot Police	M.F.P.
School of Military Engineering	S.M.E.
School of Musketry	S.M.
Royal Military College	R.M.C.
Royal Military Academy	R.M.A.
SPECIAL RESERVE.	
Royal Field Reserve Artillery	R.F.R.A.
Royal Reserve Engineers	R.R.E.
TERRITORIAL FORCE.	
Royal 1st Devon	Y. 1. DVN.
Royal North Devon	Y. N. DVN.
Lanarkshire	Y. LNK.
Lanarkshire (Queen's Own Royal Glasgow and Lower Ward of Lanarkshire)	Y. L.G.
Lancashire Hussars	Y. LCS. H.
Duke of Lancaster's Own	Y. D.L.O.
Nottinghamshire	Y. NTT.
South Nottinghamshire Hussars	Y. S.NTT.
Yorkshire Hussars	Y. Y.H.
Yorkshire Dragoons (Queen's Own)	Y. Y.D.
1st City of London Horse Artillery	H.A. 1. C. LD.
1st City of Aberdeen Battery, Royal Field Artillery	R.F.A. 1. C. AB.
Banffshire Battery, Royal Field Artillery	R.F.A. BFF.
2nd Highland Ammunition Column, Royal Field Artillery	R.F.A. 2. HLD. A.C.
1st Warwickshire Battery, Royal Field Artillery	R.F.A. 1. WK.
3rd South Midland Ammunition Column, Royal Field Artillery	R.F.A. 3. S.M.A.C.
Western Wireless Telegraph Company, R.E.	R.E. W.W.T. CO.

MARKING OF ARMS - LIST I - *continued.*

Services.	Abbreviations.
Wessex Divisional Telegraph Company, R.E.	R.E. WX. DL. T. CO.
Northern Air Line Telegraph Company, R.E.	R.E. N.A.L.T. CO.
Western Cable Telegraph Company, R.E.	R.E. W.C.T. CO.
London Balloon Company, R.E.	R.E. LD. BAL.
1st North Midland Field Company, R.E.	R.E. 1. N.M
Hertfordshire Battalion	H.T.F.
1st Battalion City of London	1. LD.
9th Battalion County of London	9. LD.
Wessex Divisional Company, A.S.C.	A.S.C. WX. DL.
South-Western Brigade Company, A.S.C.	A.S.C. S.W. BDE.
North Scottish Royal Garrison Artillery	R.G.A. N.S.
Argyllshire (Mountain) Battery, Royal Garrison Artillery	R.G.A. A.R.G.
Engineer and Railway Staff Corps	R.E. E.R.S.
City of Aberdeen (Fortress) Royal Engineers	R.E. C. AB.
Lowland Mounted Brigade, Transport and Supply Column, Army Service Corps	A.S.C. LOW. M.B.
Eastern Mounted Brigade Field Ambulance	{ R.A.M.C. E.M.B.F.A.
1st East Anglian Field Ambulance	{ R.A.M.C. 1st E.A.F.A.
1st Eastern General Hospital	{ R.A.M.C. 1st E.G.H.
1st London General Hospital	{ R.A.M.C. 1st L.G.H.
2nd London Sanitary Company	{ R.A.M.C. 2nd L.S.CO.
MILITIA.	
The Channel Islands Militia—	
The Royal Militia of the Island of Jersey { Artillery	M R.J.A
Engineers	M. R.J.E.
Light Infantry	M J.L.I.
Medical Corps	M J.M.C.
Royal Guernsey { Artillery	M R.G.A.
Infantry	M R.G.
Royal Alderney Artillery	M R. ALD. A.
The Bermuda Militia { Artillery	M BER. A.
Engineers, Submarine Miners	M. BER. S.M.
The King's Own Malta Regiment of Militia	M. K.O. MTA.
The Royal Engineers (Militia), Malta Division	M. MTA. S.M.
VOLUNTEERS.	
The Bermuda Rifle Volunteers	V. BER.

Appendix 3. The Marking of Arms, 1912

LIST II.

The following are the abbreviations to be used in marking arms of corps which bear the titles detailed below. Examples of the mode of combining abbreviations of titles common to several corps with the numerals, &c., that are necessary to distinguish each individual corps bearing the common title, are given at the end of the appendix.

Infantry Regiments.	Abbreviations.
The Royal Scots (Lothian Regt.)	R.S.
The Queen's (Royal West Surrey Regt.)	W.SR.
The Buffs (East Kent Regt.)	E.K.
The King's Own (Royal Lancaster Regt.)	LAN.
The Northumberland Fusiliers	N.F.
The Royal Warwickshire Regt.	WK.
The Royal Fusiliers (City of London Regt.)	R.F.
The King's (Liverpool Regt.)	LL.
The Norfolk Regt.	N.K.
The Lincolnshire Regt.	LIN.
The Devonshire Regt.	DVN.
The Suffolk Regt.	SK.
Prince Albert's (Somersetshire Light Infantry)	ST.
The Prince of Wales's Own (West Yorkshire Regt.)	W.Y.
The East Yorkshire Regt.	E.Y.
The Bedfordshire Regt.	BD.
The Leicestershire Regt.	LEIC.
The Royal Irish Regt.	R.I.
Alexandra, Princess of Wales's Own (Yorkshire Regt.)	YK.
The Lancashire Fusiliers	L.F.
The Royal Scots Fusiliers	S.F.
The Cheshire Regt.	CH.
The Royal Welsh Fusiliers	W.F.
The South Wales Borderers	S.W.B.
The King's Own Scottish Borderers	K.O.S.B.
The Cameronians (Scottish Rifles)	S.R.
The Royal Inniskilling Fusiliers	IN. F.
The Gloucestershire Regt.	GR.
The Worcestershire Regt.	WR.
The East Lancashire Regt.	E.L.
The East Surrey Regt.	E.SR.
The Duke of Cornwall's Light Infantry	CLL.
The Duke of Wellington's (West Riding Regt.)	W.RID.
The Border Regt.	BR.
The Royal Sussex Regt.	SX.
The Hampshire Regt.	HTS.
The South Staffordshire Regt.	S.STF.
The Dorsetshire Regt.	DT.
The Prince of Wales's Volunteers (South Lancashire Regt.)	S.L.
The Welsh Regt.	WEL.
The Black Watch (Royal Highlanders)	R.H.
The Oxfordshire Light Infantry	OX.
The Essex Regt.	EX.
The Sherwood Foresters (Nottinghamshire and Derbyshire Regiment)	DY.
The Loyal North Lancashire Regt.	N.L.
The Northamptonshire Regt.	NN.
Princess Charlotte of Wales's (Royal Berkshire Regt.)	BRK.
The Queen's Own (Royal West Kent Regt.)	W.KT.
The King's Own (Yorkshire Light Infantry)	Y.L.I.
The King's (Shropshire Light Infantry)	SH.
The Duke of Cambridge's Own (Middlesex Regt.)	MX.
The King's Royal Rifle Corps	K.R.R.
The Duke of Edinburgh's (Wiltshire Regt.)	WTS.
The Manchester Regt.	MAN.
The Prince of Wales's (North Staffordshire Regt.)	N.STF.
The York and Lancaster Regt.	Y & L.
The Durham Light Infantry	DM.
The Highland Light Infantry	H.L.I.
Seaforth Highlanders (Ross-shire Buffs, The Duke of Albany's)	SEA.
The Gordon Highlanders	GOR.
The Queen's Own Cameron Highlanders	CAM.
The Royal Irish Rifles	R.I.R.
Princess Victoria's (Royal Irish Fusiliers)	I.F.
The Connaught Rangers	CT.
Princess Louise's (Argyll and Sutherland Highlanders)	A. & S.H.
The Prince of Wales's Leinster Regt. (Royal Canadians)	LEIN.
The Royal Munster Fusiliers	M.F.
The Royal Dublin Fusiliers	D.F.
The Rifle Brigade (The Prince Consort's Own)	R.B.

OFFICERS TRAINING CORPS.

Senior Division.

Universities.	Abbreviations.	Universities.	Abbreviations.
Aberystwyth	AYH.	Leeds	LDS.
Bangor	BAN.	London	LDN.
Belfast	BFT.	Manchester	MHR.
Birmingham	BHM.	Nottingham	NTTM.
Bristol	BRIS.	Oxford	OXF.
Cambridge	CAM.	Reading	RDG. U.
Dublin	DN.	Royal Agricultural College	R.A.C.
Durham	DRM.	St. Andrew's	ST.AN
Edinburgh	EDIN.	Sheffield	SFD.
Glasgow	GGW.		

Junior Division

Units.	Abbreviations.	Units.	Abbreviations.
Aldenham School	ALD.	Charterhouse School	CHE.
All Hallows School	A.H.	Chatham House College	C.H.C.
Archbishop Abbot's School	A. AB. S.	Cheltenham College	CM.C.
Ardingly College	ARD.	Chigwell School	CGL.
Ardrossan Academy	A.A.	Christ's Hospital	CH.H.
Army School, Maidenhead	A.S.M.	Churcher's College	CH.C.
Beaumont College	BT.C.	City of London School	C.L.S.
Bedford Grammar School	B.G.S.	Clifton College	CL.C.
Bedford Modern School	B.M.S.	Cork Grammar School	C.G.S.
Berkhamsted School	BKD.	Cranbrook School	CK.S.
Bishop's Stortford School	B.S.S.	Cranleigh School	CRH.
Blundell's School	BDL.	Dartford Grammar School	D.G.
Bournemouth School	BMH.	Dean Close School	D.C.
Bradfield College	BDD.	Denstone College	DEN.
Bridlington Grammar School	BRID.	Derby School	DY.
Brighton College	BTN.	Dollar Institution	D.I.
Bristol Grammar School	BRL.	Dorchester Grammar School	D.G.S.
Bromsgrove School	BGV.	Dover College	DVR.
Buckland School	BUC.	Downside School	DOWN.
Bury Grammar School	BY.	Dulwich College	DUL.
Cambridge and County School	C.C.S.	Eastbourne College	EBN.
Campbell College	C.C.	Edinburgh Academy	E.A.
Eltham College	ELT.	Elizabeth College	EZH.
Emmanuel School	EML.	Ellesmere College	ELL.
Epsom College	EPS.	Elstow School	ELS.
Eton College	EN.	King's School (Bruton, Som.)	K.S.B.
Exeter School	EXR.	King's School (Canterbury)	K.S.C.
Felstead School	FEL.	King's School (Grantham)	K.S.G.
Fettes College	FTS.	King's School (Warwick)	K.S.W.
Forest School	FST.	Kirkcaldy High School	K.H.S.
Framlingham College	FMM.	Lancing College	L.C.
George Heriot's School	G.H.	Leeds Grammar School	L.G.
George Watson's Boy's College	G.W.B.	Leys School	LY.S.
Gigglewick School	GIG.	Liverpool College	LL.
Glasgow Academy	G.A.	Liverpool Institute	L.I.
Glasgow High School	G.H.S.	Loretto School	L.S.
Glenalmond College	GMD.	Louth School	LTH.
Gresham's School	G.S.	Maidstone Grammar School	M.G.S.
Grimsby Municipal College	G.M.C.	Malvern College	MAL.
Haileybury College	HBY.	Manchester Grammar School	MHR.S.
Handsworth Grammar School	H.G.S.	Marlborough College	M.C.
Harrow School	HAR.	Merchant Taylors' School	M.T.S.
Hereford Cathedral School	H.C.S.	Merchiston Castle School	M.C.S.
Hertford Grammar School	HFD.	Monkton Combe School	MKN.
Highgate School	HTE.	Newcastle High School	N.H.S.
Hurstpierpoint College	HPT.	North Eastern County School	N.E.C.

287

Appendix 3. The Marking of Arms, 1912

MARKING OF ARMS - LIST II - *continued*.
Junior Division-continued.

Units.	Abbreviations.	Units.	Abbreviations.
Hymers College	HYM.	Nottingham High School	NOTT.
Ispswich School	IPS.	Oakham School	OAK.
Kelly College	KY.	Oundle School	OUN.
Kelvinside Academy	KLV.	Perse School	PSE.
King Edward VII School (Sheffield)	K.E. SD.	Plymouth College	PLY.
King Edward's School (Bath)	K.E. BH.	Portsmouth Grammar School	P.G.S.
King Edward's School (Birmingham)	K.E. BM.	Queen Elizabeth's School	Q.E.S.
King Edward's Grammar School	K.E.G.	Queen Mary's Grammar School	Q.M.G.S.
King's Cathedral School	K.CDL.	Quernmore and Sidcup School	Q. & S.
King's College	KG.C.	Radley College	RAD.
King's College School	K.C.S.	Solihull Grammar School	S.G.S.
Reading School	RDG.S.	Stonyhurst College	STO.
Reigate Grammar School	R.G.S.	Tonbridge School	TON.
Repton School	RTN.	Trent College	TNT.
Rossall School	RSL.	United Services College	U.S.C.
Royal Grammar School (High Wycombe, Bucks)	R.G.S.B.	University College School	U.C.
Royal Grammar School of King Edward VI	RL.G.S.	Uppingham School	UPM.
Rugby School	RUG.	Victoria College	VIC.
St. Albans School	ST. AL.	Wellingborough Grammar School	W.G.S.
St. Bee's School	ST. B.	Wellington College	WN.C.
St. Edmund's School	ST. EDM.	Wellington College (Salop)	W.C.S.
St. Edward's School	ST. ED.	Westminster School	WME.
St. Lawrence College	ST. L.	West Somerset County School	W.S.C.
St. Paul's School	ST. P.	Whitgift Grammar School	WHT.
Sedbergh School	SBH.	Wilson's School	WIL.
Sherborne School	SHB.	Winchester College	WIN.
Shrewsbury School	SBY.	Woodbridge School	WBE.
Sidcup Hall School	S.H.S.	Worksop College	WKP.
Sir Roger Manwood School	S.R.M.		
Skinners' School	SKN.		

LIST III.

The following is a code of abbreviations to be used in marking arms of certain corps whose titles are not to be found in List I or II. Above their abbreviated corps marks the letter "Y" will be placed in the case of Yeomanry. Examples of the mode of combining abbreviations of titles common to several units with the numerals, &c., that are necessary to distinguish each individual unit bearing the common title, are given at the end of the appendix.

County and other titles.	Abbreviations.	County and other titles.	Abbreviations.
Aberdeenshire	AB.	East Midland	E.M.
Anglesey	AGS.	Edinburgh	ED.
Antrim	AM.	Essex	EX.
Argyllshire	ARG.	Fife	FE.
Ayrshire	AYR.	Fifeshire	FE.
Banff	BFF.	Fifeshire and Forfarshire	FE. & FF.
Bedfordshire	BD.	Flint	FT.
Berkshire	BRK.	Forfarshire	FF.
Bermuda	BER.	Forfarshire and Kincardine	F. & K.
Buckinghamshire	BCK.	Forth and Clyde	F. & C.
Buteshire	BE.	Glamorgan	GM.
Brecknockshire	BN.	Glamorgan and Pembroke	GM. & PB.
Cambridgeshire	CB.	Glamorganshire	GM.
Cardigan	CDN.	Glasgow	GW.
Carmarthen	CMN.	Gloucester and Worcester	GR. & WR.
Cheshire	CH.	Gloucestershire	GR.
Clare	CL.	Hampshire	HTS.
Cork	CK.		
Cornwall	CLL.		
Cornwall and Devon	C. & D.		
Cumberland	CBT.		

MARKING OF ARMS - LIST III - *continued*.

County and titles.	Abbreviations.	County and titles.	Abbreviations.
Denbighshire	DB.	Hampshire and Isle of Wight	H. & I.W.
Derbyshire	DY.	Hants and Dorset	HTS. & DT.
Devon	DVN.	Herefordshire	HF.
Devon and Cornwall	DVN. & CLL.	Herts	HTF.
Devonshire	DVN.	Highland	HLD.
Donegal	DL.	Home Counties	H.C.
Dorset	DT.	Invernesshire	IS.
Dublin City	DN.	Kent	KT.
Dundee	DDE.	Kent and Sussex	K. & SX.
Durham	DM.	Kent, East	E.K.
Durham and Yorkshire	DM. & YK.	Kent, West	W.K.
East Anglian	E.A.	Kircudbrightshire	K.C.
Eastern	E.	Pembroke	PB.
Lanarkshire	LNK.	Renfrewshire	RN.
Lancashire	LCS.	Seaforth and Cameron	S. & C.
Lancashire and Cheshire	LCS. & CH.	Shropshire	SH.
Leicestershire	LEIC.	Sligo	SO.
Limerick or Limerick City	LCK.	Somerset, North	N.ST.
Lincoln and Leicester	L. & L.	Somerset, West	W.ST.
Lincolnshire	LIN.	South Eastern	S.E.
Liverpool	LL.	South Midland	S.M.
London	LD.	South Wales	S.WAL.
Londonderry	LDY.	South Western	S.W.
Lothian	LTN.	Staffordshire	STF.
Lowland	LOW.	Suffolk	SK.
Malta	MTA.	Suffolk and Essex	S & EX.
Manchester	MAN.	Surrey	SR.
Middlesex	MX.	Sussex	SX.
Midlothian	ML.	Tipperary	TIP.
Mid-Ulster	M.U.	Warwickshire	WK.
Monmouthshire	MM.	Waterford	WD.
Montgomeryshire	MG.	Welsh Border	W.B.
Norfolk	NK.	Wessex	WX.
Norfolk and Suffolk	N. & S.	Westmorland and Cumberland	W. & C.
Northamptonshire	NN.	Wicklow	WW.
Northumberland	NTB.	Wigtownshire	WG.
Northumberland and Durham	NTB. & DM.	Wiltshire	WTS.
Northumbrian	NBN.	Worcestershire	WR.
North Midland	N.M.	York and Durham	Y. & D.
North Scottish	N.S.	Yorkshire	YK.
North Wales	N.WAL.	Yorkshire, East Riding	E.RID.
Nottinghamshire	NTT.	Yorkshire, North Riding	N.RID.
Notts and Derby	N. & D.	Yorkshire, West Riding	W.RID.
Orkney	ORK.		
Oxfordshire	OX.		

TYPICAL EXAMPLES.

The following are typical examples of the mode of combining abbreviations of titles common to several corps with the numerals, &c., that are necessary to distinguish each individual corps bearing the common title:-

Units.	Abbreviations.
REGULAR FORCES.	
1st Life Guards	1. L.G.
5th Lancers	5. L.
"A" Battery, Royal Horse Artillery	A.R.H.A.
"A" Depot, Royal Horse Artillery	A.DEP.R.H.A.
Riding Establishment, Royal Artillery	R.E.R.H.A.
1st Battery, Royal Field Artillery	1. R.H.A.
No. 1 depot, Royal Field Artillery	1D. .R.F.A.
IV. Brigade R.F.A. Ammunition Column	R.F.A. 4. BDE. A.C.
2nd Cavalry Brigade, Ammunition Column	R.H.A. 2. C.B. A.C.
II. Ammunition Park	R.F.A. II. A.P.
10th Company, Royal Garrison Artillery	10. R.G.A.
No. 1 Depot, Royal Garrison Artillery and District Establishment allotted thereto	1. DEP. R.G.A.

Appendix 3. The Marking of Arms, 1912

MARKING OF ARMS - TYPICAL EXAMPLES - *continued*

Units.	Abbreviations.
Army Ordnance Corps	A.O.C.
Armament Articifers, Army Ordnance Corps	A.A., A.O.C.
Armourer Section, Army Ordnance Corps	A.S., A.O.C.
Royal Artillery Staff, Gibraltar	GIB. (station monogram) R.A.S.
School of Gunnery, Royal Artillery	S.G. R.A.
2nd Company (Field), Royal Engineers	2 CO. R.E.
1st Air Line Company	1 A.L. R.E.
1st Cable Company	1 C.T. R.E.
1st Divisional Company	1 D.T. R.E.
1st Wireless Company	1 W.T. R.E.
1st Bridging Train	1 B.T. R.E.
1st Field Troop	1 F.T. R.E.
Training Depots for Field units	T.D. R.E.
1st Search Light Company	1 S.L. R.E.
K Telegraph Company	K.T. R.E.
Colonial Survey Section	C.S. R.E.
Supernumerary Staff	S.S. R.E.*
Establishment for Engineer Services	E.S. R.E.*
1st Battalion, The Prince Albert's (Somersetshire Light Infantry)	1. ST.
Depot, The King's Royal Rifle Corps	D.K.R.R.
2nd Battalion, The West India Regiment	2. W.I.
No. 6 Company, Army Service Corps	6. A.S.C.
Station Staff, A.S. Corps, Woolwich	W. A.S.C.
Cavalry Depot — Bristol	CAV. D. BRL.
Cavalry Depot — Dublin	CAV. D. DN.
Cavalry Depot — Dunbar	CAV. D. DBR.
Cavalry Depot — Scarborough	CAV. D. SCAR.
Cavalry Depot — Seaforth	CAV. D. SEA.
Cavalry Depot — Woolwich	CAV. D. WOOL.

SPECIAL RESERVE

Units.	Abbreviations.
Royal Field Reserve Artillery	R.F.R.A. 5 †
Royal Anglesey Royal Reserve Engineers	AN. R.R.E.
Royal Monmouth Royal Reserve Engineers	MN. R.R.E.

OFFICERS TRAINING CORPS

Units.	Abbreviations.
Belfast University	O.T.C. BFT.
Cambridge University	O.T.C. CAM.
St. Andrew's University	O.T.C. ST. AN.
Haileybury College	O.T.C. HBY.
Ipswich College	O.T.C. IPS.
King Edward's School, Bath	O.T.C. K.E. BH.
Maidstone Grammar School	O.T.C. M.G.S.
St. Albans School	O.T.C. ST. AL.

MARKING OF ARMS - TYPICAL EXAMPLES - *continued*

Units.	Abbreviations.
TERRITORIAL FORCE.	
Fifeshire and Forfarshire Yeomanry	Y. FE. & FF.
Royal East Kent Yeomanry	Y. E.K.
Wessex (Hampshire) Royal Garrison Artillery	WX. R.G.A.
Northumberland (Fortress) Royal Engineers	NTB. R.E.
5th Bn. Royal Scots	5 R.S.
Eastern Mounted Brigade Field Ambulance	R.A.M.C. E.M.B.F.A.
MILITIA.	
1st Battalion (L.I.) Royal Militia of the Island of Jersey	M. 1. J. L.I.

* Consecutive numerical marking will not be resorted to in these instances.

† The figure denotes the number of the Divisional Ammunition Column - thus the accoutrements of the Training Brigade furnishing N.C.O.s and men for the 5th Divisional Ammunition Column would be marked:-

$$\frac{\text{R.F.R.A.}}{5}$$
1 (and upwards)

Appendix 4. The List of Changes

This War Department publication, which is a basic source of information on all forms of military equipment between 1860 and 1914, was first published in January 1860. Thereafter, successive parts were published on the first of each month, generally accompanying *Army Orders* (or *Army Council Instructions*). Changes were numbered consecutively throughout - thus *LC*1 was issued on 1 January 1860 and *LC* 16976 on 1 December 1914. It is important to note that the *List of Changes* was notifying, for general information and action, decisions already taken within the War Department. As an example, the Pattern 1885 cavalry sword was formally decided upon in November 1885 but it did not appear in the *List of Changes* until 1 January 1886. The date and the War Department file reference number of decisions of this kind normally appears in the margin of the *List*.

The official title of the publication changes several times - the original being *Changes in Artillery Materiel, Small Arms, Accoutrements and other Military Stores*. From 1868, it was *List of Changes in Artillery Materiel, Small Arms and other Military Stores* and then from 1872, *List of Changes in War Materiel and of Patterns of Military Stores*. Initially, the items were under seven headings:

A   Materiel of Artillery
B   Small Arms
C   Cutlasses, Lances etc.
D   Clothing and Accoutrements
E   Harness and Horse Appointments
F   Tools
G   Barrack and Hospital Furniture and Bedding.

In 1868, a further section - F (Tents and Equipage) - was introduced and the original sections F and G were re-lettered G and H.

This system was abandoned in 1868, and thereafter the grouping was in two broad sections only - Materiel of Artillery and Miscellaneous - until 1872, when it was replaced by one of six sections, the first entitled Artillery Materiel and the rest based upon the *Vocabulary of Stores*. Later in 1872 this was rearranged into six sections as follows:

Section I   Accoutrements, Small Arms.
Section II Camp Equipment, Intrenching Tools, Harness and Saddlery, Drawing and Musical Instruments.
Section III Artificers', Earthboring and Miners' Tools.
Section IV Miscellaneous Stores
Section V   Ordnance Stores, Pontoon Equipment, all Carts and Wagons.
Section VI Barrack, Hospital and Military Prison Stores.

In 1874 a seventh section (VII) was added covering electrical stores of all kinds. Finally,

Appendix 4. The List of Changes

in 1897, the formal arrangement in sections was abandoned, but the order followed remained broadly the same.

The growth in the complexity of military equipment, particularly artillery, is illustrated by the growth in the size of the *List*. In 1860 there were 161 changes, occupying 22 pages; in 1887 there were 228 changes filling 240 pages; and in 1913 the changes totalled 412 and filled 357 pages.

A summary of the main entries relating to swords in the period from 1860 to 1914 is given below.

Cavalry
(except Household Cavalry)

Pattern 1853

*LC*562, issued 1 July 1862
Scabbard for Pattern 1853 sword, with loose rings removed and frog stud brazed on, for Cape Mounted Rifles.

Pattern 1864

*LC*887, issued 1 April 1864
Existing (Pattern 1853) cavalry sword to be fitted with new hilt of sheet steel.

*LC*2870, issued 1 March 1876
Pattern 1864 sword not to be issued in future to Royal Artillery, who will receive the 1853 pattern in lieu.

Patterns 1882

*LC*4204, issued 1 January 1883
Patterns of swords and scabbards, Cavalry, Pattern 1882, Long and Short, have been approved.

*LC*4429, issued 1 March 1884
The Pattern 1882 'Long' sword to be issued to 4th and 5th Dragoons only. All other mounted troops, except Household Cavalry, to receive 'Short' pattern.

Pattern 1885

*LC*4854, issued 1 January 1886
Pattern of this sword and scabbard have been adopted for manufacture. Detailed description.

*LC*4853, issued 1 January 1886
Pattern of buff waistbelts adopted for cavalry to carry the new Pattern 1885 cavalry sword.

*LC*5731, issued 1 May 1889
New Mark II scabbard of stouter metal introduced; weight increased to 1lb14^1/$_2$ozs.

Pattern 1890 (see also under 'General Changes')

*LC*6477, issued 1 September 1891
Notifies introduction of new Pattern 1890 cavalry sword for all mounted services, except Household Cavalry. Detailed description of sword and tests applied in manufacture.

Patterns 1899 (see also under 'General Changes')

*LC*9880, issued 1 December 1899
Patterns of the cavalry sword Pattern 1899 and scabbard, and of the cavalry sword and scabbard Pattern 1899 (Converted), adopted for manufacture. Detailed description.

*LC*9983, issued 1 February 1900
Scabbards to be marked 'P99' on the back loop plate.

Pattern 1908

*LC*14325, issued 1 October 1908
Sword, Cavalry, Pattern 1908 (Mark I) approved for manufacture. Detailed description and drawing.

*LC*15151, issued 1 August 1910
Sword knot slit increased in length and width to 0.8 inches and 0.25 inches respectively.

Appendix 4. The List of Changes

*LC*15212, issued 1 October 1910
1. Tang strengthened at juncture with blade.
2. Strengthening piece on underside of guard widened to overlap mouthpiece of scabbard.
3. Mouthpiece made concave to match the profile of strengthening piece.

*LC*15388, issued 1 March 1911
Shoulders of blade serrated to retain buff-piece.

*LC*15500, issued 1 June 1911
New pattern scabbard, Mark 1*, of thicker material, weight 1lb 9ozs to 1lb 11ozs, adopted.

*LC*15848, issued 1 March 1912
Auxiliary mouthpiece to be fitted to all Mk 1 and Mk 1* scabbards to prevent damage to wood lining and to facilitate returning the sword to the scabbard.

*LC*16089, issued 1 September 1912
1. Cross-pin through blade, in place of serration, to secure buff-piece.
2. Wood lining of scabbard to be waterproofed by soaking in melted paraffin wax.

*LC*16258, issued 1 February 1913
End of tang to be riveted over pommel nut.

*LC*16259, issued 1 February 1913
Last 4 inches of blade to be sharpened for active service.

*LC*17083, issued 1 February 1915
Guard and scabbard to be painted, pommel and ferrule to be oil-blacked.

Household Cavalry

Pattern 1882

*LC*4052, issued 1 July 1882
Pattern 1882 (Long) Mark I, with scabbard, approved for manufacture. Detailed description and drawing.

*LC*4076, issued 1 August 1882
Pattern 1882 (Short) Mark I, with scabbard approved for manufacture.

Pattern 1888

*LC*5928, issued 1 March 1890
New pattern (Household Cavalry, Pattern 1888, Long) of sword and scabbard introduced. Blade slightly curved instead of straight as in 1882 pattern. Detailed description and drawing of tests to be used in manufacture.

*LC*6601, issued 1 February 1892
A Mark II pattern scabbard adopted for future manufacture, with lower loose ring being 1inch nearer mouthpiece.

Pattern 1892 (see also under 'General Changes')

*LC*6859, issued 1 November 1892
New sword and scabbard introduced. Description and drawing, and details of tests applied in manufacture.
New Mark II pattern adopted, which differs from earlier Mark I pattern only in the grip being $1/2$ inch longer and weight accordingly increased by 2ozs.

*LC*11290, issued 1 November 1902
New pattern Mark II adopted, which differs from earlier pattern only in the shape of the crown incorporated in the guard.

Sergeants
(except Highland regiments)

*LC*54, issued 1 April 1860
Scabbard for old pattern sword of sergeants of the line altered to ring locket pattern for volunteer artillery.

*LC*560, issued 1 July 1862
Sword for Staff-Sergeants Royal Engineers with blade 2 inches shorter than earlier pattern.

Appendix 4. The List of Changes

*LC*507, issued 1 April 1862
Black leather scabbard for staff-sergeants of volunteer rifle regiments.

*LC*1377, issued 1 January 1867
New swords for staff-sergeants of line and rifle regiments, with blades similar to those of Royal Artillery and Royal Engineers.

*LC*1761, issued 1 April 1869
Sword with hilt of improved shape and smaller than previous pattern, for staff-sergeants of Royal Engineers.

*LC*2333, issued 1 October 1872
Sword knot slit of Pattern 1869 sword for Royal Engineers made larger, similar to that of the sword for staff-sergeants of Royal Artillery approved in January 1856. This modified R.E. sword to be known as Mark III. It has gun-metal hilt as in earlier 1869 pattern.

*LC*5627, issued 1 February 1889
Medical Staff Corps sergeants' sword declared obsolete and Lancaster sword-bayonets to be issued in lieu.

*LC*5629, issued 1 February 1889
New Pattern 1889 swords, with gilt hilt for dismounted Royal Engineers, infantry of the line and Medical Staff Corps, and steel hilts for dismounted Royal Artillery, rifle regiments and departmental corps. Description and drawing.

*LC*5672, issued 1 April 1889
Steel hilts of Pattern 1889 to be replaced by malleable cast-iron hilts.

*LC*6581, issued 1 January 1892
New Mark II scabbard for Pattern 1889 swords introduced.

*LC*6763, issued 1 July 1892
Mark II scabbards abolished and a lightened Mark I scabbard reintroduced.

*LC*8823, issued 1 October 1897
New Pattern 1897 sword for all dismounted services except regiments carrying claymores. (Note: Same as infantry officers' 1897 pattern).

*LC*9243, issued 1 November 1898
New Pattern 1898 sword introduced with heavier and stiffer blades than 1897 pattern.

*LC*11290, issued 1 November 1902
Staff-sergeants' sword, Pattern 1898, Mark I adopted. Differs from earlier pattern only in shape of crown on guard and in having royal cypher of Edward VII in place of Victoria.

*LC*12825, issued 1 July 1905
New Pattern 1905 sword and scabbard for all dismounted services except those regiments carrying claymores. The blade converted from Pattern 1899 cavalry sword blade. Description and drawing.

*LC*15812, issued 1 February 1912
New versions of Patterns 1898, Mark I and 1905, Mark I adopted, incorporating royal cypher of George V.

Staff-Sergeants, Highland Regiments

*LC*250, issued 1 April 1861
New scabbard with rings, locket and large shoe for sword (claymore) of non-kilted Highland regiments.

*LC*2298, issued 1 August 1872
Sergeants of kilted Highland regiments to use scabbard approved in 1861, (see 250 above) for non-kilted regiments.

*LC*6017, issued 1 June 1890
Leather scabbard with iron mounts for Staff-Sergeants Highland Volunteers sword (or pipers' sword).

*LC*7954, issued 1 October 1895
Staff-Sergeants' sword, Mark II, adopted. Detailed description and drawing.

Appendix 4. The List of Changes

Practice and Gymnasia Swords

*LC*1026, issued 1 January 1865
Practice sword for gymnasia by Wilkinson introduced, based on 1864 pattern cavalry sword.

*LC*1948, issued 1 September 1870
Lead-cutting sword and mould for casting lead approved for gymnasia.

*LC*5092, issued 1 December 1886
Practice sword, Mark II for mounted corps introduced. Description and drawing. Similar to cavalry sword Pattern 1885.

*LC*6528, issued 1 October 1891
Practice sword for dismounted corps introduced, converted from existing dismounted staff-sergeants' swords, Pattern 1889.

*LC*7090, issued 1 May 1893
Wilkinson practice gymnasia sword (see LC1026) abolished.

*LC*7090, issued 1 July 1895
New practice sword for gymnasia, Pattern 1895, adopted. Description and drawing.

*LC*8677, issued 1 June 1897
Practice swords converted from existing patterns of staff-sergeants' swords to be known simply as 'Swords, Practice, Dismounted Corps'.

*LC*9207, issued 1 October 1898
Practice swords for dismounted corps (see LC6528) declared obsolete.

*LC*9984, issued 1 January 1900
New practice gymnasia sword, Pattern 1899, introduced to replace Pattern 1895.

*LC*10042, issued 1 April 1900
Pattern 1895 swords to be converted to Pattern 1899 by reducing size of blade.

*LC*12328, issued 1 September 1904
New practice gymnasia sword, Pattern 1904, Mark I introduced to replace 1899 pattern.

*LC*13993, issued 1 January 1908
New Pattern 1907, Mark I sword introduced to replace 1904 pattern.

*LC*14972, issued 1 March 1910
Practice swords for mounted corps (see LC5092) abolished.

*LC*15152, issued 1 August 1910
Mark II version of Pattern 1907, Mark I practice sword introduced.
Mark I version to be used only in dismounted exercises.

*LC*15813, issued 1 February 1912
New Sword, Practice, Gymnasia, Pattern 1911, Mark I introduced. Hilt similar to cavalry sword Pattern 1908.

*LC*16168, issued 1 September 1912
Both versions of Pattern 1907 sword abolished.

Miscellaneous

Mountain Artillery sword, Pattern 1896
(see also under 'General Changes')

*LC*8368, issued 1 September 1896
New sword and scabbard for all ranks. Detailed description and drawing.

*LC*9359, issued 1 February 1899
New Mark II scabbard adopted, with rounded end to chape, mounts of thicker brass and steel springs in mouthpiece to retain sword.

Buglers' and Drummers' sword, Mark II

*LC*7953, issued 1 October 1895
New Mark II pattern adopted, with iron mounts for buglers' and brass mounts for drummers'. Detailed description and drawing.

*LC*12058, issued 1 March 1904
Buglers' sword, Mark II abolished.

*LC*15812, issued 1 February 1912
Mark II drummers' sword altered to incorporate new royal cypher (GRV).

294

Appendix 4. The List of Changes

Pioneer sword, Pattern 1856 (see also under 'General Changes')

*LC*12058, issued 1 March 1904
Pioneer sword abolished.

Dirks

*LC*2299, issued 1 August 1872
A dirk approved to replace claymore for pipe majors, pipers, drummers and bandsmen of kilted Highland regiments.

*LC*3504, issued 1 April 1879
A new Mark II pattern approved. Differs from earlier (Mark I) pattern in decoration of hilt.

*LC*3707, issued 1 May 1880
The Mark II dirk to be issued to pipers, drummers and bandsmen of all Highland regiments.

*LC*11290, issued 1 November 1902
New form of crown on hilt.

*LC*16582, issued 1 November 1913
A new Mark III pattern approved, usable with either Mark I or Mark II scabbard. Plain blade and different method of fixing hilt to blade.

General Changes

*LC*9206, issued 1 October 1898
Edges of Cavalry Pattern 1890, Mountain Artillery, Pioneer Pattern 1856 and Staff-Sergeants (Highland Regiments) swords to be partially sharpened in manufacture, and to be further sharpened when proceeding on active service.

*LC*10974, issued 1 April 1902
Buff-pieces of all swords to be reduced in size to prevent water getting into scabbard and to be waterproofed with melted paraffin wax.

*LC*12860, issued 1 August 1905
Only Household Cavalry, cavalry and mountain artillery swords to be further sharpened when proceeding on active service.

Select Bibliography

Note: this is not a list of all works consulted but only of those which contain information of value to the serious student. Sources which fall within the category of public records, such as Army Circulars, Memoranda, Orders and Regulations have been or are being transferred from the Ministry of Defence Central Library to the Public Record Office. Accordingly the Public Record Office should be consulted regarding the current location of particular items identified in the notes to each chapter. The National Army Museum has an excellent general military library and its staff is notably helpful. Admission, however, is strictly by Reader's Ticket only.

Place of publication of books is London unless noted otherwise.

Uniform

Broughton, U H R, *The Dress of the First Regiment of Life Guards*, (1925)

Chichester, H M and Burges-Short, G, *Records and Badges of the British Army*, (1900)

Farmer, Charles, *A Universal Military Dictionary in English and French*, (unpaginated, 1810, paginated 1816)

Goddard, T, and Booth, *Military Costume in Europe*, (1812)

Hinde, Captain Robert, *The Discipline of the Light Horse* (1770)

Hull, E, *Costume of the British Army*, (1828-30)

Millar, Oliver, *Late Georgian pictures in the collection of Her Majesty the Queen*, 2 Vols, (1969)

Miller, A E Haswell, and Dawnay, N P, *Military Drawings and Paintings in the Royal Collection*, 2 Vols, (1966)

Smith, Charles Hamilton, *Costumes of the Army of the British Empire*, (1814-15)

Spencer-Smith, Jenny, *Portraits for a King: The British Military Paintings of A-J Dubois Drahonet*, National Army Museum (1990)

Strachan, Hew, *British Military Uniforms 1768-96*, (1975)

Wilkinson-Latham, R, *Scottish Military Uniforms*, Newton Abbott (1975)

The Army in India: a photographic record 1850-1914, (1968)

Weapons

Annis, P G, *Naval Swords*, (1970)

Ariès, C, *Armes Blanches Militaires Francaises*, Paris (1966)

Aylward, J D, *The Smallsword in England*, (1960)

Blair, Claude, *European and American Arms*, (1960)

Bosanquet, Captain H T A, *The Naval Officer's Sword*, (1955)

Bottet, M, *De L'Arme Blanche (1789-1870) et De L'Arme a Feu Portative (1718-1900)*, Paris (1959)

Caldwell, D (ed.), *Scottish Weapons and Fortifications 1100-1800*, Edinburgh (1891)

Dolloczek, A, *Monographie der k.u.k.österreichisch-ungarischen Blanken- und Handfeuerwaffen*, Vienna (1896)

ffoulkes, Charles, *Inventory and Survey of the Armouries of the Tower of London*, 2 Vols, (1916)

ffoulkes, Charles, and Hopkinson, Captain E C, *Sword, Lance and Bayonet*, Cambridge (1938)

Gohlke, W, *Die Blanken Waffen und die Schutzwaffen*, Berlin (1912)

Guy, Alan J (ed.), *The Road to Waterloo*, National Army Museum (1990)- Brian Robson, '"Warranted Never to Fail": The Cavalry Sword patterns of 1796'

Laking, G, *The Armoury of Windsor Castle*, (1904)

Latham, J W, *British Military Swords, from 1800 to the present day*, (1966)

Latham, R J Wilkinson, *British Military Bayonets, from 1700 to 1945*, (1968)

Marey, Colonel H, *Mémoire sur les Armes Blanches*, Paris (1841)

May, W E, and Annis, P W G, *Swords for Sea Service*, 2 Vols, (1970)

May, W E, and Kennard, A N, *Naval Swords and Firearms*, (1962)

Mollo, E, *Russian Military Swords 1801-1917*, (1969)

Norman, A V B, *The Rapier and the Small-Sword 1460-1820*, (1980)

Peterson, Harold, *The American Sword*, revised edition, Philadelphia (1965)

Rawson, P S, *The Indian Sword*, Copenhagen (1967)

Seifert, G, *Schwert,Degen,Säbel*, Hamburg (1962)

Seitz, H, *Svardet och Varjen som Armevapen*, Stockholm (1955)

Wagner, E, *Hieb- und Stichwaffen*, Prague (1966)

Wilkinson, F, *Swords and Daggers*, (1967)

Wilkinson-Latham, J, *British Cut and Thrust Weapons*, Newton Abbott (1971)

Wise, T, *European Edged Weapons*, (1974)

Biographies and memoirs

Alexander, M, *The True Blue*, (1957)

Cassells, S A C, (ed.) *Peninsular Portrait: The letters of Captain William Bragge, Third (King's Own) Dragoons*, (1963)

Lehmann, Joseph, *All Sir Garnet; A Life of Field-Marshal Lord Wolseley*, (1964)

Lunt, J, *Charge to Glory*, (1961)

Le Marchant, D, *Memoirs of the late Major General Le Marchant*, (1841)

Thoumine, R H, *Scientific Soldier: a life of General Le Marchant 1766-1812*, (1968)

Wood, Sir Evelyn, *The Crimea in 1854 and 1894*, (1895)

Regulations and reports

Army Equipment, (7 parts), (1865)

Dress Regulations, (1822-1911)

List of Changes, (1860-1929)

Regulations for the Equipment of the Regular Army, (1865-1901)

Report of the Royal Commission appointed to enquire into the system under which patterns of war-like stores are adopted and the stores obtained and passed for Her Majesty's service (Cd 5062), (1887)

Reports on alleged failures of cavalry swords and pistols at Suakin (Cd 5633), (1889)

Special Committee on Cavalry Swords and Scabbards - reports and proceedings October 1884 to May 1885

Cavalry Swords: Report by Sir F Bramwell and B Baker Esq, War Office (1889)

Staff-Sergeants' Swords, War Office file reference 77/26. (1889)

Regimental histories

Arthur, Sir George, *The Story of the Household Cavalry*, 3 Vols, (1909)

Barrett, C B R, *The 7th (Queen's Own) Hussars*, (1914)

Campbell, Major D A, *The Dress of the Royal Artillery from 1898-1956*, Woolwich (1960)

Cavendish, Brigadier-General A E J, *The 93rd Sutherland Highlanders 1799-1927*, Privately printed (1928)

Connolly, T J, *History of the Royal Sappers and Miners*, (1855)

Cowper, Colonel L I, *The King's Own*, Oxford (1939)

Dunn-Pattison, R P, *The History of the 91st Argyllshire Highlanders*, Edinburgh (1910)

Fortescue, Sir John, *The Royal Army Service Corps*, Cambridge (1930)

Goff, G L, *Historical Records of the 91st Argyllshire Highlanders*, (1891)

Historical Records of the Queen's Own Cameron Highlanders, Edinburgh and London (1909)

Annals of the King's Royal Rifle Corps: Appendix dealing with uniforms, armament and equipment, (1913)

Leask, J C, and McCance, H M, *The Regimental Records of the Royal Scots*, Dublin (1915)

Leslie, N B, *The Battle Honours of the British and Indian Armies 1695-1914*, (1970)

MacDonald, Captain R J *The History of the Dress of the Royal Artillery*, (1899)

Wyllie, Colonel H, *The XVth (the King's) Hussars*, (1914)

Sharpe, L C, *The Field Train Department of the Board of Ordnance*, Privately printed (1993)

Articles

Antique Arms and Militaria
Vol IV, Worrall, G R, - 'The First Life Guards Trumpeter's Sword'

Army Museum '82,
Robson, Brian, 'A Royal Engineers driver's sword?', National Army Museum, (1983)

Canadian Journal of Arms Collecting
Vol II, No 2, Crook, N J, 'The British Pattern 1908 Cavalry Sword'

Classic Arms and Militaria
Vol I, No 6, Dellar, Richard, 'An Enigmatic British Cavalry Sword'

Vol I, No 7, Worrall, G R, 'British Light Dragoon Sword of 1788 - Part I'

Vol I, No 9, Worrall, G R, 'The 1796 Light Cavalry Sword - Part I'

Vol I, No 10, Worrall, G R, 'The 1796 "Waterloo Pattern" Light Cavalry Sword'

Vol I, No 11, Worrall, G R, 'The British Heavy Cavalry Sword of 1788'

Guns, Weapons and Militaria
Vol I, No 1, Worrall, G R, 'The Household Cavalry Troopers' Swords 1780-c1820'

Vol I, No 8, Worrall, G R, 'The 1912 Cavalry Officers' Sword and its variations'

Vol II, No 9, Rowntree, James, 'Some observations on "Household Cavalry Trooper's sword 1780-c1820 by G R Worrall"'

Journal of the Arms and Armour Society
Vol III, Blair, C, (ed.), 'Recollections of his father, the late Mr Thomas Gill'

Vol IV, Norman, A V B, 'Early Military Dirks in the Scottish United Services Museum'

Vol IV, May, Commander W E, 'The 5-ball type of sword hilt'

Vol V, Norman, A V B, 'Notes on some Scottish infantry swords in the Scottish United Services Museum'

Vol 9, Norman, A V B, 'The dating and identification of some swords in the Royal Collection at Windsor Castle'

Journal of the Society for Army Historical Research

Vol XLVI, Robson, B E, 'The British Cavalry Trooper's sword 1796-1853'

Vol LVI, Morrison, A W and Reeder, B W, 'Short Swords of the Foot Artillery'

Museum Supplement 47 - Dawnay, Major N P, 'Crowns and Coronets on Military appointments'

Journal of the Royal United Services Institution

Vol VI, Latham, J, 'The Shape of Sword Blades'

Vol LVI, Hall, Cornet Francis, 'Recollections in Portugal and Spain during 1811 and 1812'

The Cavalry Journal

Vol II, Mitchell, Sergeant Forbes 'The cutting power of the sword'

Vol II, Landon, Colonel H J, 'Cavalry swordsmanship in 1854'

Vol II, Poore, Major R M, 'The new cavalry sword and mounted swordsmanship'

Vol II, Van Der Byl, Major 'The Sword'

Index

Page references in italic script refer to illustrations.
Footnotes are indicated by the style 71n13 i.e. footnote 13 on page 71.

A

Abel, Sir Frederick, 45
Afghan War, Second, 3n5, 32, 38-9, 100
Alexander, Captain James (42nd Foot), 181
Alison, Lieutenant-General Sir Archibald, 45
American War of Independence, 5, 142
Andrews (swordmaker), 112
Annesley, Colonel Arthur Lyttleton, 39, 71n10
Anstruther, Major (Royal Artillery), 215
Arabin, Lieutenant-Colonel William (2nd Life Guards), 124
Arbuthnot, Colonel Henry Thomas, 43, 45-6, 71n13, 115-6, 118
Austria
    cavalry sabre (1775), 18
    superiority of equipment and training, 17

B

Baden-Powell, Major-General Sir Robert, 56, 73n38
Baker, Benjamin, 52
Baker, Colonel Thomas Durand, 38-9, 70n5
Balaclava, Battle of (1854), 30, 31-2, 195
bandsmen, 195, 256-61, *196, 254-5, 258-60*
Baynes, Captain Henry (Royal Artillery), 227
Beaumont, Battle of (1794), 14, 17
Beechey, Sir William (painter), 80, 146, 209n3
Bell-Smythe, Major J A (1st Dragoon Guards), 61
belts, Sam Browne, 100, 139, 192-3, 208
Bengal Lancers, 3n5
bibliography, 296-301
Biddulph, Lieutenant Thomas (1st Life Guards), 132
Bienvenida, action at (1812), 21
blades
    claymore, 175
    cut-and-thrust, 16, 28, 61, 120-1, 142
    fullers, 9, 14
    pipe-backed, 84, 86-7
    ramrod-back, 84, 86

saw-back, 232
scimitar, 16, 202
Boer War - *see* South African War
Bombay Light Cavalry, 86
Booth, Ensign Charles (52nd Foot), 150
Bowden, Private Samuel (Royal Horse Guards), 114
Bragge, Captain William (3rd Dragoons), 21
Bramwell, Sir Frederick, 52, 72n28
broadsword, 77, 80, 107, 126, 172-4, 181, 183, *173, 179, 182, 184, 185-6*
buff-piece, 68
buglers, 251-6
Burnaby, Lieutenant-Colonel Frederick G (Royal Horse Guards), 116, 123n28

C
cabbage cutter, 240
Callow, Lieutenant-Colonel John (3rd Dragoons), 77
Call, Major C F (India Stores Department), 45
Calvert, Major-General Harry, 148
Cambridge, H R H the Duke of, 105n39, 115, 118, 215
Canadian Militia, 57
Cann, Drummer William, 252
Carnegie of Tarrie, Captain John (2nd Dragoons), 87, *88*
Cathcart, Major-General Lord, 126
Cavalry and Guards Club, 124
Cavalry Officers' swords, 74-102
Cavalry Troopers' swords
    1788-1878: 4-32
    1878-1914: 38-70
Cavalry, Inspectors-General of, 41
Celtic decoration, *85*
chape, 174
Clarke, Major-General Sir Alured, 209n3
claymore, 175 - *see also* broadsword
Coast Guard, 245
colonels' powers, 2, 4
Commander-in-Chief, 1
Committees on swords
    1828: 26-7
    1845: 45-7
    1855: 30-1
    1861: 32

    1903-04: 57-61
    1906-08: 61-6
Conway, General Henry Seymour, 5, 33n2
Copley, J S (painter), 127
costs of swords, 18, 48, 64, 66, 107
Craven, Thomas (swordmaker), 108
Crimean War, 3n2, 30-2, 36n45, 181, 219, 239, 243, 244
crowns on swords, 121, 123n35
cuirassiers, French, 21
Cunliffe, Daniel (painter), 188, 191, 252, 262n6
Custance, Major William Neville (6th Dragoon Guards), 30-1, 36n44, 44

D
Dayes, Edward (painter), 145, 172, 178, 226
Dighton, Denis (painter), 82, 86, 127
Dighton Junior, Robert (painter), 103n11, 108, 126
dirks, Scottish, 195-6, *196*
dismounted swords, 82
Dorville, Colonel Philip (1st Dragoons), 87
Drahonet, A-J Dubois (painter), 110, 112, 114, 130, 181, 230, 252, 256
Drake, Captain W T (Royal Horse Guards), 127
Dress Regulations
    1822: 87-8, 93-6, 131, 134, 156, 243
    1831: 132, 134
    1832: 181
    1833: 227-8
    1834: 132-4, 137, 139, 159
    1846: 137
    1854: 161
    1855: 164
    1857: 90, 137, 235
    1864: 87-8
    1872: 137, 164
    1874: 235
    1883: 183
    1891: 164
    1900: 88, 208, 235
    1911: 185
drummers, 193-5, 251-6, *194, 236, 253-4*

E
écusson, 208, 237, 257
Eden Commission, 39, 71n11
Edward VII, King, 66, 121
Egypt, campaigns in
    British 1801: 80, 84, 204, 227
        1882: 114
    French 1798: 84
Enfield, Royal Small Arms Factory
    Chief Storekeeper, 26
    manufacture, 26-8, 30-1, 41-2, 115-6, 278
    Superintendent, 41-2, 43, 118, 214
equerries, royal, 207-8
equipment, army, 284-95
espontoon, 142
Ewart, Sergeant (2nd Dragoons) at Waterloo, 21

F
Farrington, Lieutenant-Colonel A (Royal Artillery), 226
Fencibles, 174, 197n10
Ferrara, Andrea, 172
ffoulkes, Charles, 156
Field Marshals, 208, 272
fifers, 251
Firmin & Sons (sword suppliers), 220
flank companies, 175, 178
Ford, Lieutenant John (79th Foot), 174-5, 197n8
Fox, Colonel Malcolm, 60, 61, 68, 165
Fraser, Sir W A (1st Life Guards), 134
French Army sword (1816), 24
French, Major-General Sir John, 56, 57, 66, 73n45
Frith & Sons (steelmakers), 47
frock swords, 126, 159
frogs, 14, 108, 145, 215
Fuentes d'Onoro, action at (1811), 22

G
Garcia Hernandez, Battle of, 22
General Officers
    Board of Cavalry (1796), 18

  Board of (1787-88), 5-6
  swords, 202-10, 272, *205-6*
George III, King, 146, 209n3
George IV, King, 87, 95, 130, 209n5
Germany (Solingen), 5-7, 48, 50, 237-9
Gill, Thomas (swordmaker), 6, 28, 33n6, 77, 87, 107
Glasgow Art Gallery and Museum, 9, 12, 14, 104n29
Glynn, Company Quarter-Master-Sergeant (Grenadier Guards), 269
Goldie, Troop Corporal-Major Robert (Royal Horse Guards), 114
Gossett, Lieutenant Arthur (Royal Horse Artillery), 228
Graham, Sir Reginald Bellingham, 80
Granby, John, Marquess of, 1, 124
Gregory, Francis (10th Light Dragoons), 103n6
Griffith, Lieutenant-Colonel Henry Darby (2nd Dragoons), 30, 32
grips
 aluminium, 62
 brass, 77
 dermatine, 64, 68
 ebonite, 215
 ebony, 143, 198n12
 fishskin, 9, 59, 87
 gryphonite, 64, 66
 horn, 143
 iron, 252
 ivory, 143
 leather, 9, 28
 shagreen, 77
 silver wire, 82, 90
 vulcanite, 59, 62
 walnut, 68
guards
 basket, 5, 87
 bowl, 24, 54, 59, 66, 102
 knucklebow, 5, 143, 148
 stirrup, 148
 three-bar, 24, 28, 77
gutta-percha, use in experiments, 68

H

Hadden, James (3rd Dragoon Guards), 86
Haig, Major-General Sir Douglas, 56, 57, 66, 73n45
Hall, Cornet Francis (14th Light Dragoons), 22
handkerchief cutter, 267-9, *268*
hardening, oil and water, 53
Harvey, Samuel (swordmaker), 6, 28, 33n6
Hayes, Michael Angelo (painter), 181
Hertzberg, *Fabrique Royale*, 9
hilts
    basket, 14, 124, 183, 188
    beaded, 143
    boatshell, 80, 126
    cross-bar, 183
    disc, 21, 22
    five-ball, 143, 169n5
    four-bar, 112, 132
    Gothic, 156, 181
    honeysuckle, 87, 90, 98, 126
    knucklebow, 9, 74
    ladder, 86, 87, 90, 126
    mameluke, 80, 90, 202
    Scottish variations, 186-8
    scroll, 90, 188
    stirrup, 22
    three-bar, 98, 102, 156
Hope, Major-General Sir John, 178, 213
Hoppner, J (painter), 124
Household Cavalry
    officers' swords, 124-139
    troopers' swords, 106-121
Hunter, G R, 45
Hutton, Captain Alfred, 60, 61, 64
Hutton, Lieutenant H W (4th Dragoon Guards), 84

I

Indian Army, 22-4, 228
Indian Political Service, 208, 210n13, *207*
Infantry Officers' swords, 142-168

J

Jagger, Trumpeter Thomas, 256
Jardine, Major J B (5th Lancers), 61

K

Keane, Lieutenant-Colonel Edward (6th Dragoons), 26
Kelly, Captain Edward (Royal Horse Guards), 127
Kempson, Lieutenant C H (1st Dragoons), 92
Kempt, Major-General Sir J, 210n11
Kent, H R H the Duke of, 148
King-Harman, Colonel W H, 51, 215
Kirwan, Major B R (Royal Artillery), 61
knots - *see* sword knots

L

langets, 9, 21, 24, 34n24, 183, 209n7
Latham, J F, 45
Latham, John, 90, 157
Lawrenson, Major-General John, 32, 37n47
Le Marchant, Major-General John Gaspard, 7, 14, 16-18, 24
lead-cutting swords, 266-9, 270n20, *268*
Lear, Colonel, 105n35
Legermuseum, Delft, 14
levée swords, 134, 159, 207, *91, 96-7, 99*
Liège, weapon purchases through, 239
Limbert, Cornet John (1st Life Guards), 30-1
locket, 174
Loutherbourg, P J (painter), 197n7
Lowe, Major-General Sir Drury Curzon Drury, 45, 71n19

M

Macdonald, Sergeant D (42nd Foot), 189
Mackay, Captain Colin (78th Foot), 178
MacRae, Captain Duncan (78th Foot), 175
Mansel, Major-General, 14
Manufacture of swords
    1889 specification, 52-3, 62-4
    Enfield, 26-8, 30-1, 41-2, 48
    English decline, 28, 48, 278-9

English-German rivalry, 5-7
Solingen, 5-7, 48, 50, 237-9
Mappin, F J, 45, 47
Marindin, Lieutenant Samuel (2nd Life Guards), 130
Marsland, Lieutenant W E (1st Dragoon Guards), 87
McDowell, Lieutenant-General Sir Hay, 169n7
McLeod, Lieutenant-Colonel Norman (42nd Foot), 174
Mellifont, George, 77
Mercer, General Cavalié (Royal Artillery), 80, 146, 227
Militia, 2, 213, 257
Millar, Major-General W (Royal Artillery), 26
Miller, Lieutenant William (8th Hussars), 27
Mole, Robert, & Son (swordmakers), 28, 39-40, 42-3, 46, 48, 64, 208, 219
Moore, Major-General Sir John, 209n3
Mountain Artillery
    origins, 228-30
    pattern sword 1896, 20

N

Napier, Colonel T S, 60
National Museum of Ireland, Dublin, 112
Northcote, James (painter), 209n3
Nottingham, Pattern Room, 116

O

Onslow, Lieutenant-Colonel, 215
Ordnance
    Board of, 242
    Master-General of, 1, 3n2
Osborne, Henry (swordmaker), 17, 18, 28

P

Pallasche fur Kurassiere, 18, 127
Parry, Lieutenant Sidney (1st Life Guards), 132
pattern swords: *List of Changes*, 290-5
pattern swords: Cavalry
    1864-99 dimensions table, 70
    1788 Heavy Cavalry, 9-14, *11, 13, 15, 78-9*
    1788 Light Cavalry, 9, *8*

1796 Heavy Cavalry, 18-22, *19-20, 83, 85, 128*
1796 Light Cavalry, 18, 22, *23, 81*
1821 Heavy Cavalry, 24, 26, *25, 89*
1821 Light Cavalry, 24, 26, *25, 94*
1853 Cavalry, 28, 32, 38, *29*
1864 Cavalry, 32, 38-9, *31*
1880 Cavalry, Experimental, Converted, 39, 41
1880 Cavalry, Experimental, New, 40-2, *40*
1881 Cavalry, Long and Short, 42-3, *44*
1881 Cavalry, Experimental, 42
1882 Cavalry, Long and Short, New, 42-3, *44*
1885 Cavalry, 48, *49*
1890 Cavalry, 53, *55*
1899 Cavalry, 54, *55*
1903-06 Cavalry, Experimental, 61-4, *63*
1904 Cavalry, Experimental, 57-9, *58*
1905 Cavalry, Experimental, 59-60, *60*
1906 Cavalry, Mark I, Experimental, 64-6, *65*
1908 Cavalry, Mark I, 66-8, *67, 69*
1908 Cavalry, Mark I, India, 68, *69*
1904 Cavalry, Officers, Experimental, 59, *59*
1912 Cavalry Officers, 100-2, 139, *101-2*

pattern swords: General Officers
    1831 General Officers, 204-8, *206*

pattern swords: Household Cavalry
    1882 Household Cavalry, Long and Short, Mark I, 116-8, *117*
    1888 Household Cavalry, Long, 120, *117*
    1892 Household Cavalry, 120-1, *119*

pattern swords: Infantry Officers
    1786 Infantry Officers, 142-5, *144*
    1796 Infantry Officers, 145-6, 202, *147*
    1822 Infantry Officers, 156-7, *157-8, 162*
    1845 Infantry Officers, 159, 161, *162*
    1895 Infantry Officers, 165, *166*
    1897 Infantry Officers, 165-8, *166-7*

pattern swords: Sergeants
    1857 Staff-Sergeants, Highland Regiments, Mark I, 191, *190*
    1861 Staff-Sergeants, line regiments, 213
    1866 Staff-Sergeants, line regiments, 213-4
    1889 Staff-Sergeants, 215, *216*
    1895 Staff-Sergeants, Highland Regiments, Mark II, 191, *192*
    1897 Staff-Sergeants, 217

    1898 Staff-Sergeants, 217
    1922-29 Staff-Sergeants, 192-3
pattern swords: others
    1798 Highland Regiment Officers, 172-4
    1803 Grenadiers and Light Infantry Officers, 148-50, *151-3*
    1820 1st Life Guards, 110, 116
    1857 Royal Engineers Officers, 235, *236*
Paulet group (68th Foot), 252
Persian influence, 82
picquet weight swords, 159, 161, 168, *166*
pioneers, 261, *260*
pipers, 193-5, 201n50, *194*
point
    hatchet, 12
    spear, 21, 24
pommel
    flattened ball, 127
    lion's head, 127
Poore, Major R M (7th Hussars), 61
Porter, Captain George (1st Troop of Horse Guards), 124
Powell, Major A L, 61
practice swords, 264-6, *265*
Prosser, John (swordmaker), 24, 84, 156
Prussian Army
    Cavalry sabre, model 1811, 24
    Infantry officer's sword, 169n13

Q
quillons, 9, 98, 134, 257

R
Reeves, Charles, patent tang, 28, 64
regimental administration, 18th century, 2, 3n3
Regiments and Corps
    Cavalry
        1st Life Guards, 30, 46, 107, 110, 126, 132, 139, 256, 272, *111, 131*
        2nd Life Guards, 107-12, 126, 132-9, 267, 271, *111, 113, 133, 135-6,138, 255*
        Royal Horse Guards (Blues), 46, 56, 106-7, 126, 134, 272, *113, 115, 125, 136,138*
        Horse Grenadier Guards, 106-7, 124, 132, *109*
        1st (King's) Dragoon Guards, 87, 90, *91*

2nd Dragoon Guards, 16, 42
3rd Dragoon Guards (Prince of Wales's), 14, 86, 170n16, *15*
4th Dragoon Guards, 14, 39, 41, 42, 77, 92, *78, 85, 93*
5th Dragoon Guards, 39, 42, 51, 90
6th Dragoon Guards (Carabiniers), 30, 90-1, 100, 102, *91-2, 255*
1st (Royal) Dragoons, 21, 22, 42, 45, 87, *93*
2nd Dragoons (Royal Scots Greys), 21, 30, 31-2, 42, 50, 51, 86-7, *88*
3rd Dragoons, 21, 77, *96*
4th Dragoons, 24, 84, 86
6th Dragoons (Inniskillings), 9, 41, *10*
4th Light Dragoons (Hussars), 39, 41, 42, 46, 91-2, *92*
7th Light Dragoons (Hussars), 45, 46, 82, *76*
10th Light Dragoons (Hussars) (Prince of Wales's), 7, 46, 47, 74, 80, 102, *75, 81, 102*
12th Light Dragoons (Lancers), 51, 95, 102n2
15th Light Dragoons (Hussars), 5, 45, 46, 77, 82, *4, 78, 97*
16th Light Dragoons (Hussars), 80, *75*
30th (Princess of Wales') Light Dragoons, 77, *76*
8th Hussars, 26, 27
11th Hussars, 30, 31-2, 39, 41, 53, 98
14th Hussars, 46, 51
18th Hussars, 46, 56, 98, 105n39, *97*
19th Hussars, 51, 53, *99*
20th Hussars, 41, 46, 50-1
21st Hussars, 42
9th Lancers, 91, 95
16th Lancers, 45, 95, *96*
17th Lancers, 26, 95, *94*

Artillery

Royal Artillery, 32, 38, 145, 218, 226-234, 248n18, 273, *229, 233*
B Battery, 39, 41
G Battery, 41
H Battery, 42
I Battery, 42
K Battery, 39, 41
M Battery, 39, 41
Royal Field Artillery, 231, 248n18
Royal Garrison Artillery, 248n18
Royal Horse Artillery, 227-8
Royal Irish Artillery, 247n1
Mountain Artillery, 228, *229*

Infantry

1st (Grenadier) Guards, 170n22, 220, *221*

2nd (Coldstream) Guards, 220, *222*
3rd (Scots Fusilier) Guards, 195, 220, *221, 258*
1st Foot (Royal Scots), 172, 178, 213, *179*
2nd Foot, 145
4th Foot, 170n18
5th Foot (Royal Northumberland Fusiliers), 168, *167*
7th Foot (Royal Fusiliers), 257, *212*
12th Foot, 148
20th Foot (Lancashire Fusiliers), 168
21st Foot (Royal Scots Fusiliers), 172, 181, 195, *182*
23rd Foot (Royal Welsh Fusiliers), 153, 159, *155*
24th Foot (South Wales Borderers), 168
25th Foot (King's Own Scottish Borderers), 172, 197n1, *180, 184*
26th Foot (Cameronians), 172, 183, 188, *189*
30th Foot, *258*
32nd Foot, 86
42nd Foot (Black Watch), 172, 174, 175, 181, 185, 188, 189, 211, 251-2, *190*
43rd Foot, 150, 153, 193, *154*
51st Foot, 153, *154*
52nd Foot, 150, *153*
60th Foot (Royal Americans), 153, 159
65th Foot, 170n18
68th Foot, 252
71st Foot (Highland Light Infantry), 172, 174, 175, 183, 185, *176-7, 184*
72nd Foot (Seaforth Highlanders), 172, *182*
73rd Foot (Black Watch), 172
74th Foot (Highland Light Infantry), 172, 183, 188, *184*
75th Foot (Gordon Highlanders), 172
78th Foot (Seaforth Highlanders), 175, 178, 181, *176, 179*
79th Foot (Cameron Highlanders), 174, 188, 191, *187*
84th Foot, *149*
87th Foot, 213
90th Foot (Perthshire Light Infantry), 178, 188, *180*
91st Foot (Argyll and Sutherland Highlanders), 183, 185, *186*
92nd Foot (Gordon Highlanders), 178, 188, 213, *187*
93rd Foot (Argyll and Sutherland Highlanders), 178, *173*
95th Foot, 153, *144, 155*
116th Foot (Perthshire Highlanders), 174, *173*
Rifle Brigade, 153, 156, 159

Corps

Army Hospital Corps, 213, 219-20, 244-5, 275, *244*
Army Pay Department, 165, 246, 275

    Army Veterinary Department, 245-6
    Commissariat, 213, 241, 274, 275
    Control Department, 241, 275
    Land Transport Corps, 240-1, 275, *240*
    Medical Staff Corps, 219-20, 244
    Military Stores Department, 241, 243, 275
    Military Train, 240-1, 275
    Ordnance Stores Department, 165, 213, 242, 275
    Royal Army Dental Corps, 246
    Royal Army Educational Corps, 246
    Royal Army Medical Corps, 219-20, 243-5, 275
    Royal Army Ordnance Corps, 242-3, 275
    Royal Army Pay Corps, 246, 275
    Royal Army Service Corps, 88, 239-42, 275
    Royal Army Veterinary Corps, 245-6, 275
    Royal Corps of Signals, 246
    Royal Electrical and Mechanical Engineers, 246
    Royal Engineers, 1, 90, 218-9, 234-9, 249n32, 274, *236, 238*
    Royal Military Artificers and Labourers, 218, 234, 249n32
    Royal Pioneer Corps, 246
    Royal Sappers and Miners, 218, 252
    Royal Staff Corps, 1, 3n2, 239, 249n36, 274
    Royal Waggoners, 239-40, 245
    Royal Wagon Corps/Train, 239-40, 249n38, 274
Reynolds, Sir Joshua (painter), 124
ricasso, 14, 161
Richard I, King, 266
Rifle Regiments, 153, 156, 159, 188, 217-8, 274, *160*
Rimington, Brigadier-General M F, 57, 73n45
Roberts, Field Marshal Lord, 57
Roberts, Private George (1st Life Guards), 110
Robinson, Corporal Thomas (2nd Life Guards), 112
Romney, George (painter), 170
Royal Armouries, Tower of London, 12, 14
Royal Navy, 143
Royal North British Dragoons - *see* 2nd Dragoons
Rungeling, Kettle-Drummer George (Royal Horse Guards), 114
Runkel, John Justus (sword supplier), 6-7, 33n6, 146, 276

S

Salamanca, Battle of (1812), 22, 24
Sam Browne belt, 100, 139, 192-3, 208
Sanderson & Company (steelmakers), 47
scabbards
    brass, 108
    iron, 9, 22, 28
    leather, 9, 14, 40, 46, 56, 59, 82, 164
    steel, 27-8, 39, 56, 64, 164, 183
    steel and leather, 100
    wood, 9, 57, 64, 139
scimitar, 16, 202
Scobell, Major-General Henry, 57, 61, 73n45
Scottish infantry swords, 172-196
Scottish United Services Museum, Edinburgh, 12, 14, 21, *11*
Secretary at War, 1, 3n1
Seele, J B (painter), 18
sergeants
    Scottish regiments, 189-93
    other regiments, 211-224
Shaw, Sergeant (1st Life Guards), 22, 110
silladar system, 2
Small Arms, Chief Inspector of, 64
Smithies, Private James (1st Dragoons), 21
Smith, Lieutenant-Colonel Charles Hamilton (painter), 14, 107, 126, 150, 208, 213
Solingen, 5-7, 48, 50, 237-9
South African War (1899-1902), 54-57, 139
South African War, Royal Commission on, 38, 56-7
Spanish pattern hanger, 231-2
spontoon, 142
Staff Officers, 202-4, 208, 209n8, *205*
Stanley, Colonel (Royal Horse Guards), 107
State sword, 137
Steele, Colonel, 88
Strathmore, 10th Earl of, 124
Stubbs, George (painter), 7
Suakin, campaigns around (1884-88), 47, 50-1, 214
supply of swords
    Board of Ordnance, 24, 28
    private manufacture, 28
sword knots, 126, 150, 174, 271-5

T

Talana Hill, Battle of (1899), 56
Talbot, Colonel the Hon. R A J (1st Life Guards), 123n30
tang, 28, 64
Taylor, Lieutenant-General Sir Herbert, 26-7, 35n37
testing of swords
    1788 views of English and German makers, 6-7
    1788 recommendations, 7
    1855 committee tests, 30-1
    1880-82 Cavalry pattern, 39-43
    1885 Cavalry pattern, 46-7, 50, *31*
    1889 recommendations, 52
    foreign swords, 61
    marking of blades following, 278
    unofficial regimental testing, 30-1, 45, 50, 51, 123n30
Thackwell, Lieutenant-Colonel Joseph (15th Hussars), 26, 36n38
Tickell, Major E S (14th Hussars), 61
training in swordsmanship, 38
Trotter, Captain John (2nd Life Guards), 130
trumpeters, 256
Tullibardine, Marquis of (Royal Horse Guards), 56
Turton & Son (steelmakers), 45

U

United States Army
    Cavalry pattern (1913), 68
    Dragoon sabre (1833), 26
    Engineers (*c*1805), 146
    General and Staff Officers, 104n15
    Infantry Officers (1812-1840), 143
    Infantry Officers (1840), 146
    Topographical Engineers (1838), 26
United States Marine Corps, 204

V

Vivian, Major-General Sir Richard Hussey, 26, 35n8
Volunteers, 2, 213, 257, 269n1

W

Waite, John Musgrove, 267
War-like stores, Royal Commission on, 43, 50, 71n13
Waterloo, Battle of, 21, 22, 86, 110, 114, 127
Wellington, Arthur, 1st Duke of, 82, 202, 209n9, 227, 228
Weyersberg, Kirschbaum & Company (swordmakers), 48
Wheeler, Lieutenant L J (6th Dragoon Guards), 91
Wildman, Major Edward (6th Dragoon Guards), 84
Wilkie, Sir David (painter), 114
Wilkinson & Son (swordmakers), 28, 45, 64, 74, 88
Windsor, Royal Collection at
    drawings and paintings, 7, 18
    swords, 7, 12, 22
Winterbottom, Regimental Corporal-Major, 110
Wolfe-Murray, General Sir James, 61
Wolseley, General Lord, 50, 52, 114-5, 118
Wood, Colonel E A (10th Hussars), 45
Wood, Field Marshal Sir Evelyn, 32
Woolley, James (swordmaker), 6, 28, 33n6, 107
Worrall Collection, 36n40
Wyatt, Lieutenant-Colonel (23rd Foot), 153

Y

Yeomanry, regiments and swords, 22, 26
York, Field Marshal the Duke of, 124

Z

Zoffany, John (painter), 174
Zululand, 183